Contemporary Philosophy and Religious Thought

An Introduction to the
Philosophy of Religion

Contemporary Philosophy and Religious Thought

An Introduction to the Philosophy of Religion

Malcolm L. Diamond

Professor of Religion
Princeton University

McGraw-Hill Book Company

*New York   St. Louis   San Francisco   Düsseldorf
Johannesburg   Kuala Lumpur   London   Mexico   Montreal   New Delhi
Panama   Paris   São Paulo   Singapore   Sydney   Tokyo   Toronto*

CONTEMPORARY PHILOSOPHY AND RELIGIOUS THOUGHT

An Introduction to the Philosophy of Religion

Copyright © 1974 by McGraw-Hill, Inc. All rights reserved.
Printed in the United States of America. No part of this publication
may be reproduced, stored in a retrieval system, or transmitted, in any
form or by any means, electronic, mechanical, photocopying, recording, or
otherwise, without the prior written permission of the publisher.

1234567890DODO798654

This book was set in Times Roman by Black Dot, Inc. The editors were
Alison Meersschaert and Phyllis T. Dulan; the designer was Joseph
Gillans; and the production supervisor was Thomas J. LoPinto.
R. R. Donnelley & Sons Company was printer and binder.

Library of Congress Cataloging in Publication Data

Diamond, Malcolm Luria.
    Contemporary philosophy and religious thought.

     1. Religion—Philosophy. 2. God. I. Title.
BL51.D48   200'.1   73–17084
ISBN 0–07–016721–4
ISBN 0–07–016720–6 (pbk.)

To My Father
Walter J. Diamond
and in Memory of
My Mother
Jeannette C. Diamond

Contents

PART FOUR   TRADITIONAL ARGUMENTS FOR THE
                EXISTENCE OF GOD

PART FIVE   PAUL TILLICH: RELIGION AS ULTIMACY

Preface for Teachers

The question of the existence and nature of God—the central issue of Western religious thought—is the focus of this book. I do not, however, assume the importance of this issue; rather I explore the reasons that belief in God has been regarded as both important and compelling by Christians and Jews and the reasons that sceptics have challenged this belief.

The text combines a "problems" and a "thinkers" approach. It deals with such problems as the proofs for God's existence, verification, faith, miracles, and religious experience. In considering different approaches to these problems, I present a number of thinkers who have played a major role in shaping twentieth-century religious thought, among them Rudolph Otto, Martin Buber, William James, Sören Kierkegaard, and Paul Tillich.

In an effort to overcome a common deficiency of introductory texts—brief explanations that assume too much prior knowledge on the part of students—problems and thinkers are both treated at length. Terms such as *analytic, contingent, numinous,* and *subjective* are unavoidable, but every effort is made to explain them in ordinary English and to use illustrations from everyday experiences, relevant to students' interests, in bringing these terms to life.

Religious existentialists and philosophical analysts are generally regarded as antithetical types. The existentialists often write with an urgency and passion that is prophetic, whereas analysts are, as the name suggests, detached—even when they are favorably disposed to religious claims. I have been drawn to both movements and try to write from inside them, emphasizing the importance of both approaches.

The format of the book has been dictated by considerations that have proved effective in my teaching. One of them involves the relationship between exposition and criticism. The thinkers considered are hard to follow. In order to let the main patterns emerge, I present their thought without interrupting the exposition with critical reflections. Critical sections appear at the end of individual chapters.

Part One on Theology and Verification provides a working vocabulary for the text and logically serves as the initial one. Part Two on Religious Experience and Part Three on Religious Existentialism deal with nonrationalistic approaches to God. They are introduced at this point because, generally speaking, students are more engaged by them than by the rationalistic arguments for the existence of God—teleological, ontological, and cosmological—that follow in Part Four. Some teachers may, of course, prefer to move directly to Part Four before discussing Parts Two and Three. Part Five presents an extensive survey of the thought of Paul Tillich, an extraordinary thinker who is not only important in himself but who comes to grips with almost all of the important topics considered in this text. The final part, therefore, serves as a review as well as a source of fresh insights which add to the student's understanding and help him to formulate his own critical approach to religious belief.

The text grew out of a course on the Problems of Religious Thought that I have taught at Princeton University for a number of years. I loved doing it. The students were alive. They forced the issues, and their questions and objections led me to rework and clarify my approach to the material. I am deeply grateful for their help, and I hope that this book reflects it.

Support from Princeton University and the Danforth Foundation provided a year's leave of absence for reflection that was free of the distractions of academic routine and for uninterrupted bursts of writing.

Among those who helped by reading and criticizing the book are David Burrell, Robert Cassidy, Van A. Harvey, Edward Langerak, Thomas V. Litzenburg, Basil Mitchell, Kenneth V. Nelson, Paul Nelson, G. Dennis O'Brien, John P. Reeder, Jr., Richard M. Rorty, William L. Rowe, Edward W. St. Clair, Robert A. Segal, Axel Steuer, and Paul Van Buren. They are, of course, not responsible for the faults that remain.

At McGraw-Hill, Phyllis Dulan helped greatly in preparing the manuscript for publication; Cheryl Mehalik provided assistance in processing the manuscript; and Alison Meersschaert, Philosophy and Religion Editor, provided important advice and encouragement as well as sharp editing.

Denise Landry typed an exasperating number of revisions with patience and incredible efficiency.

Malcolm L. Diamond

Preface for Students

Reinhold Niebuhr said, "There's nothing as irrelevant as the answer to a question that nobody asked." I would add that there's nothing as irrelevant as the refutation to a point that nobody made. To get inside a book like this, it is not enough to have a conversation's worth of curiosity. You have to have questions that you really want answered and points that you really want to make—a question like "Does God exist?" and points like "Religion is just a matter of feeling" and "Faith is a matter of wish-fulfillment."

You have to care enough about these questions and opinions to make an effort to grapple with the answers that have been presented by leading religious thinkers. This requires the kind of effort you would put into learning a science or a foreign language. In a subject like mechanics, the words "mass" and "inertia" are defined in terms of mathematical symbols which immediately alert you to the special effort required to grasp their meaning. Two technical terms that will be considered in the Introduction, *anthropomorphism* and *transcendence*, are English words and other English words are used to define them. You are, therefore, tempted to think that you can master them by taking lecture notes or by reading a few sentences in a book. In the case of anthropomorphism this works. It means ascribing human characteristics, like love, to God. Defining transcendence is another matter. The preliminary definition provided in the Introduction will give you a sense that it means beyond. As used in the context of religious thought, it refers to God as beyond all other beings. Yet a word of this kind cannot be mastered at the start of a book like this. It can be understood only at the end when you have worked through the kinds of problems that lead religious thinkers to use the term and when you have made the effort to understand the different senses in which they use it.

Students generally have a passion to know where their professor stands on the issues so that they can tell where his biases probably lie. This is understandable and justifiable. On the other hand, I often find myself resisting requests to "declare myself." Finding out the position of a professor can also serve as the basis for misconstruing his views as authoritative. I do not regard my views in this light. My major concern is not to engage the reader with my positions but with important problems and figures in the field of religious thought. With this reservation in mind, let me state a few things about my outlook.

In the matchup between existentialistic believers and analytic sceptics that characterizes so much of the book and is brought to final focus in the Epilogue, my termperament is with the existentialists but my intellect is with the analysts.

It would take an autobiography to explain how I, as a Jew reared in the orthodox tradition and one who still resonates to its melodies, have come to a deep involvement with Christian thought as well as with that of my own tradition. One reason is that compassion, the strand of Jewishness that I value most highly, is also central to Christianity, even though adherents of both traditions have honored this ideal largely in its abuse.

In this book I try to communicate the importance of religion and to show that an educated person cannot formulate beliefs responsibly without taking account of philosophical challenges to them.

Malcolm L. Diamond

Acknowledgments

I am grateful to the following publishers and periodicals for permission to quote long passages from the books and articles listed.

G. Allen, for Basil Mitchell, ed., *Faith and Logic*.

Blackwell, for Ronald Hepburn, "From World to God" (*Mind*, 1963).

Dover, for William James, *The Will to Believe*.

Harcourt Brace Jovanovich, for E. M. Forster, *A Passage to India*.

Harper & Row, for Martin Buber, *The Eclipse of God*; Rudolph Bultmann, *The Presence of Eternity*; Paul Tillich, *Dynamics of Faith*.

Macmillan, for Martin Buber, *Between Man and Man*; Paul Edwards, ed., *The Encyclopedia of Philosophy*.

Macmillan Services, Ltd., for A. E. Taylor, *Does God Exist?*

Open Court, for Norris Clarke, S.J., "A Curious Blindspot in the Anglo-American Tradition of Anti-theistic Argument" (*The Monist*, 1970).

The Philosophical Review, for Norman Malcolm, "Anselm's Ontological Arguments."

Princeton University Press, for Soren Kierkegaard, *Concluding Unscientific Postscript*; Soren Kierkegaard, *Fear and Trembling* and *Sickness unto Death*.

SCM Press, for A. Flew and A. MacIntyre, eds., *New Essays in Philosophical Theology*.

Scribner, for Rudolph Bultmann, *Jesus Christ and Mythology*; Fredrick Ferré, *Basic Modern Philosophy of Religion*.

Vedanta Press, for *The Bhagavad-Gita*, trans. by S. Prabhavananda and C. Isherwood.

Yale University Press, for Carl Becker, *The Heavenly City of the Eighteenth Century Philosophers*.

I wish to thank the Cambridge University Press and Professor H. D. Lewis, editor of *Religious Studies*, for permission to reprint portions of my essay "Miracles" which appeared in that periodical in 1973.

Introduction: The God of Theism

The question of the existence of God is obviously of great importance. If God exists then there is a power beyond all human power that is concerned with what happens to individuals and communities. If there is a God who is all-powerful, all-knowing, and perfectly good, then, no matter how bad things seem, there is hope. The affirmations of faith that follow communicate the urgency of belief as expressed in two major religions— Christianity and Judaism.

The apostle Paul proclaimed the glad tidings of the redemption that came through the death of the Messiah (that is, Christ), who was executed like a criminal. He was crucified—which in that day was as common a mode of execution as the electric chair today (the Christian faith later converted the cross into a religious symbol). The message of redemption through the sacrificial love of Jesus Christ was, in St. Paul's terms, an obstacle to the Jews, who expected a triumphant Messiah, and nonsense to the Greeks, who did not see how the fate of one individual could involve the salvation of all people. In proclaiming the message to both Jews and Greeks, St. Paul was whipped, tortured, and imprisoned. After

1

reviewing his sufferings, he closes on the following triumphant affirmation of faith:

> Then what can separate us from the love of Christ? Can affliction or
> hardship? Can persecution, hunger, nakedness, peril, or the sword? . . .
> and yet, in spite of all, overwhelming victory is ours through him who loves
> us. For I am convinced that there is nothing in death or life, in the realm of
> spirits or superhuman powers, in the world as it is or the world as it shall be,
> in the forces of the universe, in heights or depths—nothing at all in all
> creation that can separate us from the love of God in Christ Jesus our Lord
> (Rom. 8:35–39).

The Jewish faith is rooted in a particular people. Their enslavement in
Egypt prefigures Jewish history. There were few periods when the Jews
were in control of their government and their destiny. They were subject
to many persecutions culminating in the horrors of the Nazi era. Yet all
over the world, at the Seder, the special meal that inaugurates the
Passover holiday, Jews read the following affirmation of their faith:

> That which has stood for our fathers stands for us
> For it was not only one tyrant that rose against us to destroy us
> Rather, in every age, they rise against us to destroy us,
> But the Holy One, blessed be he, saves us from their hands.

Jews repeated and *meant* these words during the darkest days of the Nazi
era, and there are Jews who mean them today. They believe that God
preserves their people from one generation to the next for purposes of his
own.

In proclaiming the God of love and power, religions like Judaism and
Christianity are not only concerned to provide us with grounds for hope
but they are also concerned to provide us with guides for action. Jesus, in
the Sermon on the Mount, characterizes God as perfect and urges his
followers to imitate God:

> You have heard that it was said, "You shall love your neighbor and hate
> your enemy." But I say to you, Love your enemies and pray for those who
> persecute you, so that you may be sons of your Father who is in heaven; for
> he makes his sun rise on the evil and the good and sends his rain on the just
> and on the unjust. . . . You, therefore, must be perfect, as your heavenly
> Father is perfect (Matt. 5:43, 44, 48).

THE PROBLEM OF ANTHROPOMORPHISM

A text like the Sermon on the Mount has the directness of poetry. Yet
Jesus is not merely trying to stir our emotions. He tells of the heavenly

Father, the most important of all realities, and, in the name of this reality, he urges us to behave in certain ways. In other words, belief in a God who is perfect stands at the center of Jesus' teachings and of the religion he founded. This belief triggers hard questions like "Does this God exist?" and "How does the heavenly Father that Jesus talks about differ from our earthly fathers?"

From the earliest periods of Western thought, philosophers have had problems with the application of words like "father" to God. To apply it to God is to use language anthropomorphically, that is, to attribute human characteristics to God. What then, are we to make of it? Is talking about God as Father intended only to evoke certain feelings in us, or does it have hold of something that provides a clue to the way things are in the world? This problem has been around just about as long as people have talked of God. Critics of religion charge that men create gods in their own image and that if cows could think they would imagine a bovine deity. In "The Cotter's Saturday Night" Robert Burns wrote: "An honest man's the noblest work of God." The atheist Robert Ingersoll replied: "An honest God's the noblest work of man."

The anthropomorphism of the biblical portrait of God was a problem throughout Christian history. Many Christians have regarded the words of the Bible as divinely inspired in the sense that they are not only literally true, but immune to the very possibility of error. Yet they must then cope with verses like "The man and his wife heard the sound of the Lord God walking in the garden at the time of the evening breeze" (Gen. 3:8). A God who walks is a God who has a body, and, in our experience, all embodied beings are limited. A limited God might be more powerful than human beings but he would hardly be the answer to the religious quest. He would not be a God of infinite love and limitless power who can provide hope in the face of the evils that afflict mankind.

In response to problems like that of anthropomorphism, the Church soon developed theoreticians of the faith called *theologians.* They were concerned with clarifying the nature of God to those already inside the fold and with defending Christian beliefs from the criticisms of those outside it. Purging the faith of anthropomorphism was an important aspect of both the inner and outer directed thinking of the theologians. In doing so, the earliest theologians used the categories of Greek philosophy. Theologians have also used every other philosophy that has developed in the Western world in the effort to expound and defend the faith.

Theologians are philosophically trained thinkers who deal with philosophical difficulties involved in the teachings of a specific religious tradition. Philosophers of religion, as I use the term, deal with the same problems. The difference is that the term *theologian* carries the implication of being an official spokesman for a religious tradition. The term *philosopher of religion,* as I shall use it, does not imply that the individual is a spokesman for a religious point of view. He does not undertake to show that his views conform to the beliefs of a religious tradition with which he identifies.

THE GOD OF THE THEOLOGIANS

A working definition of God will help to focus both the claims of theologians and the problems of establishing the existence of this God: God is an omnipotent, omniscient, and eternal person who is pure spirit. He is both transcendent and immanent. He created the universe and human beings are his special creation. He loves them, interacts with them, and desires their love.[1] The stress on the personal element in the concept of God is characteristic of three of the great religions—Judaism, Christianity, and Islam. Their view of God is generally referred to by the technical term *theism.*

The odd qualities that occur in the definition are intended, in part, to stress the absence of all limitations in God. He is not merely like other persons, powerful, knowing, and good to a certain degree; he is infinitely powerful (omnipotent), he knows everything that can conceivably be known (omniscient), and he is perfectly good. Human persons are born and die but God is eternal, that is, he does not begin to exist and his existence is without end. Unlike human beings, God does not have a body; he is pure spirit. He is not, however, like a ghost because he is utterly beyond, that is, he transcends space and time. By this, theologians mean that if every reality in the universe were to cease to exist, God would not. Yet God is also immanent, namely, his reality permeates the universe to such an extent that there is no place and no being that is not saturated with his presence. In other words, he is not limited by being locatable in space and time, but he is also not limited by being apart from all the beings that are located in space and time. He created everything and he sustains all beings. He interacts with human beings in the course of history with the ultimate goal of eliciting love from them both in relation to one another and in relation to himself.[2]

This book will focus on the problems raised by this idea of God. I will present arguments used by religious thinkers to justify their claims about this unique reality and the objections to these arguments on the part of philosophical sceptics.

Part One pivots around the charge that the theistic idea of God is so confused that theologians have no idea of what it means. The sceptics charge that theologians talk about God creating the world and about God's love for us without specifying rules that would enable us to understand exactly how the activities of the invisible God differ from those of visible human agents. As a result these sceptics propose that theology be eliminated from the list of subjects that are worthy of serious philosophical study.

Part Two considers the appeal to religious experience as a way of witnessing to the activity of God. It is a mode of experience which they think is appropriate to God's distinctive reality. Its uniqueness is brought out by comparing it with other modes of firsthand experience like the red of a sunset and the impact of great art. It is then argued that religious experience yields knowledge of God that is so direct that it is self-validating. In other words, there is no need to go outside the experience itself in order to check on whether it is an experience of a reality that is external to the self or merely a projection of personal fantasies onto the cosmos.

Part Three presents religious existentialism, which is one of the most influential theological movements of the twentieth century. The existentialists consciously reject sciences, like physics, as the model for knowledge of God, and they refuse to play the game of showing the reasonableness of Christianity (or of any other religion). Instead, they stress commitment to religious beliefs even when the evidence points the other way. In doing so, they strain language to the utmost. Of course, other types of religious thinkers are forced to use seemingly contradictory language like the claim that God is both transcendent (utterly beyond the world) and immanent (present in every part of the world). The existentialists, however, are distinctive in that they seem to revel in it, especially when dealing with the claim that Jesus Christ is wholly divine and wholly human.

Part Four discusses points of view that are at the opposite end of the spectrum from religious existentialism, namely, the efforts to achieve knowledge of God by rational arguments and proofs. The ones considered have acquired the status of classical statements of the rational approach; they are the teleological, ontological, and cosmological arguments.

Part Five is devoted to an extended discussion of Paul Tillich's thought. He is one of the most important religious thinkers of the twentieth century because he is sensitive to the problems of religious thought and tries to cope with them by working toward a suitable method of approaching the meaning of God and the knowledge of his reality. In doing so, he uses all the approaches that are considered in this book. His thought is, therefore, not only important in its own right, it also provides a helpful reexamination of the other approaches. Finally, it should be noted that although all the thinkers studied in this book realize that knowledge of God must, in one way or another, be based on methods that depart from those used in dealing with other realities, Tillich's approach is by far the most radical.

Part One

Theology
and Verification

Verification is a most impressive adaptation of scientific thinking to philosophical purposes. The term was set at the center of the philosophical stage by the work of the logical positivists who were part of the broad movement of twentieth-century analytic philosophy.[1] They met in Vienna in the twenties and formed a philosophical school with a revolutionary program. Many of them were competent mathematicians and physicists who were concerned with adapting the techniques of these disciplines to philosophical advantage. They were convinced that philosophy did not progress because traditional enterprises like metaphysics and theology weighed it down like the albatross on the neck of the Ancient Mariner. They devised the test of verification in an effort to eliminate them from the philosophical arena.

In the case of theology the revolutionary character of the positivists' program is easy to state.[2] Atheists argue the case for the existence of God and reach the conclusion that God does not exist. Agnostics take the position that the question cannot be resolved one way or the other. The positivists believe that the issue is not even worth arguing because (in a special philosophical sense that we shall soon come to appreciate) the claim that God exists is meaningless.

The positivists tried to bury theology. Religious thinkers can take comfort from the fact that positivism has passed from the philosophical scene while theology is still very much a part of it. Nevertheless, the importance of positivism for contemporary religious thought is not merely historical. Its terminology is still used by thinkers throughout the English-speaking world. Indeed, mastery of this terminology is a precondition of philosophical literacy. Furthermore, knowledge of God is a central concern of religious thinkers; they often deal with it in terms of faith. Since the logical positivists were exceptionally clear as to what they meant by knowledge, it is instructive to compare their views with what religious thinkers, especially the existentialists, mean by faith.

The positivists used verification as an instrument to cut theology away from the living body of philosophy. Many theologians who were sympathetic to the positivists' concern for clarity and rigor tried to show that verification could be used in a positive way to advance the cause of religious thought. In the subsequent parts of the book I intend to show that verification is an important tool for the sympathetic presentation, as well as for the criticism of religious thinkers who had never heard of the term verification. Religious existentialists, for example, engage in verification, but—with the notable exception of Paul Tillich—their ignorance of its philosophical importance, or their indifference to it, leads to haphazard and inadequate results.

Part One will be concerned with: (1) the goals and terminology of the positivists, (2) the problems they met in trying to formulate an adequate version of the test of verification, (3) the failure of their effort to eliminate theology from serious philosophical consideration, (4) sampling of answers to the positivists' challenge by religious thinkers who were sympathetic to verificationism, and (5) discussion of the reasons that most contemporary religious thinkers do not appeal to miracles as a way of answering the positivists' challenge.

Chapter 1

The Goals and Techniques of the Logical Positivists

The logical positivists' challenge to theology must be understood in the wider context of the issue of religion and science because their movement trades heavily on the prestige of science. Our scientifically oriented culture is less hospitable to religious beliefs than were the cultures that spawned the three great theistic religions (that is, religions that believe in a personal God—Judaism, Christianity, and Islam). Without disproving the teachings of these faiths, science has led to a downgrading of their status and to the rise of considerable scepticism about the validity of belief in the existence of God. The mood is captured in a cartoon that was drawn by an undergraduate in the sixties. A freshman home for his first vacation steps off the train. Mom, Dad, and Sis rush eagerly to greet him and he proclaims: "I don't believe in God!"

TECHNOLOGY MAKES AN IMPACT ON THE SCIENTIFICALLY UNSOPHISTICATED

One reason that science has made such a tremendous difference to the status of religious belief is its ability to reach people who have no sense of what science is all about. In this respect science is like religion and very different from philosophy. The moral teachings of the German philosopher, Immanuel Kant (1724–1804) have direct relevance to the lives of all of us. However, there is no way of being impressed with his teachings if you cannot follow his reasoning, and this is very hard to do, even for people with philosophical training. Before the rise of science, most challenges to the theological status quo came from philosophers, which limited their impact. For instance, in the twelfth century Aristotle's teachings were adopted by a number of theologians who used them to challenge the prevailing platonic consensus. At that time doctors of theology had to shift gears in order to deal with this challenge, but the mass of believers were unaffected by it. They were not interested in philosophical formulations of Christian teachings. The great company of believers were attuned to the promise of eternal life. They hoped that the joys of a future life would compensate them for the sufferings of their present one. Karl Marx derided this hope in his definition of religion as "the opiate of the masses," and it has been satirized by the Wobblies (The International Workers of the World). They sneered about bosses who cheated the workers and then paid preachers to promise them "pie in the sky by and by." Yet before the rise of science, this promise didn't look too bad. At least religion promised the masses "pie," that is, it promised them something relevant to their desires, which is more than could be said for Aristotle, whose teachings were slanted to the elite. What makes pie in the sky much less appealing today is the success of the scientific enterprise.

On the theoretical level, the impact of science would not have been all that great, because on this level, it is as abstruse as philosophy. The reason that the challenge of science to religious belief proved more formidable than that of any philosophy is that technology makes a palpable difference to the life of every man, whether he understands scientific theory or not. Science, in its technological manifestations, can deliver "pie" here and now. We can produce food, automobiles, and the rest in incredible quantities. Most people are not apt to be satisfied with promises of plenty in a future life; they want it *all*, and they want it *now*.

THE REVOLUTIONARY GOAL:
ELIMINATE METAPHYSICS AND THEOLOGY

It is generally understood that the rise of science challenged theology. It is less widely appreciated that it also constituted a serious challenge to philosophy. One of the most impressive features of science is its ability to progress. Newtonian science may have been overthrown by the developments of the twentieth century, but this has not led to a return to pre-Newtonian views like those of Ptolemaic astronomy. By contrast, philosophy seems static. The history of philosophy has often been written in terms of the debates between metaphysicians who were oriented to what they claimed were invisible realities and philosophers who were oriented to the observable world. The realities that metaphysicians claimed to uncover varied greatly in character from the Forms of Plato to the general substances of the English philosopher John Locke (1632–1704). The meaning of these particular concepts is of no concern to us in this context; what is important is a sense for a major characteristic which all metaphysical realities share. W. T. Stace, a contemporary philosopher, expresses it by referring to metaphysics as "any type of thought which depends on the distinction between an outer appearance and an inner reality, and which asserts that there is a reality lying behind the appearances which *never* itself appears."[3] In this sense theologians who talk of the transcendent God are also metaphysicians. According to theologians, we see God's creation but we *never* see God.

Metaphysicians have always generated opposition. As a philosopher recently put it: "Philosophical debates are hottest between those philosophers who want to make certain entries in the list of what there is in the world and other philosophers who do not want to let them get away with it."[4] The debates raged, but philosophy did not progress. Instead, in each generation the same types of philosophical schools seemed to emerge, making the kinds of points that had been made by their predecessors. The only significant change seemed to be in the technical terms that were used to make them. Given the pretentions of philosophers, especially of metaphysicians, to achieve a higher type of knowledge than that available to scientists, this was a deplorable state of affairs. It led Immanuel Kant to draw an invidious comparison between metaphysics and the natural sciences:

> If it [metaphysics] be a science, how comes it that it cannot, like other science, obtain universal and permanent recognition? . . . Everybody, however ignorant in other matters, may deliver a final verdict, as in this domain there is as yet no standard weight and measure to distinguish sound knowledge from shallow talk.[5]

Kant's effort to establish weights and measures for metaphysics is one of the most impressive intellectual achievements in history. Yet his version of metaphysics also failed "to obtain universal and permanent recognition." The logical positivists adopted a number of Kant's important technical terms. The crucial ones were—*analytic, synthetic, a priori,* and *a posteriori*—terms that will soon be clarified. Kant used them in an effort to reform metaphysics, but the positivists used them in an effort to eliminate it. They thought that philosophy could only achieve progress that was comparable to that of science if metaphysics, and theology as well, no longer received serious attention from philosophers.

Anyone unfamiliar with the history of philosophy can hardly appreciate the startling character of this proposal. The cultural prestige of philosophy and even its subject matter seemed inescapably bound up with metaphysics and theology. As far as prestige is concerned, the issue hinges on the contrast between human beings and animals. Both use their senses to observe physical objects, but only humans can reason. Metaphysicians and theologians used reason to claim knowledge of realities of a higher order than the mere physical objects which animals can also observe. These alleged realities transcend, that is, they are utterly beyond the reach of the senses. Since God is an illustration of these transcendent realities, the high stakes involved are obvious.

The proposal to eliminate metaphysics and theology was not only a threat to the philosophical mystique, it threatened to leave philosophy without a subject matter. Scientists work by means of *observations*, and they are very successful at it. The study of *nonobservable* realities like God seemed to be the special subject matter of philosophy. The proposal to eliminate them from philosophy seemed like proposing to revise *Hamlet* by eliminating the Prince of Denmark.

The positivists were not the first philosophers to engage in sharp criticisms of arguments to transcendent realities. Empiricism, that is, the view that all knowledge is rooted in sense experience, is a traditional philosophical position. It was directed against rationalist metaphysicians who thought they could attain knowledge of transcendent realities on the basis of deductive reasoning of the kind used in mathematics. The pre-positivistic empiricists who opposed the rationalists tended to begin with sense experience and to be less rigorously deductive in their approach to knowledge. I have already noted that John Locke, one of the leading English empiricists, wrote of "general substances" which are, in his scheme, metaphysical entities that are not accessible to the senses. This is enough to show that the pre-positivist empiricists did not try to eliminate metaphysics and theology; indeed, they had metaphysical and theological positions of their own. Furthermore, they expended a great deal of their energies in trying to show what was wrong with the arguments of rationalist metaphysicians and theologians. These were the ancient "never get anywhere" disputes that Kant was complaining about in the paragraph quoted above.

In part, the positivists represented a continuation of the empiricist tradition but they were also, as they claimed to be, revolutionary. Their effort to eliminate metaphysics differed radically from the traditional empiricist criticisms of individual metaphysical arguments. What was at issue will be clearer if we consider an analogy.

Imagine a great university that admits anyone who applies. The faculty then works over each and every candidate, some flunk out, and others graduate. Now let us suppose that a number of young professors with new ideas reject these traditional procedures. They are convinced that the university will never progress in its task of advancing knowledge as long as time is wasted in flunking candidates who shouldn't have been admitted in the first place. They propose a preliminary examination that will be taken by all candidates for admission. It is designed to be as simple as possible: as an objective examination that can be graded by a computer. By means of it, they propose to eliminate candidates who are obviously unworthy. Those who pass and are admitted as qualified candidates for the degree are then examined just as carefully as under the old procedures. In the end, some graduate, and others do not. The important gain of this new system is that the faculty confines its efforts to a select group of promising candidates, even though some of them will still fail to work out.

The traditional empiricists used techniques that were rather like the old admission procedures. They studied all metaphysical and theological works and tried to refute statements like "The Absolute is perfect" or "God is omnipotent." The revised admission procedure mirrors the goals of the logical positivists. They thought they had a preliminary check on philosophical works that would determine, with a minimum of time and effort, whether books that contain statements like "The Absolute is perfect" were worth studying in detail. If a work failed to pass, it was set aside as worthless, and the positivists didn't even bother to argue with its author. If it passed, it would be studied very carefully. It might be found wanting, but at least the positivists would have assured themselves beforehand that the study was worth the effort.

The preliminary examination applied to philosophical work by the positivists was the test of verification. Before we can understand their use of it, we shall have to examine its construction within the framework of the analytic-synthetic distinction.[6]

THE ANALYTIC AND THE SYNTHETIC

"True," for a philosopher, is like the assayer's statement that "This mineral is gold." It has been inspected and certified. It is the real thing. The positivists, like all philosophers, are careful about stamping "true" on any statements. There are many types of sentences which could never, because of their grammatical form, be used to make true statements. These include questions like "What's for dinner?" exclamations, "O boy!" and imperatives, "Bring it now!" The grammatical form of a sentence that can be labeled "true" is the declarative, as in "Two plus three equals five" and "John F. Kennedy was elected President of the United States in 1960."[7] The distinctive feature of the positivists' challenge to metaphysics and theology is the effort to drive a wedge between proper grammatical form and proper philosophical form. In saying that "The Absolute is perfect," the metaphysician makes a declarative statement which is grammatically correct. He intends it as a cognitive claim, that is, a claim to know that something is true. The positivists thought that they could show that statements of this kind were incapable of being true. Therefore, metaphysicians who write these sentences cannot be making genuine cognitive claims.

The positivists introduced a radical restriction on the kinds of statements that had a capacity for being true. They insisted that all such statements were members of one of two mutually exclusive classes—the *analytic* and the *synthetic*. Countless statements from the philosophical tradition could not, by this standard, be true because statements like "The Absolute is perfect" or "God is omnipotent" are, according to the positivists, neither analytic nor synthetic. Metaphysicians and theologians protested against the arbitrariness of this restriction. The positivists proudly acknowledged the extreme and radical character of their procedures; however, they denied that this restriction was arbitrary. It was rooted in their admiration for mathematics and science, which are the two most successful modes of knowing that men have achieved.[8]

The Analytic: The Necessary Truths of Mathematics and Logic

The positivists derived their use of the "analytic" by reflecting on the character of true statements made in mathematics and logic. The main features of analytic statements, as the positivists understood them, are:

1 Analytic statements are necessarily true; their denials are contradictions.
2 They are known to be true a priori.
3 They do not convey factual information.

Necessity   Philosophers have always been fascinated by mathematics. Statements like "Two plus three equals five" have been their ideal illustrations of true statements because of a peculiar property, they are not merely true, their truth is necessary. You cannot consider them false even for the sake of argument or fantasy. For the sake of argument we can imagine that the statement "John F. Kennedy was assassinated in 1963" is false. And for the sake of fantasy, we may, in reading the comic strip "Mandrake the Magician" pretend that the statement "All men are visible to agents with normal vision" is false because Mandrake is supposed to be able to make himself invisible. Mathematical statements like "Two plus three equals five" cannot be treated this way. Provided that we keep our symbolism and rules constant, even the most clever author of science fiction cannot change their truth value. They are true for everyone, at every time, and every place.

The analytic is not confined to mathematics. A limitless number of verbal statements have the same coercive power, for example, "All bachelors are unmarried" and "It is snowing or it is not snowing." These statements, like those of mathematics, are analytic and necessarily true because their truth depends on purely logical considerations. It is impossible to deny their truth because to do so involves one in contradiction and contradictions are necessarily false. The logical structure of an analytic statement may not appear on the surface, but it is there. Consider the statement "All bachelors are unmarried." Remember that a crucial part of the definition of a bachelor is a person who is *unmarried* and male. The statement can then be rewritten by letting "A" stand for unmarried, and "B" for male. It then reads, "All A&B are A." To deny the truth of this statement by talking of a married bachelor would involve a contradiction because A&B can only be true if both A and B are true. Therefore, we cannot affirm the truth of A&B and simultaneously declare A to be false. To do so would be like saying, "A white horse is *not* white."

A Priori   An important feature of analytic statements is related to their logical character. They are known a priori, that is, they are known to be true independently of observations of the world. To check on the truth of the analytic statement "All bachelors are unmarried," we need only to reflect on the meaning of the terms and on the rules of the English language. We do not need to go out into the world and make observations like polling all bachelors in order to find out whether or not they are married.

The a priori character of analytic statements explains a peculiarity of our intellectual interaction. If someone challenges the truth of the statement "Alan Jones is unmarried" (a statement of fact which is not analytic), he calls the statement into question. If someone challenges the truth of "All bachelors are unmarried," he calls his understanding of the statement into question. If he persists in challenging the truth of this statement and of other statements like it, we would come to question his basic intellectual capacities.

Not Factually Informative   In the domain of necessity there are two kinds of statements. They are either *analytic*, that is, necessarily true, such as, "A square has four sides" (because a square is, by definition, a four-sided figure), or *contradictory*, that is, necessarily false, as in the case of "This square has three sides." A contradiction is the simultaneous affirmation of "*A* and not *A*" where the sense of *A* does not change. The statement is contradictory because it amounts to saying that "A square has four sides and a square does not have four sides."

Analytic statements are necessarily true. Their truth is known with certainty because, as we have seen, it follows from an analysis of their logical structure. This certainty is, however, purchased at a price; analytic statements are not informative about states of affairs in the world. Analytic statements merely elaborate the rules governing our use of words and other symbols. Like all matters relating to the analytic, this point is obvious once you grasp it, and baffling until you do. An illustration may help. It will deal with the analytic statement, "It is snowing or it is not snowing," which certainly seems to be about a state of affairs in the world, namely, about the weather.

I am at Aspen during the ski season, but there's no snow. I have no prospect of coming back, and I am brooding about my bad luck in front of the fire in the basement lounge of a ski lodge. There are no windows so I can't see out. Suddenly a friend bursts into the lounge shouting exhuberantly: "It is snowing!" I jump out of my chair and break for the stairs so that I can run to the picture window on the next floor and watch the beautiful stuff come down.

Now let's try an instant replay on this scenario. I am at Aspen during the ski season and there's no snow. I am brooding in the windowless basement of a ski lodge when my friend bursts in and shouts: "It is snowing!" As I jump out of my chair and break for the stairs, he adds: "Or it is not snowing." Collapse and fadeout!

The point is that the analytic statement "It is snowing or it is not snowing" only appears to be about the weather. This becomes clear when we realize that its truth is compatible with any weather whatever—with rain, sleet, or sunshine as well as with snow. Actually, the statement is not about the weather at all. Rather, it serves to illustrate the operation of "or" as a logical connective. We know that this statement is true a priori, that is, by inspecting the statement. We do not have to check the weather to know it because any statement with the logical form "*A* or not *A*" is necessarily true. In this case we substituted "It is snowing" for *A*, but the results would still be necessarily true if we changed the statement to

"There are microbes or there are not microbes," "It is purple or it is not purple," and "It is a miracle or it is not a miracle." We can be sure that these statements are not informative about germs, colors, or religion. Like the statement about snow, they serve only to show how "or" functions logically. To deny their truth is impossible, but they are not capable of conveying information about states of affairs in the world. The truth of an analytic statement is compatible with any state of affairs whatever because analytic statements are not informative with regard to any state of affairs.

The exposition may have given the impression that the analytic is trivial; it is *not*. After all, the analytic embraces two of the most important intellectual disciplines—mathematics and logic.

In addition, analytic statements may be said to be informative in some rather special, but important, senses of that term. A person who first comes to realize the truth of an analytic statement increases his personal store of information in the psychological sense. It is not, however, information about states of affairs in the world. For example, someone may know what a cube is without being aware of the fact that it has twelve edges. If this is pointed out, he receives additional information. It is, however, only information about the defining characteristic of cubes. Once you know some of them, the rest of the characteristics are logically tied in. It only requires reflection, or proper stimulation, to bring them to conscious awareness. Contrast the statement "A cube has twelve edges" with the statement "The lobby of the Empire State Building is cubical." In order to check on the truth of the second statement, awareness of the defining characteristics of cubes is not enough, we must go out into the world and do some measuring.

The most important sense in which the analytic may be regarded as informative is that it provides information about the rules that control the use of symbolic systems. Without this information regarding mathematical and symbolic systems, we could hardly hope to do significant work in any field. Indeed, without this information we cannot even speak a language because we will not know how to hang words together. In this connection, we might consider the exchange between Alice and Humpty Dumpty in Lewis Carroll's *Through the Looking Glass.*

Humpty Dumpty: There are 364 days when you might get un-birthday presents . . . and only *one* for birthday presents, you know. There's glory for you.

Alice: I don't know what you mean by "glory."

Humpty Dumpty: Of course you don't—till I tell you. I meant "there's a nice knock-down argument" for you.

Alice: But "glory" doesn't mean "a nice knock-down argument!"

Humpty Dumpty: When I use a word, it means just what I choose it to mean—neither more nor less.

Alice: The question is whether you *can* make words mean different things.

Humpty Dumpty: The question is, which is to be master—that's all.

It is important to note that if Humpty Dumpty's linguistic policies were actually in force, this delightful interchange could not take place. There could be no linguistic communication because words would not have fixed meanings. They could not even be used for the purpose of saying that "glory" means "there's a nice knock-down argument."

The analytic then, is important, and it is even, in some special senses, informative. Analytic statements deal with the internal relations of words and numbers. They deal with the way that words and numbers must necessarily relate to one another if they are to be used meaningfully. They do not deal with the way that words and numbers are used to refer to states of affairs in the world. They do not deal with matters of fact.

The Synthetic: The Possible Truths of Fact

According to the positivists, there is only one other class of statements that is capable of being true—the *synthetic*. The defining characteristics of the synthetic can be contrasted with those of the analytic.

1   It is possible for synthetic statements to be either true or false.
2   Their truth or falsity is determined a posteriori.
3   They convey factual information.

Either True or False   In contrast to analytic statements, which are necessarily true and contradictions that are necessarily false, it is possible for synthetic statements to be either true or false. To appreciate the difference, we need only add the word "not" to an example of each class. Vary one of the standard examples of an analytic statement in this way, and it yields "It is not the case that bachelors are unmarried," which cannot possibly be true; it is a contradiction. On the other hand, we have already considered a good example of a synthetic statement, "Alan Jones is unmarried." Add the word "not," and the result, "Alan Jones is *not* unmarried," makes just as much sense as the original statement that he *is* unmarried. Both statements may be either true or false. To find out whether either of them is actually true or false, we must check them out by means of observations.

A Posteriori   In checking on the truth of synthetic statements by observations, we use our senses, primarily, sight, hearing, and touch. In checking on "Alan Jones is unmarried," we would observe his habits, his residence, and we would check the records at Town Hall to see if we could find a marriage license with his name on it. Philosophers call this method of checking the truth of statements *a posteriori*. It means roughly, "after," that is, the truth of the statement is determined after observation, which contrasts sharply with the a priori.

Factually Informative We have already considered examples of the factually informative character of synthetic statements. "It is snowing" is used to provide information about a state of affairs "out there." "Alan Jones is a bachelor" is intended to tell us something specific about a particular person. These synthetic statements convey information that cannot be derived from mere reflection on the meaning of the words used in them.

A final illustration may be useful in clarifying the distinction between the analytic and the synthetic. In the game of chess the statement "Bishops are those pieces which move diagonally" is analytic. It tells us about the patterns in which bishops necessarily move, but it doesn't inform us about specific moves in any particular game of chess. By contrast, a newspaper account of a championship match will contain statements like "Fischer, playing white, moved his queen's bishop to K5." This move was not necessary. Within the rules of chess, he might have moved differently. The specific move is a matter of fact; the statement of it is synthetic.

Pseudo-synthetic

The positivists claimed to have uncovered a type of statement that appears to be synthetic, that is, factual, but which is not the genuine article. They used the prefix "pseudo," that is, pretended or unreal, to set them apart. *Pseudo-synthetic* statements are, therefore, grammatically similar to genuine ones, and like them, they appear to convey information about states of affairs in the world. Positivists charged that pseudo-synthetic statements are incapable of doing any such thing because they lack all capacity for being true. The instrument by which the positivists tried to demonstrate this was the test of verification. Before discussing this test in detail, it will be useful to develop a sense for the kinds of analyses that led positivists to categorize statements as pseudo-synthetic.

The status of a statement is a matter of language and it might seem that a mere inspection of the words of a statement would enable us to classify it, but the issue is more complex. The determination of the status of a statement is affected by such factors as the philosopher's use of his words and his openness to evidence that challenges the truth of his statements.

The Refusal to Accept Counter-Evidence   A common application of the term "pseudo-synthetic" results from circumstances in which a metaphysician or theologian makes a statement that seems to be straightforwardly synthetic. The positivist asks for a specification of the kinds of evidence that would determine its truth or falsity. The thinker who made the statement refuses but insists, all the same, that the statement tells us something about states of affairs in the world. The positivist then charges that the statement in question is pseudo-synthetic. The application of this line of analysis to the theological statement "God loves us as a father loves his children" will be treated later (see pp. 46 ff). At this point it will be more helpful to consider examples that are neither theological nor philosophical.

We all know people who are addicted to making large-scale generalizations about minorities. These are often derogatory, but in an effort to keep psychological sensitivities low and logical awareness high, let me present a few flattering ones: "All Irishmen are charming," "All Jews are intelligent," and "All Blacks are graceful." The statements are intended to be synthetic because the person making them assures his hearers that these are characteristics they can expect to find in each member of certain identifiable groups. In that case, one instance of a surly Irishman, a stupid Jew, or an awkward Black should be enough to show that each of the statements is false. If the person making the statement accepts the counter-evidence and admits that his statement is false, all is in order. His statement was both intended to be synthetic (factual), and it proved to be genuinely synthetic because he was receptive to observations that showed that the statement was untrue.

Yet people who make generalizations of this kind are notoriously reluctant to accept counter-evidence. Tell a person who claims "All Irishmen are charming" that you have an Irish friend who is not charming and you are apt to get answers like: "When you get to know him better you'll see that he *really* is charming" or "If he isn't charming then he can't *really* be Irish." Under cross-examination it becomes clear that the person intends to make a synthetic statement, but he refuses to let any observations count against its truth. In that case, the positivists insist that the statement is pseudo-synthetic.

Pseudo-synthetic Statements Cannot Be Either True or False
We are now in a position to understand the positivist's claim that pseudo-synthetic statements lack "truth-capacity" as well as truth. The positivists maintained that there were two and only two procedures that were appropriate to determining the truth of a statement: either the a priori procedures used for analytic statements or the a posteriori ones that

are applied to synthetic statements. In the case of a pseudo-synthetic statement both are ruled out by the person making it. The a priori is ruled out by his intention to use the statement to convey factual information. Positivists insist that he should in that case, be willing to accept the a posteriori method of checking on synthetic statements which involves verification by means of observations. Yet the person making the statement resolutely refuses to specify any observations that would be relevant to determining its truth or falsity. According to the positivists, he has ruled out *all* procedures by which the truth of his statement might be determined and it is shown to be without any capacity for truth.

Since pseudo-synthetic statements have no capacity for truth, it is obvious that they are not actually true. What is less obvious is the further point urged by the positivists, namely, that pseudo-synthetic statements cannot be false either. They fall outside the range of statements that can be either true or false. It follows that in the positivists' scheme of things, "false" is something of a compliment. Of course, it is not nearly as much of a compliment as "true," but at least a false statement like "Adlai Stevenson was elected President of the United States in 1952" is genuinely synthetic. It might have been true, it merely happens to be false. By contrast, a pseudo-synthetic statement cannot possibly be false any more than it can be true. Therefore, the positivists declared that pseudo-synthetic statements were "factually meaningless."

When positivists refer to a statement as "factually meaningless," they are using the word "meaningless" (and its contrast term "meaningful") in a special sense. It can only be understood in the context of their philosophical program.

If supposedly synthetic statements are found to be capable of being either true or false, they make a genuine cognitive claim. Positivists certify them as genuinely synthetic and regard them as "cognitively meaningful" or "factually meaningful" ("empirical" may be substituted for "factual"). The terms are often used interchangeably, but as I use them cognitively, "meaningful" is broader than "factually meaningful." A statement is *cognitively meaningful* if it is *analytic or genuinely synthetic.* A statement is *factually (or empirically) meaningful,* if and only if, it is *genuinely synthetic.* Since pseudo-synthetic statements are incapable of being either true or false, it is clear that they are both "cognitively" and "factually" meaningless. There is no point in making an effort to determine whether or not they are true or false because they cannot possibly be either true or false.

As used in this context, the word "meaningless" is misleading. It suggests that a statement like "God loves us as a father loves his children," which is labeled "pseudo-synthetic," cannot be understood.

This is not the case. Soon after the positivists introduced the notion of cognitive meaninglessness, philosophers began to criticize it. They noted that the positivists obviously understood a great number of allegedly cognitively meaningless statements. After all, unless the positivists understood them, they would not have been able to demonstrate (at least to their own satisfaction) that they could not possibly be true.[9] By claiming that metaphysical and theological statements were factually (or cognitively) meaningless, the positivists were not (in general) asserting that these statements were utterly unintelligible gibberish. The positivists were, rather, trying to expose the pretentiousness of these statements. It is precisely because they are not gibberish that they seem to convey information about the world. Yet the positivists were convinced that they were incapable of doing so. "Factually meaningless" can therefore be paired with "pseudo-synthetic" as terms that expressed the positivists' confidence that they had seen through the deceptive appearances of metaphysical and theological statements.

Far from claiming that metaphysical and theological statements were utterly meaningless, the positivists actually assigned a special type of meaning to them, namely, "emotive meaning." According to the positivists, a statement like "God loves us as a father loves his children" cannot, when understood literally, be either true or false. Therefore, it cannot have factual meaning. It can, however, have emotive meaning which involves the fairly consistent set of emotional responses it elicits from people who have been conditioned to expressions of this kind.[10]

Furthermore, the positivists conceded the sincerity of the metaphysicians and theologians who made pseudo-synthetic statements. They were not accusing these thinkers of deliberately trying to mislead their readers.[11] After all, the positivists' claim to revolutionary significance was bound up with the fact that the cognitive meaninglessness of metaphysical and theological statements was not easily uncovered. These statements had been regarded as cognitively meaningful by generations of philosophers, even by pre-positivistic empiricists who often challenged their truth.

The question of why previous generations of philosophers had been deceived is an interesting one.[12] A possible explanation involves the appeal to a cultural gap: scientists achieved unprecedented knowledge of the world, but it took a long while for the implications of scientific method to sink in. The positivists obviously thought that they were the first philosophers who fully understood these implications. They declared that scientific statements are genuinely synthetic and that metaphysical and theological statements are parasitic on them (as well as on common sense statements of fact). A theological statement like "God loves us" seems to be just as synthetic as the statement "Hydrogen atoms have one electron." Theologians who make statements of this kind want to provide important information about the world. Yet, unlike scientists, they do not specify observations that would verify the truth of their claims. The possibility of checking on the truth or falsity of supposedly synthetic statements by means of observations is what the issue of verification is all about.

VERIFICATION: THE TEST FOR FACTUAL MEANINGFULNESS

An obvious question arises at this point: How do we determine whether a supposedly synthetic statement is capable of being true or false? In answering this question the positivists proposed the test of verification which has also been called the empiricist criterion of meaning. It was intended to be as quick and simple as the litmus paper test that determines whether a solution is acidic or alkaline. The positivists probed the scientific method in an effort to find the element that made scientific work so successful. They were certain that it could not be common sense; after all, sophisticated scientific work like theoretical physics is written in a notation that is almost purely logical and mathematical. A literate person who has not studied the field cannot even read a page of it. It is so abstract that scientists themselves may forget that their theories relate to states of affairs in the world. Yet, the theories generate expectations. If the observations made conform with the results that the theory leads the scientists to anticipate, then, to that extent, the statement of the theory is verified; it is true. If the observations fail to conform to the expectations, then (provided that the accuracy of the experiments and similar factors have been checked out) the theory is falsified. Once falsified it can be discarded, and scientists are free to pursue more fruitful lines of inquiry. In this way science can progress.

Verification is the positivists' adaptation of the role of experimental work in science to philosophical purposes. If a grammatical and philosophical analysis shows that a statement is supposed to be synthetic, positivists ask, How can it be verified? If it is *not* possible to specify observations that would verify it, then it is pseudo-synthetic. It has failed the preliminary examination and is not worthy of serious philosophical consideration. It can be stowed in a "dead file" under "factually meaningless."

If it is possible to specify observations that would check out a supposedly synthetic statement, one can proceed to do so. If the observations correspond to the state of affairs communicated by the statement, it is true; if they do not match, it is false. In verifying "This book has white pages and black print" one has only to look at the book in his hands to see that it is true. The statement "This book has yellow pages and red print," is checked out in the same way. It is false, but it is a perfectly meaningful synthetic or factual statement that might have been true.

The verification of a common sense statement like "This book has white pages and black print," is the easiest type to understand. It is also the kind of statement that is least relevant to a discussion of verification and theology. On the one hand, it is not even clearly relevant to the verification of scientific hypotheses. They are verified by observations, but the relation is not as simple as it is in the case of checking on the colors of a book.[13] On the other hand, it should be obvious that theological statements about God are not *intended* to be verified by direct observations. God is not like a unicorn or a flying saucer, that is, an object that is supposed to be observable but whose existence is called into question because no reliable observations ever turn up. After all, theologians claim that God is utterly beyond sense experience; this is part of the meaning of "transcendent."

The issue of verification and theology pivots around the positivists' claim that verification plays a crucial and successful role in scientific work and that it is not operative at all, or not successfully, in the work of theologians. To appreciate the complexity of the issue we shall have to consider some of the problems that emerged in connection with the test of verification as well as two important variations on it—falsification and confirmation.

Chapter 2

From Positivism
to Analysis

Since the mid-fifties, there have been few philosophers who accept the label *logical positivist*. The central concerns of the logical positivists are still part of the philosophical scene, but their positions have been either rejected or refined. Their successors are a large company of empiricist philosophers. All of them practice philosophy by exploring the nature of language and its spectrum of legitimate meanings (in the philosophical, not the dictionary sense). They agree that the gleaning of factual information is best left to scientists. They remain hostile to speculative systems of philosophy in the grand style of G. W. Hegel and F. H. Bradley. Their work, however, is much more varied than that of the positivists, and some of it is even reminiscent of what metaphysicians have done in the past. These contemporary empiricists are called by many names, but generally by the name *philosophical analysts*, or simply, *analysts*.

There is no sharp line dividing the analysts from their positivist predecessors. The work of refining positivism was largely a self-critical enterprise. The positivists' ability to nail down the reasons for the inadequacy of the various formulations of the test of verification is evidence of a rigor that contrasts favorably with much of the traditional metaphysical and theological writing that they rejected.[14] Some of the positivists of the Vienna Circle, such as Rudolf Carnap, Herbert Feigl, and C. G. Hempel, became leading figures on the analytic scene. So too did A. J. Ayer whose *Language, Truth and Logic* (1936) did so much to bring positivism to the attention of philosophers in the English-speaking world. These thinkers abandoned or modified positivistic conclusions while retaining the respect for science and the bias against metaphysics and theology that characterized their earlier work.

On the English scene, analysis has been less oriented to science and mathematics and more concerned with articulating and emphasizing the importance of ordinary language to philosophy. Gilbert Ryle and J. L. Austin have been significant representatives of this tendency, but the greatest influence was that of the late work of Ludwig Wittgenstein. He provided an impetus to the abandonment of positivistic rigidity in favor of more supple approaches to meaning and also to the wider range of concerns that contemporary analysts manifest. By lecturing on these matters at Cambridge during the thirties and forties he influenced a generation of philosophers, among them were Elizabeth Anscombe, Peter Geach, Norman Malcolm, and John Wisdom. His influence became much wider when a number of his books were posthumously published during the fifties.

There are many reasons for the demise of positivism as a self-confident and integrated movement. A major one is the fact that the test of verification, which was supposed to enable philosophy to progress in a manner comparable to scientific progress, itself became mired in difficulties of a peculiarly philosophical kind.

STATEMENTS OF THE TEST ARE NEITHER ANALYTIC NOR SYNTHETIC

The positivists claimed that only two classes of statements were capable of being true and therefore cognitively meaningful: the analytic and the synthetic. They soon suffered the embarrassment of having their philosophical opponents note that standard statements of the test of verification were not members of either class. It follows that by the positivists' standards they were cognitively meaningless, and therefore, no threat to metaphysics and theology.

The test of verification can be formulated as follows: A statement is factually meaningful if and only if there are observations that could, in principle, verify it. Critics of positivism used a variety of arguments to show that this statement is cognitively meaningless.[15] I will present a small sampling of them.

Analytic

As we have seen, the positivists claimed that analytic statements are necessarily true because their denials involve us in contradictions. The truth of statements like "All bachelors are unmarried" is, therefore, universally acknowledged. When we consider the statement of the test of verification, things are quite different. (1) No contradiction is involved in denying that a statement is factually meaningful if and only if there are observations that would, in principle, verify it. (2) When the positivists first formulated their statement of the test, they were a radical minority. Most philosophers at the time not only thought that the statement of the test could be denied without contradiction, but they thought that the *denial* of the *statement* of the test was *true*. Therefore, the positivists could not claim that the statement of the test was cognitively meaningful on the grounds that it is analytic because it lacks the necessity and universality required for analytic status.

Synthetic

The other option is to claim that the statement of the test of verification is synthetic. Positivists would then have to assume the burden of specifying the observations that would verify the statement that a statement is factually meaningful if and only if there are observations that would, in principle, verify it. Yet factual meaningfulness is simply not the sort of concept that can be verified by observations. Therefore, this route was also closed to the positivists and they were forced to concede that statements of the test were neither analytic nor synthetic. The positivists' opponents seized on this admission to claim that the statement of the test was cognitively meaningless and could be safely ignored. The positivists' response was to insist that it was nevertheless useful and important.

Proposal

Faced with this unhappy state of affairs regarding the status of the statement of the test of verification, the positivists denied that it was a statement (or an "assertion" or a "proposition," which are often interchanged with "statement"). C. G. Hempel put it in the following terms: "One might think of construing the criterion as a definition which indicates what empiricists propose to understand by a cognitively significant sentence; thus understood, it would not have the character of an assertion and would be neither true nor false. But this conception would attribute to the criterion a measure of arbitrariness which cannot be reconciled with the heated controversies it has engendered. . . ."[16] To elaborate: as a *proposal* the statement of the test of verification (which Hempel refers to as "the empiricist criterion of meaning") would have the *grammatical form* of an *imperative sentence* in the first person plural, that is, the form of sentence that begins with the phrase, "Let us." In that case, the proposal might be put as follows: Let us restrict factual meaningfulness to statements that are verifiable in principle. This would, on *grammatical* grounds alone—without further philosophical analysis—preclude the possibility that the proposal could be cognitively meaningful because, as we have seen, only *declarative sentences* can be either analytic or synthetic (see pp. 13f). As Hempel notes in the case of the proposal, which is an imperative, the question of its truth or falsity does not even come up. This means that the statement of the test cannot be true. In that case, the positivists' insistence on restricting factual meaningfulness to statements that are, in principle, verifiable by observations, seems utterly arbitrary. The positivists may propose to do so. However, given the fact that the statement of the test cannot possibly be true, the positivists' opponents are free to propose different definitions of factualy meaningfulness.

Although the positivists conceded the point that the statement of the test of verification was itself neither analytic nor synthetic, they were confident that its practical benefits would compensate for the theoretical flaw of its status as a statement. Yet success in practice is a standard that varies according to one's purposes. At first, the positivists were happy with the way the test worked in practice, because it seemed to do the job of excluding metaphysics and theology without damaging the status of scientific or common sense statements. Obviously, metaphysicians and theologians would not be at all happy with this sort of "practice." They were, therefore, by no means prepared to ignore the theoretical flaw pertaining to its status, and to accept the test of verifiability as a useful proposal.

In any case, the positivists themselves discovered flaws in the way the test operated in practice. This made it far less useful for the positivists' anti-metaphysical and anti-theological purposes.

THE DIFFICULTIES OF VERIFICATION
AND ITS REFORMULATIONS

Once the point of the test of verification is understood, it seems almost intuitive. Therefore, it should be easy to formulate an adequate statement of it, but this task proved to be anything but easy. One way of coming at the issue is to consider A. J. Ayer's point that a crucial consideration in appraising the adequacy of a criterion of factual meaningfulness is that it should yield acceptable results in noncontroversial cases.[17] Examples of statements that philosophers today find noncontroversial are "There is molten metal at the earth's core," "All crows are black," and "Horses exist." They are common sense statements whose factual meaningfulness seems obvious. Similarly, the factual meaningfulness of statements of well-established scientific laws, like the law of gravity, seem noncontroversial. Yet, as we shall soon see, positivist versions of verification that denied factual meaningfulness to metaphysical and theological statements also denied them to these seemingly noncontroversial common sense and scientific statements. This is an unacceptable result and constituted a critical breakdown in the positivists' program.

Many criticisms have been directed against the positivists' versions of verification; I shall present four.[18] The positivists quickly overcame the first but they were never able to solve the problems connected with the other three.

    1   Countless statements that the positivists regarded as factually meaningful could not be verified because of practical difficulties.

    2   The test of verification was too restrictive. It excluded metaphysics and theology, but it also resulted in branding as meaningless many scientific and common sense statements that the positivists regarded as meaningful.

    3   An effort to recast the test in terms of falsification proved to be too restrictive in this same sense.

    4   The test was modified to confirmation in order to include as factually meaningful some standard scientific and common sense statements. This proved too permissive, it also "passed" metaphysical and theological statements.

VERIFIABILITY: STATEMENTS THAT CAN BE VERIFIED IN PRINCIPLE

Early in the game, positivists introduced a major modification of their test. Initially they insisted that the only statements which were factually meaningful were those which could actually be verified like "This book has white pages and black print." The positivists were soon to acknowledge the excessive restrictiveness of this criterion. "There is molten metal at the earth's core" is probably true, but it is a statement whose truth we cannot actually verify. Even at our present state of advanced technology, there is no way of burrowing to the center of the earth. However, we are familiar with molten metal and if we could reach the center of the earth, we would know what to look for in the effort to verify this statement. The statement, "There is a gold sphere, twenty feet in diameter, at the earth's core" is almost certainly false. If we could get to the earth's core, it would be easy to falsify it, because in this case as well, we would know what to look for. The crucial point is not whether the statement would turn out to be true or false; it is whether there are *conceivable* observations that would, in principle, verify or falsify it. The statements we have just considered seem to be factually meaningful, yet the highly restrictive version of verification first used by the positivists denied them this status.

The positivists successfully overcame this difficulty. They modified their earlier position and conceded factually meaningful status to statements that could be verified *in principle* ("We'd know what to look for, if we could get there"), even though, for *practical* reasons, they cannot be verified in fact.[19]

To elaborate, the statement "There are twenty daemons at the center of the earth" is supposedly synthetic like the statements about molten metal and the gold sphere. There is, however, a crucial difference; daemons are defined as being inaccessible to the senses. Therefore, even if we could burrow to the center of the earth, we wouldn't know what to look for when we got there. For this reason, the statement "There are twenty daemons at the center of the earth" is unverifiable *in principle*. Positivists would, with maximal confidence, classify it as pseudo-synthetic, and declare it to be factually meaningless.

Verification Is Too Restrictive: It Eliminates Common Sense and Science

The test of verifiability, that is, verification in principle, may be phrased: A statement is factually meaningful if and only if there are observations that could, in principle, verify it. The difficulties of verifiability involve the use of such apparently simple words as "all," "some," and "exists." This discussion will focus on "all," a word that is unproblematic in ordinary English, but which proves treacherous in the context of verification.

"All crows are black" seems to be a straightforward synthetic statement. It is intended to convey information about a state of affairs in the world, and it can be checked by observations. It is almost certainly true, as well as factually meaningful. Philosophical reflection, however, uncovers a peculiarity of this statement arising from the word "all." In order to appreciate it, compare the statement "All crows are black" with "This crow is black." The statement about "this crow" is conclusively verifiable. To establish its truth, we have only to look at the crow being pointed to. The statement about "all crows" seems to allow for the same verification procedure; looking at crows. However, no matter how many crows are checked out in the course of history, there is always the possibility that an exception will turn up: A yellow bird, born of two black crows, and incontestably crowlike in all other respects, in other words, a yellow crow! Therefore, *as long as it is not qualified by a limitation of time* (as in "All crows *now living* are black"), the statement "All crows are black" is not verifiable—not even *in principle.*

At first it might seem as though the difficulty with "All crows are black" is like the problem associated with one of our earlier statements: "There is molten metal at the earth's core." Both statements cannot be verified, but both seem factually meaningful and probably true. Actually, the two statements are quite different. There is a technological problem associated with the statement about the core of the earth. Anytime we could manage to get there, we would have no difficulty in verifying this statement. Therefore, it is factually meaningful. There is also a merely practical difficulty involved in verifying the statement "All crows *now living* are black"; it would be hard to assemble them. By contrast, the difficulty with the statement "All crows are black" is *logical.* The statement is not verifiable, even in principle, because we cannot, logically cannot, exclude the possibility of contrary evidence emerging at some future date. "All crows are black" is then, by the test of verifiability, factually meaningless, which was upsetting to the positivists because it is the kind of noncontroversial statement whose meaningfulness they had no desire to challenge.

From the positivists' standpoint, an even more regrettable consequence of this excessive restrictiveness of the principle of verifiability is the fact that scientific laws are caught in this same net. The law of gravity, for example, has the same logical form as the statement about crows: "All bodies falling freely from rest will accelerate at a rate of 32 feet per second per second." The statement is universal ("All bodies") and it is unrestricted with regard to time. According to the test of verifiability, it too is factually meaningless. This was especially embarrassing for the positivists. The application of their most distinctive principle resulted in the denial of meaning to well-established scientific laws. This meant that, if valid, their work would undercut the prestige of science. This was a case of the positivists sawing off the limb they were sitting on, because the appeal of their program was heavily dependent on this prestige.

Falsification Is Too Restrictive

A leading philosopher of science, Karl Popper, was sympathetic to the positivists' effort to discriminate the factually meaningful statements of science from the nonempirical statements of the metaphysicians.[20] He thought that the positivists had got off on the wrong foot by working with verifiability. No matter how many observations verify a scientific general-ization, it is always possible that an exception to it will be observed in the future. For this reason Popper thought that verifiability was not the distinctive feature of science; its distinctive feature is *falsification.* "All bodies falling freely from rest will accelerate at a rate of 32 feet per second per second" is a scientific law now regarded as true. Countless observations have verified it, but none are conclusive because one properly certified exception to it will falsify it, that is, it will force us to label it "false." To label a statement "false," is, as we have seen, to concede that it is factually meaningful. It might have been true, but it happens, as things go in the world, to be false. Popper concluded that falsifiability rather than verifiability is the litmus paper type of test that the positivists had been seeking in their effort to discriminate between scientific and metaphysical statements. It can be phrased: A statement is factually meaningful if and only if there are observations that could, in principle, falsify it.

The test of verifiability founders on statements that deal with every member of a class. Falsification, as Popper himself noted, ran into trouble in coping with statements that deal with at least one member of a class. Consider the statement, "Unicorns exist." It can be rephrased as "There is at least one unicorn." This is a noncontroversial statement whose truth would be denied by everyone; but no one, including the positivists, would want to deny that it is factually meaningful. Furthermore, it seems as though it would be easy to falsify it. We begin by considering the description: a white animal, with the body of a horse, and a long thin horn protruding from its forehead. We then try to find a beast that actually conforms to this description. If no relevant observations are made, we would say that the statement is falsified. Here we seem to have a clear-cut case of a supposedly synthetic statement passing the test; it is found to be factually meaningful, although false. Nevertheless, reflection on the logic of this statement shows that it cannot, in principle, be falsified, even though it is almost certainly false. The statement, "All crows are black," is not restricted with regard to time. Therefore, no matter how long the quest for a unicorn might prove fruitless, there is always the possibility that one will turn up. The same analysis can be applied to any claim that some kind of thing exists, for example, a scientific claim about genes, "There is a gene that produces sexless human beings." It is, as far as we know, false, but no one would want to claim that it is factually meaningless. The test of falsification would, however, strip it of factual meaning. It is clear that the test of falsification, like verification, denies meaningfulness to statements of common sense and science whose meaning the positivists had no desire to challenge.

It is not surprising that falsification is no more effective than verification, because there is a logical relation between universal and particular statements that links verification and falsification. The denial of a universal statement is expressed in terms of a particular statement, and the denial of a particular statement is expressed in terms of a universal statement. Thus the denial of "All crows are black" (a universal statement which, as we have seen, is nonverifiable) may be formulated in terms of the particular statement "There is at least one nonblack crow" (which, we have seen, is nonfalsifiable). By the same token, the denial of the particular statement "There is at least one unicorn," which served as the key example of a nonfalsifiable statement, is the universal (and therefore nonverifiable) statement "All animals are non-unicorns."

The test of verification is so important that another attempt at an adequate formulation is worthwhile. After all, there does not seem to be anything conclusively verifiable or falsifiable about theological statements like "God loves us as a father loves his children" or metaphysical statements like "The Absolute enters into, but is itself incapable of, evolution and progress." By contrast, even though "All crows are black" is not conclusively verifiable, it is conclusively falsifiable. One validated instance of a yellow crow would falsify it, in the way that the actual existence of black swans conclusively falsifies "All swans are white." In like fashion, even though the statement "There is at least one unicorn" (or "Unicorns exist") cannot be conclusively falsified, the discovery of a unicorn would conclusively verify it. (We would only need to find an actual white animal with the body of a horse and a horn like an ibex.) One might, therefore, suggest that the statement of the test be modified as follows: A statement is factually meaningful if and only if it is *either* conclusively verifiable *or* conclusively falsifiable. In that case universal statements like "All crows are black" would be factually meaningful because they are conclusively falsifiable. The negation of this statement, namely, the particular statement that "There is at least one nonblack crow" would also be factually meaningful because it is conclusively verifiable. This would seem to answer all the difficulties encountered so far.

Unfortunately, there are a limitless number of statements which turn out to be factually meaningless by this criterion, but which are instances of the kind of statement whose factual meaningfulness seemed noncontroversial to the positivists. Examples are: "Beyond every star there is another one" and "For any substance there exists some solvent."[21] The words "every" and "any," like "all," are of unrestricted generality, that is, they are used to make a universal statement. We have seen that when unrestricted to time, they are not verifiable. "Some" and "another" mean "at least one," which are the marks of particular statements; we have seen that, when unrestricted to time, they are not falsifiable. The revised statement of the test asks only that a factually meaningful statement be *either* verifiable *or* falsifiable. However, statements of this kind—which logicians refer to as involving mixed quantification (universal and particular)—are *neither* verifiable *nor* falsifiable because the universal part is not verifiable and the particular part is not falsifiable. Furthermore, the universal and particular components cannot be detached from one another without changing the meaning of the statement. Therefore, this revised criterion, like the others, forces the positivist to brand as pseudo-synthetic statements whose factual meaningfulness he has no desire to challenge.

With the greatest reluctance the positivists concluded that both verification and falsification were too restrictive. A rigorous application of either test eliminated scientific babies with the metaphysical bath water.

Confirmation Is Too Permissive

The positivists' reaction to the excessive restrictiveness of verification and falsification was predictable. They modified their criterion of meaning in the effort to make it restrictive enough to exclude metaphysics and theology, but permissive enough to include science.

Reams of literature have been written on this subject. Almost all of it is highly technical, as might be expected, since the issue concerns the theoretical frontiers of logic in its relation to the philosophy of science.[22] In dealing with it here, I shall include only enough material to enable us to understand its relevance to theology.

The problem that emerged in connection with the positivists' test for eliminating theology is that many common sense and scientific statements also fail to be verifiable or falsifiable. Positivists located the difficulty in the demand for conclusiveness. This is especially clear in the case of falsification because this test is modeled on crucial scientific experiments. ᵀf one valid exception to a scientific generalization turns up, we then label the statement of the generalization as "false." Verification may also be thought of in pretty much the same terms, namely, in terms of a single conclusive case; "This book has white pages and black print" is conclusively verified if you look at it.

The answer to the difficulty seemed obvious: eliminate the need for *conclusive* verification or falsification. The positivists substituted the test of confirmation, roughly—a statement is factually meaningful if and only if there are, in principle, observations that would count as evidence for its truth and observations that would count against it. These observations would not count conclusively for its truth, they are partial confirmations of its truth, hence, the term *confirmation.*

Positivists thought this modified test would work because, as we have noted, they were certain of one basic distinction between scientific statements on the one hand, and metaphysical and theological statements on the other. Observations are relevant to establishing the truth of science; they are not relevant to establishing the truth of metaphysics and theology. The positivists were right, up to a point. God, the subject of the most important theological statements, is not observable, not even in principle. Therefore, statements about him, like "God divided the waters of the Red Sea," cannot be conclusively verified by observations, but very few theologians would concede the point that there are no observations that could *confirm* the truth of their statements. If the demand for conclusive verification and falsification is abandoned, many theologians could specify observations that count for the truth of their statements. Indeed, in Chapter 10 we will consider an argument that appeals to the intricacies of human organs like the eye as evidence for the statement, "The world was designed by a being of infinite intelligence." To appreciate this, or any similar line of theological argument, we must refine the notion of confirmation to take account of indirect as well as of direct checks.

Countless statements can be verified conclusively by direct inspection. "This book has white pages and black print" is an example that has come up a number of times. Since you have the book in your hands, you can look at it and verify it.

Statements which cannot be verified directly can often be confirmed indirectly. They are confirmable by evidence that counts for or against their truth. In some cases, the evidence is the observation of one part of a process that we have, on other occasions, observed fully. Thus, "Johnny has been eating chocolate ice cream," where the evidence is a brown smudge on his chin. In this case we say that the smudge counts as confirmation of the statement. We could not verify it directly, because we did not actually see him eat it. It is, however, a solid indirect check because we have often observed him eating ice cream and watched him produce just this kind of smudge.

In other cases, we have evidence that confirms a statement about a nonobservable reality. Statements about subatomic particles are a case in point. Electrons cannot be observed directly, but we regard certain types of behavior of drops of oil between charged plates as evidence that confirms the existence of electrons.[23]

The existence of God cannot, as has been repeatedly noted, be verified by direct inspection, but theologians can argue that the orderly patterns of the stars provides indirect confirmation of the existence of the Creator. Of course, the connection between the statement "God created the heavens and the earth" and the astronomical observations which are relevant to its confirmation are not all that clear. They must be considered in the context of a given theology. Scientific work, however, involves the same problem. Considerable mastery of physics is required for the appreciation of the connection between statements about electrons and the evidence that confirms them.

Theologians may, therefore, argue that if *confirmation* is the test, their statements, by the positivists' own standards, are factually meaningful. Basil Mitchell provides an important illustration on this point (see pp. 51 ff.).

When positivists weakened the test to make sure that it did not exclude science and common sense they came up with confirmation. From their standpoint, it was too permissive. It failed to exclude metaphysics and theology.

THE LOOSENING UP OF CONTEMPORARY EMPIRICISM

During the forties leading empiricists who were sympathetic to the positivists could see that positivism was not going to succeed. One of the main reasons was the failure of verification to serve as a quick litmus paper test that would eliminate metaphysics, theology, and other "meaningless" subjects. There were other considerations as well, and I will touch on some of them.

Quine's Rejection of the Analytic

An important milestone on the road to the post-positivist scene was the appearance, in 1953, of W. V. Quine's essay "Two Dogmas of Empiricism."[24] He does not elaborate on the difficulties of the test of verification. They were relatively old hat by that time and he assumes them. He trains his fire on the analytic. This was a rude jolt to the positivists. By 1953 they knew very well that they were in trouble on verification, but their view of the analytic rested on the self-evident and necessary character of logic. It was a bulwark of their program. Yet Quine denied that any statements were necessary in the sense that the positivists claimed necessity for analytic statements.

Quine tried to show that the analytic is a philosophical chimera. The technical details of his treatment and the question of whether his position will ultimately be validated is extremely complex.[25] The important point in this historical context is that his assault on the analytic contributed to the passing of positivism from the center of the philosophical stage. Quine is a brilliant logician and epistemologist who is very much inside the empiricist family. He was respected by the positivists and their admirers. By attacking what had been regarded as an especially strong point of positivism he seriously undermined the movement.

The Break with Dogmatism

Many philosophers were inclined to take the positivists at face value and to regard their enterprise as a vigorous manifestation of the scientific spirit within the philosophical camp; as time went on, they began to wonder whether the positivists were not merely partisan. There was something prejudicial and dogmatic about the tortuous efforts of the positivists to achieve a version of the verifiability principle with the right combination of permissiveness ("science-in") and restrictiveness ("theology-out"). A scientific inquiry into meaningfulness should have been more open-ended. It might have begun with a sense of the meaningfulness of certain types of statements and of the meaninglessness of other types, but the investigators would have been open to the possibility that things might not turn out that way. The positivists, by contrast, clung to their favorite whipping boys: platonic, hegelian, heideggerian, and *theological* statements. It was assumed that they are factually meaningless, come what may![26] The job was to find the philosophical broadsword that would hack them from the scene without injuring any innocent scientific or common sense bystanders. In displaying this unscientific type of dogmatism the positivists repeated mistakes of past generations of philosophers, especially the one of dividing subjects into two vast classes like the material and the mental or the subjective and the objective.

Among the post-positivistic analysts comprehensive terms like *subjective* and *objective* are suspect. These terms embrace and obscure so many important distinctions that Gilbert Ryle calls them "umbrella-words."[27] He refers to a large cover that has a considerable variety of objects sheltered under it. Some of the positivists' distinctions came to seem embarrassingly like these overblown terms of traditional metaphysicians and theologians. Morton White, after paying tribute to the creative impetus of the early positivists, was sharply critical of the dogmatic spirit which all too quickly set in and led to an emphasis on umbrella words.

> . . . ancient metaphysical generalizations about everything being fire or water were erased and replaced by equally indefensible universal theses, according to which all logical statements are like this, and all physical statements are like that, and all ethical statements are very different from both.[28]

Wittgenstein: Meaning as Use

The impetus to break with the dogmatism represented by the umbrella words of positivism received its strongest support from Wittgenstein's later work. Wittgenstein was by no means the first philosopher to make the point in print; his authority was a function of his enormous prestige. He was a philosophical "loner" who had never been a member of the Vienna Circle, but his *Tractatus Logico-Philosophicus* (1921) was a major influence on the development of logical positivism. Everyone knew that he had been rethinking his position during the thirties and forties and the posthumous appearance of his *Philosophical Investigations* (1953) was one of the major events of the century.[29] In the later work he repudiated the rigidities of the positivism that his earlier work had inspired. He insisted strongly that the incredible variety of cognitively meaningful language cannot be forced into prefabricated molds. Conclusions that may be drawn from his later work are:

1 Cognitive meaning should not be restricted to the cases that conform to the standards of mathematics and physics.

2 In any case, even within these disciplines, meanings are far more complicated than can be indicated by the sweeping terms *analytic* and *synthetic*.

3 It is a mistake to consider the meaning of individual words and statements without paying close attention to the nuances of their larger linguistic context. "White" and "black" must be understood in the context of the function of color terms in ordinary English. One of Wittgenstein's major contributions was to show that this is far more complicated than we usually take it to be. A child may be able to say "black" when you point to a black chair, and "white" when you point to a white one, without really grasping the meaning of black and white. He might associate the colors with the shape of the chairs or with the texture of the materials used to cover them. Therefore, checking on whether someone has mastered color words cannot be done by simplistic tests that are confined to the verification of isolated statements like "This book has white pages and black print." Wittgenstein's analysis is obviously even more relevant to disciplines with complex fabrics of meaning like law, physics, architecture, and, of course, theology. As he put it: "For a *large* class of cases—though not for all—in which we employ the word 'meaning' it can be defined thus: the meaning of a word is its use in the language."[30]

In philosophy important insights do not generally resolve issues, rather they form the basis of fresh approaches to them. This was the case with Wittgenstein's theory of "meaning as use." It helped to get contemporary empiricists out of the analytic and the synthetic ruts, but it did not resolve all the important questions of cognitive meaning. Initially, some thinkers misunderstood it; they thought it involved the consequence that "anything goes." Some religious thinkers, for example, hailed this departure as a conclusive answer to the challenge of the positivists because the word "God" certainly has a meaning in English and it is well established. Part of this meaning involves the idea that God is an existing reality. It would, therefore, seem that according to Wittgenstein's standard of "meaning as use," God must exist. Obviously, this line of reasoning is too simplistic. Even if we accept Wittgenstein's statement that the meaning of a word is its use in the language, there are complications that should be noted. One is that Wittgenstein did not claim that his standard of meaning applies to all cases. Another is that God is obviously a controversial case. In addition, we realize that we are not stuck with the common use of words, but that we often react critically to them. Take, for example, the use of "daemon" in a culture where daemons are believed to exist. Existence is, for them, part of the meaning of daemon. Yet people of *our* culture will not accept the existence of daemons on this basis. Indeed, as noted earlier, the rise of science has called the meaning of God into question in our western culture. Although believers still regard existence as part of its meaning, vast numbers of sceptics challenge this use. Therefore, sceptics reject facile efforts to invoke Wittgenstein's prestige on behalf of the claim that God exists by an appeal to generations of believers who have used the term "God" to refer to an actual agent.[31]

On the other hand, *critics* of theology can also be too facile. Wittgenstein's theory of meaning as use is an antidote to the all too common practice of demanding that theologians produce evidence for "God exists" that would be comparable to evidence for "The Abominable Snowman exists." This is misguided because the term "God" is not used to refer to a reality that is supposed to be observable. Wittgenstein alerts us to the need to consider terms like "God" and statements like "God loves us" in their theological contexts.

Wittgenstein himself did not publish formal statements about religion during his lifetime.[32] His appeal to contemporary religious thinkers is a function of his approach to meaning as use.

A considerable number of contemporary religious thinkers were influenced by Wittgenstein.[33] Some of them invoke his name merely for the purpose of making the point that positivism didn't eliminate theology. Others, who regard themselves as philosophical empiricists, apply his thought more directly and positively to their own work, as in the following statement by Basil Mitchell:

> How will philosophers of this persuasion [that is, post-positivistic analysts who have been influenced by Wittgenstein] tend to approach theology? Three things are, I think, clear.

1   They will not, as did the Idealists, put forward . . . a world-view or philosophy of life, which might conflict with Christianity; because they regard the development of such world-views as no part of a philosopher's business.

2   They will not . . . rule out theological statements from the start on the ground that they are meaningless, as the logical positivists did.

3   They will ask the same sort of questions about theological statements as they do about statements of other kinds, viz., "How are they verified? What sorts of arguments or observations tend to confirm or refute them?" In short, "What is their logic?"[34]

Mitchell, of course, does not regard the kind of verification or confirmation that is appropriate to scientific hypotheses as the model for theological statements, which is the point of his question: "What is *their* logic?" Mitchell's answer will be given when we consider his parable The Partisan and the Stranger in the next chapter. (See pp. 265, for another illustration of Wittgenstein's influence on contemporary religious thought.)

Chapter 3

Theology and Analysis

By the time that Wittgenstein's *Philosophical Investigations* began to take hold, it was clear that the deployment of verification as a preliminary examination would not eliminate theology. This chapter deals with major theological responses to the challenge of verification, but it is important to realize that the field is so extensive that I am only scratching the surface.[35]

WISDOM'S "GODS": THE COMPLEXITIES
OF PHILOSOPHICAL ANALYSIS

John Wisdom's "Gods," which appeared in 1946, is one of the most influential essays on religious thought to appear in this century. Part of its influence may be attributed to the elusiveness of Wisdom's style. He does not state positions, but suggests them by means of imaginative illustrations.

By the time he wrote "Gods," Wisdom had been greatly affected by Wittgenstein, and this essay shows it. Wisdom does not isolate theological *statements* like "God is the sustainer of the universe," or

"God loves us," and then subject them to the test of verification. He focusses on theological *arguments* and explores their complexities and their changing patterns.

Idle Disputes

To understand Wisdom's discussion of arguments between atheists and believers it is important to realize that he had previously formulated a standard of utterly futile arguments or, as he calls them, "idle disputes."[36] He illustrated it by means of two fanciful and apparently conflicting explanations of why a watch is not working. One expert claims that the source of the trouble is a leprechaun that's messing up the works; the other one claims that it's a brownie. It seems like a genuine difference as to the facts; the sort of thing that could be settled by opening the watch and looking inside to see which expert is right. Yet when the experts are pressed, this apparent difference vanishes. Neither leprechauns nor brownies turn out to be the sort of things that can be seen, heard, touched, tasted, or smelled. Furthermore, neither expert is willing to propose a test that will settle the issue; there are no observable consequences of either hypothesis. We cannot, for example, leave milk near the watch on the grounds that leprechauns will drink it whereas brownies will not. Therefore, the difference between the experts is merely verbal, and the dispute is an idle one. It is clear that "idle" is to disputes as "pseudo-synthetic" is to statements.

When he explores the nature of the disputes between theists and atheists, Wisdom deals with two different questions. It is important to keep them distinct even though he himself failed to do so.

    1   Can an empirical dispute change its character in such a way that it is no longer a dispute about the facts and yet is not an idle dispute?

    2   Assuming that this has happened in the case of the dispute between theists and atheists, what kind of dispute are they now engaged in?

It is obvious that if he is to answer the first question affirmatively, Wisdom must provide a convincing answer to the second question. Unfortunately, his use of the parable of the invisible gardener (which will now be considered at length) to provide a vivid answer to the first question has led to misunderstandings of his answers to the second one.

How the Argument between Theists and Atheists Has Changed

In answering the first question, Wisdom begins by showing us how things were in the days before science discredited the idea of God's miraculous intervention in the world. He refers to the story of Elijah's challenge to the priests of the pagan deity, Baal (1 Kings 18:20–40). Altars to Baal and to Jaweh (the Lord of Israel) are erected. The true God is to prove himself by consuming his altar with fire. Here the dispute involves observable consequences, namely, which altar will be consumed. When the fire from heaven consumes the altar to Jaweh, the Israelites shout: "Jaweh is God." Here is an example of a dispute which is not at all idle.

Wisdom then shows how the dispute between atheists and theists has changed. Theologians are now too much oriented to science to propose a test by miracle (see Chap. 4). It is in this context that he tells his parable of the Invisible Gardener.

> Two people return to their long neglected garden and find among the weeds a few of the old plants surprisingly vigorous. One says to the other, "It must be that a gardener has been coming and doing something about these plants." Upon inquiry they find that no neighbor has ever seen anyone at work in their garden. The first man says to the other, "He must have worked while people slept." The other says, "No, someone would have heard him and besides, anybody who cared about the plants would have kept down these weeds." The first man says, "Look at the way these are arranged. There is purpose and a feeling for beauty here. I believe that someone comes, someone invisible to mortal eyes. I believe that the more carefully we look the more we shall find confirmation of this." They examine the garden ever so carefully and sometimes they come on new things suggesting that a gardener comes and sometimes they come on new things suggesting the contrary and even that a malicious person has been at work. Besides examining the garden carefully they also study what happens to gardens left without attention. Each learns all the other learns about this and about the garden. Consequently, when after all this one says, "I still believe a gardener comes" while the other says, "I don't," their different words now reflect no difference as to what they would find in the garden if they looked further and no difference about how fast untended gardens fall into disorder. At this stage, in this context, the gardener hypothesis has ceased to be experimental, the difference between one who accepts and one who rejects it is now not a matter of the one expecting something the other does not expect. What is the difference between them? The one says, "A gardener comes unseen and unheard. He is manifested only in his works with which we are all familiar." The other says, "There is no gardener" and with this difference in what they say about the gardener goes a difference in how they feel towards the garden. In spite of the fact that neither expects anything of it which the other does not expect.[37]

The dispute has changed from one about the facts to a dispute about their responses to the garden as a whole. In other words, they have both looked at and investigated the same area; the atheist experiences it as untended, the believer experiences it as tended.

Wisdom uses this parable to show how an argument can shift in character. Prescientific generations of Christians might have differed with atheists about the facts. Sophisticated contemporary theologians differ with them in more complicated ways. Wisdom did not intend the parable of The Invisible Gardener to serve as a model for sophisticated theological arguments. The invisible gardener cannot serve as a model for God because gardeners are the kinds of things that are supposed to be visible. By contrast the word "God" is not intended to refer to a visible being. It is unfortunate that Anthony Flew's passionate and important challenge to the meaningfulness of theological language is marred by a misunderstanding of this point. Flew suggests both that the invisible gardener is a model for God and that Wisdom's account of the dispute over the garden is intended to serve as a model for disputes between sophisticated theologians and atheists.[38]

Flew's interpretation is, however, plausible because the garden can readily be taken for the world as a whole and it seems as though the invisible gardener must stand for God. Indeed, if that were not Wisdom's intention, then the man who continues, against the evidence, to believe in the presence of an invisible gardener must be operating under a delusion.

Wisdom left himself wide open to Flew's unsympathetic interpretation. A more sympathetic one cannot be attempted within the framework of the parable of The Invisible Gardener. It must come, rather, from an examination of Wisdom's subsequent efforts to elaborate the nature of the dispute between sophisticated theists and atheists.

THE ARGUMENT BETWEEN SOPHISTICATED THEISTS AND ATHEISTS

Having shown to his satisfaction that an empirical argument can cease to be an argument about facts and yet not become an idle dispute, Wisdom examines the nature of the dispute between sophisticated theists and atheists. Wisdom, like the religious existentialists, (who are treated in Part Three) shifts our focus from mathematics and science to the subtleties and complexities of human interaction; to the sorts of things handled by judges, historians, and novelists.[39] Indeed, one of the important developments of religious thought in the twentieth century is the way that thinkers like Wittgenstein and Wisdom, who represent one wing of the broad analytic tradition, have, by dealing with problems of *knowledge*, come to many of the same insights that religious existentialists arrived at by reflecting on the implications of *faith*.[40] In the following sections, Wisdom considers issues that existentialists call *subjective*. The disputants have procedures that enable them to argue rationally, but they do not have agreed-upon (*objective*) standards for resolving the disputes.

The Legal Model Against the use of mathematical or scientific models of argument, Wisdom appeals to the legal model.[41] In legal arguments there are special cases where both sides agree on the facts; the conflict then centers on their arrangement and presentation. "For sometimes when there is agreement as to the facts there is still argument as to whether defendent did or did not 'exercise reasonable care,' or was not 'negligent.'"[42] After big trials, jurors don't disagree very much about facts, because all the facts available are presented to all the jurors. They differ in the way they see the facts and in the frameworks into which they set them. Therefore, on the basis of the same set of facts, one juror may vote "guilty" and another for acquittal.

Wisdom shifts to legal examples (and to others that will soon be considered) in order to suggest that the positivists' obsession with the appeal to "the facts" was misguided. There is more to *empirical* judgement than that. "It is possible," he notes, "to have before one's eyes all the items of a pattern and still to miss the pattern."[43] It is clear that Wisdom believes that the patterns in which facts are arranged and the connections that are drawn between one set of facts and another, has as much to do with factual meaningfulness as does the narrower question of establishing the facts. "What is so," he insists, "isn't merely a matter of 'the facts.'"[44] Wisdom regards legal arguments of this kind as illuminating models for theology. A statement like "God loves us" should not be regarded as if it were intended as a common sense statement of fact. A great many facts are relevant to establishing it, but it is part of a religious outlook. It ought, therefore, to be evaluated within the context of the patterns of the experiences and beliefs that are the framework of Christianity.

Beauty "The difference as to whether God exists involves our feelings more than most scientific disputes and in this respect is more like a difference as to whether there is beauty in a thing."[45] With this remark Wisdom broadens the scope of his treatment. The legal analogy is designed to show that narrow views of induction and deduction won't do for dealing with theological arguments. He then turns to beauty and love to show that our feelings can be strongly engaged in arguments and yet the arguments need be neither idle nor irrational.

If two people stand in front of a painting, they cannot disagree about "the facts" of it because the facts are before them on the canvas. Nevertheless, people in that situation disagree, even violently, about the meaning and the worth of paintings. The positivists regarded these disagreements as emotive. They claimed that they merely reflect the feelings and associations of the participants, and therefore that those disputes have no cognitive content. Wisdom rejects this view. He insists that these disputes are not idle because there are rational procedures for conducting these arguments. The individuals involved can go over the painting connecting some parts with other aspects of experience, say of other paintings. The hope is that the connections will trigger similar responses in the other individual and persuade him to share a similar perspective on the painting.

Consider a person who appreciates art but is repelled at his first exposure to Jackson Pollack's action paintings, which seem a totally disordered mass of color that has been haphazardly flung onto the canvas. A friend who is familiar with his taste might note that he admires the later works of the Italian master Tintoretto. He would then try to associate the energy of Pollack to the way in which Tintoretto's later paintings seem to burst out of the frames that enclose them. In this process of what Wisdom calls "connecting" works, the individual who is anti-Pollack may develop an appreciation for his work. On the other hand, he may "disconnect" Tintoretto from Pollack by noting that Tintoretto's representational art provides examples of magnificently rendered bodies, robes, and other recognizable aspects of experience, whereas Pollack is utterly nonrepresentational. The dispute would be hard to resolve, but Wisdom maintains that it is not idle. The parties are not disputing the facts but are arguing over matters relating to patterns and perspectives on the facts. They are doing so in reasonable terms and both critics might have their views of the Jackson Pollack paintings significantly altered.

In the context of the discussion of theology and verification, the moral of Wisdom's essay is clear: What is so isn't merely a matter of "the facts." Therefore, theological statements can have empirical meaning in the broad sense, without being verifiable in a clear-cut way.

FALSIFICATION AND THEOLOGY

In the early fifties, the debate on the cognitive meaningfulness of theological statements shifted to the issue of theology and falsification. The interest was sparked by a fascinating discussion in which all the participants followed the example set by Wisdom in his essay *Gods*. They deal with the issue in terms of parables or striking illustrations.[46]

Flew's Statement of the Challenge

The passion with which Anthony Flew introduced falsification as a challenge to the factual meaningfulness of theological statements goes a long way toward accounting for the continuing interest in this issue. Previous positivistic criticisms of religious language had generally been bloodless discussions of the logic of "God exists." By focusing on the statement "God loves us as a father loves his children" (which I shall shorten to "God loves us") Flew linked his challenge to one of the perennial problems of Christian thought, namely, to the problem of evil.[47] Furthermore, this statement has deep biblical roots. In the Book of Hosea (11:1) we read: "When Israel was a boy I loved him, I called my son out of Egypt." The New Testament is full of talk about the loving concern of the heavenly Father, culminating in the statement: "God is love" (1 John 4:9).

As Flew understands it, the statement "God loves us" is not only intended to be informative (synthetic), but the information conveyed is clearly regarded by believers as being one of the most important truths that we can know in orienting ourselves to reality. Flew's searing assault on the meaningfulness of the statement "God loves us" contrasts the love of earthly fathers with the love that believers attribute to the heavenly father.

> Someone tells us that God loves us as a father loves his children. We are reassured. But then we see a child dying of inoperable cancer of the throat. His earthly father is driven frantic in his efforts to help, but his Heavenly Father reveals no obvious sign of concern. Some qualification is made— God's love is "not merely human love" or it is "an inscrutable love," . . . and we realize that such sufferings are quite compatible with the truth of the assertion that "God loves us as a father (but of course, . . .)." We are reassured again. But then perhaps we ask: what is this assurance of God's (appropriately qualified) love worth, what is this apparent guarantee really a guarantee against? Just what would have to happen not merely (morally and wrongly) to tempt but also (logically and rightly) to entitle us to say "God does not love us" or even "God does not exist?"[48]

Flew thinks that the obvious conclusion to be drawn is that the statement "God loves us" is not true, but he thinks that theologians shrink from the obvious. In an effort to make them face up to it, Flew invokes the test of falsification. He challenges theologians to specify an observable set of circumstances that would falsify the statement "God loves us." In effect, Flew confronts theologians with the following unpalatable options (unpalatable to them, not to Flew).

Analytic One clearly meaningful option would be to declare that "God loves us" is analytic. In that case it would be necessarily true, but it would no longer be doing the job that believers want it to do. Believers want a guarantee that a limitless power will console us, somehow, for human suffering. If the statement "God loves us" is analytic, it can offer no such guarantee. It can only express the theologians' definition of

"God," that is, their intention of inextricably associating the word "love" with the word "God." This verbal formula would be logically impeccable, but religiously vacuous.

Synthetic Theologians might insist that "God loves us" is a genuine synthetic statement. In that case they would claim that "God loves us" means that we are loved by a center of consciousness that is aware of all states of affairs and that is infinitely powerful. This is a strong claim. It is, in Flew's view, factually meaningful because he thinks it is falsifiable in principle. Indeed, although this is not his main point, he thinks that it has actually been falsified. Human suffering through the ages has falsified, many times over, the claim that we are loved by an all-knowing and all-powerful God.

Pseudo-synthetic In order to appreciate the force of Flew's pseudo-synthetic option, it is important to consider the impact of science on contemporary religious thought. Before the rise of modern science and technology the empirical option was not closed to religion. Therefore, we sometimes find the biblical authors appealing to observable tests that will verify their claims. This is, of course, obvious in the case of Elijah and the priests of Baal that Wisdom cited, but it is also true of the Deuteronomic authors who promised the people that if they obeyed God they would prosper in material terms (see the books of Deuteronomy, Joshuah, and Judges). It is also clear that the miracle stories in both the Old Testament and the New Testament are intended to provide backing for the faith by appeal to extraordinary occurrences in the observable order. By contrast, other biblical authors urged believers to persist in their faith even when the observable evidence runs against their beliefs (Second Isa., Job).

In the discussion of miracles which follows in the next chapter, I shall show why the rise of science led many sophisticated theologians to the conclusion that theology cannot successfully compete with science in dealing with the observable order. As a result the overwhelming majority of contemporary religious thinkers have abandoned all types of appeal to observables. They would not be prepared to have the parents of the child suffering from inoperable cancer test faith empirically. For example, by praying to God for help and then saying that if the child is cured, the statement "God loves us" is true, and that if the child suffers and dies, the statement is false. Instead, theologians emphasize the mystery of divine transcendence and qualify the meaning of "God loves us." They fall back on such traditional moves as saying that God's love is so mysterious that we cannot understand it, or of saying that we limited human beings cannot see the whole picture. These theologians argue that if we could see reality as a whole, we would be able to realize that God does love every human being, even the child dying of inoperable cancer.

Flew claims that the statement "God loves us" is clear and important but that qualifications of this kind erode its power. By clinging to the verbal formula "God loves us" theologians persuade themselves that they are talking about the old time religion of the biblical authors, but he claims that this isn't so.

> Someone may dissipate his assertion completely without noticing that he has done so. A fine brash hypothesis may thus be killed by inches, the death by a thousand qualifications.[49]

At the tail end of this process, the statement still appears to be synthetic, but as actually used by the theologians, it is compatible with any state of affairs whatever, including the suffering of a child dying of inoperable cancer. Therefore, the statement "God loves us," as used by most theologians is not genuinely synthetic. Flew's third option, the one he is clearly concerned to stress, is that this statement is pseudo-synthetic and therefore, factually meaningless.

Hare: "Bliks" Are Not Falsifiable, But We Use Them to Assess the Facts

R. M. Hare's reply to Flew stresses a point that has gained wide acceptance. Language, even when we restrict our consideration to its empirical functions, has many levels or strata.[50] One important kind of statement is what Hare calls a "blik." A blik is not verified or falsified by evidence, it is rather, a basic view of the world which is used to assess the evidence. A person who has a blik sees the world in terms of it. Hare's main illustration is sensational. A student has a blik whose content can be expressed by the statement "All members of the faculty are trying to kill me." This may seem to be factual; however, on examination it develops that it is not a straightforward statement of fact that is subjected to day-to-day checks. On the contrary, the student takes its truth for granted and uses it as the basis of judging the behavior of members of the faculty. If some members of the faculty are hostile, this serves him as verification of the statement, "All members of the faculty are trying to kill me." If, on the other hand, some members of the faculty go out of their way to be friendly, he proceeds to interpret their conduct as a diabolical effort to throw him off guard. He appeals to his blik to falsify the statement, "These professors do not intend to harm me." On this basis Hare concludes that the student's blik, expressed by the statement, "All members of the faculty are trying to kill me," is an empirically meaningful statement which is not falsifiable.

Subsequently, Hare states: "It was Hume who taught us that our whole commerce with the world depends upon our blik about the world; and that the differences between bliks about the world cannot be settled by observation of what happens in the world."[51] This shows that Hare thinks that something important is at stake. He does not coin the term "blik" merely to toy with the delusions of a paranoid student. Bliks are "mind-sets" which express the basic categories by which we experience the world and they play an important role in science. Hare merely suggests this point, but it is vitally important to the philosophy of science. There are certain fundamental assumptions of science that cannot be verified by any amount of scientific work because they are themselves assumed without argument by scientists, that is, they are presupposed in scientific work. An example is: Every observable occurrence can be explained by the application of the scientific method. This statement is not verified by scientific work, but rather, it is an assumption (whether conscious or not) that makes scientists look for their types of explanations regardless of what they observe (see p. 62).

In general, it appears increasingly difficult to come up with a philosophical touchstone, like verification or falsification, that will discriminate sharply between scientific and religious statements. John F. Miller, III, has shown that, like theologians, philosophers of science qualify and qualify again rather than give up the truth of their fundamental statements, like "Every event has a cause." Alastair McKinnon has shown that the strata found in statements relevant to religion are comparable to those found in science.[52] That is why it is important to keep the success of technology in mind in any discussions of the broad issue of religion and science or the narrower issue of theology and verification. Scientists have achieved remarkable success in explaining, predicting, and controlling events in the observable world. Those of us who cannot follow their abstruse theories are bound to be impressed with science when we use television sets and electric typewriters. The cognitive success of science cannot, therefore, be undercut by harping on the problems that continually plagued verificationism. These problems only show that philosophy is a difficult subject and that it is hard—as demonstrated by the story of positivism—to attain conclusive results in it. It does not show that religious thinkers can point to *practical* developments in the field of religion that are comparable, from the standpoint of knowledge, to the technological fruits of science.

Hare may therefore, be right in suggesting that physicists—the very figures that the positivists regarded as ideal scientists, operate with bliks. It would not follow that physics and religion ought, as cognitive enterprises, to be set on the same level. The appeal to bliks can, however, be refined into an important response to the challenge of falsification which discriminates between scientific and theological statements at the *theoretical* level.

Mitchell: Theological Statements Can Be Confirmed and Disconfirmed

Basil Mitchell's contribution to the debate on theology and falsification is a religiously relevant response to Flew's religiously relevant challenge.[53] Mitchell's contribution pivots around his parable of The Partisan and the Stranger, a parable which says a great deal about the way that faith operates in the lives of believers and is relevant to existentialist discussions of faith (see Part Three).

In the parable, a partisan, that is, a member of the resistance to the Nazis, meets a mysterious stranger. In a conversation of great intensity he is persuaded that the stranger is the secret head of the resistance. They never have another direct meeting, but the partisan continues to see the stranger in contexts that confronts him with a swirl of conflicting evidence. Sometimes the stranger seems to help the resistance, at other times he appears as the chief of the Nazis and arrests members of the movement. Other members of the resistance decide that the stranger is really an enemy, but the partisan who had the intimate conversation with him persists in his trust.

Mitchell uses this parable to meet Flew's challenge head on.

1 He refuses to qualify the meaning of "love" in the statement "God loves us." This is the point of his admitting that the stranger's work in arresting members of the resistance does count against the truth of the statement, "The stranger is on our side."

2 Mitchell insists that theological statements are factually meaningful. To make good on this claim, he, in effect, shifts the issue from Flew's challenge, which is expressed in terms of conclusive falsification, to the test of confirmation and disconfirmation.

In the biblical story of Elijah and the priests of Baal, we have a conclusive test of fire (see p. 43). Elijah's claim that the Lord God of Israel is the true God is conclusively verified, and the priests' claim that Baal is the true God is conclusively falsified. By contrast, in Mitchell's parable tests are applied, but they are not conclusive. When members of the resistance are unaccountably released, the events confirm, or count for the truth of, the statement "The stranger is on our side." On the other hand, when members of the resistance are unexpectedly captured, the statement is disconfirmed because these events count against its truth.

One reason for the lack of conclusiveness in Mitchell's parable is that it is not possible to quantify the test. Even when quite a few members of the resistance have been captured, it is open to the partisan to argue that "The stranger is on our side." He can, for example, claim that the stranger must permit these tragic episodes to occur because, if he interfered too openly on the side of the resistance the Nazis would discover his true identity and his usefulness to the movement (as well as his life) would come to an end. Furthermore, it is obvious that the partisan who had the special conversation with the stranger is in a different situation from the rest of his comrades. His conversation was a source of privileged access to the stranger (what Martin Buber would call an I-You relation; see Chap. 6). As a result, he sets the evidence in the context of that special relation. Therefore, evidence that would conclusively falsify the statement "The stranger is on our side" for other members of the resistance, might well not do so for the partisan who talked directly to him.

Mitchell's important contribution is to show that the logic of confirmation is permissive enough to render theological statements factually meaningful. Theologians can claim that their statements are factually meaningful even though, like the statement "The stranger is on our side," they cannot be conclusively verified or conclusively falsified.[54]

One final point: it should be noted that Flew's challenge is itself unclear.[55] At times he deals with falsification: "What would have to occur or to have occurred to constitute for you a disproof of the love of, or of the existence of, God?"[56] In demanding disproof he must be asking for conclusive falsification as the test for the factual meaningfulness of theological statements. In that case, he is demanding something that need not be provided. As we have seen, using conclusive falsification eliminates seemingly noncontroversial common sense and scientific statements that the positivists had no desire to challenge (see p. 32).

At other times, Flew asks only that theologians specify circumstances that would count against or disconfirm their statements or assertions: " . . . sophisticated religious people . . . tend to refuse to allow, not merely that anything actually does occur, but that anything conceivably could occur, which would count against their theological assertions and explanations."[57] In light of the failure of the positivists' program, it might be argued that theologians ought not to feel obligated to answer this challenge. After all, the various versions of confirmation and disconfirmation have not been shown to be adequate statements of a test for factual meaningfulness. Yet a refusal on the part of theologians to state circumstances that would count against the truth of a statement like "God loves us as a father loves his children" would make the statement irrelevant to human concerns. Mitchell's use of the parable of the Partisan and the Stranger shows how a believer responds to the fact of suffering as something which counts against the truth of "God loves us." Therefore, he successfully replies to what might be called the challenge of disconfirmation. Flew, in his response to Mitchell, actually concedes this point; but then Flew notes that the problem of evil may be raised to plague theologians even after they have successfully met this challenge.[58] Flew may or may not be justified in his position regarding the problem of evil, but this is, after all, another issue.

THEOLOGY IS STILL A GOING ENTERPRISE

A considerable number of brilliant philosophers tried to discredit theology as a cognitive enterprise. They used the test of verification (or falsification or confirmation) in an effort to dismiss it without detailed examination. During the heyday of positivism most contemporary empiricists thought they had succeeded. In 1955, Gilbert Ryle provided an interesting statement of the view that theology is going, going, going, . . . even if not quite gone:

> The theological fire has died down, but it has not quite gone out and the kettle of theological philosophy, though far from even simmering, is not quite stone cold. Some philosophers, some of the time, do take some interest in tensions between theological, scientific and moral ideas. Others are at least polemically interested enough to deny that theological dictions convey any ideas at all. But most of us, most of the time, do just forget about the subject.[59]

Ryle made these observations in the mid-fifties. His assessment did not seem all that farfetched, not merely to positivists and other contemporary empiricists, but to many religious thinkers who devoutly desired to find legitimate reasons for challenging it. Yet, in the two decades that have followed Ryle's remarks, philosophical interest in theological issues has not abated; it has increased. A debate which took place about five years earlier foreshadowed subsequent developments.[60] In it, A. J. Ayer, one of the most aggressively anti-theological of the positivists, challenged F. C. Copleston, S.J., a Thomist who is the leading historian of philosophy in our time.[61]

Ayer opened the debate with a typically strong blast: ". . . one thing which those of us who are called logical positivists tend to have in common is that we deny the possibility of philosophy as a speculative discipline. . . . Consequently, we reject metaphysics, if this be under-stood, as I think it commonly has been, as an attempt to gain knowledge about [states of affairs in] the world by non-scientific means."[62] He then invokes the principle of verification to show that metaphysical statements are pseudo-synthetic and factually meaningless. Copleston replies by claiming that Ayer is misguided in thinking that he can use verification as a neutral instrument which tests for factual meaningfulness in the way that a Geiger counter tests for radioactivity. Far from its being a neutral instrument, it is merely a sophisticated way of asserting the basic conviction of positivism, namely, that all knowledge is rooted in observa-tions by means of the senses. Yet this position cannot be simply assumed as valid, it must be argued for. As Copleston puts it:

> If you say that any factual statement, in order to be meaningful, must be verifiable, and if you mean by "verifiable" verifiable by sense-experience, then surely you are presupposing that all reality is given in sense-experience. If you are presupposing this, you are presupposing that there can be no such thing as a metaphysical reality. And if you presuppose this, you are presupposing a philosophical position which cannot be demon-strated by the principle of verification.[63]

Copleston is accusing Ayer of circular argument in the vicious sense. Verifiability is a valid test only if the positivists' observation-oriented approach to experience is valid. Yet the only reason that Ayer offers for accepting this approach to reality is the principle of verification itself. Copleston continues by stating, "It seems to me that logical positivism claims to be what I might call a 'neutral' technique, whereas it presupposes the truth of positivism . . . it looks to me as though the principle of verifiability were excogitated partly *in order* to exclude metaphysical propositions from the range of meaningful propositions."[64] In other words, Copleston claims that the test of verification is not something that the positivists uncovered in an open-ended quest for meaningfulness, but rather, that it is contrived to suit their philosophical prejudices.

Ayer concedes the point that no version of verifiability has, thus far, proved successful, but he appeals to its practical benefits as justification for its use. "I claim for my method that it does yield valuable results in the way of analysis. . . . "[65] This claim is combined with a counterclaim namely, that metaphysicians and theologians employ methods that do not yield valuable results because, as he tells Copleston:

> . . . you fail to supply any rules for the use of your expressions. . . . All that I require is that some indication be given of the way in which the

expression relates to some possible experience. It is only when a statement fails to refer, even indirectly, to anything observable that I wish to dismiss it as metaphysical.[66]

Copleston regards Ayer's approach to meaningfulness as dogmatic, prejudicial, and restrictive. He claims that as soon as one departs from patterns appropriate to mathematics, common sense statements of fact, or scientific statements, Ayer cries, "Foul!" The only conditions under which Ayer will concede the cognitive meaningfulness of metaphysical and theological statements is a condition that is unacceptable to any self-respecting metaphysician or theologian, namely, that they transform their statements into analytic or scientific (synthetic) statements. Copleston puts it this way:

> A metaphysical proposition is testable by rational discussion, but not by purely empirical means. When you say that metaphysical propositions are meaningless because they are unverifiable in your sense, I do not think this amounts to more than saying that metaphysics is not the same thing as empirical science.[67]

This debate took place in 1949. At that time most philosophers in the English-speaking world would have felt that Father Copleston was stubbornly refusing to concede that the "jig was up" with his kind of metaphysical theology. Yet it was positivism's days that were numbered. After the appearance of Wittgenstein's *Philosophical Investigations* in 1953, theologians who made the kinds of points that Copleston makes here could draw support from the work of one of the founding fathers of contemporary empiricism. Theologians could insist that the meaning of the word "God" can only be determined by its use in religious and theological language. It is arbitrary and dogmatic to say that it cannot have cognitive meaning unless it conforms to the pattern of mathematical symbols on the one hand or of electrons on the other. Against Ayer and other empiricists who demonstrated the pseudo-synthetic character of theological statements, theologians could protest that these statements are not "pseudo" anything; they are genuinely theological. Indeed, Ayer himself was soon to acknowledge this point.[68] In Wittgensteinian terms, theology and metaphysics are legitimate "language games" with their own distinctive assumptions and rules.

The moral of the story seems quite clear, even to leading positivists like A. J. Ayer and C. G. Hempel, who have continued to be outstanding representatives of contemporary empiricism in the post-positivistic period. It involves pessimism about the possibility of coming up with an adequate statement of the test of verification, combined with the recognition that the test has not served as a preliminary examination that could eliminate metaphysics and theology from the philosophy.

In 1951 C. G. Hempel published his important survey of the problems associated with the test of verification. He concluded it on the following note: "It is to be hoped that before long . . . our last version of the empiricist meaning criterion [the test of verification] will be replaced by another, more adequate one."[69] Some fifteen years later he indicated that empiricists had to continue to hope because they had still not come up with an adequate statement of the test.[70]

In little more than two decades the empiricists shifted from confidence in verification as a device that would trigger a philosophical revolution to the pious hope that the device itself might be made to work. In this connection, the contrast in the two editions of Ayer's *Language, Truth and Logic* is especially striking. In the first edition (1936) he was confident to the point of being cocky. Ten years later, in the introduction to the second edition, he wrote:

> Although I should still defend the use of the criterion of verifiability as a methodological principle, I realize that for the effective elimination of metaphysics it needs to be supported by detailed analyses of particular metaphysical arguments.[71]

This statement is, to put it mildly, ironical because the test of verification was designed as an instant purgative which would eliminate metaphysics without the need for "the detailed analyses of particular metaphysical arguments." After all, "detailed analysis" is what the pre-positivistic empiricists applied to metaphysics; there was nothing revolutionary in that.

In any case, revolutionary or not, detailed analysis of particular theological arguments and of individual religious thinkers will be presented in the balance of this book. These presentations will be informed by contemporary empiricism in *both* exposition and criticism. The confrontation is, I believe, a fruitful one.

Chapter 4

Miracles

The challenge of verification sharpened the attacks made on religion in the name of science. A consideration of the problem of miracles will underscore this point.

One of the most widespread misunderstandings of the effect of science on religious beliefs is the notion that science proves that miracles can't happen. This, in a way, is what many people mean when they claim that science disproves religion. They think that religious beliefs are based on the miraculous accounts of the Bible such as the Red Sea dividing when Moses put his magic rod over it and Jesus raising Lazarus from the dead. They insist that, since science proves that such miracles cannot occur, science demonstrates the falsity of religious beliefs. They are wrong on both counts. In the first place, the truth of religious beliefs does not stand or fall on the issue of miracles. In the second place, although science does affect the believability of miracles, it is not easy to specify exactly how it does so. In the effort which follows, a few misunderstandings will have to be cleared up.

A considerable number of miracles were reported in the Bible, and they have been accepted as true by generations of believers, including theologians. Traditionally, theologians did not regard them as clinching arguments for the existence of God. They did not ask nonbelievers to accept the existence of God, or any other religious beliefs, on the grounds that God had caused the waters of the Red Sea to divide for Moses and the Israelites, or of any other wonders. They accepted God's existence and rule in advance of any miracle. Miracles were signs of his power; devices used by God to gain the attention of mankind and to intensify the sense that, in the words of Isaiah, "The whole earth is full of his glory" (Isa. 6:3). Before the rise of science, the beliefs regarding miracles were not front and center for most Christian thinkers. They provided supporting evidence for beliefs that theologians regarded as acceptable on other grounds.[72]

The coming of science changed the status of miracles within Christian thought. Leading English scientists of the seventeenth and eighteenth century, like Robert Boyle, were Christians who wanted empirical support for their religious beliefs. They wanted it to be comparable to the empirical evidence that confirmed their scientific hypothesis.[73] They appealed to biblical miracles in an effort to provide it. This set miracles at the center of religious controversies and they have remained there into the present century.

The close connection between earlier challenges to religion that were mounted in the name of science and the challenge of verification is sharply focused by Raeburne Heimbeck's recent study in *Theology and Meaning*.[74] He presents a sophisticated survey of the original criterion of empiricist meaning and of the many modifications that have succeeded it. He concludes that theological statements are factually meaningful because there are observations that are relevant to their verification. These observations were, presumably, actually made by witnesses of the events described in the Bible. He concentrates on two of them: (1) The crossing of the Red Sea and (2) the resurrection of Jesus Christ.[75] The observations involved are, to say the least, startling. Heimbeck claims that an observer of the crossing of the Red Sea by the Israelites would have at one moment seen a raging sea. When Moses put his magic rod over the waters, they would divide and liquid water would behave like ice, that is, it would stand in "walls" through which the Israelites passed. The believer then claims that an event as utterly extraordinary as that could not happen without the supernatural intervention of the transcendent God.

Selectivity is another feature of the appeal to miracles as the answer to the challenge of verification. The resurrection of Jesus Christ verifies the truth of Christian statements and only of Christian statements. It would not serve equally well to verify theological statements of other religions like Judaism and Islam. If Jesus of Nazareth actually died on the cross, was then buried in a sealed tomb, and rose from the dead to appear to his disciples, the claim that he was the Christ is verified or, at least, confirmed.

If there are acceptable grounds for believing that the biblical miracles took place as reported, then this answer to the challenge of verification is adequate. Statements about God would definitely be linked to observable consequences and they would, therefore, be factually meaningful. Even the most hard-nosed positivist would then be forced to admit that it is worth investigating their truth or falsity.

Belief in miracles certainly has not vanished from the western religious scene. Many orthodox Jews, Roman Catholics, and conservative Protestants believe that the miracles reported in the Bible actually occurred. There are important contemporary theologians who not only agree that the biblical miracles occurred, but who claim that miracles continue to occur. A leading Anglican theologian, Austin Farrer, wrote: "The miracles of the saints never cease; a hundred years ago the sainted Curé d'Ars multiplied bread and healed the sick and lived himself by a continuous physical miracle, nor has he lacked successors since."[76]

Despite the fact that some important theologians like Farrer defend the traditional view of miracles, from the time of Friedrich Schleiermacher (1768–1834) many important religious thinkers have rejected it. Five of them will be treated at length in this book: Rudolph Otto, Martin Buber, Soren Kierkegaard, Rudolf Bultmann, and Paul Tillich. They reject the view that miracles are extraordinary occurrences that can only be attributed to God's supernatural intervention into earthly affairs for two reasons: (1) They think that belief in miracles distracts believers. It leads them to search for observable wonders instead of focusing on religious virtues like trust, love, and hope. (2) Defending the traditional view of miracles involves theologians in sharp conflicts with science. Religious thinkers who reject the traditional view of miracles claim that by doing so they are freed from the need to defend supernaturalism and can then more effectively affirm the truly important elements of their faith.

In the sections which follow I will present my own statement of the kind of thinking that underlies the rejection of the traditional view of miracles on the part of so many outstanding religious thinkers.

MIRACLE: THE DEFINITION INVOLVES OCCURRENCE AND INTERPRETATION

All too many people think of a miracle as a happening, a happening of a most extraordinary kind. Some of the events reported in the Bible like

Jesus raising Lazarus from the dead and the waters standing in "walls" at the Red Sea illustrate this very well. Actually, the happening is only one part of what is meant by the term miracle. A definition of the traditional view would run as follows: A miracle is an extraordinary event that shatters the fabric of our understanding of nature to the extent that we are impelled to attribute to it a cause that is supernatural (above nature), namely, the active agency of the transcendent God. The issue of miracle must be treated in terms of the two main elements in this definition: (1) the possibility of the *occurrence* of an event that is so extraordinary as to shatter the patterns by which we understand nature, and (2) the *interpretation* of this event as having been caused by the supernatural action of God.[77]

MIRACULOUS OCCURRENCES

A miraculous occurrence is a happening that is so utterly extraordinary as to shatter the framework of our understanding of nature. Obviously, this is a culturally determined notion.[78] The framework of the understanding of nature cannot be dissociated from particular times and places. In earlier periods of history earthquakes and eclipses were happenings that conformed to my definition, today, in our scientifically sophisticated culture, they are not.

In order to separate the element of occurrence from that of interpretation, I shall, for the moment, ignore the biblical accounts of miracles. They confront us with problems regarding the historical accuracy of the stories (see pp. 67 ff.). Instead, I shall focus on the contemporary scene and deal with the Roman Catholic shrine at Lourdes. I am persuaded that some utterly extraordinary cures have taken place there. Interesting corroboration was provided by an article in the August 9, 1971 issue of *Newsweek*. A three-year-old girl with terminal cancer whose bones had been eaten away by the disease was immersed in the waters of Lourdes. Her condition continued to deteriorate for the next two days, but on the third day, it happened! Not only was the disease arrested, but the bones in her skull grew back. Her Protestant doctor—a highly trained observer, who was thoroughly familiar with the case—said that "miracle would not be too strong a word to use."

In this same story, the reporter notes that "not surprisingly, many doctors believe that Lourdes's record of sixty-two authenticated miraculous cures since 1858 could be statistically duplicated for that period in any large hospital." In other words, these doctors do not believe that God intervenes in a special way at Lourdes. Whether these doctors are right or wrong about their statistical hunch, one thing is clear. The reliability of the accounts of instantaneous cures at Lourdes is not the interesting philosophical issue, but rather, the problem of interpreting the evidence. In order to isolate this crucial philosophical point, let's imagine the following situation in which the evidence for an utterly extraordinary happening is exaggerated and overwhelming.

The Roman Catholic Church authorities are nettled at the continued scepticism of the world community regarding miraculous healings at Lourdes. Therefore, they offer the scientific community a challenge saying: "Test the cures in any way that you like; we will cooperate." A crack team of medical scientists, biochemists, physiologists, and psychologists converge on the shrine. With the cooperation of the church authorities they thoroughly examine all the afflicted people who come to the shrine for cures. The scientists use the most sophisticated instruments available to record the precise disfigurations of every malformed or diseased part of each supplicant's body. Then one of the children undergoes a miraculous cure. A totally withered leg of a two-year-old girl is immersed in the waters and is instantaneously changed to normal appearance. X-ray checks before and after the event prove that it is the same leg. Subsequent tests show that it is now fully functional. There are absolutely no known medical theories to account for the instantaneous healing. It is an utterly extraordinary disruption of the patterns of nature. The scientists, who constitute the most sophisticated set of observers that could possibly been found to check it out, are unanimous in their verdict: "It has occurred!" This enables us to focus on the philosophical question: How is this occurrence to be interpreted?

THE INTERPRETATION OF MIRACULOUS OCCURRENCES

Given the circumstances, the Roman Catholic interpretation seems relatively straightforward. It attributes the instant and astonishing cure to the supernatural intervention of God. Furthermore, they have an analysis that accounts for the power of God to intervene in this way.[79] God, the God of the Bible, is the creator of heaven and earth. He established the patterns which they normally manifest. He is appropriately called Father because he governs the world like a father. An earthly father governs his home according to certain regular patterns. Children are expected to be in bed by a specified hour. However, under unusual circumstances, the father who established the patterns may choose to vary them. He may let the children stay up far beyond their normal bedtime in order to give them a special treat, such as going to a film, or watching an exceptional program on television. So too, with God. He governs nature according to regular patterns. Many of them were as familiar to the people of biblical times as they are to us. If not, people of biblical times could not have had a sense for the miraculous exception.[80] On rare occasions, for special purposes, God varies those patterns, just as an earthly father does. Furthermore, he unquestionably has the power to do so, because, like an earthly father, he is varying the patterns that he has himself established. According to Catholic teaching, in the case of Lourdes, he varies the patterns of human physiology through the instrumentality of the Blessed Virgin Mary. That is why the withered leg of the two-year-old girl was cured.

As already noted, medical scientists can accept the report of a miraculous healing at Lourdes, and reject the supernaturalist interpretation of it. They would feed this occurrence into the body of scientific data and try to devise a hypothesis that explains it. They might proceed by studying the human organism to ascertain whether there are rare combinations of tissues that are like extremely rare types of blood; by checking people to see whether there are special psychological types who have rare properties that affect the capacity to heal; and, of course, they would check the chemical composition of the waters of Lourdes. In light of the fact that the occurrences at Lourdes are so far beyond anything that can be accounted for at the present state of medical science, the search for a scientific pattern of regularity would take a long time, perhaps quite a few generations. Scientists might ultimately succeed. They might discover that if rare physiological and psychological types were immersed in waters of an utterly rare type like those of Lourdes, under circumstances of the kind of psychological intensity generated at Lourdes, *then*, this kind of instantaneous healing takes place. The physiological type might occur only once in every one million persons; the psychological type might occur only once in every ten million persons; and this unusual specimen with afflictions like cancer might come to the waters of Lourdes, in the requisite frame of mind, only once in a half century. Nevertheless, this concurrence of the right physiology and psychology with the right chemistry would constitute a natural interpretation of the cures. Regardless of how rare the occurrence might be, scientists would claim that "*if* physiological type y (with certain kinds of afflictions) came together in the same person with psychological type x and was immersed in chemical waters type z, *then* instantaneous healing would result." This would exemplify the "if . . . then . . ." pattern which is typical of scientific hypotheses and laws. It would link many disparate occurrences into a natural and lawful pattern.

Thinkers who favor the naturalistic interpretation of extraordinary cures can offer additional arguments on behalf of the scientific approach. Scientists operate with a high degree of prediction and control. They might, for example, isolate the special ingredient in the waters of Lourdes and expose all afflicted people to it.

This contrasts favorably with the religious interpretation of the Roman Catholic Church which admittedly affords us no way of predicting or controlling the cures. Even if the requisite factors are present, there is, according to the Church, no way of telling whether a miraculous healing will occur, because it involves the grace of God which cannot be predicted. To pursue the comparison between the heavenly Father and earthly fathers further: All the conditions for the special treat of a late bedtime may be present, but an earthly father may still refuse to allow the child to stay up. So too, all the conditions for a miracle may be present, but the heavenly Father may still withhold that final act of will, the gracious "yes" that is the cause of the miraculous healing. Furthermore, the "if . . . then . . . " pattern of the scientists is *natural* insofar as all the factors, however rare they may be, are earthly factors that can be checked out in a public way, but the action of God, through the mediation of the Blessed Virgin Mary, is supernatural.

The Roman Catholic Church does not claim that the factors involved in miraculous cures are public in the sense that any person of normal intelligence could, if properly instructed, follow them. The *healing* is public, but just as God's grace is involved in its taking place, so too grace is involved in being able to apprehend its supernatural causes. Without God's gracious acquiescence, individual men are incapable of being aware of his activity.[81] Even if God's grace has a "law" of its own, it would take an infinite intelligence like God's to discern it. The "law" would remain inaccessible, in principle, to our limited intellects.[82] We never, for example, learn why some supplicants are miraculously cured, whereas the prayers of others go unanswered.

The unanswered prayers of countless supplicants represent a further difficulty for the supernaturalist standpoint. According to the Roman Catholic Church, God is loving and merciful as well as just. The Church also teaches that very young children who have been baptized are innocent of sin. Therefore, even if we were to concede the dubious point that the sins of adults justify their suffering from afflictions like cancer, this justification would not be present in the case of a four-year-old child. It seems capricious if not immoral of God to be gracious to such a tiny fraction of the children who are brought to shrines for healing.

All the points that have been made in favor of the naturalistic approach to instantaneous cures at Lourdes could be acknowledged by the supernaturalist without shaking his faith in the validity of his approach. He could reply that the scientists in seeking a natural interpretation would—for a very long time—be unsuccessful. By contrast, the supernatural interpretation is already operative and fits neatly. In light of this, the scientists' insistence on pursuing a natural explanation seems dogmatic.

The logic of this conflict between supernaturalists and naturalists involves an ironical reversal of the usual pattern. In this case it is the secularists, or anyone else who holds out for naturalistic understanding, who seem to be "waiting for Godot." Nevertheless, I intend to show that people who hold out for scientific explanations are not dogmatic, but reasonable. I shall do so by considering two issues: (1) exceptions to scientific laws and (2) the autonomy of scientists.

THE CASE FOR THE NATURALISTIC INTERPRETATION

A strong argument that is often advanced by naturalists is that we cannot accept supernatural explanations of observable occurrences because that would involve accepting two classes of exceptions to scientific laws.

Natural Exceptions

They show that the current scientific view of lawful regularity is mistaken. They will be repeated whenever the same circumstances occur. Scientists would, of course, have to take account of them. They would have to devise new laws that would apply to these exceptional occurrences as well as all the previous data.

Supernaturally Caused Exceptions

They would be repeated only if God, in his mysterious grace, wills them to be repeated. These special cases would, presumably, *not* be scientifically relevant because they would not be exceptions to natural regularities—the only ones that concern scientists. Therefore, scientists could ignore these miraculous occurrences with impunity.

In a recent essay Guy Robinson spelled out the deplorable consequences of accepting these two classes of exceptions to a scientific law. "Scientific development would either be stopped or else made completely capricious, because it would necessarily be a matter of whim whether one invoked the concept of miracle . . . to explain an awkward result, or, on the other hand, accepted the result as evidence of the need to modify the theory one was investigating."[83] In effect, Robinson is arguing that the price of accepting these two classes of exceptions to a scientific law is too high.

I would like to strengthen Robinson's case by linking it to the question of the autonomy or self-regulation of scientists. I claim that accepting the possibility of a class of supernatural exceptions to scientific laws would involve the sacrifice of scientific autonomy. I shall deploy this argument by sketching a farfetched scenario.

Imagine that the government of the United States has scheduled thermonuclear tests on an island in the Pacific. A well-known pacifist, who is a priest, determines to stop it. He fails to influence the government's policy and the tests proceed. He then prays in the hope that he can at least keep the explosions from polluting the atmosphere.

The military leaders give the signal to fire a bomb. The exploding mechanisms are properly triggered, but there is no gigantic mushroom cloud. They rush to check the machinery. To their astonishment they find that all the pointer readings and other available data indicate that the 1,000-megaton bomb being tested had actually exploded. It seemed to have gone off, in the sense of energy exchanges, yet there had been no visible signs of an explosion, nor had any damage been done to the island. They try to fire the bomb again, but it is futile. It is dead, and the money invested in it has gone down the drain. Baffled, the military leaders order another 1,000-metagon bomb to be exploded. It is with the same astonishing result.

At this point, the military leaders are dissatisfied with the scientists on hand who cannot handle these amazing occurrences. They call for a full-scale investigation. One of the leading physicists in the country undertakes the job of research and assembles a crack team.

Let's assume that these scientists are prepared to allow for the possibility of supernatural exceptions to the scientific status quo. They investigate the possibility that the extraordinary patterns displayed by the thermonuclear weapons are attributable to the prayers of the priest. We are now in a position to see why, allowing for the possibility of supernatural explanations, naturally observable occurrences is something that would, in effect, drive working scientists to opt right out of the scientific enterprise.[84] In a situation of this kind, these scientists would not be able to investigate the effectiveness of the priest's prayers because, as scientists, they would not be able to determine whether the exception was supernatural. Therefore, the head of the investigating team would have to phone the Pope to ask him to send one of *his* investigating teams (the Vatican has trained personnel to investigate claims of the miraculous) to the area. The conversation might run something like this:

Scientist: Your Holiness, this is Professor Grendl, and I have a problem. Thermonuclear tests are taking place in the South Pacific under the auspices of my government, and all sorts of incredible things are happening. Gigantic discharges of energy are taking place with no observable effects on the environment. My government has called me in to investigate it.

The Pope: Fine, from what I hear you're just the man to do it. Go ahead!

Scientist: Well, Your Holiness, it isn't that simple. These investigations cost a fortune, and our present administration is economy-minded. So, we don't want to spend all that money investigating these extraordinary occurrences unless we're sure that these exceptions are ours. I mean unless we're sure that they're *natural* exceptions. Now, you must have heard about the priest who is conducting a prayer vigil in this area. Some people say that his prayers are being answered miraculously and that's why the bombs are discharging without damaging anything and without polluting the atmosphere. Could you send one of your best teams out here to check this out?

By this time, the point should be clear. Scientists cannot function as scientists if they have to appeal to leading figures in some other enterprise to tell them what to do. Scientists, as scientists, must operate with autonomy, that is, they must set their own rules and referee their own games. Even though no logical prohibition prevents scientists from accepting the supernatural interpretation of an extraordinary occurrence, on the functional level, it involves a sellout of science.

The discussion of autonomy has helped to determine the price of accepting the class of supernaturally caused exceptions to supernatural laws, but it does not settle the question of whether the price is worth paying. Supernaturalists argue that in undercutting the work of scientists we interfere with a merely human enterprise, whereas, the naturalistic interpretation cuts us off from the possibility of responding to the grace of God.

The answer that I offer on behalf of the naturalistic interpretation is practical. It recommends reliance on scientific explanations without pretending to be a conclusive refutation of supernaturalism.

In discussing the interpretation of miraculous occurrences, we are dealing with naturally observable events like the sudden healing of a totally withered leg. We are not dealing with such elusive phenomena as intelligence and freedom. Any educated person knows that the record of scientists in handling observable occurrences is vastly superior to that of magicians, shamans, witch doctors, faith healers, and other types who have claimed to both understand and control nature. It is, therefore, unreasonable to propose a policy, like the sacrifice of autonomy, which would interfere with the work of scientists at the operative level.

To summarize: It is reasonable to reject the supernatural interpretations of "miraculous" occurrences because (1) the record shows that, in the long run, scientists come up with explanations of events that seem—even for long periods of time—to defy natural explanation, (2) to accept supernatural interpretations of events that can be naturally observed would impede the work of scientists at the operative level by forcing them to sacrifice their autonomy, and (3) by contrast, naturalistic interpretations of naturally observable events do not require a sacrifice of any concepts that are important and integral to religion.

The natural/supernatural contrast should not be equated with a contrast between science and religion. Leading religious thinkers of the past two centuries have fought the tendency to identify Christian faith with supernaturalist views that claim that the activity of God *must* be invoked to explain extraordinary observable occurrences. They have insisted that we can understand God's relation to men on the model of freedom. I do not wish to explore the complexities of philosophical discussions of freedom and determinism. For my purposes I need only note that no philosopher who defends the notion of freedom would claim that a free decision could enable a human being to jump out of a twelfth-story window and to fly up instead of falling down. So too, religious thinkers who reject the traditional view of miracles insist that God's relation to mankind must be understood within the fabric of scientific understanding. This position does not force religion to demand a sacrifice of the scientists' autonomy or of any other significant operative principles of science.

BIBLICAL MIRACLES

The discussion to this point has been restricted to the belief that miracles occur in the present. However, most believers do not deal with them in contemporary terms. They stress the miracles of the Bible, but the biblical accounts of miracles are even more problematic than claims to miraculous cures at a shrine like Lourdes. In the case of instantaneous cures at Lourdes we have seen that the supernatural interpretation is unacceptable from the standpoint of science. Biblical accounts of miracles are equally problematic from this standpoint, but they involve another major problem. There is the problem of whether or not we ought to believe that the events—such as Moses at the Burning Bush and Jesus walking on water—actually happened. What follows is based on David Hume's essay on miracles in Book X of his *Enquiry*.[85]

The more extraordinary an occurrence is, the less we ought to believe someone who tells us it happened. Obviously, if we are told that we can see it for ourselves this serves to modify our scepticism. If someone claims that he saw a man walk on water and proposes to take us to see him do it again, we are no longer quite so sceptical.

This pattern does not apply to the biblical accounts because we cannot hope to see the biblical miracles for ourselves and people who believe them don't offer to show us similar occurrences. Therefore, our willingness to accept the accounts depends on the credibility of the biblical witnesses. Hume proposes a severe test for the believability of witnesses who report the utterly extraordinary: " . . . no testimony is sufficient to establish a miracle, unless the testimony be of such a kind that its falsehood would be more miraculous than the fact that it endeavors to establish."[86] To illustrate: if a friend told you that he'd seen a violet hippopotamus with orange polka dots flying across the campus, you would not be rationally entitled to believe him unless it were more probable that such an animal actually had been flying across the campus than to suppose that your friend was on drugs and having a bad trip. Clearly, it is the latter possibility that is more likely.

Furthermore, when Hume proceeds to set down his standards for the credibility of witnesses, we can really see the magnitude of the decline in the prestige of religion under the impact of science. Traditionally, the prophets and apostles were regarded as the most virtuous and praiseworthy of men. They were also regarded as the recorders of the words of God, the agents of God's interventions in history, and the key witnesses to his mighty acts. In the prescientific culture of the West, it was assumed that the biblical miracles had these ideal witnesses attesting to their authenticity. Therefore, they were regarded as being worthy of belief by intelligent people.

Once science had come on the scene, Hume applied scientific standards of credibility to men who claimed to have witnessed utterly extraordinary occurrences. Hume insisted that to be believed, such events should have been witnessed by observers who were (1) numerous, (2) intelligent, (3) well-educated, (4) honest, (5) in the position of having a lot to lose if they are mistaken in their accounts (this would cut down on carelessness), and (6) operating publicly in a well-known part of the world.[87]

Once these scientifically oriented standards of credibility are adopted, the biblical witnesses are demoted. Instead of being regarded as ideal types, they are looked upon as the sort of witnesses we'd be most inclined to suspect. The men who recorded the biblical accounts were not dispassionate observers but partisans of a new and struggling faith. Among the other disabilities from which they suffered (from a scientific point of view), is the fact that none of them could have been well-educated in Hume's sense because they all operated with prescientific standards of expectation and evidence. In addition, they were operating in an obscure part of the world, and the events they described were not public in the scientific sense. Peter preached the glad tidings concerning Jesus as the Christ or Messiah. Yet, he acknowledged the fact that the post-Resurrection appearances of Jesus were not public—in the sense of being observable to all—but rather, that they were restricted to the disciples (Acts 10:41).

The credibility of the biblical accounts of miracles are eroded even further by the application of the scientific attitude and method to the study of religion. Here we find that the belief in miracles, and the kinds of miracles reported, are functions of certain stages in the development of various cultures. In other words, the reports of miracles in different religions follow certain fairly predictable patterns.[88]

The challenge of science to supernaturalistic types of religion is a rough one. Conservatives are not apt to get very far in urging us to accept the supernaturalist interpretation of miracles because scientifically oriented philosophers can skewer them on the horns of a dilemma. On the one horn the sceptics challenge the accounts of miracles and refuse to concede that they occurred. As we have seen, this is a pretty effective challenge when leveled at the biblical accounts of miracles. On the other horn, scientifically oriented philosophers insist that if something happens that is extraordinary enough to rate the designation "miraculous," there must be a natural explanation for it.

The argument has not demonstrated that the conservative point of view is wrong, much less that it is impossible. If you believe in the Judeo-Christian God, creator of heaven and earth, a God to whom all things are possible, then you can follow the supernaturalists in incorporating the insights of scientists into the religious point of view. Scientists, according to supernaturalists, uncover the regularities that God ordains but only by the light of faith can we understand the irregularities, that is, the miracles, that he performs to enlighten our sinful souls. Since supernaturalists' communities have a long tradition of faith behind them, you can find considerable practical benefits from this way of approaching experience. There are the gratifications of hymn-singing and other forms of ritual, and the considerable support of a well-integrated community. In addition, you may be enriched by looking out at the world from inside a pretty well-developed worldview.

Yet, few people in our day will opt for the supernaturalist's position. The benefits of technology are so vast and so public that, in general, people want to affirm science. Supernaturalists who accept the traditional view of miracles are often characterized as being, culturally speaking, "out of it." A good example is the film *Inherit the Wind* where an ultraconservative Protestant, William Jennings Bryan, is shown mounting a major effort to keep the evolutionary theory from being taught in the schools of Tennessee. Yet, supernaturalists are not without resources in coping with this rejection by the dominant culture. They can claim that it is the cross they bear in witnessing truly to Jesus Christ.

MIRACLES WITHOUT SUPERNATURALISM

Many religious thinkers reject the supernaturalist understanding of miracle without rejecting the idea of miracle as such. A good example is provided by Martin Buber's treatment of the crossing of the Red Sea.[89] The supernaturalist account stresses fantastic details like the dividing of the raging seas when Moses put his rod over them and their standing firm as the Israelites passed between them on dry ground. By contrast, Buber focuses on the natural details which are also given in the fourteenth chapter of Exodus. They involve such clearly natural phenomena as fog and wind. The only extraordinary thing about them is the way they work together to enable the Israelites to escape. First the dense fog hides them from the Egyptians, then a strong wind blows the fog away and makes the waters of a marshy area unusually shallow. The Israelites, traveling light, manage to cross it. The Egyptians spot them and try to overtake the Israelites, but the Egyptians are encumbered with chariots, horses, and the weight of their armor. They bog down in the mire and give up the chase.

Buber's version of this miraculous event factors out the extraordinary details and deals with the quality of the experience. The fog, the wind, the marshy waters are all natural, but the Israelites experience the redeeming hand of God in and through the series of natural circumstances. From that point on, God is known to them as "the Redeemer of Israel." This becomes a central category of Jewish experience and it used in interpreting their subsequent history.

Approaches to miracles like the one exemplified by Buber have advantages and disadvantages when compared with the supernaturalist interpretations. The supernaturalist approach is very problematical from the scientific point of view. It asks us to believe that water—contrary to everything we know about its behavior—stood in "walls" at the Red Sea in order to allow the Israelites to pass safely through. Furthermore, Christian and Jewish supernaturalists are inconsistent. They are highly critical of reports of miracles when they encounter them in religions like Hinduism and Buddhism, but they are less critical when they deal with biblical accounts of miracles.

Buber's approach avoids these disadvantages but it does not come off as well on the question of verification. Supernaturalists, who accept extraordinary details like raging waters dividing and standing in walls, can insist that only God's supernatural intervention could have caused it. Similarly, when Elijah challenged the priests of Baal to the test of fire, there was something in the nature of a crucial experiment about it. If fire consumed the altar of Baal, he would be regarded as the true God; if fire consumed the altar of Jaweh, the Lord of Israel, then he would be hailed as the true God.

By contrast, the view exemplified by Buber stresses the natural details involved in an incident like the crossing of the Red Sea. It follows that Buber's version of the miracle can be interpreted in other ways.[90] It need not be regarded as an act of God. It could, for example, be taken as a matter of luck; the right factors came together at the right moment.

In general, positivists and other contemporary empiricists have conceded the factual meaningfulness of supernaturalism.[91] However, they regard this view as so hopelessly outmoded by the development of scientific standards of believability that they do not even bother to challenge the truth of its factually meaningful statements. They trained their fire on sophisticated religious thinkers like Martin Buber and Rudolf Bultmann who accept the traditional view of God while rejecting the supernaturalistic framework of belief that characterized people of biblical times (see especially, Chap. 9). These religious thinkers are more vulnerable to the challenge of verification than supernaturalists, but a close analysis of Buber, Bultmann, and Tillich should show that they are not as vulnerable as the positivists thought they were. In part this is because, as we have seen, unexpected difficulties were encountered in formulating an adequate version of the test of verification. In part it is also because the thinking of Buber, Bultmann, and the rest, is so complex that it is difficult to understand just what role verification plays in it.

One of the main points of this book is to try to trace the broad kinds of verification that are found in many types of religious thought.

Part Two

Religious Experience

One theological response to the challenge of verification is the appeal to religious experience. Some theologians claim that statements about God can be checked out in the same way as statements about ordinary physical objects, namely, by direct firsthand experience. Statements like "This book has white pages and black print" can be checked out by sense experiences (in this case the sense of sight) whereas statements about God deal with a transcendent reality that is beyond sense experience. The problems relating to this fundamental dissimilarity between our experience of God and our experience of physical objects will occupy us throughout this section.

Religious experience will be treated in the context of the challenge of verification, but it would be a terrible mistake to suppose that this is the most important thing about religious experience as far as believers are concerned. To them the experience is important as the direct sense of God's presence. In other words, "religious experience" is an intellectual label for those moments in which religion comes alive. As such, they are regarded by believers as the most precious moments of their lives. They enhance their lives and provide the assurance that, as one thinker has put it, "Man is not alone."[1]

Experience is a catchall term that has a wide range of associations. In its broadest sense it used to express the notion that we are affected by and actively participate in an ordered world of things. Some of the narrower meanings of the term have associations that appeal to theologians, and some have associations that appeal to sceptics. Before turning to a consideration of religious experience itself, I should like to explore some of these associations.

Theologians are drawn to the notion that when we talk of experiencing something we often refer to a reality "out there" that is independent of the apparatus we use in becoming aware of it. In this sense we can talk of an experience of a sunset or a symphony, and it is in this sense that the theologian wants to talk of our experience of God. Experience also has the association of expertise and theologians want to talk of great religious figures like Moses and Mohamet as having had a great deal of experience of God so that they may be considered experts in religious matters.

Experience can, however, refer to things that are not independent of the individual who has them. A splitting headache or a vivid nightmare does not have anything "out there" that corresponds to it. Sceptics stress meanings of this kind in rejecting appeals to religious experience that are designed to show that God is an independent reality.

The treatment which follows will be devoted to an extended discussion of the thought of Rudolf Otto and Martin Buber, two thinkers whose accounts of religious experience are powerful but contrasting. Otto stresses the special character of religious experience and of the uniqueness of its object, that is, God or the Holy One. Buber, on the other hand, tries to call our attention to the religious dimension of ordinary experiences.

Chapter 5

Rudolf Otto: Phenomenologist and Theologian

The name of the theologian Rudolf Otto (1869–1937) is, more than that of any other thinker, associated with the notion of religious experience. His book *The Idea of the Holy* crackles with the sense of the urgency of the experience and the power of God's presence.[2] Before considering his special approach to religious experience, it is important to note that he rejects supernaturalism of the kind associated with the traditional view of miracles. In commenting on Darwinian thought he accepts the naturalistic account of the origin and development of life.

> But there can be no doubt that *natural* factors and *natural* laws were and are the conditions of life's origin and development; and although we do not yet, and possibly never shall, know what they are, it is by reason of, and in accordance with, such *natural* factors and laws that life began, and it would no doubt always arise in exactly the same way where these were set in motion.[3]

Otto claims that the traditional supernaturalistic view of miracle is, ironically, a form of rationalism. It places the religious emphasis on empirical factors in the same way that scientists rest their theories on these observables. In other words, religious empiricists and sceptical empiricists share the same assumptions and are looking for the same things; they merely arrive at different conclusions. By contrast, Otto shifts the focus to the inner life. "The difference between rationalism and its opposite . . . resolves itself rather into a peculiar difference of *quality* in the mental attitudes and emotional content of the religious life itself."[4]

Otto's view of the religious life differs greatly from that of his philosophical master, Immanuel Kant, who thought that religion is derivative from the experience of moral obligation.[5] Otto, by contrast, insists that religious experience is unique. He stresses the special character of religion, that is, its discontinuity with all other modes of experience. "If there be any single domain of human experience that presents us with something unmistakably specific and unique, peculiar to itself, assuredly it is that of the religious life."[6] The heart of religious experience is the encounter with holiness.

"Holy" is another of those words that is hard to define. After reading some of the illustrative passages in this chapter, a reader who does not know what it means should develop a sense for it. Among other things, it means separate, powerful, and valuable beyond measure. Holy objects are set apart from all other things, and they must be handled with extreme caution. Indeed, almost all religions have special classes of men, generally called priests, who alone are considered pure enough to handle holy objects. A dreadful story from the Book of Samuel illustrates the point (2 Sam. 6:6, 7). The Ark of the Covenant, the most holy object in Israel, is being carried to the newly established capital of Jerusalem by the orders of King David. It is loaded on an oxcart. The animals stumble and Uzzah grabs the Ark in an effort to keep it from falling. Despite the fact that his motivation was one of respect for the holiness of the Ark, he is struck dead—just as if he had touched a high voltage wire. Since he is not a priest he is not qualified to touch this holy object, even with the best of intentions.

Rudolf Otto was a Christian thinker who fully affirmed monotheism, that is, the view that God is a single reality. For purposes of analysis, Otto distinguishes rational and nonrational elements in the holy one. The situation is comparable to a child who is one individual, but has been influenced by both parents. There is no possibility of *experiencing* the child in terms of pure "mother-influence" elements and pure "father-influence" elements. Certainly the child cannot be broken down into these two components. However, when we discuss the character of a child, we can, by using words, focus on one set of influences to the relative exclusion of the other. In this way, Otto distinguishes the nonrational element, which he calls the "numinous," from the rational element. The numinous is "wholly other"; there is nothing to which it can be meaningfully compared, whereas, the rational element of the holy is, for Otto, primarily moral. It is the element captured by Jesus in the statement: "There must be no limit to your goodness, just as your heavenly father's goodness knows no bounds" (Matt. 6:48).

Otto hammers home the importance of the nonrational side of religious experience to the point where he seems to revel in it, but he had no intention of subordinating the moral element in religion to the nonrational. He was fully aware of the fact that without the moral element religion sinks to the level of superstition and fanaticism.[7] His strong emphasis on the nonrational was not a function of his preference for it, but of his historical situation. During the century after Kant, the nonrational element was so thoroughly subordinated to the rational one that religion came to be regarded as a somewhat vivid and popular version of moral philosophy. Otto was trying to call attention to the nonrational factor in the experience of God, and to do so, he had to stress the fact that holiness, which is widely regarded as a central category of religion, involves more than moral perfection:

> To be *rapt* in worship is one thing; to be morally *uplifted* by the contemplation of a good deed is another; and it is not to their common features, but to those elements of emotional content peculiar to the first [religion] that we would have attention directed as precisely as possible.[8]

Otto tries to bring people to full awareness of the holy, which involves the numinous element, by means of techniques similar to those used in courses in music appreciation. A professor of music may be convinced that everyone has a capacity for appreciating the power and meaning of Beethoven's late quartets; however, he may have to urge students to resist the temptation to assimilate this kind of music by means of the appealing and accessible world of pop music.

Otto's course in "religious appreciation" involves a number of techniques:

Taunting Otto clearly thinks that religious experience is not only a good thing, he thinks it is the best thing. Yet, instead of trying the hard sell, he tells us that he doesn't much care whether we read him or not. If we fail to do so, clearly it will be our loss. Early in *The Idea of the Holy*, he writes:

> The reader is invited to direct his mind to a moment of deeply-felt religious experience, as little as possible qualified by other forms of consciousness. Whoever cannot do this, whoever knows no such moments in his experience, is requested to read no farther.[9]

Clearly this passage is rhetorical device on Otto's part. He is certain that everyone has deeply felt moments of religious experience, and he wants the reader to continue. As we shall see, he is persuaded that many people turn away from the full force of religious experience (mostly because they are terrified by it) and refuse to explore its implications.

Comparisons   We noted that a good teacher of music appreciation wants to emphasize the distinctive character of the late Beethoven quartets; he wants the student to *dissociate* them from other forms of music. Nevertheless, the teacher may initially have to ask the student to do the very opposite, namely to *associate* the quartets with his previous experience of music. So too Otto, even though he is mainly trying to isolate the distinctive element in religous experience, finds that he must appeal to similarities between religious and other types of experience.

> We can co-operate in this process [of bringing an individual to awareness of the unique features of religious experience] by bringing before his notice all that can be found in other regions of the mind, already known and familiar, to resemble, or again to afford some special contrast to, the particular experience we wish to elucidate. Then we must add: "This *X* of ours is not precisely *this* experience, but akin to this one and the opposite of that other. Cannot you now realize for yourself what it is?" In other words, our *X* cannot, strictly speaking, be taught, it can only be evoked, awakened in the mind; as everything that comes "of the spirit" must be awakened.[10]

As we shall see, Otto's major comparison is between religious experience and our experience of great works of art.

Quotation   A good teacher of music appreciation would not merely talk about music, he would illustrate it by means of recordings or preferably by means of live music. Otto is aware of the need to confront his reader with important examples of religious experiences and he quotes extensively from both occidental and oriental religions. I shall follow his example.

Coining New Words   Otto is concerned about pointing out the distinctive element in religious experience—the one that shatters the fabric of our ordinary states of consciousness. For this reason, he coins his own words in order to develop a terminology that will not be associated with *familiar experiences*. In other words, he tries to use unfamiliar words to symbolize these unfamiliar experiences. The words he used were taken from Latin. He used a great number of these terms. I will deal with the four that I regard as especially important: *numinous, mysterium, tremendum,* and *fascinans.*

OTTO AS A PHENOMENOLOGIST

Otto is an excellent *phenomenologist of religion.* The word "phenomenon" is one that stresses the passive, receiving side of experience. It is

rooted in the Greek word meaning "appearance." Roughly, a phenomenon is that which appears *before* it is worked over by means of checks
that are consciously applied. If you see a roundish red thing coming at
you, then this appearance as it is (before you start applying labels to it), is
the phenomenon. It is the way "whatever it is" actually appears to you.
Subsequently, you may decide that it is a cement mixer, a sports car, or a
queer reflection from the road, but the phenomenon is what appears to
you before you check out these possible ways of taking it.[11]

A long standing source of confusion in philosophy is the view that
that "roundish red thing" is a "raw" description which simply deals with
phenomena as given, that is, which deals with them in an utterly naïve and
unintellectual way. In his *Philosophical Investigations* Ludwig Wittgenstein showed that this is not the case.[12] The ability to use color words like
red, and shape words like roundish, involves considerable sophistication.
Nevertheless, the perception and identification of objects are activities
that admit to degrees. Some philosophers are more concerned with their
own categories than they are with the specific and distinct appearances of
the objects. They rush to judge the kinds of things that are possible, and
the kinds of things there are before they study the kinds of things that
actually appear to them. Ironically, the early positivists, who were so
much oriented to science, provided a good example of philosophers who
were all too quick to apply labels. They filed a considerable number of
diverse statements under the heading "factually meaningless." It was in
reaction against the philosophical tendency to program our responses to
phenomena by means of intellectual labels that Wittgenstein came up with
the remark: "Don't think, but look!"[13] Many scholars of religion regard
Otto as a man whose "looking" at religious phenomena was pretty
perceptive, even though his "thinking" about them was inadequate.

THE NUMINOUS

Otto's crucial term is the *numinous.* It refers to the nonrational element in
the experience of God. As noted earlier, it cannot actually be separated
from the rational element either in God himself or in religious experience.
Yet it can, for purposes of discussion, be focused upon separately.

The term numinous involves Otto's effort to point to the similarities
between religious experience and sense experience. His effort to do so is
heavily indebted to Kant, but it is better to present Otto without reference
to Kant because he misuses Kant's categories.[14]

Sense experience can, for intellectual purposes, be broken down
into passive and active elements. The mind, for example, is passive to
stimuli like light which comes to it from outside. This aspect of picking up
external stimuli is called *intuition* which, in this context, has nothing to do

with the unreasoned hunches that are referred to by the phrase "woman's intuition." Intuitions are not themselves rational, but they are necessary to the formulation of rational judgments about what there is "out there." In a single integrated process, intuitions are worked over by the basic structures of the mind. The result is rational judgments of a more or less specific nature like "red sports car" or "red roundish object."

Otto claims that in religious experience the mind operates in the same way. Although he does not use the term intuition, he suggests that in religious experience the mind intuits a nonrational *other* that stimulates it. Unlike the intuitions of sense experience, the source of religious intuition is nonsensible, it is the numinous reality of God. When the mind works this over intellectually (and this is done inescapably even in the most primitive religions), the person makes the judgment "the holy one," or "God." In focusing on our basic experience of the numinous, Otto says a great deal about it, yet it is Ronald Hepburn who provides the clearest description:

> Otto memorably described . . . the numinous as a stunning but not horrifying experience, a blend of wonder, ecstasy, and fear at what is too great to be coped with intellectually. It is none of these feelings *exactly*; beyond them all is some element of quite inexpressible strangeness. . . . Its impact is . . . compelling and authoritative.[15]

Otto's more precise accounts of religious experience do not focus on the term "the numinous," but rather, he breaks up the numinous into major components. These are indicated in the quotation from Hepburn where wonder is linked to what Otto calls the "mysterium" fear to the "tremendum," and ecstacy to the "fascinans."

Mysterium Tremendum et Fascinans

Otto is certain that all human beings have a capacity for religious experience. He is also certain that we have all, in one way or another, been exposed to realities that would stimulate our sense of the holy. Yet he thinks that many of us fail to develop our capacity for religious experience, and we fail to have what he regards as the most valuable of all experiences, namely, conscious rapport with God.

Otto, as previously noted, uses strange Latin words to try to blast us out of the comfortable ruts of the normal, so that we come to notice the uncanny aspects of experience. The main terms that will be considered here, *mysterium, tremendum,* and *fascinans,* have obvious English equivalents, mystery, tremendous, and fascinating. Otto, of course, wrote in German and his Latin terms have equivalents in that language as well. Otto chose to use Latin because the words in ordinary spoken languages have been devalued; a difficult catch in baseball is called tremendous; a man who can talk a bit more interestingly than most is described as fascinating; detective stories that require a bit of ingenuity to clear them up are called mysteries. It would, therefore, hardly serve Otto's purpose to describe the numinous as a "tremendous and fascinating mystery."

Otto is emphatically oriented to the "beyondness" of the holy. The *mysterium* points to the element that is beyond our comprehension, the *fascinans* points to the element of attraction that is beyond our control, and the *tremendum* points to the element of awesome power that is beyond any force that we can imagine.

Before turning to consideration of the individual terms, *mysterium*, *fascinans*, and *tremendum*, it is important to recall the meaning of the term phenomenon, namely, that which appears. Otto is an effective phenomenologist because he is sensitive to what appears, and he evokes a sense of religious experience in his readers. Once again, I must note that for Otto, God himself is the important thing. God is a reality that cannot be broken down into different elements. It is also true of religious experience in its "live" sense, that is, when an individual is having it. Inevitably, the discussion of aspects of the unified experience confuses the issue. It makes it *seem* as though the *mysterium* could be dissociated from the *fascinans* and the *tremendum*, and that they can be dissociated from one another, although this is not so.

Mysterium Since *mysterium* is one of his central categories, one would expect Otto to provide a full scale discussion of it. He doesn't. In fact, what he says about the *mysterium* boils down to one point—the distinction between a difficult problem and a mystery. Problems do not overwhelm us, they are intellectual difficulties or puzzles that intrigue us. The point of a problem is to formulate it clearly and to try to devise techniques for solving it. It may be extremely difficult. We haven't yet discovered a solution to the problem of finding a cure for cancer. Nevertheless, we are convinced that medical scientists will eventually come up with one. Problems are the special domain of science. The scientist is struck by a phenomenon he cannot explain, and he formulates it as a problem in terms of clear, but as yet unanswered, questions. He then tries to devise effective techniques for getting the answers.

Mysteries share one important characteristic with problems.[16] They are phenomena that arrest our attention, but that we cannot explain. Yet where problems are unexplainable in fact, at a particular time (even a relatively simple one like an algebra problem is not answerable by the student when he first reads it), mysteries cannot be explained even in the remote future. They are inexplicable *in principle*.

Otto claims that the sense of the *mysterium* is more than a merely problematic phenomenon. It is something we directly experience as so utterly overwhelming that the person who encounters it knows, immediately and indubitably, that there is no possibility of coming up with an explanation of the mysterious reality.

Martin Buber, whose view of religious experience will be considered in the following chapter, has provided a clear statement of the *mysterium*:

> All religious reality begins with what biblical religion calls the "fear of God." It comes when our existence between birth and death becomes incomprehensible and uncanny, when all security is shattered through the mystery. This is not the relative mystery of that which is inaccessible only to the present state of human knowledge and is hence in principle discoverable [that is, what has been referred to as a problem]. It is the essential mystery, the inscrutableness of which belongs to its very nature; it is unknowable.[17]

Otto, like Buber, deals with the *mysterium* in experiential terms that make it distinctively religious.

> The truly "mysterious" object is beyond our apprehension and comprehension, not only because our knowledge has certain irremovable limits, but because in it we come upon something inherently "wholly other," whose kind and character are incommensurable with our own, and before which we therefore recoil in a wonder that strikes us chill and dumb.[18]

Fascinans and Tremendum   Otto repeatedly emphasizes the utter uniqueness of religious experience. Yet, in an effort to get people to become consciously aware of what they actually experience but often fail to notice, Otto is forced to draw on parallels between religious experience and other types of experience. The experience of the holy is one which is similar to other areas of experience in which we simultaneously want to look and to look away. The dual aspect of vivid experiences is what Otto gets at with the terms *fascinans* (want to look) and *tremendum* (want to look away). I was about ten years old when I saw Boris Karloff play the monster in *Frankenstein*. At his first appearance I experienced one of the parallels to Otto's account of religious experience. I looked, looked away, and then peeked through my fingers. The *fascinans* expresses the powerful attraction. It is characteristic of adolescents in relation to sex. It draws them on with almost uncontrollable and insatiable curiosity, yet it is also characterized by the *tremendum*, since it arouses their deepest anxieties and makes them shrink back from the experience they so desperately seek. The attraction of the *fascinans* cannot, in reality or in our experience, be separated from the overwhelming power of the *tre-*

mendum that makes us recoil from the reality that irresistably attracts us.

The central statement of holiness in the Bible, which is found in the sixth chapter of Isaiah, communicates the *tremendum.* Isaiah has a vision in which the train of God fills the Temple and the angels chant: "Holy, Holy, Holy, is the Lord of Hosts, the whole earth is full of his glory." This experience was not only a fulfillment for the prophet, whose sense of mission dated from it, but his expression of it has become a source of religious experience to countless people since his time. The chant "Holy, Holy, Holy" is central to Jewish prayer, to the Catholic mass, and it appears frequently in Protestant worship. Yet the prophet's initial reaction was to recoil and almost collapse, "Woe is me! I am lost, for I am a man of unclean lips and I dwell among a people of unclean lips; yet with these eyes have I seen the King, the Lord of Hosts."

It is not uncommon for certain religious figures to be granted so many experiences of God that they become overly familiar. They either lose the sense of the *tremendum,* or they suspect that there is more to God than what they have experienced. They ask for the privilege of experiencing the holy with the full power of the *tremendum.* Their request is granted, and they are overwhelmed.

The story of Abraham arguing with God is one of Otto's own illustrations (Gen. 18:16–33).[19] Abraham had been the servant of God and had experienced God directly and intensely. He learns that God proposes to destroy Sodom, the home of his sister and his brother-in-law, Lot. He pleads with God to spare the city on the grounds that it would be unjust of God, the Lord of justice, to destroy the righteous inhabitants along with the wicked ones. God agrees to spare the city if fifty righteous ones are to be found in it. Abraham is swept up with the force of his argument, but is suddenly overwhelmed by the sense of his own unworthiness and creatureliness. "Behold I have taken it upon myself to speak to the Lord, I who am but dust and ashes."

In the Bhagavad-Gita, a classic of Hinduism, we have a dialogue between Arjuna, a warrior prince who is about to fight his own kinsmen, and Krishna, who is the High God Vishnu, incarnate as a man, and acting as Arjuna's charioteer.[20] Krishna has been teaching Arjuna about his proper duties as a warrior and a man, when Arjuna, not content with knowing God in his human form, asks to see him as Vishnu, saying:

> O Supreme Lord, you are as you describe yourself to be: I do not doubt that. Nevertheless, I long to behold your divine form. If you find me worthy of that vision, then reveal to me O master of yogis, your changeless Atman.

The narrator then tells us that the vision was granted and describes it in words that are designed to shatter our sense of ordinary experience.

> Then Sri Krishna, Master of all yogis, revealed to Arjuna his transcendent divine form. Speaking from innumerable mouths, seeing with a myriad eyes, of many marvellous aspects, adorned with countless divine ornaments, brandishing all kinds of heavenly weapons, wearing celestial garlands and the raiment of paradise, anointed with perfumes of heavenly fragrance, full of revelations, resplendent, boundless, omnipresent. Suppose a thousand suns should rise together into the sky: such is the glory of the shape of the infinite God.

Arjuna was overcome by what he experienced.

> Then was Arjuna, the lord of mighty riches, overcome with wonder. His hair stood erect. He bowed low before God in adoration, and clasped his hands. He addressed Krishna in a choking voice:
> "Well, it is that the world delights to do you honor, Mightiest! How indeed should they withhold their homage? You are what is not, what is, and what transcends them. Take our salutations Lord, from every quarter!
> "Infinite of might and boundless in your glory, carelessly I called you 'Krishna' and 'my comrade'—took undying God for friend and fellow-mortal. Overbold with love, I was unconscious of your greatness. Did my words offend? Forgive me Lord Eternal. Author of the world, the unmoved and the moving, you alone are fit for worship."

Arjuna concludes his response on a note that recalls the end of the Book of Job. Job, having challenged God and indicted him for injustice, finally is granted direct experience of God and says: "Therefore, I despise myself and repent in dust and ashes" (Job 42:6). In similar fashion, Arjuna says:

> Therefore, I bow down prostrate, and ask for pardon. Now forgive me God, as friend forgives his comrade, father forgives son, and man his dearest lover. I have seen what no man ever saw before me: Deep is my delight but still my dread is greater. Show me now your other form, O Lord, be gracious.

Krishna's prayer was answered, and he was released from the dread of the *tremendum* that had snuffed out the delight of the *fascinans*.

The Effectiveness of Otto's Categories

Otto's description of religious experience, what is more technically known as his phenomenology, is stimulating, but it is far from being definitive. His emphasis on its dreadful character needs to be supplemented by descriptions of the less turbulent aspects of religious experience, as in William James' description of the "once-born" type of believer.[21] Yet, in the years since 1917, when *Das Heilige* was published,

Otto's terminology has become an important element in discussions of religion. The effectiveness of his terminology is attributable to two main factors: (1) The term "numinous" did what Otto wanted it to do. It freed religion from subordination to morality and other forms of experience; it focused on the uniqueness of religion. (2) The terms *tremendum* and *fascinans* caught on because they capture a duality that is characteristic of many religions. I will cite a few of them.

In Hindu popular religion the laughing elephant god Ganesha symbolizes the joyful, the almost playful aspect of reality—the fascinans. The other sides of the statues of Ganesha, like the reverse side of a coin, have representations of the ferocious and demonic god Kirttimukha, who is a good symbol of the *tremendum*. The High Gods of Hinduism manifest the same duality. Vishnu being the beneficent preserver of existence (*fascinans*) and Shiva the destroyer who represents the destructive ravages of time (*tremendum*). Although as High Gods, each of them incorporates the opposite element as well as the one with which they are primarily associated.[22]

Within Western religion, which is dominated by the biblical portrait of God, we observe the same duality. This is misrepresented by the inaccurate cliché that the God of the New Testament is a God of love and mercy (*fascinans*) whereas the God of the Old Testament is a God of wrath and judgment (*tremendum*). Actually, both testaments contain eloquent testimony to both aspects of the duality.

Turning first to the Old Testament, we have already considered the treatment of holiness in the sixth chapter of Isaiah. It was linked to the *tremendum*, Isaiah was overwhelmed by it and felt impure. By contrast, in the eleventh chapter of Hosea, holiness is specifically related to compassion. Israel is condemned for its faithlessness, and is shown to be utterly corrupt, so much so, that it ought to be destroyed. Yet God says: "My heart recoils within me, my compassion grows warm and tender: I will not execute my fierce anger. I will not destroy Ephraim [the Northern Kingdom of Israel], for I am God and not man, the Holy One in your midst."

The classic expression of the twofold aspect of God is found in the thirty-fourth chapter of Exodus where the shift from the *fascinans* to the *tremendum*, in the space of a short statement, is startling: "The Lord, the Lord, a God merciful and gracious, slow to anger, and abounding in steadfast love and faithfulness. Keeping steadfast love for thousands, and forgiving iniquity and transgression and sin, but who will by no means clear the guilty, visiting the iniquity of the fathers on the children and the children's children to the third and fourth generation."

As far as the New Testament is concerned, we have to purge our

minds of contemporary sentimental images of Jesus. Otto himself emphasized the numinous qualities found in New Testment accounts of
Jesus, and this means that the *tremendum* is present as well as the
fascinans. Sometimes the contrasts are as sharp as the one we just
considered in the Book of Exodus. In the seventh chapter of Matthew we
have the moving statement: "Ask and it will be given you; seek and you
will find; knock and it will be opened to you. If you who are evil know
how to give good gifts to your children, how much more will your father
who is in heaven give good things to those who ask him?" Yet this
statement which so poignantly communicates the *fascinans* is immediately followed by one which reflects the *tremendum*: "Enter by the narrow
gate; for the gate is wide and the way is easy that leads to destruction and
those who enter by it are many. For the gate is narrow and the way is hard
that leads to life, and those who find it are few."

Both elements are present throughout the Gospels, just as they are
present in all important religions, because reality confronts us with the
twofold aspect of fulfillment and annihilation and Otto's categories of the
fascinans/*tremendum* are gripping because they capture a duality that is
present in religion as well as in life.

OTTO'S "ARGUMENT" FOR THE EXISTENCE OF GOD

Otto's style is difficult to follow. He not only uses many special terms
such as *mysterium, tremendum,* and *fascinans,* he also uses Kantian
terminology with special twists of his own. In working through the tangled
skein of his thought, I find an argument for the existence of God based
on religious experience. After all, the German title of Otto's book is *Das
Heilige* which means "the holy." Otto's purpose is distorted by the title
chosen by the English translator, namely, *The Idea of the Holy.* Otto is not
so much interested in the concept of holiness as in the reality of the holy,
that is, of God.

The statement of Otto's "argument" for the existence of God that I
am about to present is consistent with his views. However, I am sure that
readers who are familiar with Otto will be able to find passages that
conflict with my interpretations. This assurance is based on my conviction
that his views are inconsistent.[23] Nevertheless, I have done my best to be
faithful to his appeal to religious experience in mounting a sustained
(though I think ineffective) argument for the existence of God. There are
two major themes: (1) the effort to use Kantian categories to argue that
our knowledge of God is a priori and (2) the parallel between religious and
aesthetic experience.

In talking of Otto's "argument" for the existence of God, the word is set in quotation marks because Otto is not interested in presenting a formal argument of the kind that will be treated in Part Four. On the contrary, he is convinced that all of us directly experience the reality of God and that there is no need to argue for God's existence. Given the fact that in our times millions of people do not believe in God, Otto's position is a strange one. I will lay it out in terms of what I take to be his answers to four basic questions. (1) Does everyone have religious experience, and if so, how? (2) If all people do have religious experience, why do so many of them deny the existence of God? (3) If everyone has a basic capacity for religious experience and everyone experiences the same god, why are there so many different religions? (4) Since God cannot be seen, why should we believe that our religious experience is experience of a reality that is external to us and not merely imaginary?

Everyone Has a Capacity for Religious Experience

Otto has an important stake in claiming that *everyone* has the capacity for religious experience. If God were to grant this capacity to some people and not others, then countless people would be shut out from experience of God through no fault of their own. It would be hard to square this with the view that God is holy, which involves, among other things, moral perfection.

Otto uses Kant's category of the a priori in discussing the universal capacity for religious experience. As I said earlier, his misuse of Kant's terminology is the weakest part of the book. Instead of presenting his program in Kantian terms, I will bring out his points by means of illustrations.

Otto describes the a priori as follows: "Now this is the criterion of all a priori knowledge, namely, that as soon as an assertion has been clearly expressed and understood, knowledge of its truth comes into the mind with the certitude of firsthand insight."[24] When we express and understand an a priori statement like the mathematical one that "Two plus three equals five," we are certain of its truth. Otto transfers this to religion: in claiming that our knowledge of God is a priori, he can claim that we are certain that God exists.

Otto claims: "A Priori cognitions are not such as everyone does have . . . but such as everyone is *capable* of having. The loftier a priori cognitions . . . do not . . . occur spontaneously, but rather are 'awakened' through the instrumentality of other more highly endowed natures."[25] Otto here calls attention to another feature of the a priori, namely, that the ability to handle it, in fields like mathematics, is an inborn capacity, that is, a basic part of the mental equipment of normal human beings. Yet it is obvious that, as Otto says, not everyone actualizes his potential for it. If we do not, for example, study geometry, we will not actualize our capacity for performing the Pythagorean theorem. In other words, the truth of mathematics and other forms of a priori knowledge is not determined by sense experience. Nevertheless, we need teaching to stimulate us into actualizing our capacity for acquiring this mode of knowledge.

When Otto refers to "loftier a priori cognitions," he is referring to our inborn capacity for experiencing the numinous, a capacity he refers to as "divination." It is this capacity that enables him to account for the fact that we can, in religious experience, have knowledge of God who, as Otto insists again and again, is "wholly to other." This knowledge would be impossible if God himself had not implanted the capacity for divination in us.

Otto claims that all of us have divination, that is, the capacity for religious experience, present in us at birth independently of experience. Yet we need other people, especially the great religious leaders like Moses, the Buddha, Jesus, and Mohamet to trigger the sense of the holy in us. We do not meet what Otto calls these "highly endowed natures" directly, but our parents and religious teachers confront us with their teachings and with stories of their lives. In this way they play a role long after their own eras.

There is, of course, an important difference between religious and geometrical experience. Countless people do not study geometry, and so they never actualize their capacity for doing geometry, which is a purely intellectual activity. Religious experience, on the other hand, has an intellectual component, but it is by no means purely intellectual. Therefore, people can be stimulated to the actual experience of the holy in a wide variety of ways. The impact of a great religious leader is an important and an especially worthwhile way of coming to an experience of the holy, but since "the whole earth is full of his glory," anything at all—from a sunset to a melody—can trigger a religious experience. To pursue this comparison with music, even though a simple melody provides musical experience, it takes a master like Mozart to exalt us. So too, according to Otto, we need great religious leaders to take us to the pinnacle of religious experience.[26]

Many People Shy Away from Religious Experience

Otto's analysis of religious experience involves the claim that every individual has a capacity for it and that life provides ample occasions for this capacity to be used. It would seem that everyone should acknowledge the reality of God, but countless people have denied it. Otto's thought provides answers to this question.

The experience of God is the most fulfilling one that individuals can know but, as we have seen, it is also threatening. Thus, Jesus urges his hearers not to concentrate on the powers of this world, no matter how formidable they seem, because they are insignificant when compared to the power of God. "And do not fear those who kill the body, but cannot kill the soul; rather, fear him who can destroy both body and soul in hell" (Matt. 10:28). Martin Buber, in a memorable passage, captures this sense of the threatening character of the true God:

> An important philosopher of our day, Whitehead, asks how the Old Testament saying that the fear of God is the beginning of wisdom is to be reconciled with the New Testament saying that God is love. Whitehead has not fully grasped the meaning of the word "beginning." He who begins with the love of God without having previously experienced the fear of God, loves an idol which he himself has made, a god whom it is easy enough to love. He does not love the real God who is, to begin with, dreadful and incomprehensible.[27]

Otto can claim that even though everyone is given the experience of God, and, therefore, has a basis on which to acknowledge his reality, many people shy away from the confrontation and pretend that *all* experience is a routine affair.

One God, Many Religions

Otto claims that many people have religious experience but shy away from both the experience and its implications because it is overwhelming. This is why there are so many atheists. It does not account for the diversity of religions. After all, according to Otto, people have the faculty of divination, and they all use it to tune in the same reality, namely, God. One would, therefore, suppose that all individuals who stand up to the fearful character of religious experience and let the holy come through would wind up with the same view of God. Clearly they do not. Otto takes account of the problem by comparing religious and aesthetic experience: " . . . false recognitions of the holy are later rejected and wholly or partly extruded as inadequate or simply unworthy, as soon as a higher level of development and purer religious judgment have been reached. There is a precisely parallel process in another department of judgment, that of aesthetic taste."[28]

Otto clearly relies on a "progress" view of culture which he applies to art and religion. Most people today would apply it only to science. At this stage of history there are different schools of literary criticism and strong differences of opinions within the individual schools. The same applies to religion; there are many different ones and there are strong differences within the individual traditions. Otto puts it this way:

> . . . those [religious] judgments that spring from pure contemplative feeling also resemble judgments of aesthetic taste in claiming, like them, objective validity, universality, and necessity. The apparently subjective and personal character of the judgment of taste, expressed in the maxim *de gustibus non disputandum* [there is no disputing tastes], simply amounts to this, that tastes of different degrees of culture and maturity are first compared, then so opposed to one another that agreement is impossible.[29]

Astonishingly enough, Otto regards this as a temporary state which will be overcome as the human race further develops its rational capacities. He believes that everyone will ultimately be brought to a universal judgment with regard to artistic matters.[30]

Otto transfers his analysis to judgments in religion by talking of the religious experience by means of still another special term, *contemplation* which involves reflection on the reality of God as it impinges upon the self:

> Where, on the basis of a real talent in this direction "contemplation" grows by careful exercise in depth and inwardness, there what one man feels *can* be "expounded" and "brought to consciousness" in another; one man can both educate himself to a genuine and true manner of feeling and be the means of bringing others to the same point; and that is what corresponds in the domain of "contemplation" to the part played by argument and persuasion in that of logical conviction.[31]

Otto clearly hopes for the day when the rational element of all human beings will be so fully developed that we will all be led to recognize the validity of judgments in the field of religion. For Otto that meant the truth of the Lutheran version of Protestant Christianity. In the meantime, he hopes to be an example of "one man" who can "bring to consciousness" in us what he himself feels and experiences, namely the holiness of God.

The Reality of God

Otto, as noted earlier, is not merely interested in the idea; he wants to convince us of the reality of the holy. "It is one thing merely to believe in a reality beyond the senses and another to have experience of it also; it is one thing to have ideas of 'the holy' and another to become consciously aware of it as an operative reality, intervening actively in the phenomenal world [that is, in the world that we register with our senses]."[32] Yet we can acknowledge the validity of Otto's description of religious experience (his phenomenology) without conceding the reality of the object of that experience, namely, God. I once had a dream of a praying mantis with the head of a friend. It was terrifyingly vivid, but there was no reality which corresponded to it. Since we cannot observe God we have every reason for raising the question as to whether God, that is, the object of religious experience, is illusory.

The first point to be made is important to any discussion of religious thought, and not just to Otto; it will come up repeatedly throughout this book. The transcendent God is not supposed to be accessible to sense experience. God is not like a flying saucer, that is, he is not a reality that ought to be observable, but is, somehow, never reliably observed. To understand the word "God" is to appreciate the fact that the reality to which the term refers is beyond the senses. Any reality that is observed could not be God; it could only be an idol.

Otto therefore insists that in order "to divine" God, that is, to have a proper sense of his reality, we must not only rely on our own religious experience, we must allow ourselves to be influenced by the experts. Otto himself draws a parallel between religion and music.[33] He speaks of people with a limited capacity for appreciating music as being at the lowest level. At the next level we have performers who understand music, and at the highest level we have the composers who create it. In the same way, there are, according to Otto, the great majority of people who have only a limited capacity to respond to God. At a higher level we find the prophets who understand more of the holy because they more fully appreciate the rational side of God. Finally, at the highest level we find the great religious leaders and consumately, Jesus of Nazareth. The great majority ought, therefore, to allow the experts to evoke and shape their capacity for divining God. They ought to follow the lead of the experts in accepting the reality of God and in understanding the rational and moral elements of the holy.

Otto and the Subjective-Objective Contrast

In order to evaluate Otto's argument I will have to try to clarify the subjective-objective contrast as it functions in religious thought. These words serve as striking examples of what Gilbert Ryle calls umbrella words in that too many ideas are covered by them without proper regard for important distinctions (see p. 37). Although I initiate this discussion in connection with Otto's thought, it is important to note that it is equally important to the other thinkers who will be treated in detail.

Objective as External Contrasted with Subjective as Imaginary When I grope through my room in the darkness of the night and bump my shin on a chair leg, the chair is objective. The pain is imposed by an object external to me. My sense of touch and sight testify to the independent existence of the chair. On the other hand, if I grope around in the dark, hear an unfamiliar sound, and sense the presence of a menacing stranger in the room, I may turn on the light and discover that no one is present. The sound may have been external to me, but the mysterious stranger was subjective, that is, a figment of my imagination. He was not an independent reality. This sense of the objective-subjective contrast depends on the use of observations to check the contents of the mind.

Objective as Agreed upon Standards of Judgments and Applications of Those Standards The other relevant objective-subjective contrast deals with the attainment of agreement on standards of knowledge and on the application of standards to specific cases. Physics is objective in the sense that physicists can agree on the standards for sound judgment and on specific applications of those standards, as for example, to the judgment that the helium atom has two electrons. What makes the widespread agreement that physicists achieve all the more remarkable is that their theories are complex and also that they constantly deal with nonobservables like subatomic particles.

In the context of this second use of the objective-subjective contrast, subjectivity refers to personal and cultural factors that lead people to come down on different sides of a given judgment. Russians are culturally conditioned to have different views of democracy than Americans; a taut personality may prefer Arturo Toscanini's performances of Beethoven whereas a person of a more easygoing temperament might prefer those of Bruno Walter. These factors that vary from one individual subject to another are called subjective.

Physicists attain widespread agreement despite personal and cultural differences. Individuals as different in temperament as Albert Einstein and Edward Teller can, as physicists, agree on the judgments about the significance of various experiments. So too can American and Russian physicists despite their cultural differences. That is why physics has served as the model of an objective intellectual discipline. Of course, the extent of the agreement among physicists is not total, but it is, nevertheless, very great.[34]

It should be obvious that in politics, art, and religion, we do not find anything like the same degree of agreement that is found in physics. This point will be developed later in connection with criticisms of Otto (see p. 97). Here it is important to note that religious thought is considered by many thinkers to be subjective in two closely connected senses: (1) a factual claim that there is no consensus on either procedures for settling disputes or on specific judgments and (2) the reason that there is no widespread agreement is that subjective (personal and cultural) factors make agreement unobtainable. Individuals are regarded as being too strongly influenced by their personal temperament and their cultural conditioning to disengage themselves from their involvements. Therefore, they cannot overcome their differences on procedures, for example, on how to go about settling the question of the existence of God, much less on specific judgments, as for instance, on whether or not Jesus Christ is God's only begotten son.

Phenomenology and Objectivity *Phenomenology*, as noted earlier, is a philosophical term that is rooted in a Greek word meaning appearance. This might suggest the traditional philosophical contrast between appearance (for example, a stick that is half immersed in water appears to bend sharply at the surface) and reality (the fact that the stick is actually straight). In point of fact, phenomenology is intended to fend off preoccupation with this distinction and with all other philosophical categories that distract us from focusing on the way things actually appear.

God is clearly not observable, in principle as well as in fact. Yet God is experienced as a reality that is other than the self, in other words, as an objective reality in the first sense of the word "objective." In this connection, Otto's quotation and criticism of a statement by William James is especially illuminating. First, the quotation from James that deals with the human response to the divine:

> It is as if there were in the human consciousness *a sense of reality, a feeling of objective presence, a perception* of what we may call "something there. . . . "[35]

Otto thinks that in this passage James provides an excellent example of a philosopher whose "holiness-receptor" is working well in the sense of being attuned to the reality of God, but whose rational side messes up the data he receives.

> James is debarred by his empiricist and pragmatist standpoint from coming to a recognition of faculties of knowledge and potentialities of thought in the spirit itself, and he is therefore obliged to have recourse to somewhat . . . mysterious hypotheses to explain this fact. But he grasps the fact itself clearly enough [and] is sufficient of a realist not to explain it away.[36]

The "fact" referred to by Otto is that when we pay attention to the phenomenon, that is, to the appearance of God, there is no "as if" about it. God comes through as the object of the experience, in a sense similar to the way another person is manifested as external to the self. "But this 'feeling of reality,' the feeling of a 'numinous' *object* objectively given, must be posited as a primary immediate datum of consciousness."[37] These experiences verify statements about God's existence and nature.

We are now in a position to appreciate the startling and even daring character of Otto's argument for the objectivity of our knowledge of God:

1   From the phenomenological standpoint, God appears as objectively given in the first sense of "objective" that we considered. God appears to us as an "other," that is, as *independent* of human subjectivity.

2   What is distinctive about Otto's approach to the knowledge of God is that he claims that it is objective in the second sense of the term that we considered. Otto claims that *we can agree on procedures for settling disputes about the existence of God* and that *we can reach agreement with regard to specific judgments about him.* We can, for example, agree that God is the *mysterium tremendum et fascinans.*

This last claim sets Otto in outright opposition to religious existentialists who insist that our knowledge of God is inescapably subjective in this last sense of the term (see Part Three, especially Chapter 8).

CRITICISMS OF OTTO'S "ARGUMENT"

Readers who are stirred by Otto's *Idea of the Holy* might protest against the effort to evaluate it philosophically on the grounds that it should be evaluated like a course in music appreciation. In that case, the standard would be personal and emotional. If it opens some people to religious experience, it is effective as far as these individuals are concerned; this is all we can ask of the book. Yet Otto does argue for the objective reality of the holy; in other words, he claims that individuals who have religious experiences encounter a reality that is independent of their imaginations. He argues his case by means of appeals to the a priori and also by means of the parallel between religious experience and experience of art. Therefore, it is certainly legitimate to point out dissimilarities that undercut Otto's points.

An Appearance Can Be Objective
in the Phenomenological Sense and Still Be Illusory

Otto's "argument" is daring in its objectivity, but it is not convincing. Let us assume that he is right in claiming that there is no "as if" about the *appearance* of God; in other words, phenomenologically speaking, God appears to us as an independent reality. Nevertheless, it may still be the case that God is an illusion rather than an independent reality.[38] We can distinguish between appearances that are subjective and appearances that are objective and then between entities that are subjective (illusory) and objective (real).

Someone says: "It's incredible! That cloud looks exactly like a bear." The appearance of the bear is clearly recognized as subjective by the person making the statement. He knows that it is not a bear. Although the appearance of the bear is subjective, the status of the cloud is objective, in the sense that the cloud is really out there.

Now I'd like to illustrate a different situation: an objective appearance (in other words, phenomenologically objective) of something that is, in the first sense of the term, subjective, that is, illusory. Think of the distinction in terms of the following, two-sentence exchange:

A.: I see a clump of trees about five miles off but from the way it shimmers I know that it isn't a real oasis, it's a mirage.

B.: If you know that it's not the real thing, it can't be a mirage because mirages as *phenomena* are always objectively given.

It is the nature of an illusory oasis, namely, a mirage, to appear to be real. Yet that characteristic of its appearance does not endow it with objective status. Travelers who try to drink at these oases whose appearances are objective are terribly frustrated.

Oases are, however, entities that are supposed to be observable. We determine that—despite its objective appearance—the mirage is illusory, by checking it out with our senses. We try, for example, to feel the trees and taste the water. We have seen that this does not apply to God because God is not supposed to be observable. This leaves us with the second sense, namely, agreed upon procedures that enable us to arrive at agreement on specific judgments. We have seen that Otto tries to make good his claim to objectivity in this second sense, by means of an appeal to the a priori and by means of his parallels between religious and aesthetic judgments. I do not think he succeeds.

Otto claims that religious experience is, like mathematics, an inborn capacity that is actualized in specific situations. Once it is used it has the same independence of observations as mathematics. Religious experience is, however, neither clear nor coercive. It is not clear because different things count as religious experience within different religious traditions and even within different branches of the same religions. It is, for example, obvious that different branches of Christendom interpret the faith experience in different terms. Some of them—like the Baptists— stress stormy conversion experiences, others a steady development of understanding and serenity. This is the basis of William James' distinction between twice-born and once-born types.[39]

Of greater importance in this context is the fact that religious experiences do not seem to be coercive in a sense that even remotely resembles the way that mathematics is coercive. People can have religious experiences without interpreting them as experiences of God. Ronald Hepburn tells of a recurring dream of a landscape on a high plateau; no people are present, but rather, the scene is dominated by stark columns like those found on temples and towers. Somehow the experience communicated exaltation, but also a sense of dread, of numinous awe, which haunted him for a number of days after the dreams. Many years after he first had the dream and its after-experience of the numinous, he found himself on a hill on the outskirts of Edinburgh. He recognized it as the mysterious "paradise-landscape" of his dreams. He then remembered his first visit to the hill which took place when he was a small child. At that time the hill seemed immeasurably high and the columns frighteningly tall. He came to see that this experience of an ordinary place had launched him on a repeated dream experience of the numinous, which he had regarded as an encounter with the "wholly other," that is, with God. In commenting on this realization of the source of the dream, Hepburn writes:

> In being "explained" the dream has not lost its interest or much of its value. But one lesson could not be dodged, that the transition from "numinous awe" to "therefore experience of the transcendent"—of the "wholly other"—is far from a reliable one. . . . [40]

A follower of Otto who is persuaded that religious experiences provide knowledge of the reality of God could avoid the negative implications of Hepburn's story with two different moves: (1) insist that no one can have a genuine religious experience and subsequently deny that God exists; he would, therefore, conclude that Hepburn's experience wasn't the real thing and (2) admit that Hepburn's religious experience was genuine but claim that Hepburn, having registered the numinous, frittered away his sense of God's reality by misapplying Freudian categories to the experience.

The first move mentioned would render Otto's position invulnerable to criticisms of the kind made by Hepburn. Any sceptic who claimed to have had a religious experience would be dismissed out of hand. His scepticism would be regarded as a sufficient basis for the conclusion that his experience could not possibly have been genuine. However, the survey of verificationism in Part One should have made it clear that invulnerability of this kind can only be purchased at a very high price, namely, the price of reducing a genuine synthetic statement to one that is pseudo-synthetic. A follower of Otto who takes this line will simply not accept counter-evidence to the statement, "A person who has had a genuine religious experience must believe in God." The link between the phrase "genuine religious experience" and "belief in God" then becomes a matter of definition rather than of inquiry. Countless people might follow Hepburn's pattern. They insist that they had undergone experiences like those described by Otto, and they would, nevertheless, deny the existence of God. Otto's follower would not be fazed. He would dismiss all of them with the judgment that their experiences couldn't have been the real thing.

The second move mentioned above makes better sense. In this case Otto's follower is prepared to concede the possibility that a sceptic could have genuine religious experiences. The argument then proceeds along philosophical lines as believers and sceptics debate the merits of conflicting interpretations of religious experiences. The criticisms of Otto which follow should be taken as a contribution to this debate.

The Parallel to Aesthetics and the Problem of Reference

Otto claims that religious experience is similar to aesthetic experience in that objective judgments can be made in both fields. This is a startling claim. Even well-established aesthetic judgments are open to serious challenge. The English composer Benjamin Britten does not share the consensus regarding Beethoven; he is sharply critical of his music. As for Brahms, Britten despises him.

Otto is, however, justified in claiming that there is a consensus with regard to greatness in art, and a follower of Otto's could claim that Britten's judgments are eccentric. Against this, the sceptic can note that even though there is a consensus on the identity of the great composers there is no consensus on the methods for arriving at these judgments. However, even if we were to concede Otto's point that objectivity, in the second sense of the term, is to be found in aesthetic matters, there is a radical difference between judgments in religion and aesthetic judgments. It involves the problem of reference. I will explain it with illustrations of arguments in the two fields.

One critic says: "If you are stirred by Furtwängler's Beethoven, how can you be so negative toward Klemperer's? Both play deliberately and let the music breathe." The answer would be: "I get a sense of where the music is going in Furtwängler even though the pace is slow, but in Klemperer, I lose all sense of direction." They could then play recordings by both conductors and compare passages in an effort to settle this. Klemperer's admirer would focus attention on certain passages in an

effort to persuade the other person that what they both admire in
Furtwängler is present in Klemperer. They might wind up the argument
agreeing to disagree, but, at times these techniques do succeed in
changing views (see p. 46).

In similar fashion, two students might argue about Western and
Oriental religions. One of them might be negative toward Oriental
religions on the grounds that the only experiences which are important to
Oriental religions are those in which the worshiper loses all sense of
individuality. The other might object by citing the passage from the
Bhagavad-Gita where Arjuna, in encountering the high God Vishnu,
retains a sense of his individuality (see pp. 83f). This might, and should
be, persuasive, but a counterargument is possible by means of an appeal
to other passages from Oriental religions in an effort to show that the
Arjuna-Vishnu episode is untypical. They would continue by considering
individual passages and arguing their relevance to the point at issue.

The very possibility of this sort of argument about religion, as well
as aesthetics, shows that Otto is right in claiming that judgments in religion
and art are not utterly chaotic and disputes not necessarily idle.

Just about everyone considers Mozart and Beethoven great composers. In the domain of religion, we similarly find an almost unanimous
agreement on the greatness of Moses, Jesus, and Mohamet (see p. 88). It
is for this reason that even the sceptical English philosopher C. D. Broad
concedes the point that there is a rational basis for trusting experts in the
field of religion.[41] This makes Otto's parallel look good.

There is, however, an important difference between aesthetic and
religious experience that undercuts the effectiveness of Otto's parallel. If
two critics differ about the worth of Botticelli's *The Birth of Venus* or
about the Furtwängler and Klemperer interpretations of Beethoven, their
observations of the work of art itself anchors the reference of their
argument. They are disputing about the painting right there on the canvas
or about the sounds emanating from the stereo set. In the case of religious
disputes, the reference is far more elusive.

Otto claims that God exists, but he rightly insists that God cannot be
observed. This is a central problem of religious thought because, ordinarily, when we refer to something as existing, we need sense experience. At
least, we need it when we are not referring to a mathematical entity like
the square root of two. Sense experience is crucial to our ability to
identify and reidentify specific things, as Stuart Hampshire put it:

> What then is the relation between perception and existence which is vaguely
> indicated in the empiricist thesis: "Any knowledge outside mathematics
> must ultimately be derived from perception and introspection?" The

connection is to be found in that fundamental form of statement: "This (That, It) is a so-and-so," which is an identification made in the presence of the object referred to.[42]

In other words, what makes us secure in the judgment that *The Birth of Venus* exists is the fact that we can point to it. We may have all sorts of differences about its artistic worth and importance, but these arguments presuppose our ability to point to the painting itself, to observe it by means of the senses.

It is *relatively easy* to get a consensus on sense experience. Art experts may differ about the worth and importance of *The Birth of Venus*, but they will not differ on the size of the canvas or the color of the paints used to represent the rippling water. God, by contrast, is a transcendent reality that cannot be sensed. In and of itself, this is not a reason for deciding that God does not and cannot exist. Yet the fact that God cannot be pointed to considerably undercuts the effectiveness of Otto's parallel to aesthetic experience.

This dissimilarity is also compounded by the dissimilarity—already noted—between judgments about the holy and judgments in the field of geometry. These dissimilarities make Otto's "argument" considerably less persuasive than it might seem at first reading. There is, therefore, no overriding reason for us to accept the judgments of the "experts" in the field of religion with regard to the reality of God.

Divination as a Contrived Category

Otto proclaims the transcendence of God in the most uncompromising terms: "The truly 'mysterious' object [of religious experience] is beyond our apprehension and comprehension, not only because our knowledge has certain irremovable limits, but because in it we come upon something inherently 'wholly other' whose kind and character are incommensurable with our own. . . . "[43] If God, the "wholly other," is beyond our apprehension and comprehension, that means that God cannot even be "picked up" by us (apprehended) much less understood (comprehended). In that case, it would seem that we could have no way whatever of identifying God, much less of pointing to him.

Otto's answer to this problem is the claim that we all possess "divination," the special built-in capacity to register God. It is not, like our sensory apparatus, a natural capacity for spotting natural objects. It is, rather, a special supernatural capacity that we have for tuning in on this one supernatural reality.

There is no way of conclusively demonstrating that Otto is mistaken. If we point to the vast numbers of people who seem to lack the capacity for divination, Otto can always claim that they have the capacity, but they either fail to use it, or they run away from the "holiness input" it provides because the encounter with the holy one is so terribly threatening to them. Nevertheless, there is something contrived about Otto's appeal to divination. It does one job and one job only. It seems to have been invented to explain how it is that we can possibly become aware of a reality that is "wholly other" than every other reality that we can possibly apprehend or comprehend. Furthermore, there don't seem to be sharply defined rules that regulate divination. It certainly isn't comparable to geometry in this respect.

The sense in which Otto's view of religious experience is contrived should become clearer when we consider the thought of Martin Buber. Buber also uses a distinctive vocabulary to talk about experience of God. Yet Buber does not restrict his approach to religious experience; he applies it to all experience. Therefore, someone who has never, to the best of his knowledge, had religious experience, can check out Buber's language to see how it squares with all sorts of experiences. By contrast, Otto's approach is apt to shut out the person who has never consciously experienced God.

Chapter 6

Martin Buber: On Meeting God

Martin Buber's thought is saturated with the sense of holiness.[44] He is, like Otto, aware of its threatening quality, but he does not emphasize it. Instead, he emphasizes central themes of the Jewish tradition. Every moment of life and every individual being we encounter can be holy; to live authentically an individual should infuse everyday routines with holiness.

Buber's book *I and Thou* is his most influential statement of the way in which everyday life can be permeated by holiness, yet its language is hardly everyday language. It is poetic, obscure, and allusive. Buber's terminology and his ideas stand in need of considerable interpretation. It is, however, important to realize that an interpreter who emphasizes the strangeness of Otto's terminology treats Otto fairly, but a similar emphasis in interpreting Buber introduces violent distortions. Buber's terms are intended to shed light on routine experiences and not to shatter them.

In this connection it is important to consider Walter Kaufmann's reasons for introducing a fundamental change in the presentation of

Buber's thought in his recent translation of *I and Thou.* In the original
German, the title is *Ich und Du.* There is nothing unusual about the word
"du." It is the second person singular that is commonly used in addressing
children, and by adults who are familiar with one another. The original
English translation of "du" as "thou" was unfortunate because "thou" is
an archaic term that is never used in speech. The one context in which the
word "thou" is frequently used is in translations of the Bible, where it is
used in addressing God. Therefore, "thou" has a religious association
which "du" does not have. Kaufmann substitutes the word "you" for
"thou" in his recent translation of the book (though he retains "thou" in
the title; otherwise people might have thought it was a different book).
Kaufmann, however, capitalizes the word "You" to indicate the special
meaning Buber gives it when writing about the "I-You" relation, or "the
World of You." Yet Kaufmann rightly insists that these special uses
ought not to be made even more strange than they are by the process of
translation.[45] Buber's "world of You" is not a special "holy place"
removed from our ordinary world. As we shall see, it simply is the
ordinary world, sparkling with the light of God, an emphasis which is
profoundly Jewish. It was intensified in the teachings of the Hasidic sect
which exerted a great influence on Buber. The following saying is typical:
" . . . there is no rung of being on which we cannot find the holiness of
God everywhere and at all times."[46]

BUBER'S APPROACH TO EXPERIENCE

Although Buber is one of our most perceptive commentators on religious
experience, oddly enough, one of the best ways of introducing his thought
is to clarify his negative attitude toward the word "experience."

Experience is a primary example of an umbrella word under which
too many distinctions are huddled. Otto is favorably disposed toward it
because of two of its associations, namely, to objectivity and certainty.
When Otto writes of religious experience, he stresses the point that it is
experience *of* the holy, that is, of God. It is not merely a fantasy, like a
dream, which is internal to the mind. Furthermore, "experience" carries the
implication of being immediate rather than something one merely hears
about. For Otto, claiming that one has had religious experience is to claim
firsthand relation to God. The association is positive because it has the
overtone of the certitude that is carried by the direct experience of colors
like red or sounds like a trumpet.

Buber, by contrast, is not only negative toward the word "experience," he is almost repelled by it. He associates the word with superficial-
ity and self-absorption. His attitude toward the word makes it seem

perverse of me to classify his thought under the heading of "religious experience," but once we get clear on usage, the procedure is appropriate. The most general use of experience in English is free of the associations that trouble Buber. The word is often used as a neutral catchall for any content that individuals can meaningfully register. It is then refined by distinctions that deal with activities like imagining, thinking, and perceiving, and by distinctions in quality such as pleasurable, violent, and superficial. Therefore, I propose to present Buber's central category, the I-You relation, as a special mode of experience.[47]

The I-You and the I-It: Not a Person/Thing Distinction

Buber fervently affirms the reality of God, but his approach to him involves a comprehensive approach to total experience—what the Germans call a *Weltanschauung*, literally, a world-outlook. He does not confine himself to religion, which enables him to provide important insights for people who cannot agree with his view of God.

I and Thou begins on an oracular note in which Buber names two basic attitudes that we adopt toward other beings.

> The world is twofold for man in accordance with his twofold attitude. The attitude of man is twofold in accordance with the two basic words he can speak. The basic words are not single words but word pairs. One basic word is the word pair I-You. The other basic word is the word pair I-It.[48]

The two words that are paired with "I," namely, "You" and "It," suggest that the distinction involved is the difference between our attitude toward persons and our attitude toward things. Anyone familiar with Kant would hear overtones of his imperative: "Act so that you treat humanity, whether in your own person or in that of another, always as an end and never as a means only."[49]

What Buber is getting at is something more radical than this Kantian distinction. Buber claims that when we are most truly human, we do not and ought not to treat any being whatever—human or not—merely as a means and not as an end in itself. The I-You and the I-It attitudes both cut across the person/thing distinction. Any being whatever, including human beings, can be an It and any being whatever, including things, can be a You.

The I-It

Buber's major concern was with the I-You, not the I-It. So much so that there is a temptation to deal exclusively with the I-You and to define the

I-It as "whatever is *not* I-You." However, it is important to develop a sense of what Buber means by the I-It, because the positivistic approach to knowledge is an excellent example of what the I-It is all about.

Control   Some years ago the makers of a pain-killing drug presented a series of commercials about people who couldn't cope. They suffered from headaches and similar ailments and were on the verge of giving up. A helpful friend told them about the marvellous new medication. They used it and, of course, had instantaneous relief! The commercial ended with a solemn voice intoning: "You're in control again!"

We all have a passion for keeping things under control, and this is the thread that runs through the variety of phenomena that Buber groups under the broad term *I-It*. In the I-It attitude the individual controls situations by remaining calculating and detached. The professor sees to it that no conversation becomes open-ended enough to run past his office hours. The novelist keeps his characters from developing a momentum of their own that might carry the book beyond the projected number of pages. The student inhibits his interest in an assignment to make sure that it doesn't consume more time than any one course is worth.

In the I-It attitude detachment is preserved, come what may. The individual refuses to "let go" to the point where the cost of the experience might exceed his estimate. He is in control.

What makes Buber's position an extreme one is his claim that it isn't the character of the object, the activity, or the philosophy that determines its status as an "It." The crucial factor is the attitude that the individual manifests.

It seems obvious that the I-It attitude of detached control can be directed to minerals, tables, computers, and credit cards. Yet it can equally be directed to parakeets, dogs, and *people*. What's more, it frequently *is* directed to people; elevator operators, for example, are generally treated as impersonally as the buttons in automatic elevators.

As for activities—although the activity of checking out someone's credit rating is a natural for the I-It—from Buber's point of view, the glamorous activity of gathering material for a novel is also I-It. A novelist circulating in a cocktail party in order to focus on special character types is not relating to people; he's using them.

By this time, it should be obvious that Buber's thought cuts across traditional distinctions; this is one reason for its considerable influence. As we shall see, this effort to cut across the person/thing distinction is an important source of his influence on contemporary religious thought. It is relevant to efforts to extend knowledge beyond the limits that the positivists staked out.

Positivism: Knowledge and Control The positivists restricted knowledge to mathematics, science, and to common sense statements of fact. This gave the impression that these were the only things they cared about. Although it may have been true of some of them, generally speaking, the positivists were morally concerned and culturally sensitive. As individuals the positivists had a wide range of interests, but their movement was forged by their concern for the integrity of two words: "true" and "know." They wanted truth and knowledge to be restricted to areas where their use could be controlled by clear rules. Mathematics is the most obvious case, but physics, chemistry, geology, biology, and a few other sciences do reasonably well at setting up procedures that enable them to control these words. As for common sense, there are great difficulties involved in getting an adequate theory of how we know the truth of a statement like "This page is white." On the operative level, however, we manage pretty well. We achieve a consensus on the use of "know" and "true" with regard to statements of fact.

In morality, art, politics, and religion the words "true" and "know" are used, but agreement on their application is hard to come by because the procedures for applying them are fuzzy. The positivists charged that traditional philosophers do great harm by talking about truth and knowledge in fields like religion and morality. They are, invariably, unable to make their claims good, and the public gets the idea that all uses of the words "true" and "know" are infected with a lack of clarity and uncertainty. This results in widespread cynicism.

As far as Buber is concerned, the positivists represent the standard case of philosophers who cling to the I-It attitude. He thinks that their limits on our use of the words "true" and "know" are arbitrary. He is convinced that what we experience in the I-You relation is profoundly true, even though it cannot be checked out like mathematics or physics.

Buber is not negative toward the I-It attitude in and of itself. The following description of I-It knowing and of the world it spawns makes it clear that he values the I-It for the same reasons that positivists value science—it is both public and reliable.

> The world [of It] is somewhat reliable; it has density and duration; its articulation can be surveyed; one can get it out again and again; one recounts it with one's eyes closed and then checks it with one's eyes open. . . . It is only *about* it that you can come to an understanding with others; although it takes a somewhat different form for everybody, it is prepared to be a common object for you. . . . Without it you cannot remain alive; its reliability preserves you. . . . [50]

Buber's problem is not with the I-It as the indispensable floor; it is with philosophies, like positivism, that mistake this floor for a ceiling. "And in all seriousness of truth, listen: without It a human being cannot live. But whoever lives only with that is not human."[51]

The I-You

I-You: two personal pronouns connected by a hyphen. The words suggest a relation between persons and the suggestion is not altogether erroneous. The relation between human beings is the model for Buber's I-You, yet he expands it by dividing the potential partners of the I-You relation into three groups, or as he puts it, "spheres of relation." Human beings are the standard case and Buber refers to the human sphere as the "main portal."[52] The other two spheres, which he refers to as "side portals," are comprised of natural and cultural objects. In the sphere of nature there is a progression from the inanimate to domestic animals who can communicate with us to the point where they seem at the threshold of speech.[53] Potential partners to the I-You relation in the sphere of culture refer to all manufactured, that is, man-made articles whether they are tools like fishhooks, or products of high culture like mathematical theorems.

On first reading it seems as though Buber is stretching language too far when he embraces natural and cultural objects in the I-You relation. It is almost as though he is determined to shock us. One of his best known illustrations was an I-You encounter with a tree, and trees cannot even be aware of other beings; neither can Greek columns, yet Buber also reports on an encounter with a column.[54] He tells the story of his I-You relation with a pet horse, and although the horse had awareness, it couldn't speak.[55] However, the net of the I-You only seems overextended if we refuse to think about the kinds of experience that drove Buber to insist that the I-You is not confined to relations between human beings. If we "let go" in relation to trees, columns, horses and the rest, we are apt to have experiences that are characterized by many of the most important elements of a deeply realized human relation—even if the fully realized give and take of speech is absent.

What Buber is doing is to suggest a radical revision in the concepts we use in thinking about the world. One of the most basic conceptual distinctions we make is that between persons and things. Buber does not entirely abandon this, but rather suggests that it be downgraded in importance. The thing/person contrast is static. It is an observer's contrast that is based upon defining characteristics of things, on the one hand, and people, on the other. Buber proposes to displace this contrast from the center of our consciousness and speech and to substitute the It/You contrast which is a participant's contrast. Whether the "other" that one encounters is It or You is not a matter to be determined by detached examination of a set of characteristics that can be captured by a photograph or any other "still" portrait. Buber's contrast depends on the *quality of the relation* between the self and others. It is therefore clear, or at least it should be, that Buber's It/You contrast is not contrived for the special purpose of getting his view of God off the ground. It is an overall approach to total experience, of God, and everything else.

Buber claims that many of the things that we experience when, at our best, we relate well to human beings, are also experienced in our relation to beings that are not human. One way of getting at Buber's point is to explore your own most meaningful relations to other beings and to see whether his account rings true.[56] I will do that with one of mine.

Even in the jet age, going abroad involves considerable expense and effort and we all feel the pressure of acquiring the experiences that an in-group tells us we are supposed to have. So, I find myself striding through the long halls of the Uffizi Gallery in Florence seeking the experience of great art, but the works keep their distance. They remain "Its" to me because I am overanxious to fully experience these paintings which are certified as great works of art by means of stars.

Thus, I enter the room of Leonardo da Vinci's *The Adoration of the Magi* determined to experience the painting in a meaningful way. As I turn toward it, another painting catches my eye and I am intrigued. I look at the tag: it is *The Crucifixion with Magdalen* by Signorelli. Since the painting has no stars at all in the catalogue, it is obvious that the experts do not think much of it. The moment confronts me with a challenge. If I stay with this painting and become absorbed with it, I will not have time for the Leonardo, much less for the other certified great paintings in the gallery. Nevertheless, I stay with the Signorelli and encounter it as a You. It communicates a distinctive perspective on the crucifixion. The figure on the cross is the only one that seems real. It alone has color and appears three dimensional. The world that serves as a backdrop to the image of the crucified Savior is completely devoid of vitality.

Obviously this relation is different from an I-You relation between human beings. It is therefore important to explore features of this experience that lead Buber to extend the I-You category beyond encounters between human beings.

Grace: Planning-Spontaneity-Response   The I-It is characterized by control. We can totally plan an I-It experience. We can plan a date, plan a visit to an art gallery, or plan any experience that we can afford in terms of time and expense. All that is required is a confrontation with another being. We cannot, however, plan our way into an I-You relation. Buber writes of an I-You encounter with a fragment of mica; he just chanced to come upon this mineral glistening in the sun.[57] In the same way, we may have an I-You relation with a friend we just happen to meet.

In these cases there is *no* element of planning, but in general, I-You encounters involve some degree of intention. The only way that you can have an I-You relation with the original of a Signorelli painting is to plan a visit to the Uffizi.

Planning may be a necessary condition of an I-You relation with a given work of art but it is certainly not a sufficient one. To wake up in Florence on a summer morning and say: "I'm going to have an I-You relation with Signorelli's crucifixion today," is, in fact, one way of guaranteeing that you won't have it. Excessive self-consciousness chokes off the spontaneity that is an indispensable part of an I-You relation. The same applies to love. We never speak of planning our way into love. We *fall* in love. An I-You relation, like love, is a happening. This is just as true of a genuine I-You encounter with a tree as it is of the encounter with Signorelli's painting.

Yet, when we are spontaneously addressed by the other, we are free to back away from the I-You and retreat into an I-It experience we can control. I might have rushed past the Signorelli in order to more "profitably spend" my time on the Leonardo. To let go and enter the open-ended I-You relation involves a risk.

This threefold reaction of planning-spontaneity-response is what the religions call grace. It is central to Buber's account of the I-You.

> The You encounters me by grace—it cannot be found by seeking. . . . The You encounters me. But I enter into a direct relationship to it. Thus the relationship is election and electing, passive and active at once.[58]

Relation: The Self Is Loose But It Does Not Disappear   We've all experienced those wonderful intense "raps" in which we keep going till dawn. "Where did the time go?" Chronological time and geographical location fade away in that kind of situation. What is important about the time is the rhythm of the give and take of the experience. What is important about the place is that the other is present.

> I do not find the human being to whom I say You in any Sometime and Somewhere.[59]

In my encounter with the Signorelli painting I was no longer aware of being in the Uffizi Gallery in Florence at two thirty in the afternoon. The important time was the lived duration of the I-You relation with the painting, the place was right there in its presence. "The basic word I-You can only be spoken with one's whole being. The basic word I-It can never be spoken with one's whole being."[60]

In entering an I-You relation nothing can be held back. A person must really let go. Furthermore, "comparison shopping" even at the most refined cultural level kills the possibility of an I-You relation. You can't step into an I-You relation to the Signorelli crucifixion while wondering whether it's as powerful as Grünewald's. "Nothing is present but this one. . . . Measure and comparison have fled."[61]

In the I-You relation excessive self-consciousness—that is, the level of the anxious inner conversation where you ask yourself: "Is it worth it?"—fades out. There is, however, no loss of self-consciousness in the sense of losing one's identity. The You "teaches you to encounter others and to stand your ground in such encounters." [62] In relating to Signorelli's painting I am aware of myself, but I am not excessively self-absorbed. I am not observing myself with the "third eye" to see how I'm doing.

Buber did not reject the self and everyday life. He was concerned about fulfilling them, but this involves the risk of participating in the unreliable I-You relations.

> What has to be given up is not the I but that false drive for self-affirmation which impels man to flee from the unreliable, unsolid, unlasting, unpredictable dangerous world of relation into the having of things.[63]

That is how Buber regards the positivists. They flee from the troubling philosophical implications of I-You relations into the security of the analytic and synthetic.

GOD AS THE ETERNAL YOU

There are readers of *I and Thou* who are deeply stirred by Buber's account of the I-You relation, but who are put off by the fact that the book culminates in the relation to God, the eternal You. Buber does not try to argue readers out of their rejection of God; like Otto, he appeals to experience in an effort to show that God is always present to everyone, even though countless people are not aware of his presence. Buber is also like Otto in his awareness of the "otherness" of God, the awesome power that Otto referred to by the term *tremendum.* Yet his comment on Otto shows how much Buber is concerned to emphasize the obvious and everyday character of religious experience:

> Of course, God is "the wholly other"; but he is also the wholly same: the wholly present. Of course, he is the *mysterium tremendum* that appears and overwhelms; but he is also the mystery of the obvious that is closer to me than my own.[64]

This statement seems contradictory: "the *wholly* same" and "the *wholly* other" are phrases that seem to cancel one another. Buber deliberately talks this way to reflect the conflicting types of religious experiences that have led men to use so many different names for this ultimate reality. What links all of them is the presence of God in the I-You relation.

> Men have addressed their eternal You by many names. . . . But all names of God remain hallowed—because they have been used not only to speak *of* God but also to speak *to* him . . . when he addresses with his whole devoted being the You of his life that cannot be restricted by any other, he addresses God.[65]

God as Present in Every I-You Encounter

Buber's philosophy is a fully integrated worldview. His approach to religious experience does not involve a special capacity like Otto's divination. Experience of God as the eternal You emerges from the fabric of all experience. " . . . in every You we address the eternal You in every sphere according to its manner."[66] Buber's use of the term "the eternal You" is intended to emphasize the continuity of religious experience with other experience, and also, the sense in which God is always open to human beings, that is, always ready to be a You to everyone. It is not intended as a sophisticated substitute for the word "God." He makes the point clearly in *I and Thou*: "Some would deny any legitimate use of the word God because it has been misused too much. Certainly it is the most burdened of all human words. Precisely for that reason it is the most imperishable and unavoidable."[67]

Buber's most helpful suggestion regarding the relation of the eternal You to the many I-You encounters of everyday life is to compare God to a poet and the poems to the many individual partners to I-You relations.

> When we really understand a poem, all we know of the poet is what we learn of him in the poem—no biographical wisdom is of value for the pure understanding of what is to be understood: the *I* which approaches us is the subject of this single poem. But when we read other poems by the poet in the same true way their subjects combine in all their multiplicity, completing and confirming one another, to form the one polyphony of the person's existence.
>
> In such a way, out of the givers of the signs, the speakers of the words in lived life, out of the moment Gods there arises for us with a single identity the Lord of the voice, the One.[68]

There are readers who respond rapturously to Buber's accounts of I-You relations. Yet they insist that they do not experience an eternal You at the fringe of the encounters nor do "moment Gods" arise out of them. In an effort to deal with the variations among Buber's readers on this crucial point, I will introduce a variation on his example of the poems and the poet.

Imagine a beginning class in music appreciation that is devoted to the study of symphonies. The instructor opens it by playing Beethoven's Seventh Symphony and comments on the composer's style. The following week he plays a record and says it is Mozart's Fortieth. The students dutifully note this, but one of them says: "I'd bet that it's a Beethoven symphony." The teacher doesn't say anything but plays a different record and announces: "This is another Beethoven symphony, the Fourth." The same student protests: "But this one doesn't sound like Beethoven!" He turns out to have been right both times. The instructor had deliberately misled these students, who had never listened to symphonies before, in order to check out their sense of style. Throughout the course, this student displays a remarkable gift for identifying composers after hearing only one or two of their works. Most of the other students gradually develop a sense for it, but they often make mistakes. Some students, even at the end of the course, were never able to identify any composers.

According to Buber, God emerges from the many individual encounters as the You who is always present. A parallel to the sense for musical style is to claim that some people sense the presence of the eternal You as soon as they have I-You encounters; some come to it out of the cumulative impact of many encounters; and some never recognize God, no matter how many I-You encounters they have.

There is another problem involved in the notion that God is present in every I-You encounter, and it may be indicated by varying the illustration. When we turn on an FM set in the middle of the performance of a symphony we've never heard before, we can try to identify the composer and to verify our identification. The FM announcer usually follows through with the statement "You have just been listening to a performance of Hayden's Fourty-Fourth Symphony in E minor, etc." There is, however, no conclusive way of telling whether we are right in recognizing God as the eternal You who is present in the many I-You encounters.

The example is improved if we imagine that the scores of Beethoven's nine symphonies are available but that their composer is unknown; indeed, that there is no way of knowing whether they are the products of a single composer. We, presumably, would vary considerably in our judgment of whether one individual produced all of them and in our sense of the character of their composer or composers. Yet, we could not conclusively check our views. In the same way, some people experience

God as present in and through every I-You encounter. However, the way in which they come to do so varies greatly, and they cannot convince sceptics that there really is one eternal You who is present in all encounters. Furthermore, among those who acknowledge the presence of God in the many I-You relations, there is considerable variation in their sense of the character of God. Just as there is no way of conclusively resolving the differences between believers and sceptics about his existence, there is no way of conclusively settling differences among believers regarding his character.

God as a Particular Partner to an I-You Encounter

Buber's talk of God as the eternal You who is present in every I-You relation can lead to two mistaken impressions: (1) "God" is a general term that stands for what is common to all I-You relations—a term we might call "Youness"—(2)"God" is a symbol that designates the sum total of the I-You encounters that take place in the world. In either case, Buber could be accused of denying that God is a reality that transcends the world. Buber, however, strongly stresses the transcendence of God. God is present in the I-You relations that take place in every sphere of encounter, but his reality is not exhausted by the enumeration of these I-You encounters. "All spheres are included in it, while it is included in none." Again, "God embraces but is not the universe; just so, God embraces, but is not myself."[69]

There is no limit to the ways in which men can encounter God as a special partner in the I-You relation. After all, if Buber claims that any being whatever can be a partner in an I-You relation, then a relation with any being whatever can propel us into a direct relation with God. The God who emerges at the fringe of the limitless variety of I-You encounters with trees, sunsets, symphonies, poems, and the rest, is the true God. Yet, the individual who encounters God *only* in this way is a religious freelancer, who knows God as, let us say, the Author of Nature or as The One Behind the Many. From Buber's point of view, this is valid as far as it goes, but the believing Jew or Christian who, like the freelancer, encounters God at the fringe of each I-You encounter, has another major mode of access to God. The believer relives, or enters into the spirit of, the climactic episodes that shaped his religion. In reliving the saga of Moses he meets God as the one who freed the Israelites from slavery in Egypt. This is made explicit in the Passover *Haggadah* where the Jew is told: "In every generation a man is obligated to regard himself as though he had gone out of Egypt. . . . Because it was not only our fathers that the Holy One Blessed be He redeemed, rather, he redeemed us along with them."

Buber claims that towering figures like Moses, Jesus, and Mohamet had especially potent encounters with God. They were not only direct, in the way that all I-You encounters are direct, but they were creative. They established fresh ways of approaching God—ways that then shaped a tradition. The record of these formative experiences are preserved in sacred scriptures like the Bible and the Koran. These books serve succeeding generations as reservoirs of genuine relation to God. It is not the words on the page, taken in themselves, which provide an encounter with God; they are only capable of doing so if they come alive for the individual believer. Buber writes: "The word of God crosses my vision like a falling star to whose fire the meteorite will bear witness without making it light up for me, and I myself can only bear witness to the light but not produce the stone and say, 'This is it.' "[70]

To vary Buber's example, suppose that we attend a concert at which we have an I-You encounter with an incandescent performance of Beethoven's Quartet in C Sharp Minor. The performance is taped and later released as a record. I cannot play the record, listen to the sounds, and say: "This is it." The recording is a witness to the I-You relation, but in playing it, I may continually experience it as a sequence of sounds which remain I-It. On occasion the music may come through in such a way that I again experience the You. Since spontaneity is involved, there is no way of programming myself for the I-You experience, and its occurrence cannot be predicted. Yet, when it occurs, the You is reencountered. In the same way, the words of the Bible are merely I-It on one reading after the other. Unpredictably, they can grasp the reader and serve as vehicles to an encounter with the God of Abraham, Isaac, and Jacob. The believer then experiences God in more specific terms, in terms of a tradition whose outlines are the product of the epochal encounters of great figures of the past.

Isaiah's vision in the Temple has served as an especially fruitful medium of encounters with God because it has been incorporated in the prayer books of Judaism and Christianity (see p. 83). Believers read or chant the words: "Holy, holy, holy, the Lord of hosts, the whole earth is full of his glory" (Isa. 6:3). If the words come alive, they experience the overwhelming majesty of the God that Isaiah encountered.

Buber regards the great founders and leaders of the religious traditions as instructors who awaken us to the sense of the holy. Without their help, we may go through life experiencing the alternation of It, You, and It again, but failing to see the large mosaic that is spelled out by the individual stones of experience. We may fail to see that all Yous live in the light of the eternal You.

There is no limit to the qualities of God that are registered in these experiences. Yet Buber singles out responsiveness as most important.

> Every You in the world is compelled by its nature to become a thing for us
> or at least to enter again and again into thinghood [the I-It]. . . . Only one
> You never ceases, in accordance with its nature to be You for us.[71]

Human beings are sometimes accessible and sometimes withdrawn. God
alone is eternally You, that is, always open, always prepared to enter into
relation with us as a You.

Jesus, suffering on the cross, quotes the Psalmist by crying: "My
God, my God, why hast thou forsaken me?" (Matt. 27:46; Ps. 22:1). He
expresses his sense of abandonment, but he addresses God as one who is,
nevertheless, a present reality. "To be sure," Buber writes, "whoever
knows God also knows God's remoteness and the agony of drought upon
a frightened heart, but not the loss of presence."[72]

Why the Existence of God
Is Not Acknowledged by Everyone

Every religious thinker who believes in the transcendent God must cope
with the problem of unbelief. We have seen that Otto had to cope with the
problem of how people can deny the existence of a being as overpowering
as the *mysterium tremendum et* (and) *fascinans*. The problem is especially
acute in Buber's case because he takes presence as the crucial quality of
the eternal You. God not only exists, but Buber insists that he is always
available to men as a partner to an I-You encounter. He must, therefore,
provide some account of why countless people claim that God does not
exist. Buber's answer is somewhat similar to Otto's in that Buber also
stresses the threatening character of religious experience. Indeed, Buber
extends the analysis to all I-You experiences; people are upset by the
insecurity involved in them. Early in *I and Thou* he calls attention to one
of the most difficult aspects of human existence: "This, however, is the
sublime melancholy of our lot that every You must become an It in our
world."[73] It is sublime because only human beings can experience the full
I-You relation, which is mutual in terms of both awareness and speech. It
is melancholy because we cannot sustain the relation. The need to carry
out life's functions, to provide our daily bread, forces us back to the I-It
attitude where the You is changed to an It. Every being that has come
through to us as an actual You is destined to become an It again, that is, a
thing that is only potentially or latently a You. "Love itself cannot abide
in direct relation; it endures, but in the alternation of actuality and
latency."[74]

T. S. Eliot, in the first of the *Four Quartets* wrote: "Human kind
cannot bear very much reality." This might serve as the text of Buber's
analysis of what happens with regard to the alternation of It and You.

People back off from the uncertainty and insecurity of the You, which involves spontaneity. They run away from the I-You relations into I-It experiences that can be controlled. Buber claims that people "flee from the unreliable, unsolid, unlasting, unpredictable, dangerous world of relation into the having of things."[75]

When men flee from the I-You to the I-It, they have something they can get hold of, the words of a poem, the notes of a symphony, the painting on a canvas, or the bodily aspects of another human being. God is a special case. If men flee from the I-You, then they cannot refer to God at all, because God is not an object that can be sensed. He has no observable features. Therefore, "It is . . . only the relation I-You in which we can meet God at all, because of Him, in absolute contrast to all other existing beings, no objective [I-It] aspect can be attained."[76]

Although God is eternally You, that is, always open to an I-You relation with human beings, he is also eternally elusive. He has no I-It aspect and can therefore *only* be met in the I-You relation. God, the most important reality of all, is therefore the most unpredictable and uncontrollable.

We are now in position to understand one important part of Buber's answer to the problem of unbelief. Human beings are frustrated by the fact that God is exclusively You and they devise techniques that are intended to force him to be present on demand. "The eternal You is You by its very nature; only *our* nature forces us to draw it into the It-world and It-speech."[77] People brandish symbols of God in an effort to guarantee religious experiences. In this way they make God into an object and try to drag him into the It-world.

Techniques designed to insure the presence of God cannot work; coercive techniques can only be effective on an It, and God is pure You. Nevertheless, people expect them to work. When they fail, as they must, countless people draw the wrong conclusion, namely, that God does not exist. The response to the Bible is a good example of this process. Many people are brought up with the view that the Bible is an infallible record of God's own words, and therefore, free of error. When they study subjects like evolution, they decide that the Bible is shot through with errors and conclude that God does not exist.

Buber regards this as an almost perverse response. The Bible is not a record of God's own words, but a record of human recollections of encounters with the eternal You.[78] Therefore, the Bible does not have God's presence locked into its words; it is primarily an especially effective springboard to encounters with the eternal You. When a person discovers that the words of the Bible are not literally true, Buber thinks that he should continue to read the Bible in the hope that the words will light up for him so that he may encounter the eternal You in and through them.

> God's address to man penetrates the events in all our lives and all the events
> in the world around us, everything biographical and everything historical,
> and turns it into instruction, into demands for you and me. . . . Often we
> think that there is nothing to be heard as if we had not long ago plugged wax
> into our own ears.[79]

Keeping open to the possibility of encounters with the eternal You is the
right way of responding to the failure of I-It devices, but Buber claims
that it is especially difficult under the conditions of contemporary culture.

Encouraged by the success of science, positivists and other empiricists seek to make all experiences measure up to scientific standards
of public verification and control. When moral and religious statements
are unable to meet this test, they ban them from the cognitive field. In
responding to this kind of scepticism, Buber does not present careful
arguments which are designed to expose the limitations of verification; he
blasts away at the cultural tendency that produces it. His hope is that we
will be shocked into a state of new sensitivity to the experience of the
reality that is eternally You.

> In our age the I-It relation, gigantically swollen, has usurped, practically
> uncontested, the mastery and the rule. The I of this relation, an I that
> possesses all, makes all, succeeds with all, this I that is unable to say You,
> unable to meet a being essentially, is lord of the hour. This selfhood that has
> become omnipotent, with all the It around it, can naturally acknowledge
> neither God nor any genuine absolute which manifests itself to men as of
> non-human origin. It steps in between and shuts off from us the light of
> heaven.[80]

KNOWLEDGE OF THE YOU AND OF THE ETERNAL YOU

It is extremely difficult to interpret Buber's view of the role of knowing in
I-You encounters because he was not interested in technical questions of
epistemology. I once heard a philosopher ask him whether there was an
element of knowledge in the I-You encounter. Buber said that the only
way of dealing with the question was to reflect on I-You relations. He
then retold the story of his encounter with the tree.[81] Unfortunately, he
let it go at that and did not deal with the issue of whether the encounter
involved an element of knowledge. In what follows, I accept Buber's
advice and think about specific I-You encounters, but I take the extra step
of working out a position on the question of knowledge and the I-You
relation.

You Can't Know Your You and Have It Too

Buber's I-It and I-You are contrast terms. The I-It is an experience in which the self is detached from the other and self-conscious about the game that is being played. It is analyzing, checking, and seeking to use and to control the other. The self in the I-You relation does not plan and calculate. There is a meeting and the self is addressed by an other; spontaneity is crucial to the I-You. There is no possibility of analyzing the qualities of this other and of checking them out because the very effort to do so forces the self into the I-It attitude of detachment and plummets one out of the I-You relation.

> Even as a melody is not composed of tones, nor a verse of words, nor a statue of lines—one must pull and tear to turn a unity into a multiplicity—so it is with the human being to whom I say You. I can abstract from him the color of his hair or the color of his speech or the "color" of his graciousness; I have to do this again and again; but immediately he is no longer You.[82]

From the epistemological standpoint, there are many different issues packed into this statement. Clearly, Buber cannot be denying that some knowledge of the You is possible during the relation itself. If the You is a woman one loves, one certainly continues to be aware of her identity after the I-It has been superseded by the I-You. What fades out as the I-It gives way to the I-You is not conscious awareness, but the kinds of awareness that are only compatible with an attitude of detachment, namely, analysis, comparison, verification, utilization, and preoccupation with one's reactions.

Buber's important and valid point is that during an I-You relation we cannot consciously isolate the features of the You and see how they hang together to make her the special person she is. To make an effort of this kind, we would have to become detached and adopt the I-It attitude. In this sense, you cannot know your You and have it too. The I-You relation is a happening that involves give and take with no holding back. Certain types of self-conscious reflection, like those just mentioned, are incompatible with it.

One of the major criticisms that I will direct against Buber is that he drives this insight beyond the point of legitimate application. First, it is important to make clear, as best I can, that from Buber's standpoint checkability (in all its forms, verification, falsification, and confirmation) must be consigned to the I-It. In this way he sets I-You relations with all beings, and, of course, with God, beyond the range of empiricist analysis.

Checkability and the You

We have seen that some knowledge of the You is present during the I-You relation itself; a person can, for example, identify the You as a familiar friend. Yet this sort of knowledge is so basic that Buber ignores it. He focuses on more interesting features of the You which are not observable: for example, on the worth and importance of the You. He claims that these features are only genuinely present for the duration of the I-You relation, but that during this relation they cannot be isolated, analyzed, and verified. In this connection I shall again reflect on Basil Mitchell's potent parable, The Partisan and the Stranger (see pp. 51f). The partisan, a member of the resistance, has only one I-You encounter with the stranger who claims to be its secret leader. On the basis of this meeting he decides that the stranger is trustworthy and is prepared to stake his own life and that of his comrades on his knowledge of the stranger's character. The statements "I know that the stranger is on our side" or "The stranger is trustworthy" are rooted in his I-You encounter. What is involved is not merely the partisan's sense of the stranger during the time of their meeting, but his sense of how the stranger will act under pressure.

In general, the most important features of the You cannot be verified by direct inspection. The partisan could have directly verified the color of the stranger's eyes, but his trustworthiness cannot be verified in this way. Yet, we noted that there is a way of confirming the statement "The stranger is trustworthy." When he reappears in his disguise as the head of the Gestapo, the partisan can see what happens to the members of the resistance. If they are captured and executed, this counts against the truth of the statement; if they are captured and yet manage mysteriously to escape, the statement is confirmed.

Buber introduces a factor that makes even this degree of inconclusive confirmation of the qualities of the You highly problematic. He claims that the evidence that is relevant to confirming or disconfirming the statement is inaccessible in principle because it is "locked into" the I-You relation.

When we check a statement like "The stranger is trustworthy," the person we encountered in the relation is inaccessible in principle because the relation is over. Even if the stranger is actually in the room with him as the partisan tries to verify the statement, he would be inaccessible as a *You* because the act of checking involves the detachment of the I-It. Yet the "You" of the stranger is not totally inaccessible because the partisan can remember the I-You encounter and check his judgments against the memory. "Qualities, to be sure, had remained in his memory after every encounter, as belonging to the remembered You. . . ." [83] Checking out the qualities of the You is a rational affair. It involves an effort to deal with elements of the partner that are genuinely there, independently of the specific relation. In other words, to say "The stranger is trustworthy" is to claim that this particular person will, when confronted with events like the arrest of members of the resistance, prove to be someone they can count on. After all, that is what the word "trustworthy" means. If Buber were not prepared to allow that much, then the word "trustworthy" would lose its capacity to communicate.

Buber, however, is concerned to set the I-You relation on a higher level of truth where it is immune to the I-It modes of checking out the truth of statements. After an I-You encounter, the partisan remembers the stranger. Certain features, which are objective or I-It like the color of his eyes and the slope of his shoulders, can be reliably checked when the stranger reappears in Nazi uniform. If this were not the case, then the partisan would have no way of knowing that the Gestapo chief and the stranger were the same person. However, the I-You quality of trustworthiness is not reliably observable. Even if the partisan has another meeting with the stranger, the quality of trustworthiness may not come through. Yet this would not prove that this quality had not been present on the occasion of their first meeting and it would not prove that the stranger is not, in fact, trustworthy. In that sense, the partisan's I-You knowledge of the trustworthiness of the stranger is not subject to verification or falsification. It is present in the memory of the partisan and it cannot be erased.

Knowledge of God, the Eternal You

Throughout his career, Buber was more concerned with meeting God than talking about him. He claims that no amount of philosophizing can win through to this encounter which provides the overarching meaning or purpose of life.

> [The fact] that meaning is open and accessible in the actual lived concrete [of specific I-You encounters, especially with the eternal You] does not mean it is to be won and possessed through any type of analytical or synthetic investigation or through any type of reflection upon the lived concrete.[84]

Buber, as we have seen, regards the Bible as a specially potent record of encounters with the eternal You which can, when individuals of our own day find that they come alive, serve as a springboard to a direct relation to God. In this sense, he accepts Pascal's contrast between the God of the philosophers and scholars, a God who is only an idea, with the God of Abraham, Isaac, and Jacob who is experienced as a presence, a You.[85]

Indeed, Buber also rejects the God of the theologians by saying that it too "is a logicized God."[86]

Buber's attitude toward philosophical and theological approaches to God is a source of a great deal of confusion. It underlies his incredible statement: "I am absolutely not capable nor even disposed to teach this or that about God."[87] The statement is incredible because as Paul Edwards, an analytic philosopher, notes: "Buber appears to possess a good deal of communicable knowledge both about God's nature and his intentions concerning human beings."[88] Buber writes that "only one You never ceases, in accordance with its nature to be You for us" and that God "limits himself in all his limitlessness, he makes room for the creatures."[89] Buber's books are full of statements of this kind, and Edwards quotes quite a few of them. Yet even more important than individual passages is the fact that Buber speaks of God as the eternal You and the absolute person.[90] These terms communicate Buber's view that although we encounter God in a personal relation, he is not a limited reality like human beings. We are, for example, sometimes open to the I-You relation, but he is always open; we are able to be engaged in an I-You relation with only one You at a time, God can be simultaneously present as a You to all human beings.[91]

Despite his explicit disclaimer, Buber clearly teaches a great deal about God and his denial is a function not of his practice, but of his suspicion of philosophical and theological approaches to God. He thinks that they approach God in the spirit of the I-It. Such an approach is justifiable in the case of all other beings who can be encountered in the I-It as well as in the I-You. Whereas, Buber insists that God is unique in that he is either to be approached as a You, or he cannot be approached legitimately at all. Buber, therefore, wants to avoid discussions of God in the I-It level of knowledge.

> I have occasionally described my standpoint to friends as the "narrow ridge." I wanted by this to express that I did not rest on the broad upland of a system that includes a series of sure statements about the absolute, but on a narrow rocky ridge between the gulfs where there is no sureness of expressible knowledge but the certainty of meeting what remains, undisclosed.[92]

Buber as we can see, is not opposed to talking about God. In doing so, he tries to avoid two "gulfs," that is, two basic mistakes both of which result from illegitimately reflecting on I-You relations in an I-It manner. (1) The sceptic experiences the multitude of I-You relations but he refuses to recognize the one eternal You who addresses him through them. He dissolves the reality of this presence in a sequence of arguments which are designed to show that there is no God. (2) Theologians experience the full presence of the eternal You and acknowledge the reality of God. They then make the mistake of freezing the living presence into logically consistent characteristics (at least they are intended to be consistent), and, in doing so, they too dissolve the reality of the presence.

Buber, in opposition to the sceptics, insists that we cannot validly deny the reality of the one who is present in all I-You encounters. In opposition to theologians (or to his characterization of theologians) he insists that we cannot have any sure knowledge of God, a position that is consistent with his overall outlook. As we have seen, he denies that there can be sure knowledge of any partner to an I-You relation.

The Special Problems of Knowing the Eternal You

There are many problems packed into Buber's experiential approach to God and into his existential affirmation of the reality of the God he experiences. I-You knowledge of any partner to a relation is highly problematic, but knowledge of the eternal You is far more problematic than that of any other You. To appreciate the point we need only note that the mysterious stranger of Basil Mitchell's parable is problematic as a You, but not as an It. When he reappears as head of the Gestapo, the partisan can readily identify him by means of observable I-It features like his height and the color of his eyes. These observable features provide an I-It reference for the subject of the statement, "The stranger is trustworthy." The partisan is referring to that individual in the Gestapo uniform, an individual he can point out.

In this context, it is worth recalling Buber's view that God is the only partner of an I-You relation that has no observable or I-It aspect. "It is . . . only in the I-You relation that we can meet God at all, because of Him, in absolute contrast to all other existing beings, no objective aspect can be attained."[93] This means that the problems of checking out an encounter with the eternal You are compounded. To begin with, there are the same problems that are involved in checking out any other You. The further problem is that once the encounter with the eternal You is over, there is no I-It presence that can be pointed to. In other words, in the case of all other partners to the I-You relation, knowledge of their special (and nonobservable) qualities like trustworthiness is problematic. In the case of God, knowledge of his *existence* is as problematic as knowledge of his attributes, like power or love.

Buber's approach to religious experience sets God beyond the reach of checkability. God's existence and his qualities cannot be checked out during the relation with the eternal You because the effort to do so would end it by forcing the individual to adopt the I-It attitude. They cannot be checked out after the relation because the presence of the eternal You is not accessible to the individual who adopts the I-It attitude and tries to check it out. Therefore, God's existence cannot possibly be proved or disproved and it is not even possible to confirm or disconfirm it. Proof and checking are I-It activities, and God, who is only accessible in the I-You relation, transcends them. Proof and checking are not only impossible, but Buber insists that they are not desirable. Because it is impossible to achieve them, we can and should live by faith.

When we consider why proof and checking are neither possible nor desirable, we come to the existentialistic side of Buber's thought. Since religious existentialism is the topic of Part Three, I will say only enough to indicate the differences between Buber and Otto. In Otto, two senses of objective were presented: (1) existing independently and (2) checkability by accepted methods that result in agreements on specific issues. Otto regards statements about God as objective in both senses. Buber agrees with Otto on the first sense, but differs on the second.

With regard to the second sense of objective, Otto thinks that universal agreement on aesthetic and religious judgments is attainable in principle, even though it will not occur in the foreseeable future. Buber does not regard this goal as either attainable or desirable. For Buber truth is what Kant called a regulative ideal or what he himself calls a border concept.[94] Buber, like Kierkegaard, agrees with the spirit of a statement by the German thinker Gotthold Lessing (1729–1781):

> If God were to hold out enclosed in his right hand all truth, and in his left hand just the active search for truth, though with the condition that I should on this search always and eternally err, and should say to me: "Choose!" I should humbly take his left hand and say: "Father, give me this one; absolute truth is yours alone."[95]

Buber thinks that personal and cultural factors influence our relation to God to the extent that we can never, in principle, achieve objective agreement on these issues. God is eternally present; he can be found everywhere and in relation to everything. Yet there are special springboards to the relation with the eternal You, namely, the sacred texts of the religions. When they come alive the worshiper experiences God in specific terms that have shaped and been transmitted by a given religious tradition. Generally speaking, religious texts come alive only for people who have been sensitized to them by participation in a given religious tradition. If the texts are those of Theravadin Buddhism, the experience will not involve a personal God. If the tradition is Judaism, Christianity, or Islam, and the texts of the Bible or of the Koran come alive, the individual encounters God as a personal reality who confronts him directly. Buber does not think that there is any way of getting beyond the subjective sensitizing that characterizes individuals and groups in order to come up with statements about God that can be certified as objectively true. We simply cannot get agreement as to the methods for proceeding and about individual topics like Christian views of the Trinity. Of course, within the broad religious traditions like Islam and Christianity there is a considerable degree of agreement among individuals which extends beyond their personal views, but the bitter factional fights within individual religions show just how limited it is.

Differences among religious traditions is one source of Buber's view that religion is inescapably subjective. He does not believe that any broad intercultural or interfaith consensus is possible. Another source of his existentialistic point of view is his view of the inescapable element of subjectivity that is involved in affirming God.

Encounters with the eternal You, like Isaiah's vision in the Temple, provide a sense of the holy. After the vision has faded the individual has simply no way of demonstrating, to himself or to others, the truth of the statement: "Holy, holy, holy, the whole earth is full of his glory." He lives in objective insecurity, yet it is a "holy insecurity."[96] He believes that the God he encountered is an independent reality and not an illusion and he lives in the hope that he will experience future encounters with the Holy One.[97]

Buber insists that believers ought to live in the tensions brought on by the alternation between encounters with the eternal You and the mere recollection of the encounters that illuminate the relative barrenness of the I-It. There is no way of eliminating this tension. The individual who acknowledges the reality of the eternal You takes a risk of both error (God may be illusory) and action (people have been slaughtered for being faithful to their God). Buber, like other religious existentialists, thinks that taking this risk is the only way we can authentically relate to God. Nevertheless, it is important to realize that taking the risk does not make the reality of God any more objectively certain. "The risk does not ensure the truth for us; but it, and it alone, leads us to where the breath of truth is to be felt."[98]

A CRITICAL EXAMINATION OF KNOWLEDGE OF THE YOU

Buber's approach to religious experience is comprehensive and powerful, but it is also shot through with problems. In order to understand both its effectiveness and its limitations, it is important to examine the problems involved in his view of our knowledge of the partners to I-You relations and especially of the eternal You.

The It and the You Are Intricately Entangled

Buber generally sets the It and the You in maximal contrast by suggesting that the shift from It to You is as dramatic and decisive as the flick of an electric switch that floods a pitch black room with light.

> The basic word I-You can only be spoken with one's whole being.
>
> The basic word I-It can never be spoken with one's whole being.
>
> The It-world hangs together in space and time.
>
> The You-world does not hang together in space and time.[99]

Actually these sharp contrasts represent the extreme end of a spectrum. Searching my own experience I find the shift from It to You and back to be more gradual. Furthermore, the I-You experience is often mixed with I-It elements.[100] In responding to music I have known some incredibly sustained episodes that were—as far as I could tell in thinking about them later—almost exclusively I-You. I think of a recent performance of Beethoven's Quartet in F Minor by the Amadeus Quartet. In a company of three, each of us had the same reaction: an unbroken intensity of concentration that was almost uncanny. On the other hand, the first act of a performance of Wagner's *Götterdämmerung* lasted for two hours and twenty minutes. It was an utterly unforgettable experience, and I would almost use the word revelation. Yet, the intensity of concentration was nothing like that of the much shorter performance of the Beethoven Quartet. My mind was flooded by many streams of associations that were triggered by the ebb and flow of the music. The interaction between these thoughts and what was happening in the orchestra pit and on the stage was too intimate for the experience to be described as a continuing alternation of I-It and I-You. If I understand Buber's account of the I-You relation at all, I would characterize the experience of the entire act as a sustained I-You relation but one which lacked the unbroken concentration of the experience of the Beethoven Quartet. It is because they are inadequate to discriminations of this kind that I often think of the I-It and I-You categories as examples of umbrella words.

    An even more important problem is that Buber is maddeningly vague about the interaction between the It and the You. Yet in a few passages (which he fails to elaborate) he reveals an awareness of the nuances of interaction between them. In one statement he explicitly states that we do *not* move from pure It to pure You and back again:

The It is the chrysalis, the You the butterfly. Only it is not always as if these states took turns so neatly; often it is an intricately entangled series of events that is tortuously dual.[101]

In another he is very clear on the point that when we shift from the It to the You the accumulated knowledge of the I-It is not lost; it penetrates and enriches the I-You. In the context of his account of an I-You relation with a tree he enumerates the various kinds of I-It approaches we can take: that of the artist, the biologist, the botanist, the chemist, and the physicist. In all of these approaches the tree remains a fixed object, located in time and space. It is surveyed with regard to some use or other. He then describes the "letting go" that results in an exclusive I-You relation to this particular tree and comments:

This does not require me to forego any of the [I-It] modes of contemplation. There is nothing that I must not see in order to see [the tree as a You] and there is no [I-It] knowledge that I must forget. Rather is everything, picture and movement, species and instance, law and number included and inseparably fused.[102]

In discussing aesthetic experience Buber claims that the accumulation of I-It knowledge is not an end in itself. The point of acquiring it is to bring it to the I-You relation so that these climactic experiences can be enriched. He begins by considering aesthetic understanding under the rubric of I-It experience. He discusses the way that a work is created, its various observable qualities, what it expresses, and the problems of evaluating it. Then he adds:

Not that scientific and aesthetic understanding is not necessary [we must have it in order to function as human beings] . . . but it should do its work faithfully and immerse itself and disappear [that is, it should move from the center to the periphery of consciousness or even to the unconscious] in the truth of the I-You relation which surpasses [I-It] understanding and embraces what is understandable.[103]

Without making very much of the insight, Buber, in effect, concedes that there are significant gradations within what he indiscriminately characterizes as the I-You relation. Think, for example, of my experience of the Signorelli crucifixion (see p. 107). It was emphatically an I-You encounter. Now think of an authority on Renaissance art like Bernard Berenson having an encounter with the same painting. Clearly, the fund of knowledge and the critical apparatus that he brought to it would have made it harder for him to let go and enter into an I-You relation. Yet, once he did, then to say that he and I have both had I-You encounters with the same painting and to let it go at that is hardly enough. His experience is obviously richer because he is integrating an incredible amount of experience. One could write a book on the differences involved, and philosophers of art do so. For my purposes all that is required is the recognition that the I-You is not as far beyond the range of the I-It as Buber would often have us believe.

Checkability and Our Knowledge of the You

The It and the You interact to a far greater extent than Buber acknowledges, and this interaction is especially important with regard to checkability. Some time ago a soldier was accused of having set off a bomb at the University of Wisconsin which killed a graduate student. His mother said that "he couldn't have done that." Her statement was based on an accumulation of I-You encounters that gave her privileged access to his character; in that sense she certainly knew him better than anyone else. Despite the fact that her statement was primarily rooted in I-You insights, it could (contrary to Buber's position) be falsified in the I-It. A confession by this soldier would (provided it was convincing and supported by evidence that he provided) decisively falsify his mother's statement.

Even in a case like that of the partisan and the stranger where the I-You encounter is their first meeting, I-It elements come into play.[104] The partisan brings a considerable accumulation of I-It experience to that meeting. He has a great deal of knowledge of the kind of behavior and speech that is associated with virtues like sincerity and trustworthiness. When he talks with the stranger, the impressions he receives are positive; they match the patterns that he has learned to associate with these virtues. This helps him to let go and to relate to the stranger in a way that results in the conclusion: "The stranger is trustworthy." When he presents his comrades with this judgment, he is relying on the privileged access provided by his I-You encounter. However, I-It knowledge played an important role in making the I-You encounter possible. I-It knowledge can also show that he is mistaken about the qualities of the You that he has encountered.

Buber insists that nothing that happens can undermine the partisan's knowledge that the stranger is trustworthy because the I-You relation has priority. It reveals more about the true nature of the other than can be revealed by any amount of checking that takes place in the It-world. Yet Buber fails to explore the possibility of checking subtle features like trustworthiness. As noted, I-It evidence *is* relevant to the truth of the statement, "The stranger is trustworthy" (see pp. 118f). Unexpected release of some members of the resistance confirms it, and the unexpected capture of members of the resistance is disconfirming. This is the case even though only one member of the underground is able to set this I-It evidence in the context of the recollection of an I-You encounter with the stranger. Furthermore, against Buber, and with Ronald Hepburn, I maintain that it is possible for this partisan to have had a genuine I-You encounter with the stranger and then to discover that he was tragically deluded. Hepburn's example deals with the sense of bodily presence: "... When we are in an I-You situation talking with John, say, by firelight, we may quite easily make mistakes. ... I may speak to John 'sensing' his presence [as a You directly bodied against me], although unknown to me John may have quietly slipped out of the room, thinking that I was asleep."[105] To show that the statement, "John is present in the room" is false, Ronald need only open eyes.

The case of the partisan and the stranger is more complex because the partisan and the other members of his group check out the trustworthiness of the stranger but the partisan is the only one to have had an I-You relation with him. Yet this does not offer any guarantee against the partisan's being mistaken. Even though his encounter with the stranger convinced him that the man is trustworthy, it may be that the stranger is actually a Nazi. One need only elaborate on Mitchell's parable to bring this point home. Suppose that the stranger told the partisan that the local Nazi contingent had been secretly doubled in strength and they are planning to reinforce every bridge, warehouse, and all the other obvious targets of the resistance. The stranger claims that if the partisans try anything, they will be captured. He then says that he could arrange to set an alarm which would send all Nazi troops to the bridge on one side of town while the partisan's unit blows up an arms depot on the other side. If the partisan trusted the stranger and persuaded his comrades to go along with this plan, the statement, "The stranger is trustworthy," could be easily checked. The next day they would either succeed in blowing up the ammunition dump, or, if the partisan was tragically mistaken about the trustworthiness of the stranger, he and his comrades would be captured. To make it worse, the stranger might even have the partisan tortured while he rubbed in the fact that he had deceived him.

Often in important human affairs there is no practical way of checking out the truth of a statement like "The stranger is trustworthy." In cases like this, one may have to risk a great deal on untested impressions of another person's character. This does not, however, show that knowledge of the You, like the trustworthiness of the stranger, is not checkable *in principle.* Indeed, given Buber's desire to set the I-You beyond the range of the I-It, the actual situation is ironical. The only way we reliably discriminate genuine trustworthiness from an imposture is by means of I-It checks.

Human relations are both complex and subtle. The attitudes of one person to another are complicated by problems of definition like "What constitutes true friendship?" They are subtle because inner attitudes ought not to be regarded as nothing more than a function of external behavior. We all realize that a person can behave in a friendly way despite the fact that he is not genuinely friendly. In other words, he may be insincere. This is why at the extreme limit of human interaction we can insist that no amount of evidence can conclusively verify a statement like "John is a true friend to Ronald." Even if John should behave in a very warm and friendly way, it is possible to raise doubts; perhaps he inwardly loathes Ronald. There is no way of attaining as great a degree of certainty regarding the inner attitude as we can have with regard to the observable behavior.

Considerations about attitudes and behavior constitute one of the most difficult issues in contemporary philosophy—the question of the relation of mind and body.[106] They cannot be readily resolved. Martin Buber, like many other religious thinkers, generalizes from extreme cases. Even if a person might really be unfriendly while behaving in a friendly way and his unfriendly attitude might be beyond verification, it does not follow that statements like "John is a true friend of Ronald" are completely beyond checking. These statements are, in part, based on observable behavior, and we take the behavior as confirming or disconfirming the truth of the statement.

Buber, then, usually underestimates the extent to which the I-It and the I-You are subtly interfused. This is tied to his more important failure to note the extent to which I-It checking is crucial to our ability to discriminate genuine perceptions of the You from tragically mistaken ones.

Checkability and the Eternal You

We have seen that knowledge of the eternal You is far more problematical than knowledge of any other You. Ironically, the very thing that makes knowledge of God more problematical than knowledge of all other beings also makes knowledge of God less subject to the ravages of checkability. Buber tries to set partners to *all* I-You relations beyond the range of checkability, yet we have just seen that claims to knowledge of the You, like "The stranger is trustworthy" can be falsified. God, however, is not like Hepburn's friend John or Mitchell's mysterious stranger because God has no I-It aspect. He is not supposed to be observable. Furthermore, as

Wisdom notes in his reference to Elijah's contest with the priests of Baal, God is not supposed to be experimentally linked to observables (see p. 43). In other words, God is no more like an electron (nonobservable, but tied to observables) than he is like a table (directly observable) or like a unicorn (supposed to be observable but never observed). It is, therefore, extremely difficult to challenge someone's claim that "Three days ago God confronted me directly in an I-You encounter."[107]

There is no conclusive way of falsifying a claim to have had an encounter with the eternal You, or any other religious experience, but it is important to explore some of the implications of this point. Hepburn, as we have seen, had what he thought of as a numinous experience of God, but he came to regard it as the effect of a childhood experience of height (see p. 96). So too many people seem to have experiences like those that Buber describes without interpreting them as encounters with God. Donald Evans states the point clearly:

> A believer looks on a depth experience of personal encounter as a revelation of God and tries to live accordingly; that is, he is open to the "address" of the eternal You, which comes through the words and deeds of men whom he meets in personal encounter. An agnostic or atheist interprets the depth-experience in purely human terms: "Yes, human beings are mysterious; there are depths in man which can only be known in personal encounters; but why bring in God?"[108]

As we have seen, Buber's claim to knowledge of the eternal You is shot through with problems. All other partners to an I-You relation may be regarded as wholes which are greater than the sum of their observable (I-It) parts.[109] In the case of God, we are confronted by a You which has no I-It parts at all, and this makes statements about the eternal You far more questionable from the I-It standpoint than statements about any other You; indeed, it might seem to tip the balance to the agnostic or to the atheistic view.

This line of thought would not distress Buber. Unlike Otto, he is prepared to concede the point that reflection on the question of God carried on in the I-It attitude would lean in an atheistic direction. Along with other existentialists he is concerned to stress the element of risk that is involved in accepting the independent reality of the eternal You despite the atheistic drift of the objective evidence. In the following part of the book this existential approach to God will be explored in depth.

Part Three

Religious Existentialism: Faith, Revelation, and History

Religious existentialism has been the most important intellectual development in twentieth-century religion.[1] Unlike the logical positivists, the
religious existentialists were not a closely knit group, but they shared
common influences and stressed many of the same themes as they
struggled to achieve authentic expression of their various religious
traditions. Two Protestant thinkers, Soren Kierkegaard (1813–1855) and
Rudolph Bultmann (b. 1884), are the only ones considered here. It is,
therefore, important to stress that Roman Catholic, Eastern Orthodox,
and Jewish thinkers are also represented in the ranks of the religious
existentialists.[2]

Religious existentialists can be presented under a variety of formats:
they are vital interpretors of the Bible, they have revitalized important
theological doctrines like justification by faith, and they have dealt with
basic human concerns like courage and despair. I will confine my
presentation to one important theme, the existentialists' approach to
truth, because it provides religious thinkers with a significant way of

affirming traditional views of God in the face of the challenge of analytic philosophy.

The drama of nineteenth- and twentieth-century religious thought (especially Protestant) was played out against the backdrop of science. As we have seen, the technological applications of science impressed great numbers of people who had no understanding of either the scientific method or the theories of particular sciences (see Chap. 4). They respect scientists as the men who are genuine masters of knowledge. Increasingly scientific standards of believability came to dominate the culture. The miracle stories of the Bible, like the parting of the raging waters of the Red Sea (Exod. 14) and the raising of Lazarus from the dead by Jesus (John 11), seemed utterly implausible if not impossible. The rise in the prestige of science eroded the authority of the Bible and with it the believability of Christian claims. Prior to the emergence of religious existentialism as a major force in religious thought, the main theological reactions to science were conservative and liberal.[3]

Conservatives appealed to the authority of the Bible in their reaction against a culture that was becoming increasingly oriented to science. The fundamentalists, who represent the extreme wing of conservativism, insisted that all words of the Bible were inspired by God. Therefore, when read literally, they were error-proof since the all-knowing and all-powerful God could not make mistakes. They maintained that if any scientific theory, like the Darwinian view of evolution, conflicted with the words of the Bible, so much the worse for that theory. Sooner or later it would be discredited because the Bible cannot be wrong.

The liberals were open to the spirit of the scientific enterprise, and they were impressed with its methods. The biblical scholars among the liberals used the scientific method in approaching the Bible; they tried to find out when the different parts of it were written, who wrote them, and from what perspective. In doing so, they followed the patterns that scholars of the classics were using in their research on ancient texts like the epics of Homer and the dialogues of Plato. In general, they dismissed extraordinary details—like the waters dividing at the Red Sea—as legendary and insisted that they never occurred. Other biblical miracles, whose details were less extraordinary, were accepted as actually having occurred but were interpreted by means of rational categories. Some of the miraculous healings performed by Jesus were, for example, interpreted in terms of what we today would call psychosomatic medicine. Although the liberals did not accept the Bible as a source of valid accounts of miracles, they did not downgrade its status as the authoritative source of Christian teachings and as the greatest religious treasure of mankind. They preserved the traditional view of its status and authority by claiming that it was not rooted in supernatural occurrences but primarily in Jesus' moral teachings. They stressed his teaching of love to God and man, even to the enemy, and his moral injunctions like the golden rule: "Always treat others as you would like them to treat you" (Matt. 7:12).

The liberal approach is problematic because it seems to assign the Bible a unique status among religious literature on the basis of an appeal to teachings that are not unique. The two love commandments taught by Jesus: To love God with all one's heart, soul, and mind and also to love one's neighbor as oneself (Matt. 22:37–39) are not original with him. They are found in the Old Testament (Deut. 6:15; Lev. 19:18). The golden rule, far from being original with Jesus, was taught by Confucius centuries before his time and by Hillel, one of the greatest of the Rabbis, shortly before his time. If the case for biblical authority were based solely on the moral teaching of Jesus, it is hard to see how it could be justified.

Christian versions of existentialism emphasize both the distinctively Christian message that is so important to the conservatives and the acceptance of science that is characteristic of liberalism. The existentialists were especially concerned to affirm the central Christian teaching that God entered human flesh in the person of Jesus of Nazareth (the Messiah or the Christ) in order to reconcile sinful human beings to himself.

Religious existentialists wanted to transmit the traditional Christian message without tying it to assumptions about the world that have been outmoded by science. Their major technique is what I call the two-level theory of truth. The logical positivists, as we have seen, regarded the analytic (mathematics provides the best example) and the synthetic (physics provides the best example) as the only kinds of statements that were entitled to be regarded as true. Religious existentialists do not reject these types of truths, but they regard them as constituting merely one level of truth. This level is valid and self-regulating. No religious leader ought to criticize the results of the scientific investigations of a physicist or a biologist (though he may, of course, criticize the uses to which the results are put).

Religious existentialists regard the analytic and the synthetic as valid but limited because the kind of thinking involved in the analytic and the synthetic is inadequate to the most important issues of life. When individual human beings must decide on a choice of career, a marriage partner, or a commitment to a major cause, they have to move beyond the analytic and the synthetic. They must venture to a level of truth where the standards are not as reliable and agreements are hard to come by. The religious existentialists regard this as a higher level of truth because on it human beings confront more important issues. Yet the higher truth does not cancel any truths which scientists come up with at their level. Blaise

Pascal (1623–1662), the French mathematician and philosopher, who is one of the forerunners of religious existentialism, made the point neatly: "Faith indeed says what the senses do not say, but not the contrary of what they say: faith is above the senses not counter to them."[4]

Religious existentialists have not been concerned with technical issues of epistemology, that is, the theory of knowledge. In setting up their two-level theory of truth they have instead relied on the work of Immanuel Kant (1724–1804), who was one of the most influential epistemologists in the history of philosophy. They trade heavily on his basic distinction between theoretical and practical reason.[5] In using reason theoretically, a person is content to observe and personal involvement is minimized. He is concerned with reporting on the evidence for subatomic particles or on the structure of the DNA molecule, but not with changing these things. In the practical uses of reason, as in deciding on the right course of action in the struggle for racial justice, a person not only observes a state of affairs, but he evaluates it. He may then commit himself to the effort to improve the situation. In the use of practical reason personal involvement is maximized. The individual is not merely an observer but also an active agent.

Religious existentialists labeled the detached standpoint of the observer as "objective" and consigned its truths to the lower level which they contrasted with the higher level of truth that is accessible to the "subjective" participant. As a group they were suspicious of thinkers who dealt with the crucial issues of life from the theoretical standpoint. Kierkegaard set the tone by satirizing a professor who devised a theoretical proof of the immortality of the soul but who collapsed in terror when his life was in danger. His problem was that he'd forgotten his notes and that he could not remember the proof. The religious existentialists have no use for a truth about human affairs or religious matters that does not stand up to the test of day-to-day living. This emphasis is shared by an American philosophical movement called *pragmatism*. One of its leading figures, William James (1824–1910), manifests the existentialists' concern for life-relevance as well as a number of their other emphases, such as the focus on decision as an access to truth. He arrived at his position independently of the existentialists and he expressed it with greater clarity. For this reason, before turning to religious existentialism, it will be helpful to consider William James' essay on "The Will to Believe."

Chapter 7

William James: Decision and Truth

We have seen that one of the main impulses of the logical positivists is their restrictive attitude toward the key words *know* and *true*. They want to confine them to cases where the rules for application are clear and where agreement can be readily obtained on specific cases (see p. 105). With regard to synthetic (or factual) statements of truth, scientific work is their ideal. In this context, William James' essay, "The Will to Believe" is a landmark even though it is loosely argued and has been severely criticized by a number of philosophers.[6] It was written in 1896, over twenty years before the logical positivists surfaced as a philosophical movement, but it is relevant to their challenge partly because it was written in answer to an essay, *The Ethics of Belief* by William C. Clifford, a nineteenth-century forerunner of the positivists.

THE PARTISAN AND THE SCIENTIST

Clifford's major point is that overbelief is the greatest sin we can commit ". . . if a belief has been accepted on insufficient evidence. . . . It is sinful, because it is stolen in defiance of our duty to mankind. That duty is to guard ourselves from such beliefs as from a pestilence. . . . It is wrong, always, and everywhere, and for everyone, to believe anything on insufficient evidence."[7] Clifford's statement is eloquent, but James sets out to show that Clifford is wrong by claiming that this virtue is appropriate always, everywhere, and for everyone. There are circumstances in which overbelief (belief beyond the evidence) is not only justifiable but advisable. It may help to clarify the point if we compare the overbelief that is characteristic of the partisan with the tough-mindedness of the scientist.

Sports fans are good examples of the partisan. The fan is hooked on his team. He wants them to win and he lets his desires contaminate his capacity for analysis. When considering his team's prospects for the coming baseball season, he thinks of every player operating at the top of his form. He does not, for example, think of the miserable season's batting average of the shortstop but imagines him performing throughout the coming season as he did during a two-week period when he hit four home runs; he does not think of the overall performance of an ineffective pitcher but imagines him performing for an entire season as he did for the three weeks in June when he won four straight games. Of course, in evaluating the prospects of the other teams, the fan operates in the opposite way. He sees only their flaws and edits out their strengths. The fan is, then, an example of the partisan who is subjective because he lets his involvement distort his judgments.

By contrast, we think of a scientist as objective and detached. Of course a scientist may also become emotionally involved with his group, and he may be convinced that they are the best people in the field. He is then being human. However, as a scientist, he must resolutely resist the temptation to tout his associates; instead, he should examine their work closely, looking for flaws just as he would in evaluating the work of rival groups. As a human being he may be out for awards, but as a scientist he knows that he ought to be the most severe critic of his own work.

There is something admirable about scientific tough mindedness, just as there is something pathetic about the fantasies of the sports fan, but James tries to show that this is not the whole story; there are situations in which scientific toughmindedness is out of place. James was certainly not an opponent of science; indeed, he was a leading figure in the development of psychology in this country. Yet, he was nettled by Clifford's statement that "it is wrong, always, and everywhere, and for everyone, to believe anything on insufficient evidence" because it is such a drastic overstatement. James does not advocate overbelief as a way of life, but he lays out ground rules for situations where it is an appropriate response. A useful point of departure for understanding James is Kant's contrast between the theoretical and practical reason. In moral life we must weigh evidence to determine the facts, but that is only a part of a larger process of practical reasoning that culminates in decisions and actions.

OVERBELIEF IS APPROPRIATE IF IT HELPS
TO BRING ABOUT A GOOD RESULT

James' first point against the absolute prohibition of overbelief is to deal with cases where it may help to achieve a desired result. Let us say that a man is drowning in rough water about 250 yards from shore. I am not a good swimmer and the evidence that I could manage to swim out to him is far from sufficient. Yet, my belief in my ability may actually contribute toward my success in doing so. In that case, James insists that, contrary to Clifford's absolute, I am not merely permitted to believe on insufficient evidence, but I ought to believe that I can make it.

James has been sharply criticized for the position. He has, in effect, been accused of being a precursor of the "positive thinking" of the popular preacher Norman Vincent Peale and of urging us to believe that we can overcome all obstacles merely by thinking that we can do so.[8] The criticism is unjust. James does not even think that we can believe simply because we want to do so. He certainly does not claim that we can change states of affairs simply by willing them to be different than they are:

> Can we just by willing it believe that Abraham Lincoln's existence is a myth and that the portraits of him . . . are all of somebody else? Can we by any effort of our will, or by any strength of wish that it were true, believe ourselves well and about when we are roaring with rheumatism in bed, or feel certain that the two one-dollar bills in our pocket must be a hundred dollars? We can *say* any of these things, but we are absolutely impotent to believe them; and of just such things is the whole fabric of truths that we do believe in made up—matters of fact [synthetic] . . . and relations between ideas [analytic], which are either there or not there for us if we see them so, and which if not there cannot be put there by any action of our own.[9]

In the face of this blast, it is perverse to accuse James of maintaining that "if you want to believe it its true." James is only urging belief on insufficient evidence where there is a margin of doubt. The belief that I can manage to swim 250 yards in rough water may enable me to do so if I can manage about 200 yards in calm water, but not if I can barely manage twenty-five. By citing examples of this kind, James succeeds in discrediting Clifford's absolute prohibition against overbelief. He shows that in some cases it would be sinful *not* to believe on insufficient evidence.

EXISTENTIAL DECISIONS

In the rest of his essay, James draws out the implications of the point that in some cases it is sinful *not* to believe on insufficient evidence. In doing so, he makes many points that are characteristic of religious existentialists, even though his orientation and outlook were very different from theirs. James was an optimistic American and a scientist, and the pragmatic view of philosophy, which he represented, was oriented to scientific work. By contrast, even though the religious existentialists have never denied the validity of the scientific method, they have all been more concerned to warn us against its limitations than to extol its achievements.

James' major claim is especially relevant to existentialism.

> Our passional nature not only lawfully may, but must, decide an option between propositions, whenever it is a genuine option that cannot by its nature be decided on intellectual grounds; for to say, under such circumstances, "Do not decide, but leave the question open," is itself a passional decision—just like deciding yes or no—and it is attended with the same risk of losing the truth.[10]

It is important to understand the features that enable James to describe decisions as passional, or what we would call existential: They cannot be decided on intellectual grounds, and they involve momentous, live, and forced options. In developing the point I will use an illustration that is something of a soap opera.

A widow has worked hard for a considerable number of years so that she could provide her only son with an education. He has finished medical school and is now serving as an intern in a hospital. He falls in love with a nurse and plans to marry her, even though a number of doctors have told him that she "sleeps around." His mother, who has heard of her promiscuity, is furious and wants him to break up with her. He acknowledges the promiscuity but he insists that he will marry her. He believes that she will be a faithful wife.

The story confronts us with a clear-cut case of overbelief. The intern, in making the statement "Mary will be a faithful wife," admits that the evidence is insufficient. Indeed, it points the other way, that is, toward her being unfaithful. He believes in her faithfulness *in spite of* the evidence. Belief against the evidence is more typical of the existentialists than of James, but since James is being presented in the context of religious existentialism, the example is more appropriate than it might otherwise be.

Live, Momentous, and Forced Options

James characterizes the options available in situations of this kind as "live, momentous and forced." "Live" refers to the notion that genuine alternatives are present—genuine in the sense of alternatives that are both possible and desired. The doctor is, presumably, free either to marry the nurse or to obey his mother and terminate the relationship. He is also drawn to both options because he would like both to please his mother and marry the nurse. "Momentousness" is a judgment of importance and marriage is certainly one of the most important decisions any of us make. The notion of a "forced" option is contrasted with avoidable options like "Choose between going out with your umbrella or without it."[11] This option is avoidable because you can choose not to go out at all. The intern's option might also seem to be avoidable since he might drift along and fail to decide either to marry or not to marry the nurse. Yet this failure to arrive at a conscious resolute decision would, in practical terms, be a decision *not* to marry her. This is why (in the passage quoted above) James declares: ". . . under such circumstances, 'Do not decide, but leave the question open,' is itself a passional decision just like deciding yes or no."

Cannot Be Decided on Intellectual Grounds

James does not elaborate the point that options of this kind cannot be decided on intellectual grounds. I will interpret it by means of positivist standards. An issue of this kind cannot be resolved by an appeal to either of the modes of knowledge that the positivists regarded as legitimate. It is obvious that the techniques used in handling analytic statements are inappropriate. The intern cannot arrive at his decision by a process of deduction. It is not obvious that the techniques of factual investigation used to test the truth of synthetic statements are also inappropriate. The intern might find out all he can about the nurse, weigh the evidence, and then decide *on intellectual grounds* that she would or would not be a faithful wife. Indeed, this shows that not all momentous options involve existential decisions. The intellectual techniques appropriate to checking on synthetic statements are often adequate to the resolution of important issues. If the intern found out that the nurse was telling all her friends that she had fooled him that would, presumably, provide a conclusive basis for a negative decision.

James and the existentialists probe further by emphasizing something that lawyers have always known, but that philosophers frequently overlook. If a person has violated a clearly defined law, and there are many precedents on the books for the kinds of infraction he's committed, then the case will be settled out of court. The ones which are tried are cases where the answer is not clear. Existentialists focus on issues where, for a variety of reasons, there is no way of conclusively resolving the issue on intellectual grounds. One of these reasons (which James did not deal with) is the case where the person making the decision has data which are available only to him.

Privileged Access

Most philosophers have regarded emotional involvement as a source of bias which leads to attitudes like those of the sports fan. By contrast, existentialists see that it may also be a source of privileged access.[12] The intern, in proposing to marry the nurse, can echo the protest of genera- tions of lovers: "But mother, you don't know her like I do!" He is right, of course, but that does not resolve the issue. His mother claims that his infatuation leads him to see qualities in the woman that aren't really there. He vehemently protests and claims that the capacity for fidelity that he has seen is really a part of her character. It only comes through in an I-You relation in which she is trusted. Therefore, his response is, in his view, crucial to testing the truth of the statement, "Mary will be a faithful wife." Unless he trusts her and they marry, there is no possibility of bringing out this element in her character. It follows that if he listens to his mother and breaks off the relation, he will never know whether she would have proved faithful to him. This is one example of what William James means by an issue that "cannot by its nature be decided on intellectual grounds." The intern has privileged access to the nurse's character, and he is aware that his own actions will, in part, determine whether the characteristic of faithfulness will be manifest.

THE LEAP OF DECISION

Most uses of practical reason involve objective procedures. If you want to know the route to a subway station, you study a map. In this unexistential decision, you know where you want to go, you know how to research it, and practical reasoning yields an objectively valid answer.

Investigation of this kind is also relevant to existential decisions, but it serves to uncover one of their peculiarities. We know how to go about researching existential decisions, but we have no objective way of knowing when the research has yielded the right answer. To illustrate: For great numbers of people the choice of a career is programmed and no existential agony is involved. Yet, countless others find themselves torn between a number of live options. Imagine an outstanding student whose talents run to writing, history, and biology. He is considering the following careers: novelist, professor of history, biochemist, and doctor. He knows perfectly well how to investigate the options, namely, to write novels and see how they go, or to attend graduate and medical schools. The question is, how much investigation is reasonable? From the standpoint of gathering factual evidence, the more research the better. Yet at some point, although further data would be both relevant and helpful, he would have to cut off the research and come to a decision. There is no way of rationally determining the cutoff point. It involves an inescapable element of arbitrariness, which is why I paraphrase Kierkegaard by calling it the "leap" of decision.[13] This leap is not determined by rational considerations; on the other hand, it is *not* a plunge into irrationality. Given the nature of existential decisions, the "leap" is the best we can do. The element of arbitrariness that is involved in existential decision is what James means by an issue "that cannot by its nature be decided on intellectual grounds."

By reworking James I define an existential decision as involving a live, momentous, and forced option that cannot be decided upon intellectual grounds—partly because the participation of the person making the decision will effect the outcome.

THE RELIGIOUS OPTION

James applies this analysis to religious belief. He thinks it is certainly momentous because it involves our basic attitude to reality. It is a forced option.[14] A person may decide for or against belief, but James notes that a protracted failure to decide one way or the other is, to all practical purposes, the same as a conscious decision against belief. James also considers belief a live option. This is obvious to him, but it is problematic for us. We noted that he applied his thesis to a passional decision between options, whenever they can be expressed as a "genuine proposition." He was certain that the religious option could be expressed this way, but, as we have seen, the positivists used the test of verification in an effort to show that the religious option cannot be formulated in terms of genuine propositions or statements. Therefore, from their point of view, it is not even a live option.

Other critics note that James makes no effort to show why some religious options are live while others are not.[15] He seems to leave the religious option open to both superstition (at the extreme of permissiveness) and to a narrow dogmatism (at the extreme of exclusiveness).

To answer these criticisms, it is important to realize that "The Will to Believe" was not addressed to professional philosophers. James was talking to a group of Protestant college students at the turn of the century. He began his lecture by noting that most of them wanted to believe but were inhibited because of their exposure to sceptics like Clifford. James tried to eliminate these intellectual barriers. He didn't argue for the liveness of the religious option, because he knew that it was live to his audience. He didn't narrow it down because the Protestant option appealed to them, and it was (in a very watered down form) the one he affirmed. Finally, he himself took account of the danger of superstition in the following remark:

> The freedom to "believe what we will" you apply to the case of some patent superstition; and the faith you think of is the faith defined by the schoolboy when he said, "Faith is when you believe something you know ain't true." I can only repeat that this is a misapprehension . . . the freedom to believe can only cover living options which the intellect of the individual cannot by itself resolve; and living options never seem absurdities to him who has them to consider.[16]

He believed that liberal Protestant Christianity had been refined by so many centuries of reflection that he thought it had been purged of superstition. He was also convinced that rational reflection of the deductive kind employed in the analytic domain, and the factual investigations employed in the synthetic, could *not* resolve the issue.

He therefore urged his audience to believe in God on the grounds that the positive and optimistic outlook which would result could only benefit them. And, since the beliefs involved had been purged of error and superstition, they had nothing of that sort to fear in believing them.

A final difficulty concerns the relevance of the participant-observer distinction to the religious option. James' own illustration (against Clifford) concerns circumstances where the overbelief of the participant can affect the outcome. "*Do you like me or not?*—Whether you do or not depends, in countless instances, on whether I meet you half-way, am willing to assume that you must like me, and show you trust and expectation. The previous faith on my part in your liking's existence [in the fact that you like me] is in such cases what makes your liking come."[17] Yet it would be ridiculous to transpose this argument to the religious option and to claim that a previous faith on the believer's part could somehow make God exist.[18] James makes no such claim. Rather, he insists that the question of the existence of God cannot be settled one way or the other from the observer's standpoint. Therefore, the individual as participant has the right to avail himself of the benefits that flow from belief, namely, that of taking a positive attitude toward the universe.[19]

One difficulty with James' position in "The Will to Believe" is that the content of his religious option is extremely vague.

> First, we [religion] says that the best things are the more eternal things, the overlapping things, the things in the universe that throw the last stone, so to speak, and say the final word. . . . The second affirmation of religion is that we are better off even now if we believe her first affirmation to be true.[20]

As already noted, Christian existentialists agree with James in many respects, but on this point they part company. They are not interested in vague sentiments about "the more eternal things." They are interested in God and in God's reconciling love in Christ. It is fascinating to see how they use lines of argument that are so much like those of James to argue for the truth of these traditional Christian affirmations.

Chapter 8

Soren Kierkegaard:
Faith as Subjectivity

Religious existentialism begins with the work of a Danish thinker, Soren Kierkegaard (1813–1855), who remains its most powerful and provocative representative. He is also the most exasperating one. Many of his works were written pseudonymously. What is more, he did not contrive only one or two fictitious authors of his works; he came up with a number of them and scholars have had a field day in characterizing these imaginary authors and insisting that Kierkegaard cannot be understood apart from them.[21] However, I find a brilliant and consistent view of Christianity running through his writings despite the different pseudonymous authors to which they are attributed.[22]

Kierkegaard is also exasperating stylistically. Long stretches of his writing are as turgid as anything in philosophy and theology, and I am, of course, fully aware that these fields are notorious for this characteristic. The opening passage of *Sickness Unto Death* is a good example:

> The self is a relation which relates itself to its own self, or is that in the relation that the relation relates to its own self; the self is not the relation but that the relation relates itself to its own self.[23]

Yet he could also write brilliantly, often in a way that pierces to the heart of religious experience. Consider the first of his four searing preludes on

Abraham's sacrifice of Isaac. He begins with the verse: "And God tempted Abraham and said unto him, Take Isaac, thine only son, whom thou lovest and get thee into the land of Moriah, and offer him there for a burnt offering upon the mountain which I will show thee" (Kierkegaard's version of Gen. 22:1, 2). Kierkegaard then writes about the strained silence of the journey. Abraham finally resolves to tell Isaac about the meaning of their dreadful mission but he can scarcely bring himself to formulate it. Even if he did, he realizes that Isaac would not understand him. Finally, in desperation Abraham decides to sacrifice Isaac's image of him in order to preserve the child's faith.

> He seized Isaac by the throat, threw him to the ground, and said, "Stupid boy, dost thou then suppose that I am thy father? I am an idolater. Dost thou suppose that this is God's bidding? No, it is my desire." Then Isaac trembled and cried out in his terror, "O God in heaven, have compassion upon me. God of Abraham, have compassion upon me. If I have no father upon earth, be Thou my father!" But Abraham in a low voice said to himself, "O lord in heaven I thank Thee. After all it is better for him to believe that I am a monster, rather than he should lose faith in Thee."[24]

Kierkegaard was the most Christ-centered thinker in Christian history. He was not much interested in the question of the existence of God but focused obsessively on the central teaching of Christian faith, namely, that God entered human flesh in the person of Jesus of Nazareth. He was a great preacher and much of his writing consists of imaginative meditations on the poignance of God's earthly career. One of his most powerful sermons relates to a passage in the Gospel of John: "And I, if I be lifted up from the earth, will draw all to myself" (John 12:32). Kierkegaard compares Christ to a poor man who knows that he will one day be rich and thinks that "when I have become the richest of the rich, all will seek after me." In saying this he not only knows that those who now reject him will then curry favor with him, but that when they do so, they will forget both his former poverty and their rejection. And knowing this, he is able—while he is still poor—to love them.[25]

Kierkegaard's Christ-centered literature is an incredible tour de force. Christianity is freighted with the weight of middle class conformity, and a great number of his works were devoted to portraying the stultifying influence of the nineteenth-century equivalent of church suppers and sunday schools. Yet his own fresh and strenuous interpretation of Christian teachings made them seem as challenging and adventurous as daring works of art like Jackson Pollack's action paintings.

He was able to impress Christians because of his powerful insights into the mystery of God in Christ. He has been able to exert a profound

influence on comtemporary Western culture (which is no longer predomi-
nantly Christian) because he was a penetrating psychologist. He was
especially effective on the problems involved in becoming an authentic
self.

Kierkegaard can be approached from many angles. An obvious one
is the theological. It is both fascinating and instructive to see what he does
with traditional Christian themes like grace and freedom, sin, the authority of the Bible, and above all, the Incarnation. My approach is somewhat
odd because I update his thinking to show its relevance to the challenge of
contemporary empiricism.[26] It is, however, appropriate to do so because
his influence on contemporary religious thought stems from his capacity
to help religious thinkers meet the challenges of our own time, rather than
the challenges that were current in his day.

KIERKEGAARD'S STRATEGY

Kierkegaard's strategy as a religious thinker is to stress the absurdity of
Christianity but to claim, nevertheless, that it can be passionately and
validly affirmed. As he sees it, the faith hinges on the claim that God
entered history in the person of Jesus of Nazareth. He insists that it is
absurd because God, in his view, is changeless and Jesus of Nazareth, like
any other human being, changed in the course of time (see p. 157). He
insists that the biggest mistake a Christian thinker can make is to try to
avoid the derision of sceptics by trying to show the plausibility of this
claim. In doing so, the theologian necessarily alters it, so that what he
defends is no longer Christianity.[27] Instead, Kierkegaard recommends the
following reply to the jeering sceptic: "Honored sir, you speak like a fool;
of course it is absurd, as it ought to be, [yet] in spite of all objections,
which I have thought through myself in a far more terrible shape than
anyone else could bring them home to me . . . I have deliberately chosen
to believe the improbable."[28] As we shall see, Kierkegaard carried out
this strategy to the fullest extent. He was able to bring out the objections
to Christianity even more forcefully than atheists. Yet at the same time he
affirmed its truth, which was bound to make sceptics wonder whether
they were missing the point.[29] The key to understanding his strategy is to
realize that he stressed its absurdity at the objective level while affirming
its truth at the subjective one; I call it a two-level theory of truth.

Kierkegaardian Subjectivity Transposed into a
Contemporary Key

The heart of Kierkegaard's approach to the two-level theory of truth is
expressed in a definition of truth which must rank as one of the oddest

definitions of anything in any type of literature: ". . . an objective uncertainty held fast in an appropriation process of the most passionate inwardness is the truth, the highest truth, attainable for an existing individual."[30] After all, if we bring the subjective-objective contrast to bear on questions relating to truth, we generally associate truth with objectivity. We urge a person who is shouting and totally immersed in his own point of view to be objective. The idea is to disengage him from his subjective bias so that truth may be served. Furthermore, we do not usually think of truth as something that admits of degrees. A statement is either true or false, or we may find that one element of it is true and another false. Again we may find ourselves unable to determine its truth or falsity. What we find absurd is the suggestion that we should use comparatives and superlatives with regard to truth, as in true, truer, truest. Yet that is what Kierkegaard's phrase "the highest truth" suggests. Kierkegaard's view of truth seems eccentric. A clue to its meaning that modifies its strangeness is his remark that ". . . the above definition of truth is an equivalent expression for faith."[31] It is, in other words, a definition of truth that reflects Kierkegaard's understanding of what is involved in the Christian faith. Nevertheless, it is not merely a contrived definition that is designed to make the Christian faith look good. I propose, therefore, to present its broader applications by means of the concept of an existential decision that I elaborated in relation to William James. Then, I will show how Kierkegaard applies it to Christianity.

An Objective Uncertainty Kierkegaard's definition of truth begins with the phrase "an objective uncertainty." He aimed some of his best satirical shafts at the objective temper, which makes it all the more important to realize that, like James, he thinks that objectivity is fine—in its place. Yet it is a grave mistake to apply the objective approach to moral and religious issues that are beyond its scope. Thus, in a capsule statement of the two-level theory of truth Kierkegaard writes: ". . . all honor to the pursuits of science. . . . But the ethical is and remains the highest task for every human being."[32] Kierkegaard warns scientists, and others who are overly impressed with its objective techniques, that science is only effective within its proper limits.

> The modest and retiring scientist does not bring confusion into life; he is erotically absorbed in his glorious occupation. But when, on the other hand, a tumultuous scientist seeks to invade the sphere of the existential, and there proceeds to confuse the ethical, the life principle of the whole, then he is as scientist no faithful lover, and science itself stands ready to deliver him up to a comic apprehension.[33]

Kierkegaard is far more extreme than James in stressing the limits of science; he seems to think that all moral and religious issues are far beyond the scope of objectivity.

Objective As noted earlier, the existentialists' contrast between objectivity and subjectivity is rooted in Kant's distinction between the theoretical thinking of the detached observer and the thinking of the participant who must decide and act.[34] Kierkegaard refers to it explicitly in writing about "the objective tendency, which proposes to make everyone an observer. . . ."[35] There's nothing wrong with being an observer in and of itself; but it is wrong if one merely observes when one ought to participate. Kierkegaard regards the objective tendency as appropriate to judgments which the positivists were later to characterize as analytic. "In the case of a mathematical proposition the objectivity is given, but for this reason the truth of such a proposition is also an indifferent truth."[36] What Kierkegaard sought was a truth that was far from indifferent. "The thing is to find a truth which is true for me, to find the idea for which I can live and die."[37]

Kierkegaard's originality as well as his satirical gifts come into play as he discusses the other kind of truth that the positivists allowed for—the synthetic or factual. His analysis pivots on the point that people in general are aware of the capacity of subjectivity to lead to prejudice ("Whatever is mine is best") and delusion ("I am Napoleon"). In the effort to avoid these perils of subjectivity they take refuge in objectivity by sticking to "the facts and nothing but the facts." When this attitude is applied to such deeply personal matters as honesty and trust, it becomes a form of madness that is the objective equivalent of subjective delusion. To make the point, Kierkegaard tells the story of a madman who escaped from an insane asylum and headed for his home town. Suddenly the thought strikes him: "When you come to town you will be recognized, and you will at once be brought back here again; hence, you need to prepare yourself fully to convince everyone, by the objective truth of what you say, that all is in order as far as your sanity is concerned."[38] As he worries about the problem he spots a ball, picks it up, and puts it in the tail pocket of his coat. At every step he takes the ball and hits—what Kierkegaard euphemistically refers to as—his hind parts, and each time he does so, he turns to the person nearest him and says: "Bang the earth is round!"[39] The madness, as Kierkegaard observes, is not in the statement taken in itself. The madness lies in the individual's thinking that he can live authentically, or even sanely, by confining himself to the world of objective truths.

Uncertain In one of the most philosophically sophisticated chapters in his voluminous literature, Kierkegaard anticipated much of what the positivists were later to say about necessity.[40] He insisted that necessity is function of logical considerations alone. Therefore, only (what the positivists were to call) analytic statements could be objectively certain. All statements of fact (Kierkegaard was dealing specifically with historical statements) are only more or less probable. Of course, if *only* *analytic* statements are objectively certain, it follows that "objectively *un*certain" becomes an umbrella word which covers a wide range of diverse statements. Statements about the existence of God are, by this standard, objectively uncertain, but so are such straightforward statements of fact as "This page is white." However, this is less compromising than it seems because Kierkegaard's point is not to call attention to objective uncertainty in and of itself. He tries to link it to "an appropriation process of the most passionate inwardness"—a process that authentic individuals experience when they are in the midst of existential decisions.

Kierkegaard, as we have seen, thinks that people who imagine that they can approach existential decisions from the objective standpoint are just as mad as people who suffer from subjective delusions. The way to appreciate this link between the objective uncertainty that is involved in an existential decision and the appropriation process that Kierkegaard regards as integral to it is to focus on his own examples. The best known is his treatment of the story of Abraham's willingness to sacrifice Isaac. The interpretation is especially revealing because Kierkegaard wrote *Fear and Trembling* out of his anguish over having sacrificed the love of his fiancée, Regina Olsen.[41] He was, ultimately, convinced that an intense and enduring love for a woman would fatally qualify the absoluteness of his love for God. And only God is worthy of being loved "with all one's heart with all one's soul and with all one's might" (Deut. 6:5).[42] Kierkegaard obeyed his inner voice with respect to Regina, but he did so knowing that his decision was objectively uncertain. There was no way of knowing—before the decision, at the time of making it, or afterwards— whether or not it was the right thing to do. That is why, for his reflections on the subject, he took his title from St. Paul: "You must work out your own salvation in fear and trembling" (Phil. 2:12).

Appropriation Process   Kierkegaard's sense of what is involved in existential decisions comes through clearly in his approach to the Bible. He satirized the Sunday school approach that treats the Bible as a set of nice stories like Aesop's fables and points up the moral for children.[43] In the case of Abraham's aborted sacrifice of Isaac, the moral is that we, like Abraham, should be willing to offer the most precious thing we have to God. By contrast, Kierkegaard wants us to appropriate it by identifying with Abraham at the moment that he receives the divine command. We can then experience the numinous dread that permeates the story because we realize that at that point Abraham did not know that Isaac's life would be spared.

Kierkegaard's dramatic probe of the inner tensions which Abraham experiences reflects Kierkegaard's understanding of the Christian faith in its relation to morality.[44] Yet it also expresses his understanding of "the man alone," the existing individual, sweating out a decision that involves the meaning of his life. In the context of Kierkegaard's use of the phrase "an appropriation process of the most passionate inwardness" I am more concerned with his understanding of existential decisions than with his views of the relation between religion and ethics.

Kierkegaard explored the dread involved in Abraham's situation. In doing so, he came up with his most controversial category, "the teleological suspension of the ethical."[45] Briefly stated, it means that in the name of a higher principle, namely, the direct relation to God, an existing individual has the right to suspend what he himself regards as valid moral obligations and to perform acts that would otherwise be immoral. The application to Abraham is obvious. Kierkegaard was certain that Abraham regarded the taking of a child's life outrageously immoral. In response to his I-You relation to God, Abraham is willing to suspend ethical considerations and to take the life of his child. Kierkegaard's study is an effort to justify Abraham's course of action, indeed, to show that it sets the standard for authentic human existence as well as for religious faith.

In the context of *Fear and Trembling* where Kierkegaard speaks of the ethical, it becomes clear that he refers not to what we think of as moral issues but to any principle (moral, religious, or otherwise) by means of which an individual can justify his actions to his society. In other words, a principle that is universally accepted. This is made clear by Kierkegaard's contrast of Abraham with three other fathers who were called upon to sacrifice one of their children: Agamemnon, Jeptha, and Brutus.[46]

In the case of Agamemnon, the Greek fleet is ready to set sail for Troy to restore Helen to Menelaus and to punish the Trojans. It has been assembled with great effort, and it seems to be frustrated at the outset because there is no wind. Agamemnon appeals to the Oracle for a word. The dreadful command is that his daughter, Iphegenia, must be sacrificed. Jeptha, an Israelite leader, vows that if God gives him the victory over the Ammonites, he will sacrifice the first one to confront him on his return to his land, expecting, of course, that it will be an animal. His prayer is granted and on his return his daughter, who has heard the good news, runs out to greet him. She must be sacrificed. Brutus is a Roman judge. A conspiracy is uncovered; the penalty for participation is death. Among the conspirators is Brutus' son and his father must condemn him.

In all three cases fathers sacrifice that which is most precious to them, and in each case the father has a universally accepted principle to which he can appeal. In fact, the principles involved are so important to their societies that their contemporaries want the fathers to sacrifice their children. If Agamemnon were to refuse to sacrifice Iphegenia, he would lose his role as leader of the Greek forces, because, by failing to obey the Oracle, he would prevent the wind from coming and the fleet from sailing. In the case of Jeptha, a failure to fulfill his oath would bring recriminations from the Israelites. They would be sure that his broken oath would bring God's curse upon them. Brutus, as a judge, must apply the principle of justice to his own son or he would be branded as corrupt.

Within the framework of their cultures or societies all three fathers have a principle which is universal. In the case of Agamemnon it is "obey the Oracle"; in the case of Jeptha it is "fulfill the vow"; in the case of Brutus it is "decide justly without regard for personal involvement." Abraham, by contrast, does not act in the name of a generally accepted principle which provides him with communal support. As Kierkegaard presents the story (although it is not accurate in terms of what we know about Abraham's time and setting), Abraham is, from the standpoint of his community, a murderer.[47] For this reason, the inner tensions involved in Abraham's existential decision about sacrificing Isaac are far greater than those that the other fathers experience as they contemplate the sacrifice of their children.

Abraham—in trying to do the right thing—had to appropriate the meaning of God's will in fear and trembling. People of subsequent generations who read the Bible have to do the same thing if they are to understand biblical faith. Kierkegaard's purpose in *Fear and Trembling* is to dramatize the nature of Christian faith, but it is also calculated to communicate a sense of the passionate inwardness involved in existential decisions.

Passionate Inwardness The link between Kierkegaard's interpretation of Abraham as the man alone, ready to take the extreme step of killing his own child, and to other existential decisions that are not so sharply immoral in character is found in his statement that ". . . for the animal the herd defines the norm."[48] He means that the ideal Guernsey (at least from the human standpoint) is the typical Guernsey, just as the ideal poodle is the typical poodle; they are not supposed to deviate from the normal characteristics of the species.

By contrast, Kierkegaard's human ideal is the individual, the untypical person. The best examples of unusual individuals are creative geniuses. The human race advances on their backs because they venture onto uncharted waters. Kierkegaard obviously had no use for responsible committee members. His sense for creative individuality underlies many of the observations in *Fear and Trembling* in which Kierkegaard extols the particular as being higher than the universal. "The tragic hero [Agamemnon, Jeptha, Brutus] renounces himself in order to express the universal, the knight of faith [Abraham] renounces the universal in order to become the individual."[49] Kierkegaard does not want the creative individual to ignore the universal. He must not, for example, be inferior to the demands of morality. He ought to be superior to them, but to do so, he must first attain the level of acknowledging and obeying them. "For faith [Abraham's venture in being willing to sacrifice Isaac] . . . the particular is higher than the universal—yet in such a way, be it observed, that the . . . individual, after having been in the universal [that is, after having internalized its demands] now as the particular isolates himself as higher than the universal."[50]

Kierkegaard's thinking is original but strained. Against generations of faithful believers and of theologians, he insists that Abraham is, from the moral standpoint, a murderer, yet he then proceeds to claim that from the standpoint of faith Abraham rises above the universal, which, in this case, is represented by moral standards. Kierkegaard reconciles the two judgments by claiming that in relation to his role as father the universal obligation on Abraham is to love Isaac. ". . . when God requires [that Abraham sacrifice] Isaac, he [Abraham] must love him if possible even more dearly [than other fathers love their sons] and only on this condition can he *sacrifice* him; for in fact it is this love for Isaac which . . . makes his act a sacrifice [as distinct from a murder]."[51]

Abraham, like a creative genius goes beyond the universal, and is therefore unable to communicate the basis of his action to other human beings who are oriented to the common standards of their day. "The distress and dread . . . is that, humanly speaking, he is entirely unable to make himself intelligible."[52] For this reason, creative works often repel the artistic establishments of a given era. The Impressionists raised a storm in the field of painting, and Stravinsky's *The Rite of .Spring* provoked a riot at its first performance in Paris.

One of the things we mean in calling a person a genius is that their work causes us to revise our standards of merit in a given field. Yet until this sort of recognition is forthcoming, geniuses experience terrifying tensions. They are subjectively certain of the merit of their work or they wouldn't present it to the public, yet there are no objective verification procedures that can support this subjective certainty. After all, one of the things we mean by "creative" in this context is that the genius breaks with established standards. We have seen that generally accepted standards which enable us to produce widespread agreement in judging individual cases is one of the important meanings of "objective" (see pp. 92f.).

Having insisted that Abraham is—from the standpoint of the universal ethical—a murderer, Kierkegaard then reflects on Abraham's status as the "father of faith." He breaks with the conventional Abraham of Sunday school piety and paints an Abraham whose faith was characterized by fear and trembling. He then claims (in effect) that just as posterity vindicates the breakthroughs of a creative genius like Stravinsky by responding positively to the dissonances of *The Rite of Spring*, so too Kierkegaard wants posterity to vindicate *his* Abraham, the knight of faith, by responding positively to the *risk* of faith. Kierkegaard has nothing but scorn for people who admire creative individuals, whether in art, morality, or religion, but who admire them in a conventional way. This is safe; it involves going along with the judgments of posterity while overlooking the anxiety and dread that the creative individual experiences before he has achieved acceptance.

As I see it, although Kierkegaard himself never puts it this way, the creative genius—at the moment of producing a masterwork but before receiving recognition from society—provides the model for Kierkegaard's "passionate inwardness." This is a use of the phrase that is independent of Christian faith and relates to Kierkegaard's efforts to define authentic human existence. It is, however, also relevant to his understanding of faith, as with Abraham.

Truth and the Existing Individual   An existential decision is one which must be made with considerable risk because there is no way of objectively determining the right thing to do. The reasoning behind James' statement that an issue of this kind "cannot be decided on intellectual grounds" has already been discussed (see pp. 139f.). The point underlies Kierkegaard's statement that "the objective accent falls on *what* is said, the subjective accent on *how* it is said."[53] By the word "what" Kierkegaard refers to the content of a statement, for example, in the synthetic statement "This page is white," the content is the color of the page. Whenever an issue can be dealt with objectively, we want to know *what* has been determined.

Existential decisions, as we have seen, involve issues that cannot be settled by objective procedures. Kierkegaard insists that in Abraham's willingness to sacrifice Isaac, there is no objective content that can be labeled "true." The important matter is the "how"—the way in which the individual handles himself in relation to the decision. Kierkegaard has a standard of existential authenticity, although he never spelled it out in distinct terms. His treatment of Abraham suggests that an existential decision is authentic when it is made with awareness of its objective uncertainty and with willingness to take the risk of going against objective standards.

An Elaboration of Kierkegaard's Definition of Truth

We are now in position to reassess Kierkegaard's seemingly perverse definition of truth as subjectivity. I will present it with comments that summarize the previous discussion.

"*An objective uncertainty.*" A live, momentous, and forced option where there is no possibility of settling the issue by objective procedures such as the a priori used in mathematics or the observations used for checking on the truth of synthetic statements.

"*Held fast in an appropriation process of the most passionate inwardness.*" An existential decision is one where you arbitrarily cut off further research on the issue and decide in fear and trembling to do what you think is right. You know that you have no objective way of verifying or confirming the fact that it is the right decision. The attitude involved is like the inner tension experienced by a creative genius whose work is before the public, but whose merits have not yet been recognized.

"*Is the truth.*" Obviously Kierkegaard does not mean the truth of the "correspondence theory of truth," which can be illustrated by stating "This page is white," verifying it objectively by looking at the page, and then saying, "The statement is true." Kierkegaard's use of "truth" is rather like the use of truth in the phrase "the moment of truth."

"*The highest truth.*" Objective truths like those of analytic and synthetic statements are important and indispensable—at their own level. Objective procedures are inadequate where we face existential decisions in which our roles as participants are crucial. Truths which are forged by means of existential decisions are higher than objective truths because they deal with more important issues. They do not, however, conflict with truths which have been objectively determined.

"*Attainable for the existing individual.*" The existing individual cannot avoid existential decisions because he is constantly confronting forced options regarding momentous issues like marriage, choice of career, and those arising out of politics, economics, aesthetics, and religion. Since he cannot know in objective terms what the right decision might be, everything depends on the way he handles himself in coming to the decision. In fear and trembling he must take the risk of acting against the odds.

Shortly after presenting his definition of truth, Kierkegaard, as noted, adds: ". . . the above definition of truth is an equivalent expression for faith."[54] I will now present his application of his view of subjectivity to Christian faith.

Moving from the Existential HOW to the Christian WHAT

In dealing with Otto's view of religious experience I noted that there is something contrived about it. His central category of divination is custom tailored for the job of getting knowledge of God who is "wholly other"; it has no applications outside the sphere of religious experience. By contrast, Kierkegaard's views of subjectivity are wide ranging in their applications. They tell us a great deal about what is involved in trying to become an authentic individual. Nevertheless, it is important to realize that Kierkegaard's view of truth as subjectivity is derived from his analysis of Christian faith, and his own concern for this category is primarily oriented to Christianity. The "objective uncertainty" appropriated in passionate inwardness is the central Christian teaching that God entered human flesh in the person of Jesus of Nazareth who, as The Christ, is fully divine as well as fully human.

The analysis of truth as subjectivity implies that when dealing with an existential decision which cannot be handled objectively, any *what* will do, as long as you have an authentic *how*. In other words, it implies that as long as you believe with passionate inwardness, any belief that has not been objectively falsified is legitimate. Jean Paul Sartre carried existentialism to this consistent extreme. At times Kierkegaard seemed to heading in that direction, as in his comparison of the Christian and the worshiper of idols:

> If one who lives in the midst of Christendom goes up to the house of God, the house of the true God, with the true conception of God in his knowledge, and prays, but prays in a false spirit; and one who lives in an idolatrous community prays with the entire passion of the infinite, although his eyes rest upon the image of an idol: where is the most truth? The one prays in truth to God though he worships an idol; the other prays falsely to the true God, and hence worships in fact an idol.[55]

Kierkegaard, who defines faith as subjectivity, clearly favors the worshiper of idols who prays with the passion of the infinite. He seems to be saying that it is better to believe a falsehood in the right way than to believe the truth in a false spirit.

When we think about it, this contrast is, in Kierkegaardian terms, impossible. Since he has defined both truth and faith as subjectivity, he is not, by his own standard, entitled to talk about a true conception of God that can somehow be affirmed independently of the subjectivity of the worshiper. The inconsistency is revealing. What Kierkegaard is actually recommending is that we believe a specific "what," that is, Christian teachings, including the objective, that is, independent, existence of God, but with the right "how," that is, in an authentically subjective way.

Kierkegaard tried to splice authentic faith and Christian truth by linking two questions that absorbed him all his life: (1) What does it mean to be an authentic individual? and (2) What does it mean to be a genuine Christian? Ultimately, he thought that they amounted to the same thing.

The Central Christian Paradox: Jesus Christ Is Full God and Full Man Kierkegaard wrote thousands of pages about Christianity. They might all be taken as an extended sermon on the statement in the Prologue to the Gospel of John: "The word was made flesh and dwelt among us." Kierkegaard all but said as much. "If the contemporary generation [that is, contemporary with Jesus of Nazareth] had left nothing behind them but these words: 'We have believed that in such and such a year God appeared among us in the humble figure of a servant, that he lived and taught in our community, and finally died,' it would have been more than enough."[56] By this he meant that it would have been more than enough to offend objective reason and to get people to take Christianity seriously.

Kierkegaard's obsession with the claim that God entered the flesh of Jesus of Nazareth is not eccentric. It is the central item of the traditional creeds of Christendom. It is the point where Christianity decisively parted company with the parent faith of Judaism. It was made explicit by the ecumenical Council of Chalcedon in 451. The assembled bishops of the Church declared that Jesus Christ had two complete natures, one fully divine and one fully human, mysteriously united in one person which is the Second Person of the Trinity. This dogma is not confined to any one church. It has been accepted by the churches of Eastern Orthodoxy, by the Roman Catholic Church and by most Protestant denominations.

Kierkegaard regarded this central Christian teaching as objectively uncertain, and even absurd.[57] Yet, it is hard to communicate its absurdity to people reared in a Christian environment. They are so accustomed to thinking of Jesus as the God-man that they do not even find this claim odd. That is why Kierkegaard wrote that ". . . it is easier to become a Christian when I am not a Christian than to become a Christian when I am one. . . ."[58] He meant that it is difficult to get a person who was baptized at birth and brought up thinking of Jesus Christ as the God-man to appreciate the incredible character of this teaching.

The objective absurdity of the central Christian claim is that it splices that which objective reason declares to be unspliceable, namely, the divine and the human. It is beyond the pale, from the standpoint of both Hebraic religion and Greek philosophy. Kierkegaard focused on the philosophical problems. God is infinite, necessary, and eternal, whereas human existence is characterized by the opposite qualities. Human beings are finite, contingent (they are the sorts of things that might or might not exist), and temporal (see pp. 275f.). It is, therefore, inconceivable that they should merge. To understand why it is inconceivable it will be best to focus on the last pair of contrasting terms: eternal-temporal.

Kierkegaard wrote: "The eternal truth has come into being in time: this is the paradox."[59] Kierkegaard frequently used the term "paradox." He often alternated it with "absurd," so that W. V. Quine's definition of "paradox," will serve nicely for Kierkegaard's use: ". . . a paradox is just any conclusion that at first sounds absurd but that has an argument to sustain it."[60]

To appreciate the full absurdity of the claim that "the eternal truth has come into being in time" think of a mathematical truth like "Two plus three equals five." It is similar to what Kierkegaard calls "eternal truth" because it is time-invariant, meaning, it is not affected by time. It is not, for example, true when we are young, but false as we get older. It did not become true at any point in time, and it will not become false at any point in time. Of course, people become aware of time-invariant truths at different times. A child at some specific time in life becomes aware of the truth of "Two plus three equals five." That is quite another matter from claiming that the statement itself becomes true at some moment in time. It is ridiculous to say that "on July 4, 1864, in Washington, D.C., it became the case that 'Two plus three equals five.'"

The central paradox of the Christian faith, which Kierkegaard calls the absolute paradox, is that God entered the flesh of Jesus of Nazareth. God, being eternal, is time-invariant in radical contrast to the sense in which human beings vary in time. They come into being at some point in time, they grow and change in other ways with the passage of time, and then they cease to be. To say that Jesus Christ was full God and full man (the formula of the Council of Chalcedon, not merely of Kierkegaard) is to affirm of the same being that he is simultaneously A (time-invariant) and not A (not time-invariant), which seems to be a flat contradiction. Kierkegaard expressed his sense of its absurdity by writing: "The news of the day as the beginning [in time] of eternity! If God had permitted himself to be born in an inn, wrapped in swaddling clothes, and laid in a manger, could the contradiction have been greater!?"[61]

The Assault on Apologetics: Objective Props Are Rejected

Looking at the intellectual history of Christendom, Kierkegaard was outraged by one major enterprise, apologetics, which may be called the intellectual defense of the faith. It is the theological activity of external relations; the theoreticians of the Church try to make its claims good by defending them against the criticisms of nonbelievers. "If one," Kierkegaard wrote, "were to describe the whole orthodox apologetic effort in a single sentence, but also with categorical precision, one might say that it has the intent to make Christianity *plausible.* To this, one might add that, if this were to succeed, then this effort would have the ironical fate that precisely on the day of its triumph it would have lost everything and entirely quashed Christianity."[62]

Kierkegaard tore into the traditional apologetic moves with relish. He regarded them as objective props that theologians used in an effort to make belief easier. He said that anyone who tried to come to God by objective moves was like the foreigner who asked an Englishman if the road he was on led to London. The Englishman replied that it did. Yet the foreigner never reached London because the Englishman neglected to tell him that he was headed in the wrong direction.[63]

Apologetics, as far as Kierkegaard was concerned, dealt with the right subject in the wrong way. It offered proofs for the existence of God (see Part Four) and objectively valid reasons for believing in the incarnation of God in Jesus of Nazareth.[64] Kierkegaard comes alive when he demolishes apologetic efforts to show the plausibility of the central Christian claim that Jesus Christ was full God and full man. Part of his demolition was based on his understanding of the limitations of historical judgments. Since this topic will be treated at length in the next chapter, in connection with the work of Rudolf Bultmann, (who was strongly influenced by Kierkegaard), I will not develop it here. Instead, I will focus on Kierkegaard's sense of the incompatibility between historical judgments about human beings and the Christian affirmation of faith in Jesus Christ as *full God* as well as full man.

The Limits of Observation with Regard to the God-Man
Kierkegaard scores his most effective points against the objective approach to Christianity by dealing with Christians who believe that their doubts are rooted in their remoteness from the figure of Jesus. They think that if they could have witnessed his mighty acts, they would be incapable of doubt. In attacking this position, Kierkegaard bypasses the question of whether the biblical accounts of the miracles or any other details of the New Testament are valid when judged by the standards of critical historical research.[65] He proposes that we assume for the sake of argument that each detail took place exactly as reported. It follows that thousands of Jesus' contemporaries witnessed miracles like the feeding of 5,000 people with five loaves and two fish (Mark 6:34–44). Yet these

multitudes did not say: "This man is God." Indeed, even his own disciples failed to draw this conclusion so that immediately after the event the Evangelist comments: ". . . they did not understand about the loaves" (Mark 6:52). The central Christian affirmation is, according to Kierkegaard, not a function of observations. It is a matter of believing the objectively absurd and this can be done just as well by a person today as it could by the people who witnessed Jesus' earthly career.

Kierkegaard was convinced that it is impossible to have faith in Jesus Christ as the God-man on the basis of either direct observations or of historical research because there is an infinite gulf between the divine and the human. The central affirmation that "This man is God" can only be made in passionate inwardness. From the objective standpoint it is an absurdity.

In *Training in Christianity* Kierkegaard communicates his sense of the impossibility of moving from observations of Jesus of Nazareth to the conclusion "This man is God" by writing of the contrast between physical beings and pure spirits. The sight of an utterly strange track in the sand may legitimately lead to the conclusion that the animal who made it is different from any animal that has ever been seen. The one conclusion that cannot be drawn is that the track—no matter how strange it may be—was left by a spirit, because a spirit, by its nature, cannot leave tracks. He then applies the point to the central affirmation of the Christian faith: "But if God exists, and consequently is distinguished by an infinite difference of quality from all that it means to be a man, then neither can I nor anybody else, beginning with the assumption that He was a man [experience the miracles and] arrive in all eternity at the conclusion, 'therefore it was god.' "[66]

Kierkegaard resolutely destroys every effort to qualify the objective absurdity of the central Christian affirmation. Indeed, he seems to revel in it:

> Instead of the objective uncertainty, there is here a certainty, namely, that objectively it is absurd; and this absurdity, held fast in the passion of inwardness, is faith. . . . For the absurd is the object of faith, and the only object that can be believed.[67]

Kierkegaard's rhetoric might easily lead us to conclude that he affirmed the central Christian teaching of the God-man because it was absurd. There is a precedent for this in Christian history. Tertullian wrote that "because it is absurd, it is to be believed."[68] Actually, Kierkegaard did not propose that we appropriate it because it is absurd, but because *when rightly understood,* this paradox provides each human being with the chance to realize authentic individuality.

The Genuine Christian Is the Authentic Individual

One feature of Kierkegaard's thought is bound to baffle the unwary reader. He stresses the absurdity of Christian faith and yet preaches it with all the power of St. John Chrysostom, Martin Luther, Jonathan Edwards, or other great preachers of Christendom. He mines the Bible and the theological traditions of Christianity for every insight he can find, and the reader will not find any traces of doubt in Kierkegaard's formulations. It is easy enough to resolve this seeming contradiction. In vehemently rejecting Christian apologetics, Kierkegaard had no intention of cutting himself off from the wealth of Christian teachings. As long as the Christian faith is understood subjectively and is not diluted by a dose of objectivity, Kierkegaard is prepared to affirm it with unparalleled passion. In doing so, he linked the paradoxical assertion that Jesus Christ was full God and full man to the quest for authentic individuality.

Kierkegaard's thought was both Christ-centered and intensely dramatic. From the objective standpoint he had no way of showing that God existed, much less that he entered human flesh in the person of Jesus of Nazareth. However, as long as this absence of objective backing for the claim was understood, Kierkegaard felt free to let his imagination explore the workings of the mind of Christ. He reflects on verses of the New Testament like "God was in Christ reconciling the world to himself" (2 Cor. 5:19). He thinks of God in Christ as courting human sinners. He wants them to love him, but this involves a free response to his initiative. God does not want human beings to turn to him in the way that sunflowers turn toward the sun, that is, of necessity. In seeking the loving response of human beings, God the infinite enters the finite person of Jesus of Nazareth. Kierkegaard uses his powerful dramatic gifts to portray the situation in terms of a king seeking the love of a humble maiden. I shall rework it.[69]

The king, God, woos a humble maiden. Kierkegaard chooses a humble maiden as the object of God's love because the New Testament is directed to ordinary human beings and not to theological geniuses. No special gifts are required to respond to its message.

The king, in seeking her love, confronts a problem. If he appears to her in his royal regalia, she may respond lovingly, but her love will not be genuine and it will not be directed to him. It will not be genuine because she will be dazzled by the regalia which represents a splendor so far beyond her ordinary experience that her response will not be free; she will be overwhelmed. Furthermore, she will not love him because she will be responding to his appearance rather than to the man.

In an effort to overcome this difficulty the king disguises himself as a servant and confronts her on her own level. This takes care of one part of the problem; now that she is not overwhelmed by the regalia she can respond freely. Yet, there remains the question of whether or not her love is directed to him. If his disguise is totally effective, she still will not love *him* because he is, after all, not a servant but the king.

The implications of this parable for Christianity should be obvious. God does not appear in his infinite glory but confronts human beings in the disguise of the servant, Jesus of Nazareth. Yet he cannot totally hide his true nature or, in loving Jesus, people would be responding to what they take to be a man rather than to Jesus Christ who is fully divine as well as fully human. Therefore, the servant, Jesus of Nazareth, provides clues to his true nature. Human beings are free to accept them by making the leap of faith. Faith, as we have seen, involves the appropriation of this objectively absurd belief in passionate inwardness. Those who fail to make the leap may move in two different directions. Both of them, from Kierkegaard's standpoint, are misguided because both are objective. Those who fail to respond with subjective faith may either use objective arguments in an effort to prove that Jesus Christ is the God-man or they may use objective arguments in an effort to prove that Jesus of Nazareth was nothing more than a traveling preacher who repeated many teachings that were current among the Rabbis of his time.[70]

I will now show how Kierkegaard links genuine Christian faith to authentic individuality. Kierkegaard thought that every individual is confronted with a challenge. If the ordinary person—lawyer, grocer, doctor, baker, or whatever—is told of the central Christian claim that Jesus Christ was full God and full man, he has the option of experiencing authentic inwardness. The catch is that he must respond to this claim in the right way, that is, subjectively. He must recognize the objective absurdity of the claim, and, nevertheless, make the leap. ". . . when faith resolves to believe it runs the risk of committing itself to an error, but it nevertheless believes. There is no other road to faith; if one wishes to escape risk, it is as if one wanted to know with certainty that he can swim before going into the water."[71] Kierkegaard's assault on apologetics knocked every objective support out from under this faith. The individual who takes the risk must swim out over 70,000 fathoms of water with no objective life preserver to buoy him up in the midst of the dreadful insecurity of faith.[72] Kierkegaard is very explicit about the link between the risk of faith and inwardness.

> For without risk there is no faith, and the greater the risk, the greater the faith; the more objective security, the less inwardness, and the less objective security, the more profound the possible inwardness.[73]

The individual who accepts the risk of faith can, no matter how limited his talents, experience the inner life ("inwardness") of a creative individual, which is, as we have seen, Kierkegaard's standard for authentic human existence (see p. 153). It is a life which is stretched as when an artist is anxious about the response to his work before he has been acknowledged as a genius. Kierkegaard's view of inwardness sets human existence in maximal contrast to the placidity of the animal order as it has been celebrated by Walt Whitman:[74]

> I think I could turn and live with animals, they are so placid and self-contain'd,
> I stand and look at them long and long.
> They do not sweat and whine about their condition,
> They do not lie awake in the dark and weep for their sins,
> They do not make me sick discussing their duty to God.

Another one of Kierkegaard's stories catches the spirit of the link between the inner life of creative genius and that of the ordinary Christian.[75] A laborer who lived in a small village regarded himself as the most fortunate of men if he could catch a glimpse of the emperor when he paraded through his province. Yet one day the emperor confronted the laborer and told him that he wanted him for a son-in-law! The laborer was overwhelmed—he did not know that the emperor was even aware of his existence. He could have stretched his imagination to the point of thinking that the emperor might some day make him a foreman in a large factory in the capital, but to ask him to be his son-in-law, that was too much!

If the laborer believed the emperor and went to the palace, he could verify his belief by seeing if the emperor would keep his promise. Kierkegaard contrasts the laborer's story with the situation of the Christian. "And suppose now, that this was not an external reality [God is not observable like the emperor] but an inner thing, so that factual proofs [like presenting himself at the palace] could not help the laborer to certitude, but . . . it was all left to faith [that is, to subjectivity, as to] whether he possessed humble courage enough to dare to believe it. . . ."[76] In that case, the risks and the inwardness are far greater. Kierkegaard then sums up the Christian saga in terms of his theme of God courting human beings, a theme which we have already considered in terms of his story The King and the Humble Maid.

> And now for Christianity! Christianity teaches that this particular individual, and so every individual, whatever in other respects the individual may be, man, woman, serving-maid, minister of state, merchant, barber, student,

etc.—this individual exists *before* God—this individual who perhaps would be vain for having once in his life talked with the King, this man who is not a little proud of living on intimate terms with that [important] person or the other, this man . . . is invited to live on the most intimate terms with God! Furthermore, for this man's sake God came into the world, let himself be born, suffers and dies; and this suffering God almost begs and entreats this man to accept the help which is offered him! . . . Whosoever has not the humble courage to dare to believe must be offended at it.[77]

God in Christ offers himself to every man. To dare to believe the truth of the paradox of the God-man is to achieve the maximal inwardness that comes with taking the maximal risk. Manifesting maximal inwardness verifies the truth of assertions of the Christian faith, but in a profoundly subjective way. People will disagree as to whether this quality is a sign of authentic existence, and although they agree on this standard, they will disagree as to whether a given individual manifests it.

Kierkegaard and James

Earlier, I noted the relation between the version of pragmatism advocated by James and Kierkegaard's existential approach to truth. Obviously, the link between them was not historical. James, who lived half a century later, was not influenced by Kierkegaard but developed his views in the American philosophical context. It is remarkable that they turned out to have such strikingly similar approaches to truth because their temperament, backgrounds, and outlooks were so different.

Kierkegaard's central category was the absolute paradox of the God-man, which he called an objective absurdity. Trumpeting the truth of an absurdity is a procedure that would surely have repelled James. Nevertheless, Kierkegaard shared James' concern to establish standards that would guard against superstition and nonsense. Kierkegaard claims that the higher level of subjectivity goes beyond or against the understanding that operates at the objective level and writes of the true Christian:

He may very well have understanding (indeed he must have it in order to believe against [objective] understanding), he can use it in all other connections, use it in intercourse with other men. . . . He will be able to see the point of every objection [to the subjective or higher understanding of Christianity] indeed to present it himself as well as the best of them, for otherwise a higher understanding would in a suspicious way be a dubious promotion for stuff and nonsense. It is easy enough to leap away from the toilsome task of developing and sharpening the understanding, and so to get a louder hurrah, and to defend oneself against every accusation by remarking that it is a higher understanding.[78]

One of the questions that will be pursued subsequently is whether Kierkegaard took his own standards seriously enough.

Another important parallel between James and Kierkegaard concerns the status of Christian beliefs. Kierkegaard, as we have seen, stresses the traditional Christian view that Jesus Christ was both fully divine and fully human. Like James, he does not think that religious beliefs of this kind can be affirmed only on an intellectual basis. Furthermore, both thinkers reject the possibility of offering a theoretical account of truths about God. Kierkegaard never tells us how the time-invariant God can become the time-variant human being Jesus of Nazareth while remaining time-invariant. He insists that, objectively considered, it is absurd. Yet Kierkegaard insists that the affirmation of the God-man ought not be discarded because of its objective absurdity, but rather that it ought to be subjectively appropriated.

In order to understand the status of the central affirmation of the God-man in Kierkegaard's thought it will be helpful to consider William James' pragmatic view of truth which has been lucidly summarized by the contemporary philosopher Gertrude Ezorsky who characterizes the view of the lower level of scientific truth in the following terms:

> According to James the function of thought is not to copy or to image reality but to form ideas in order to satisfy the individual's needs and interests. What practical difference does it make if an idea is true? In science the truth of an idea is determined by experimental verification. Since verified ideas serve our need to predict experience and cope with our environment, scientific truth fulfils our practical interests. Hence in the context of investigation the true and the verified are one.[79]

She continued by describing with equal clarity James' view of the higher level of truth, which involves the decisions of the participant:

> Science, however, gives us no criteria for decision in the case of metaphysical and theological beliefs. Since the meaning of world-formulae [total world-views such as those involved in a faith like Christianity] are their effects on the attitudes of an individual, the individual is justified in regarding such formulae as true insofar as they provide him with "vital benefits." Thus, "On pragmatic principles, if the hypothesis of God works satisfactorily in the widest sense of the word, it is 'true.'"[80]

The lower or objective level of truth does not provide us with standards for judging religious beliefs. They can neither be sustained nor demolished at this lower level. We are, according to James, entitled to affirm them at a higher level because they provide practical benefits, that is, because they help us cope with life. It is obvious that Kierkegaard thinks that the Christian faith, especially its central teaching of the God-man, opens up distinctive possibilities for authentic existence. It ought, therefore, to be subjectively appropriated, even though it is impossible to provide a theoretical account of how one person can be fully divine and fully human.

A word of caution is in order. Kierkegaard urges the individual to become a Christian, but it cannot be done legitimately with an eye cocked toward its practical benefits. The very effort to do so in a calculating way is self-defeating. "Whoever seeks to save his life will lose it" (Luke 17:33). Faith cannot be treated like a vitamin tablet. These benefits are not available to someone who thinks he ought to believe *in order* to experience authentic existence. In genuine faith there is no element of the "put on." The individual must first appropriate the truth in fear and trembling, knowing that it is objectively absurd. The benefits of authentic individuality may follow, but there can be no guarantee. Faith involves risk; but just for that reason it can open an individual to the possibility of peak experiences.

Kierkegaard's view of faith is not a "how to" manual. He is not providing sure-fire exercises for the acquisition of faith. His view may be summarized as follows:

1 Faith cannot, of course, be based on direct observation of God.
2 It cannot be based on rational inferences from the nature of the world.
3 The individual is confronted by the central Christian claim of the God-man as it is mediated by the Church. Given the fact that the claim cannot be resolved at the objective level, the individual, in responding to it with the effort of subjective appropriation, may experience the benefits of authentic existence. He should not be inhibited by scruples arising from the level of objective reason because objectivity is not applicable to this claim.

Kierkegaard's forging of a link between authentic existence and genuine faith is one of the most brilliant efforts in the history of religious thought. It is also highly problematical; three of its major difficulties will be dealt with in the next section.

A CRITICAL LOOK AT KIERKEGAARD

Kierkegaard's dramatic powers and rhetorical gifts persuade many readers of the validity of his outlook. The criticisms which follow are an effort to counteract his power by disrupting his dramatic fabric.

Did Jesus Claim that He Was God?

Kierkegaard's work, as we noted, was obsessively focused on the claim: "The Word was made flesh and dwelt among us." The meaning could only be discerned through the passionate subjectivity of faith. The power of Kierkegaard's rejection of the objective historical approach to the Bible is that he was able to discount the negative results of biblical research even before the enterprise of higher criticism hit its stride. I have presented his crucial reason for discounting it by pointing out that no historical details regarding Jesus of Nazareth could ever justify the conclusion that he was fully divine as well as fully human.

Kierkegaard is right. Even if the higher critics had been able to show that every miracle reported of Jesus had actually happened, it would not provide objective justification for the conclusion: "This man was God!" Yet Kierkegaard, in stressing this point, ignored an important issue—the question of whether Christianity is immune from the negative results of higher criticism.[81]

Historical research into the religious attitudes of the Jews of Jesus' time render it probable that Jesus never claimed to be divine. The Jews regarded the Messiah as an instrument of God but not as God himself. Jesus, as a Jew, would almost certainly have regarded it blasphemous to claim divinity, even if he did regard himself as the Messiah who had been awaited by the Jews for centuries. Kierkegaard, in accepting the God-man formula of Chalcedon, never challenged the dogma on historical grounds; rather, he spent a lifetime trying to fathom its meaning.

Kierkegaard's view of the God-man shows the danger of holding history in contempt when dealing with important issues. The result is to make—unwittingly—some dubious historical assumptions. Objective historical research shows that it is highly unlikely that the formula of Chalcedon bears any resemblance to claims made by the historical figure of Jesus of Nazareth.

Kierkegaard might have conceded that Jesus had never claimed to be divine and still played out his scheme of the subjective appropriation of this objective absurdity—but it would have been a futile procedure. Kierkegaard insists that the New Testament does not provide objectively validated details that can support the claim that Jesus of Nazareth was both human and divine. If he were also to concede the point that Jesus himself never claimed to be divine, he would have no reason to focus on Jesus as the God-man. In that case, the element of absurdity could be even better served by choosing someone else. Since Kierkegaard maintains that inwardness is intensified in direct proportion to the objective absurdity of the claim, focusing on Pontius Pilate would have yielded more absurdity. Because Pilate, unlike Jesus, did not display admirable characteristics nor did he leave us any great teachings. Therefore, even though Kierkegaard ignores the possibility, it does seem that the negative results of historical research into the Bible are important for his scheme.

The Christian Option Was Momentous, Live, and Forced for Kierkegaard

It never occurred to Kierkegaard to make a figure other than Jesus Christ the focus of his passionate subjectivity. He never considered dealing with the incarnation of the Hindu High God Vishnu in the figure of Krishna, and he wouldn't have done so if he'd known about it. He didn't deal with the problem of authentic inwardness in general terms. As he himself wrote, he was, from the beginning, a Christian author.[82] Kierkegaard was very explicit on this point. He addresses the following observation to one who has chosen Christ:

> . . . the only possible objection would be: but you might possibly have been saved in another way. To that he cannot answer. It is as though one were to say to someone in love, yes, but you might have fallen in love with another girl; to which he would have to answer: there is no answer to that, for I only know that she is my love. The moment a lover can answer that objection he is, by virtue of that very fact, not a lover: and if a believer can answer that objection he is, by virtue of that very fact, not a believer.[83]

In Kierkegaard's Denmark everyone was born a Lutheran Christian. Yet Kierkegaard claimed that in Denmark Christianity did not exist because everyone took his religion for granted. The population had a Christianity of total conformity and Kierkegaard tried to shake them up. The question he put before them was not one of deciding whether to be or not to be a Christian, rather, he challenged them to decide what kind of Christian they were going to be. He put a maximal intellectual strain on Christian claims in an effort to get the Christians of Denmark to take their faith seriously.

Today, Christianity exists in cultures that are primarily oriented to science. In many countries religion is not sponsored by the state, and even where it is, this sponsorship no longer means very much. The major challenges to Christianity today are intellectual. For many people it no longer remains what it inescapably was for Kierkegaard, namely, a momentous, live, and forced option. They are content to dismiss it as outmoded. Kierkegaard's strategy, therefore, makes it far easier for them to dismiss Christian claims than to take them seriously.

Kierkegaard's Absolute Paradox Is Really a Contradiction

Quine, as we noted, defines a paradox as "any conclusion that at first sounds absurd but that has an argument to sustain it" (see p. 157). If the argument yields a true conclusion, Quine claims that the paradox is veridical. "A veridical paradox," he writes, "packs a surprise but the surprise quickly dissipates itself as we ponder the proof."[84] There are many Kierkegaardian paradoxes which turn out to be veridical in Quine's sense. Kierkegaard's *Works of Love* pivots around one.[85] It is a sustained reflection on the commandment, "You shall love your neighbor as yourself" (Lev. 19:18; Mark 12:31). Kierkegaard reflects on the usual definition of love which involves a feeling of attraction for another person. He wonders at the absurdity of the Bible commanding us to feel because feelings are not subject to conscious control. He dissipates the surprise by analyzing love and showing that it is *not* based on a feeling of attraction. Love is basically the transfer to others of an attitude that we generally direct toward ourselves. Each one of us should realize that our own self is the only self we've got. No matter how often we let ourselves down we never give up on ourselves. Love is a transfer of this attitude to others; don't give up on the other person no matter how often he's offended you. Give him another chance just as—again and again and again—you give yourself another chance. Kierkegaard claims that this love is within our conscious control and therefore it is legitimate for the Bible to *command* us to display it. Jesus, then, can command us to love our enemies—persons to whom we are not only not attracted but persons we actually loathe.

Having presented an example of a legitimate veridical paradox in Kierkegaard, I now propose to show how radically his presentation of the central Christian paradox of the God-man differs from it. He calls the central Christian claim, that Jesus Christ is full God and full man, the absolute paradox. His use of the adjective "absolute" sets it apart from veridical paradoxes like the commandment to love your neighbor as yourself. In referring to the God-man Kierkegaard also uses the terms "absurdity" and "contradiction." He may interchange them, but they are not interchangeable. A great deal depends on whether the teaching about Christ's two natures is absurd (a shocker), a paradox (a shocker that communicates an important truth), or a contradiction (a logical impossibility).

Kierkegaard's position is not hard to understand, he pounds it home for approximately thirty pages of sustained polemic against speculative philosophers.[86] He insists that he is not out to correct the paradox. Thinkers who correct it use philosophy to show that the absolute paradox is not really absurd, it only seems to be so. Kierkegaard devoted a lifetime to explaining the paradox, showing just where the paradox lies and why it can only be appropriated in passionate subjectivity. "An explanation of the paradox makes it clear what the paradox is, removing any obscurity remaining; a correction takes the paradox away and makes it clear that there is no paradox."[87]

Kierkegaard refuses to take the paradox away. He is convinced that any argument that dissipates the surprise or the absurdity would make Christianity objectively probable, and it would eliminate the need for faith. "For the absurd is the object of faith, and the only object that can be believed."[88] In countless passages Kierkegaard claims that the absolute paradox is absurd because it embraces a contradiction. Briefly, he says it is absurd "because it involves the contradiction that something which can become historical *only in direct opposition to all human reason* has become historical."[89]

Kierkegaard, in his desperate effort to make the apathetic Christians of his native Denmark take Christianity seriously, formulates the central Christian claim as an outright contradiction. Ironically that makes his formulation of Christian truth impossible for us. No amount of passionately subjective appropriation can make sense of a "paradox" that is really a contradiction. Kierkegaard might as well urge us to attain authentic individuality by passionately appropriating the "paradox" of the three-sided square.

Defenders of Kierkegaard could challenge this criticism on the grounds that Kierkegaard's absolute paradox of the God-man cannot be known to involve a contradiction. A three-sided square is a contradiction because in Euclidian geometry a square is defined as being a four-sided figure and we cannot simultaneously affirm that a figure has four sides and that it does not have four sides. Kierkegaard insists that God and man are distinguished by an infinite qualitative difference. In that case, we cannot get them into the same frame of reference in order to see whether they contradict one another or not.

Kierkegaard might well have responded to this defense with the statement, "I can protect myself from my enemies, but God protect me from my friends!" Kierkegaard is a thinker who made strange moves, but he knew exactly what he was doing when he made them. For his scheme of a faith as subjectivity to work, his absolute paradox had to involve a *contradiction.*

If there is no contradiction involved, then the absolute paradox is what Quine calls a veridical or true paradox. Once we see the point, the element of absurdity disappears and we are no longer surprised by it. It follows that the individual who has made the leap of faith would no longer be involved in the effort to appropriate the paradox with passionate inwardness; he would understand it objectively. A crushing irony would result because at the very moment he became a Christian he would cease to have Christian inwardness, that is, the utterly strenuous inner life of the genius who ventures onto uncharted waters. Kierkegaard, however, preserves the contradiction. He insists that the absurdity is not eliminated even after the individual is involved in the life of faith. He made the point in a number of passages:

> If I wish to preserve myself in faith I must constantly be intent upon holding fast the objective uncertainty, so as to remain out upon the deep, over seventy thousand fathoms of water, still preserving my faith.
>
> . . . it does not seem to be the case that probability increases as faith is intensified in inwardness; rather the reverse.
>
> The fruit of having been for a long time a believer is . . . a more intensive inwardness in faith.[90]

These statements must be set against others in which Kierkegaard says that after the leap of faith the central Christian affirmation is no longer absurd:

> After the believer believes, the absurd is no longer absurd—faith changes it. . . . to become a believer everyone must be alone with the absurd. While naturally it is a matter of course that for him who believes it is not absurd—faith transforms it.[91]

The apparent contradiction between these two sets of statements can be resolved by noting that they refer to different levels of truth. At the objective level the absurdity of the Christian affirmation of the God-man continues to impress the believer even after the leap of faith, indeed, it is intensified. At the subjective level it is swept up into the process of appropriating this absurdity which, as we have seen, is the authentic mode of human existence.

Kierkegaard deliberately chose to present the absolute paradox of Christianity as a contradiction because he insisted that a contradiction cannot be understood and thereby eliminated. He says that Christianity is not an imperfect sketch for an ideal philosophy that is intended to be reviewed, discussed, reworked, and completed by philosophers.[92] It is a mystery that cannot be explained by even the most brilliant minds. God in Christ offers authentic individuality to all men and not just to important philosophers. If the paradox could be explained away by great minds, then Christianity would really be directed to the associations of philosophers. Kierkegaard is persuaded that the simple man, who is astonished at the absurdity and tries to cope with it, is closer to God in Christ than the learned philosophers and theologians who write books about it.

Kierkegaard's absolute paradox is a permanent absurdity because it involves a contradiction. To eliminate the contradiction would benefit his scheme logically at the price of ruining it functionally.

Kierkegaard knew what he was doing, but in the final analysis his scheme cannot work. He moves from the lower level of objective truth to the higher level of subjectivity. Yet this move from the lower to the higher level of truth can only be justified when the issue is one which, as William James put it, "cannot by its nature be decided on intellectual grounds." When we are confronted with a contradiction, we certainly can decide the issue on objective intellectual grounds. We know that the statement in question, in this case the absolute paradox of the God-man, cannot be true.

Kierkegaard did not accidentally lapse into the contradiction. It was not an aberration from his authentic position. On the contrary, he proudly paraded the contradiction because it is integral to his understanding of Christian authenticity. In that case, the absolute paradox is not an objective uncertainty; it is an objective impossibility. Therefore, it cannot be true, subjectively, or in any other sense.

Chapter 9

Rudolf Bultmann: Sin and Grace, Revelation and History

In Rudolf Bultmann (b.1884), Kierkegaard found a strange disciple. Kierkegaard was an original. A man of moods, who broke with the crowd and railed against the conformity of Lutheran Denmark. He reveled in paradoxes and drove language to the limits of rational comprehensibility. His writings ranged widely over the entire range of culture—literature, music, art, and the drama. Bultmann is a German theologian and biblical scholar whose writings are directed to the seminaries of Protestantism. They are less original and less fascinating than Kierkegaard's, but they are also less confusing. Bultmann picks up the central Kierkegaardian themes and uses his biblical expertise to relate them to the authoritative texts of Christendom.

Bultmann follows Kierkegaard's lead in expounding faith as an activity of participants. Inwardness is also central to Bultmann, although he spells it out in categories drawn from *Being and Time* (the German original *Sein und Zeit* appeared in 1927) rather than in Kierkegaardian terms. It was written by Martin Heidegger (b.1884), an existentialist whose subsequent work has had an important influence on religious thinkers. *Being and Time* was, however, regarded as atheistic, and it influenced Jean Paul Sartre (b.1905), the French existentialist, whose atheism is emphatic and aggressive. Since Heidegger himself was greatly influenced by Kierkegaard, in adapting the categories of *Being and Time* to the purposes of Christian thought Bultmann was not wandering very far afield.

One of Bultmann's most distinctive contributions to religious existentialism is his explicit consideration of the issue of religion and science. He passionately adhered to the faith of his fathers, but he unflinchingly faced the implications of the scientific revolution.

BULTMANN'S PROGRAM OF DEMYTHOLOGIZING THE CHRISTIAN FAITH

Bultmann is, as Kierkegaard was not, a professional New Testament scholar. He mastered the scholarly apparatus for the historical and literary research into these authoritative texts of the Christian faith. He is also a believing Christian, who has mastered theology. One of the main sources of his importance is that he has used these formidable talents to work out a basic principle of biblical interpretation (*hermeneutic* is the technical term).

Bultmann does not flinch from the fact that the rise of science makes a crucial difference to the status of the Bible. He accepts the fact that people of our day are not apt to be impressed with the Gospels as a factual account of the miracles. Most of us do not believe that Jesus could walk on water, feed thousands of people with a few loaves of bread and a small number of fish, and raise a man from the dead. No amount of preaching, pontificating, or scolding will change that. The reasons have already been stated in the chapter on miracles, and they represent a good statement of the thinking that lies behind Bultmann's views (see Chapt. 4). In response to this situation Bultmann devised his *demythologizing* approach. It involves translating objective terms into existential categories.

The Importance and Meaning of Science

Bultmann talks a great deal about what modern man can and cannot believe as a result of the development of science. An important, and by no means untypical, statement is: "Man's knowledge and mastery of the world have advanced to such an extent through science and technology that it is no longer possible for anyone seriously to hold the New Testament view of the world—in fact, there is hardly anyone who does."[93]

Critics have often thought of Bultmann as having swallowed the scientific worldview whole. They accuse him of thinking that science has come up with the last word on what is and what can be.[94] Their criticism is misguided. Bultmann is sophisticated in his treatment of science. He does not regard the conclusions in force at any particular moment as final. He does not think that the methods of science are the only, or even the best way, of approaching human experience. He is, however, certain that the scientific method is the rational way of finding out what actually happens in nature. Furthermore, he accepts scientifically oriented standards of believability which determine his judgments of what *could* have happened in history.

Bultmann is convinced that however much we may have to alter our techniques of investigation in exploring different subjects, the basic principles of investigation will remain the same.

> The science of today is no longer the same as it was in the nineteenth century, and to be sure, all the results of science are relative. . . . The main point, however, is not the concrete results of scientific research and the contents of a worldview, but the method of thinking from which worldviews follow. . . . modern man acknowledges as reality only such phenomena or events as are comprehensible within the framework of the rational order of the universe. He does not acknowledge miracles because they do not fit into this lawful order. When a strange or marvellous accident occurs, he does not rest until he has found a rational cause.[95]

Bultmann thinks that a Christian who enjoys the benefits of technology is totally inconsistent if he then denies the basic assumptions of science. "It is impossible to use electric lights and the wireless and to avail ourselves of modern medical and surgical discoveries, and at the same time to believe in the New Testament world of daemons and spirits."[96] The word "impossible" is too strong. If it were impossible, Bultmann would not have to make the point. Actually, he thinks that Christians who accept the miraculous accounts of the Bible as literally true compartmentalize their lives. In ordinary affairs, they are moderns who use the most advanced products of technology; when they turn to religious matters, they try to pretend that they are living in biblical times.

Bultmann summons human beings to be faithful Christians, but he wants them to be faithful as modern people who live in a culture dominated by the rise of science. In order to do so, they must face up to a fact that is of overriding importance. The New Testament, in which the glad tidings of the coming of the Christ are proclaimed, was written before the rise of science. It is dominated on every page by an outlook which is pre-scientific. It is manifested without self-consciousness on the part of the New Testament authors because it is part of the climate of opinion of their age. A climate of opinion is pervasive and most people at a given time share it. Thus, the assumptions—involved in a pre-scientific world, for instance—are used in evaluating arguments; they are not in themselves argued for.

The view of the world has changed drastically from biblical times to the present. In biblical times supernatural occurrences were regarded as common; today, for reasons that have already been given, we seek natural explanations for all happenings that are observed (see Chapt. 4). It is important to realize, as far as Bultmann is concerned, that the shift from the biblical view of the world to the contemporary one is the *occasion* for demythologizing; it is not the *reason* for it.[97] By "occasion," Bultmann means the historical circumstances that stimulated Christians to think about the problem of communicating their message to people with a scientifically oriented outlook.[98] Yet Bultmann heatedly denies that the reason for demythologizing the New Testament is to make it easier for modern man to believe it. The reason for demythologizing the New Testament is that the central message of Christianity, the *kerygma* (from the Greek, meaning "proclamation") is independent of the mythological framework in which it comes to us.[99]

> The purpose of demythologization is not to make religion more acceptable to modern man by trimming the traditional biblical texts, but to make clearer to modern man what the Christian Faith is. He must be confronted with the issue of decision, [and] provoked to decision by the fact that the stumbling block to faith, the *skandalon* [offense] is peculiarly disturbing to man in general, not only to modern man (modern man being only one species of man). . . . It is by striving to clarify the meaning of faith that demythologization leads man to the issue of decision. . . .[100]

The kerygma, the basis of the Christian faith, is the proclamation that in Jesus Christ, God has acted decisively for the benefit of humanity.[101] It is what separates Christianity from any other religion, including Judaism, from which it was spawned.

Bultmann justifies his claim that the kerygma can be separated from its mythological framework by appealing to the New Testament itself. He claims that in the Letters of Paul and in the Gospel and Letters of John, we find the beginnings of demythologizing.[102] These New Testament authors did not go all the way because they themselves shared the mythological worldview of the time. They were not made self-conscious about it by the advent of science. Yet in his *Theology of the New Testament*, Bultmann portrays them as struggling to free the kerygma from mythology.[103]

Bultmann is convinced that the Christian message is not about miracles and other supernatural happenings. Jesus happened to live in a pre-scientific age, so his message, and the message about him, comes to us in a pre-scientific framework. The connection is accidental.[104] As far as Bultmann is concerned, there is no more need to adopt the mythological worldview in order to accept the Christian message than there is to adopt Ptolemaic astronomy in order to appreciate Sophocles' *Oedipus the King*.

Bultmann is very self-conscious about his method and he views demythologizing as a total approach to the New Testament.[105] Since the mythological worldview was pervasive, it influences every page of the New Testament, not merely such incidents as Jesus feeding thousand of people with a few fishes and loaves of bread. According to Bultmann, every verse of the New Testament must be checked in order to determine its mythological content and then to demythologize it. I will illustrate this by means of his treatment of the resurrection.

According to the New Testament Jesus died on the cross, was taken to a tomb, and placed within it. The tomb was sealed with a great rock and Roman soldiers guarded it. (Mark 15:40–47; Matt. 27:55–66). When the sabbath was over some of the women among his followers went to the tomb, hoping that they could enter and anoint his body with perfumed oils. The tomb was open. An angel appeared to them and told them that Jesus had risen and that he would appear again to his disciples (Mark 16; Matt. 27; Luke 24). Subsequently, there are varied accounts of his appearances to the disciples, including one in which doubting Thomas touches the wound in his side in order to verify the fact that it is really Jesus, the crucified one, who is appearing (John 20:24–29).

In Bultmann's view, this version of the resurrection is mythological because it makes the question of Christ's significance pivot around empirical evidence. The stories of the risen Christ's appearances to his followers provide observable evidence of his resurrection. It is checked out by three of the senses: they see him, hear him, and in one instance, they touch him. In turn, these observations provide indirect evidence that confirms the claim that Jesus Christ was fully divine as well as fully human.

Bultmann insists that this kind of talk is mythological because it deals with God in a way that is only appropriate to dealing with the *observable* aspect of human beings. Bultmann thinks that this account is incredible to modern man. He regards it as legendary just as he regards the story of Elijah and the priests of Baal as legendary. Bultmann writes: "An historical fact which involves a resurrection from the dead is utterly inconceivable." Shortly after that he refers to "the incredibility of a mythical event like the resuscitation of a corpse—for that is what resurrection means, as is shown by the fact that the risen Lord is apprehended by the physical senses."106

Bultmann finds the coming to life of a corpse unbelievable and inconceivable because he takes science seriously. In one sense he misunderstands it. No extraordinary occurrence can be ruled out absolutely, in the way that Bultmann rules out the possibility of the return of life to a corpse. Yet Bultmann makes another point which is more effective. Even if such an utterly extraordinary happening were to take place, a person with a scientifically oriented outlook would not regard it as a miracle in the New Testament sense of the term. It would be a naturally observable occurrence for which a natural explanation would be sought. As Bultmann puts it: "When a strange or marvellous accident occurs, he [modern man] does not rest until he has found a rational cause."107

At this point, it is important to reemphasize Bultmann's view that science is the occasion and not the reason for demythologizing. Bultmann's main objection to the mythological account of the resurrection is not that it is hard for modern man to believe that it happened. His main objection is that it is religiously inappropriate. It is characteristic of magic to affirm a god who makes his activities directly observable to human beings. Authentic faith, by contrast, involves risk. As we have seen in connection with Kierkegaard, it involves believing even against the objective evidence.

In summary, Bultmann rejects the fundamentalist approach to the Bible on two grounds: (1) It cannot be believed by people whose standards of credibility have been shaped by science. (2) It ought not to be adopted by people who understand the nature of Christian faith because fundamentalism tries to make belief in God more a matter of objective verification than existential risk.

EXISTENTIALISM IS AN AUTHENTIC MEDIUM FOR THE KERYGMA

Bultmann is consistent. First he purges the Bible of myth, then he interprets it in existential terms. Although Bultmann is a leading representative of religious existentialism, his style is very much that of the professional theologian. Most of his illustrations appear in the form of verses from the New Testament, as in the following:

> We are free to give ourselves to God because he has given up himself for us. "Herein is love, not that we loved God, but that he loves us, and sent his Son to be the propitiation for our sins" (1 John 4:10). "We love, because he first loved us" (1 John 4:19). The classic statement of this self-commitment

of God, which is the ground of our self-commitment, is to be found in Rom. 8.32: "God spared not his Son, but delivered him up for us; how shall he not also with him freely give us all things?" Compare the Johannine text: "God so loved the world that he gave his only begotten Son, that whosoever believeth in him should not perish, but have eternal life" (John 3:16).[108]

On rare occasions Bultmann tries illustrations from life, as when he refers to love as the kind of relation that is relevant to the existentialists' message. Yet, even these illustrations are general and abstract.

> I have said that faith grows out of the encounters which are the substance of our personal lives as historical lives. Its meaning is readily understood when we reflect upon the simple phenomena of our personal lives. The love of my friend, my wife, my children, meets me genuinely only here and now as an event. Such love cannot be observed by objective methods but only by personal experience and response.[109]

Bultmann's style restricts his appeal to theologians and other professional students of religion who find him provocative. In an effort to communicate his point of view to nonspecialists, I should like to present a sustained illustration that will put some flesh on Bultmann's program of reinterpreting the kerygma from mythological to existential categories.

Man as Sinner: Self-Encapsulated, Self-Glorying, and Self-Sufficient

Bultmann is primarily an interpreter of the New Testament. He has presented its understanding of man in a few brief strokes that are apt to jar most readers.

> The New Testament addresses man as one who is through and through a self-assertive rebel who knows from bitter experience that the life he actually lives is not his authentic life, and that he is totally incapable of achieving that life by his own efforts. In short he is a totally fallen being. This means, in the language of the New Testament, that man is a sinner.[110]

What Bultmann is driving at may come through if I develop a portrait of a good and solid citizen of contemporary American suburbia.

Jared Holmes, a successful hardworking lawyer, is proud of himself, his firm, proud of his family—and justifiably so. He lives in an elegant suburb, unscarred by dilapidated houses or by poor people, the handicapped, or the very old. He's got it made. He has an attractive wife who is an elegant hostess and four attractive children.

Jared has ambitions and plans for all of them. He knows the schools he wants his sons to go to and the corporations he wants them to lead. He knows the schools he wants his daughters to attend and the kind of men he wants them to marry. The future is tightly planned. His days are tightly organized. He gets a lot done. Time is his most precious commodity. After dinner he's either socially engaged or he works on his briefs for coming cases. Jared contributes money to many charities and other good causes, but not time. He is a regular churchgoer but attends out of respectability rather than conviction.

Jared Holmes—not the thief, the rapist, or the adulterer—is Bultmann's self-assertive rebel, the sinner who is cut off from authentic life. This is a startling claim. Far from being what most people regard as a sinner, he is a perfect example of what most of us would think of as virtuous. To appreciate the point it is important to realize that the greatest Christian interpreters of sin have never identified it with immoral acts, but with a state of alienation from God. The interpreters have differed only in the terms they have used in spelling out the alienation. Bultmann writes: "The primal sin is not an inferior morality, but rather the understanding of oneself in terms of oneself and the attempt to secure one's existence by means of what one himself establishes, by means of one's own accomplishments. It is the boasting and self-confidence of the natural man."[111] In order to spell this out in human terms, I shall consider some problems that the solid citizen I've portrayed might run into.

When Jared Holmes comes home he builds a castle of privacy around himself, by preparing a martini and withdrawing into a newspaper. It's understandable; he's been coping with people all day. The problem is that so has his wife. She's been coping with the children and now could use adult companionship. But she doesn't get it. Furthermore, Jared, though proud of his oldest son, treats him like one of his charities, giving him lots of money but little time. Although Jared justifies himself by pointing to his achievements, his estrangement from his family is intensified. His son does not understand his father's mind, only the ambitions that his father has for him. In the college of his father's choice, the son learns about the price that the blacks and others pay for American suburban affluence. He gets involved with radical groups and rebels against his family's way of life. Unfortunately, he suffers a nervous breakdown and comes home in a terrible state. His father, though worried about him, is also exasperated. "What went wrong?" he asks. "I gave him everything!"

Jared Holmes, this good citizen of American suburbia, is not a man who is consciously trying to harm anyone. Quite the contrary. It is simply ironical that the American virtues which are so highly praised—the boy scout emphasis on self-reliance and good works—often turn out to have devastating effects. The suburbanite lives in isolation from the terrible ghettos of the cities of America. Bultmann's phrase for this, borrowed from Heidegger, is "shut-upness." The suburb is sealed off from the suffering of the blacks, the poor, the aged, and the diseased. Bultmann deals with situations of this kind in terms of the Christian teaching of *original sin*. ". . . it means simply that we come into our present situation as people seeking to make our own way; that we have a history and we exist in a world which was and is governed by this view of community, and that view governs us as a matter of course; each seeks his own, and nobody pays serious heed to his neighbor."[112] Our lawyer did not create his society or his pattern of life. He is not personally a bad man. Yet his son, when exposed to the facts of American life, recoils from his pattern of life in horror and judges his father harshly.

Bultmann makes a great deal of St. Paul's rejection of self-glorification. In St. Paul's case it was glorying in his ability to know and to obey the Law, the Law of Moses. It was a rightful source of pride, but Bultmann claims that it became sinful because it led to the illusion that he could establish a right relation to God under his own will power.[113] Any genuine achievement can be turned into a source of self-glorification in which the individual thinks that he can handle reality on his own. "In this case the objective phenomena of the world, which in their objective nature are neutral, take on the character of the 'flesh' [Paul's term for the rebellious element in man], as soon as he conceives of himself and his life from the angle of the world, and seeks to attain his security on this basis. But it is precisely this—seeking to establish his own security—that is sinful."[114]

The sin is not the rightful pride the man takes in his achievements. The sin is the attitudes that follow from it. Bultmann calls them self-glorification because the individual involved comes to think too much of his achievements. He begins to boast about them and to imagine that he can handle all future problems by the same techniques. Yet Bultmann reminds us: "There are encounters and destinies which man cannot master. He cannot secure endurance from his works. His life is fleeting and its end is death."[115]

Bultmann thinks that Heidegger and other philosophers have been able to see this. That is why he can take over many of Heidegger's terms. But Bultmann insists that existentialism as a philosophy cannot help man to get out of the situations it analyzes.[116] In order to understand why, we shall have to consider grace, another central Christian teaching that is emphasized throughout Bultmann's work.

Grace: The Encounter with God-in-Christ Opens Man to Authentic Existence

Bultmann claims that existential thinking can describe the agonies of inauthentic existence, but that it cannot deliver men from them. He claims that "in practice authentic life becomes possible only when man is delivered from himself. It is the claim of the New Testament that this is exactly what has happened. This is precisely the meaning of that which was wrought in Christ. At the very point where man can do nothing, God steps in and acts—indeed he has acted already—on man's behalf."[117]

The act of God in Christ is an act in which God takes the initiative. It is an act that is offered independently of merit. The word "grace" suggests an outgoing spontaneity that benefits another person without making them feel unduly indebted.

In the mythological view grace is regarded as an invisible fluid that is miraculously infused into the soul of the sinner. Grace picks up the sinner's spirits as an injection of Adrenalin might pick him up physically. Bultmann's existential version is more subtle, so much so, that it is hard to get hold of. I will try to explain it by continuing the story of Jared Holmes the solid-citizen-sinner.

His son's rejection of the family's way of life jolts him. He is not an evil man. He wants to do something about his son, but the only thing he knows how to do is to plan and organize. He tries to plan his way into better relationships with his family. But his time-conscious, programmed planning is the disease. His outings and other forms of activities which are always overly planned don't help matters; they only make them worse. Yet, he can't help doing things that way. And even though he knows that he is, somehow responsible, he can't diagnose it. Jared can't believe that working hard to provide his family with material goods, cultural advantages, and social status is in any way a bad thing. He cannot feel that he has done anything wrong. He goes to church and the New Testament lesson for that day is the story of the rich fool (Luke 12:16–20):

> There was a rich man whose land yielded heavy crops. He debated with himself: "What am I to do? I have not the space to store my produce." And he said: "This is what I will do. I will pull down my storehouses and build them bigger. I will collect in them all my corn and other goods, and then say to myself, 'Man, you have plenty of good things laid by, enough for many years: take life easy, eat, drink, and enjoy yourself.'" But God said to him, "You fool, this very night you must surrender your life; you have made your money—who will get it now?"

The story strikes home. The solid citizen does realize that he's been trying to control things in every way. He hasn't let go, not in his own life, and not with his family. He's tried to dominate destiny.

Nothing magical has happened here, Jared has not been miraculously spared from death. He has not seen the heavens open up to disclose a heavenly vision. He has just been addressed by words, and through them, he begins to see that he has tried to control life by clinging to property and status. He has used his legal talents to carve out a niche for himself and his family, and he's proud of that. At the same time, he's lost all sense of the complexity of his own personality and drives; furthermore, he's even neglected his family.[118]

The insights don't come flooding in all at once. He picks up clues and backs away from their implications with another string of defenses about working hard to discharge his many obligations. But the seeds of a changed perspective have been planted. Jared can see that the success he has achieved through his genuine talents and hard work have not opened him to fresh possibilities of human experience. On the contrary, he has tried to insure the fact that the future will be like the past by forcing everyone around him to conform to his program.

A stimulating lecture by a philosopher might, in Bultmann's view, have the same capacity to alert Jared Holmes to his basic problems. Bultmann insists that the distinctive aspect of Christian faith, which sets it apart from mere philosophy, is the presence of a power, a liberating power. Neither philosophical nor psychological analysis can do it. Jared can only be liberated by a love that takes the initiative, a love that pulls him out of himself. Bultmann claims that the new element of love in the New Testament is not that man is commanded to love his neighbor as himself; he knew that already. "It is new, however, insofar as it has now become a possibility for man—thereby, namely, that God has loved us in Christ and that we therefore come into our now as those who are loved and thus are free to live in return."[119] Bultmann then quotes two critical verses of the New Testament. The first verse is from Romans (5:8) in which St. Paul declares that Christ died for men while they were yet sinners. God's gracious initiative is emphasized. Men did not earn God's loving sacrifice by ceasing to sin; they encountered God's love for them in the midst of their sin. The other verse is from the First Letter of John (4:19): "We love because he first loved us." Here again the gracious initiative of God is stressed. The love that human beings direct toward God is a response to his love.

What generally happens when people experience the love of God is not astonishing. It is not necessarily a mystical sense of union, or a vision like that of Isaiah in the Temple. For most people the change is like coming alive in an aesthetic sense. A person who has been bored by the Beethoven quartets for years may undergo a change and find them meaningful and momentous.

The sense of God's love, mediated through preaching and through books, may, in similar fashion, come alive. When it does, it can move strong men to tears. Yet the important change is an inner one. Nothing may take place on the surface. The lawyer who suddenly becomes receptive to the message may seem, on that occasion, to be the same as usual to the people who generally sit near him in church.

Now we are in a position to understand the role of the resurrection in Bultmann's demythologized Christianity. He breaks with the notion that it was an event that could be observed with the senses, a coming to life of a corpse and its leaving the tomb. He reinterprets it in existential terms by linking the resurrection with the cross as God's decisive and saving act in Christ. The only way it registers authentically is for the believer to hear it and to have his life changed by it. This is an existential response. It is subjective and not a happening that took place "out there" in an objectively verifiable sense. Neither the resurrection itself nor its effect on the believer is observable, nor are there generally accepted procedures for attaining agreement on interpreting these matters. Therefore, it is not objective in the second sense of the term that we considered earlier (see pp. 92f.).

> This is the way in which the cross is proclaimed. It is always proclaimed together with the resurrection. Christ meets us in the preaching as one crucified and risen. He meets us in the word of preaching and nowhere else. The faith of Easter is just this—faith in the word of preaching.[120]

Bultmann rejects all accounts of the risen Christ's appearances to the disciples as legendary. Faith is faith in the power for a new capacity for living that is made possible by God-in-Christ.

God's love comes to man while he is still a sinner. This has been an integral part of the Christian message from the beginning. St. Paul wrote: "God was in Christ reconciling the world to himself, no longer counting men's misdeeds against them" (2 Cor. 5:19). We have seen that the emphasis on God's gracious initiative is, from the logical standpoint, a needed counterweight to Kierkegaard's emphasis on the leap of faith, and I should note that Kierkegaard himself provides it.[121]

The relation between God's gracious initiative and man's response has baffled Christian thinkers from the beginning. It was a problem for St. Paul and subsequently for all the theologians of Christendom. On the one hand, we have teachings concerning the initiative of an all-powerful and all-knowing God that seem to cancel out freedom. On the other hand, there is the undeniable sense of freedom that all human beings experience in moments of decision, which is indispensable to the notion of moral responsibility. Christian thinkers often spell out the evidence on both sides of the issues of grace and freedom and affirm both teachings without reconciling them in rational terms. Bultmann's statement is typical of this trend. "There is an awareness in faith that when it occurs—that is, when there is a free decision for God—God is being allowed to act on it."[122] Bultmann here echoes St. Paul's statement: "You must work out your own salvation in fear and trembling; for it is God who works within you inspiring both the will and the deed, for his own chosen purpose" (Phil. 2:12–13).

Grace, as Bultmann uses the term, is the moment when man encounters God's love in Christ. His life is then changed.

Faith: Living Authentically with Openness to the Future

As Bultmann understands it, in the Christian scheme of things grace and faith are inextricably involved with one another. Grace is the moment of the I-You encounter with God-in-Christ when faith is born; faith is the living out of the relation to God-in-Christ that was begun in the religious experience. Bultmann writes that "to believe [in the sense of Christian Faith] . . . is qualitatively different from accepting a certain number of propositions."[123] Here is one of the basic distinctions of religious existentialists. They insist that faith is not a matter of objectively assenting the truth of a proposition in the way that one assents to the truth of the statement, "Dwight Eisenhower was re-elected president of the United States in 1956." Faith is a process; it is a *how* not a *what*. Actually, as we have seen, in relation to Kierkegaard, for religious existentialists it is more accurate to say that faith is a *what* (the content of Christian belief) that is meaningless unless it is appropriated with the right *how* ("passionate inwardness") (see p. 156). Bultmann appeals to ordinary experience in an effort to sharpen the contrast. "A theory about friendship and love will not help me to exhaust their potentialities and to experience them, but in them as an individual I have to prove myself. I have *my* life to live, as I have *my* death to die."[124]

In presenting authentic attitudes to life and death, Bultmann demythologizes the *eschaton*, the future fulfillment that is supposed to come at the end of history. He thinks that the mythological picture of Christ's second coming, followed by the last judgment cannot be believed because it involves logical confusions. The *eschaton* is, mythologically speaking, an event at the end of time, which is an incoherent notion because when we try to think of an event as the final event at the end of time, we inevitably think of it as inside the time sequence.[125] A child who is told of these final events will naturally ask: "And then what happened?" Bultmann demythologizes the view of the *eschaton* by thinking of it as the event of entering into faith. He adds Heideggerian terms explaining that the individual is now open to new possibilities for authentic existence. The difference between Heidegger's philosophy and

Christian faith is that Heidegger can tell the individual that he ought to face the dreadful anxieties of the future with resoluteness. Man ought not to let anxiety make him a prisoner of the past. "Faith includes free and complete openness to the future."[126] Existential philosophy, however, does not give him the power to make this teaching good in his life.

Bultmann spells out what he means by openness to the future in terms of a series of verses from the First Letter of St. Paul to the Corinthians:[127] "The time we live in will not last long. While it lasts, married men should be as if they had no wives; mourners should be as if they had nothing to grieve them, the joyful as if they did not rejoice; buyers must not count on keeping what they buy, nor those who use the world's wealth on using it to the full. For the whole frame of this world is passing away" (1 Cor. 7:29–31).

It is clear that St. Paul's statement contains mythological elements. He expects a final end to time as we know it. Bultmann reinterprets the passage existentially. The time that is being considered is the life of the individual. While he is in a faithful relation to God, he must affirm the ordinary relations of life such as marriage, mourning, business matters, and the rest, but he must sit loose to them. What Bultmann is driving at may become clearer if we return to the concrete illustration of the suburban lawyer.

Encountering God-in-Christ was not only a source of understanding. Jared Holmes felt a new power to drop the old patterns by which he tried to control the future. He no longer forced his family to accommodate themselves to his routine, as though he had a God-given right to control every one of the twenty-four hours of the day. Very often, when coming home, he would get involved in an unexpected game with his children, or in a conversation with his wife. Remarkably, after doing this for a while, he found that he enjoyed it more than his old martini and newspaper pattern.

He was still deeply concerned with the well being of every member of his family, but his love now had a looseness that it had never had before. He no longer felt that his children had to conform to the pattern of his ambitions. He loved them and related to them but with an element of detachment that enabled him to treat them as if they were not his children. He could treat them as individuals and personalities with destinies of their own. This is a form of verification.

Jared Holmes now gives his family more time and behaves in a more outgoing way. He cannot, however, prove that he has really changed inwardly or that the change is the result of God's love for him. Friends who know him well might insist that he has not really changed and that he is still trying to manipulate people. That he spends more time with his family could be regarded as a new trick. No objective verification is attainable.

Becoming a faithful Christian is not, in Bultmann's view, something dramatic that happens to a person and brings a full guarantee that he will live happily ever after. He has to keep working at it in order not to fall back into his old habits. "In other words, the decision of faith is never final; it needs constant renewal in every fresh situation."[128]

God's Actions as Analogically rather than Mythologically Understood

Barbarous technical terms have a way of catching on. "Demythologizing" is a good example. Many people are familiar with this term without realizing that it is only one aspect of Bultmann's program of a thorough reinterpretation of the New Testament. A more basic existential aspect of Bultmann's program is his understanding of the actions of God in analogical rather than mythological terms. He characterizes mythological language about God as language that deals with God in terms that are only appropriately used when dealing with observable beings. Mythological language speaks of God, the heavenly Father, and of Jesus Christ as seated at his right hand. God is treated as though he were locatable at a specific point in space.

In analogical language God's acts are presented in existential terms, which, as Bultmann understands it, means in ways that are unobservable *in principle.* Bultmann leans heavily on the point that a body is physical and, therefore, observable, but that the attitudes of a person, such as friendship, love, and trust are not. In Buber's terminology, observable features of persons, like the color of their eyes, are I-It. Personal characteristics, like trustworthiness, which are disclosed in I-You relations, are correlated with observable behavior like smiles and frowns. Yet the characteristics cannot be regarded as being nothing more than observable patterns of behavior (see pp. 127f.). This sort of analysis underlies Bultmann's statement about God as "Father."

> Especially in the conception of God as Father the mythological sense vanished long ago. We can understand the meaning of the term Father as applied to God by considering what it means when we speak to our fathers or when children speak to us as their fathers. As applied to God the physical import of the term father has disappeared completely; it expresses a purely personal relationship. It is in this analogical sense that we speak of God as Father.[129]

We can now understand why Jared Holmes could not prove the reality of his encounter with God-in-Christ to himself or to anyone else. The encounter, as analogically understood, is purely existential; it has no physical or objective aspect corresponding to it. Bultmann, too, sees the encounter with God as with one who is exclusively You and who has no I-It aspect at all.

An even more important implication of Bultmann's distinction between analogical and mythological knowledge about God relates to the matter of verification. In the mythological scheme it would be appropriate to check on God's personal qualities by means of observable tests in the way that Elijah proposed the test of fire (see p. 43). In the analogical scheme this kind of checking would be utterly inappropriate. There is no way of knowing whether God is really acting lovingly or not. One has the experience and lives by faith.

> The only way to preserve the unworldly transcendental character of the divine activity is to regard it not as an interference in worldly happenings, but something accomplished *in* them in such a way that the closed weft of history as it presents itself to objective observation is left undisturbed. To every other eye than the eye of faith the action of God is hidden. Only the "natural" happening is generally visible and ascertainable. In it is accomplished the hidden act of God.[130]

The friends of the suburban lawyer could only deal with the changes in his attitude and way of life in nonreligious terms. They could only see his behavior and hear his remarks. They could not experience his existential encounter with God-in-Christ. They might have thought of the change in Freudian terms, and he would not have been able to prove that they were wrong. He could only bear witness to his encounter with God in existential terms. He could not point to God independently of that encounter.

Bultmann realizes that the inability to point to God in objective terms opens him to the charge of reducing God to the status of an idea, a figment of the imagination, or to some other purely subjective status. He vehemently denies this implication. "When we say that faith alone, the faith which is aware of the divine encounter, can speak of God . . . it by no means follows that God has no real existence apart from the believer or the act of believing."[131] In other words, Bultmann, like all religious existentialists, thinks that God is objective in the first sense of the term that we considered, namely, as an independently existing reality (see pp. 91f.). To speak of God in purely existential terms is not to speak of one who is less than the transcendent God of the Judeo-Christian tradition. God is a power who is independent of human power and of human awareness, even though human beings can only know him subjectively, that is, through existential encounters.

God is the mysterious, enigmatic power that meets us *in* the world and *in* time. His *transcendence* is that of someone always having power over the temporal and the eternal: it is the transcendence of the power which creates and sets limits to our life.[132]

Bultmann's Version of the Two-Level Theory of Truth

Christian faith is not subject to objective demonstration. "It cannot be proved by logic or demonstrated by an appeal to factual evidence."[133] Bultmann, then, clearly sees that Christian faith cannot be made good in terms of the two paradigms of knowledge acknowledged by the positivists—the analytic and the synthetic. "The man who wishes to believe in God as his God must realize that he has nothing in his hand on which to base his faith. He is suspended in mid-air and cannot demand proof of the Word which addresses him. . . . Security can be found only by abandoning all security."[134] This is Bultmann's version of Kierkegaard's man of faith who is suspended over 70,000 fathoms of water. Bultmann, too, sees that man must risk all on the subjective appropriation of this objective uncertainty. The lawyer must abandon the domineering patterns which were the source of his security. He must take the risk of finding a different type, namely, the subjective security that might come from faith in God and a more authentic relation to his family. Yet a great risk is involved. If our lawyer abandons the old patterns of his false security and lets go, there is no guarantee that he will find himself in a more gratifying relation to God and to his family.

Bultmann concludes his famous essay, "The New Testament and Mythology" by stressing the objective insecurity. "It is precisely its immunity from proof which secures the Christian proclamation against the charge of being mythological."[135] There is a corollary to this that Bultmann shares with all religious existentialists. Faith is also beyond *disproof* by objective means, whether by logic or by factual evidence. This claim will be dealt with in the context of Bultmann's treatment of history.

HISTORY AND THE TWO-LEVEL THEORY OF TRUTH

One of the most fascinating aspects of twentieth-century religious thought is its emphasis on God's acts in history. One reason for this emphasis is defensive: scientists have done such a good job of explaining what happens in nature and why that it seemed superfluous to appeal to God in order to explain regularities like the course of the stars in the heavens or unusual occurrences like earthquakes or comets. The situation was captured neatly by the encounter of Napoleon with the astronomer Laplace. When the Emperor commented that in the astronomer's vast tome there was no mention of the divine author of nature, he replied: "That, Sire, is a hypothesis of which I have no need."

By pre-empting the domain of observable occurrences scientists forced religious thinkers to turn to other directions. One of them is history. Of course, history also involves observable events, but historians find it far more difficult to achieve agreement than do physicists and other natural scientists. In terms of the second use of objectivity that we considered, namely, the ability to achieve maximal agreement on standards of knowledge and on the application of the standards to particular cases, physics is an objective discipline; history is questionable. There are a number of reasons for the disparity. For one thing, it is impossible to reproduce situations in history in the way that scientists can reproduce experimental conditions in a laboratory. The United States, for example, cannot return to the year 1932, reproduce the exact circumstances of that time, and then elect Hoover instead of Roosevelt in order to test the difference that Roosevelt's election made. Another reason that history is a less objective discipline than physics is that historians are involved with the materials they study. They study human individuals and societies, often their own countries. It is difficult for them to be as detached as physicists can be about subatomic particles.[136]

Since historians have not been able to attain the measure of agreement characteristic of physicists, theologians naturally found history more open than nature to being interpreted in religious categories. However, once science provided the occasion for the turn to history, theologians came to see that they should have been stressing it independently of the rise of science. In theistic terms it makes sense to focus on history because (1) the God of theism is personal and history is the scene of the interaction between persons and (2) history is stressed within the Bible.

The prophets continually refer to God's acts in history as the basis of their insight into his nature. God redeemed the Israelites from slavery in Egypt; therefore, throughout the rest of their history he is known to them as the Redeemer. Peter, in the Book of Acts, appeals to the story of God's actions in history as the basis for his proclamation of the glad tidings of redemption. As H. Richard Niebuhr wrote: "It is not the necessity of staying alive [as a viable faith in the face of the challenges of modern culture] which forces our community to speak in historical terms. . . . The church's compulsion [to speak this way] arises out of its need—since it is a living church—to say truly what it stands for, and out of its inability to do so otherwise than by telling the story of its life."[137]

There is a great deal in the Bible besides the stories of God's momentous actions in history, but religious existentialists are convinced that the historical episodes are the crucial ones. History is the decisive scene of God's activity, the place where he makes himself most clearly known to human beings.

The Stake of Theology Is in History: It Has Happened!

When we deal with the complexities of religious thought, it is easy to lose sight of basic points. The fundamental contemporary problem of religious thought is the existence of God. Both Jewish and Christian believers insist that the most important agent acting in the universe, God, cannot be observed by the senses. This puts pressure on them to uncover features of experience that can be explained only by an appeal to the existence and activities of the transcendent God, who, of course, is not observable.

    1 In appealing to miracles theologians maintain that these extraordinary occurrences could not take place unless a supernatural God caused them (see Chapt. 4).

    2 Thinkers, like Rudolf Otto, claim that religious experience provides direct awareness of the reality of God (see Chapt. 5).

    3 Religious thinkers who advance the teleological argument claim that the intricate adaptations of parts to whole (as in the case of the way that the parts of the eye work together for the function of vision) throughout nature is best explained by the appeal to God's activities (see Chapt. 10).

    4 Theologians who deploy the cosmological argument claim that there is no rational way of accounting for the existence of the universe unless we posit the creative power of God (see Chapt. 12).

    Religious existentialists focus on the individual's struggle for authentic personal and historical existence. They claim, in effect, that the individual can encounter God in and through tumultuous experiences of subjectivity, including those that call God's existence into question. They mine the Bible for insights that will help individuals achieve authentic existence as Kierkegaard, for example, appropriates the story of Abraham's sacrifice of Isaac (see pp. 149 ff.). In itself this technique would not show why we should regard the God that is witnessed to by the biblical authors as real rather than imaginary. After all, the characters of Sophocles' *Oedipus the King* provide insights into authentic existence, and we do not regard the gods of Mount Olympus, to which his characters bear witness, as actually existing. That is why history is so important to the religious existentialists. The story of *Oedipus the King* is not historical. It did not take place in the world outside the theater and the characters could not have been observed apart from performances of the play. By contrast, the religious existentialists claim that the events reported in the Bible, at any rate the most important of them like the exodus from Egypt, did take place "out there" in the world. The characters involved in them were actual human beings who played a role in history. Kierkegaard stated the point succinctly: "The difference between poetry and history is clearly this, that history is what really occurred, whereas poetry is the possible, the imaginary, the poetized."[138] The historical claim anchors the events of the New Testament in the world. They were not imaginary; they were observed by the people who first told the stories of Jesus' activities and who provided the basis for the subsequent written accounts.

The events of history are momentous and decisive. They shape the future. Religious existentialists experience the guiding hand of the invisible God in and through these events. What is at issue is expressed vividly in the Passover *Haggadah*, the book of narratives, hymns, and ritual instructions that is read by Jews at the special meal which inaugurates the Passover holiday. The youngest boy asks the question: "Why is this night different from all other nights?" The answer which the father is instructed to give him is: "We were slaves to Pharaoh in Egypt and the Lord our God brought us out from there with a strong hand and an outstretched arm. And if the Holy One Praised be He had not brought our fathers out of Egypt why we, and our children, and our children's children would have remained enslaved to Pharaohs in Egypt."

The stake that religious thinkers have in history is then an appeal to the actual—"It *has* happened"—as contrasted with the fictitious—"Let us imagine that it happened."

The Two-Level Theory of History

Religious existentialists have a two-level theory of history that corresponds to what I have called their two-level theory of truth.[139] As we have seen, in a rough sense, the lower level of truth corresponds to what the positivists called the analytic and the synthetic. The synthetic is the domain of factual claims of common sense like "This page is white" or of science like "The helium atom has two electrons." These statements are objective in the sense that they can be verified independently of subjective factors like the heredity and the environmental conditioning of individuals; and that a wide consensus is obtained with regard to them. The religious existentialists talk of a higher level of truth involving commitment. Religious statements like "God loves us as a father loves his children" cannot, according to them, be understood independently of the subjective commitments of individuals. The two-level theory of history is a special application of this pattern. At the lower level historians deal with facts that can be handled objectively; these involve such matters as the dates of battles, the numbers of people killed, and so on. Religious existentialists regard the factual level as an indispensable condition of historical work, but it is not sufficient. The facts must be set within a framework of interpretation that enable historians to deal with such questions as why the battle took place and its influence on the further development of events. The level of interpretation corresponds to the higher level of truth and it too involves subjectivity. The two-level theory is basic to Bultmann's understanding of history. He calls the lower level of historical research into the facts *Historie*. He calls the higher level at which the facts are set into a framework of historical interpretation *Geschichte*.

Historie: Objective Research into the Facts   *Historie* is a German word that has no exact equivalent in English. It is the use of critical techniques of historical research in an effort to establish facts about the past: the who, what, when, and where. The attitude adopted by historians who engage in this kind of research should be the I-It detachment of the trained observer. Even if they are not capable of realizing it in practice, their ideal ought to be one of conducting their inquiries and checking their results without regard for their personal interests and hopes. A biblical scholar, for example, may hope that the dates in the Bible will be corroborated by information available outside the Bible. Yet if he should discover an ancient source, for instance, an Assyrian stone with dates carved on it that decisively discredit the date of a battle that is recorded in the Bible, he should be prepared to change the date. Bultmann writes: "The historian is certainly not allowed to presuppose the results of his research, and he is obliged to keep back, to reduce to silence, his personal desires with regard to these results."[140]

Professional historians are fully aware of the difficulty of researching facts. Yet Bultmann thinks that this aspect of historical work is, in principle, capable of yielding objective results. Historians ought to be able to agree on standards for determining facts and on the specific facts that have been determined:

> . . . strict methodological research can recognize objectively a certain part of the historical process, namely, events in so far as they are nothing but occurrences which happened at a certain place in space and time. . . . Of course, there are many events which cannot be fixed because the evidence is not sufficient or not clear, and also the sagacity and the ability of every historian have their limits. But that has no systematic importance; for in principle, methodical historical research can obtain objective knowledge in this sphere.[141]

Bultmann regards *Historie* as a science. Those who practice it try to develop the most accurate instruments of research. A good example is radiocarbon dating. All organic materials have carbon in them. Since Carbon 14 is radioactive, the amount of it in parchment (the organic material on which the ancients wrote) decreases with time. Therefore, measuring the amount of Carbon 14 helps researchers in dating parchment. This technique was used on the Dead Sea Scrolls, the most important archaeological discovery of modern times. Many of them contained manuscripts of books of the Bible. Scholars used the radiocarbon dating as one way of determining that the manuscripts were authentic.

Religious existentialists think that *Historie*, like any other science, ought to be free from interference with its investigations. Just as religious existentialists would not dream of invoking faith to tell a physicist how many electrons there are in the helium atom, so too they would not invoke faith to tell a historian the date of an event, like the battle of Carcemish, which is recorded in the Bible.

Geschichte: Subjective Interpretation of the Facts

In order to write history a scholar must be concerned with the facts, but he cannot remain at the factual level. He must go beyond the account of what happened, where it happened, and when it happened by dealing with the reasons for its having happened. This inevitably involves interpretations of the meaning of the events, and the level of historical interpretation is called *Geschichte*. It does not mean interpretation as contrasted with the facts, but rather it means history in the full sense of the term, the facts as they are set in a framework of interpretation. These frameworks are subjective. As Bultmann puts it: "We must remember that it is impossible to trace out a historical picture without any question [that one puts to the documents and other historical materials], and that it is possible to perceive a historical phenomenon only from a special point of view."[142]

The war that took place in the United States from 1861–1865 provides an interesting illustration of the subjectivity of historical interpretations.[143] Historians from the North and South achieve a considerable agreement about the facts. They can agree on the dates and places of battles, on the numbers of the participants, and on the casualties. Yet at the interpretive level their disagreement has been so radical that they could not even agree on the name of the war. In the North and in the rest of the country outside the South, it was called the Civil War, in the South, it was called the War Between the States. These names stand for basically different frameworks of interpretation, rooted in different views of the meaning of the American experience. As Bultmann puts it:

> Naturally, there are certain items of historical knowledge which can be regarded as definitely known—namely, such items as concern only dates that can be fixed chronologically and locally as, for example, the assassina-

tion of Caesar or Luther's posting of the ninety-five theses. But what these events that can thus be dated *mean* cannot be definitively fixed.[144]

It is obvious that American historians would respond to the war by means of interpretative frameworks that reflect their subjective involvements with the American experience. It is not obvious that this would be true of all historians. We might, for example, suppose that a Danish historian would bring an objective point of view to it because he would be free of regional loyalties. In this context it is necessary to discriminate the personal attitudes of a historian from factors that shape his outlook. In terms of his attitude a Danish historian might be detached and, to that extent, objective. However, religious existentialists would insist that, all the same, he would bring a subjective framework of interpretation to his assessment of the war. If he were aristocratic in outlook he might favor the southern point of view, if he were idealistic he might favor the abolitionists, and so on. Bultmann puts it this way:

> Certainly, as a rule, the subjectivity of the historian colors his picture of history. It depends, for instance, on the ideal which a historian has of his country and on his image of its future, how he describes its history, how he judges the importance of events, how he estimates the greatness of historical persons, how he distributes worth and worthlessness. According to their different values, different pictures will be produced by a nationalist or a socialist, an idealist or a materialist, a conservative or a liberal. And therefore the portraits of Luther or Goethe, of Napoleon or Bismarck vary in history.[145]

The perspectives or frameworks of interpretation that historians bring to their work reflect their basic orientation to life. They are deep rooted and profoundly subjective. Yet they are not as unchangeable as the color of one's eyes. They may change, but they cannot be changed by a conscious process like the one involved in deciding whether to carry an umbrella. A decision to change from, let us say, a Marxist to a Freudian perspective on history involves a process as complex as the one involved in converting to a religion or in losing one. It is a compound of a great many experiences, like those of watching the infighting of Marxist parties, and of many decisions, like the decision to read a number of Freud's books. At the end of a process of this kind the historian does not shift from a subjective to an objective framework. In the view of religious existentialists he shifts from one subjective frame of reference, the Marxist, to another, the Freudian.

The contrast that has been drawn between the objective facts and the subjective interpretations is vastly oversimplified. Working historians realize that agreement on the facts is very difficult to come by. It involves painstaking research. Furthermore, subjective considerations do not merely influence the interpretations of the facts; they influence the choice of problems, the selection of the facts, and the assessments of whether or not the evidence is adequate to establish the facts. Nevertheless, religious existentialists stress the fact-interpretation contrast in order to show that even when the facts are agreed upon, differences of interpretation will still produce radical differences in historical judgments. The situation is reminiscent of John Wisdom's example of the jury that has all the facts before it but which still produces radical differences as to the guilt of the defendant (see pp. 44f.).

Revelation in History

The important point about Bultmann's use of the *Historie-Geschichte* distinction is his application of it to the understanding of God's revelation in history. He claims that we can respond to God's decisive act in Christ at the level of *Geschichte* without our being able to achieve reliable knowledge of the life of Jesus of Nazareth at the level of *Historie*.

Revelation: God's Self-Disclosure Revelation is one of the central terms of Western theology, but a good way to approach it is to examine its nontheological uses. It involves a momentous self-disclosure of what could not be learned in any other way. If a man told his fiancée about his term in prison, it would be a momentous disclosure, but it would not be a revelation. She could have learned about it in some other way. She might have come across an old newspaper clipping that reported it, or she might have heard about it from a friend. By contrast, if a famous and self-assured actor were to tell his fiancée about the deep anxiety that he successfully masks both before and during every performance, he would be telling her something that she could not discover for herself or from anyone but him. It would therefore be revelatory, and it would be important for her to know about it. This example can also serve as a model for the theological use of revelation as the momentous self-disclosure of God, which tells men that which they could not discover for themselves.

Rudolf Bultmann defined revelation as "that opening up of what is hidden which is here absolutely necessary and decisive for man if he is to achieve 'salvation' or authenticity; that is, revelation here is the disclosure of *God* to man."[146] Bultmann adds that this disclosure can take place as an "occurrence that puts me in a new situation."[147] This definition stresses the fact that these disclosures are the product of God's initiative. They provide the individual with new possibilities for authentic existence.

God's decisive act is recorded in the New Testament. It is an historical account, but the facts are not the important thing. The New Testament itself sets the facts in the Christian framework of interpretation which involves *Geschichte*, but a *Geschichte* which is holy. If the individual appropriates this framework, he may receive a power to live authentically. Yet, as Bultmann notes, there is only the possibility; there is no guarantee because we are dealing with faith and not magic.

There Are No Hard Facts Concerning the Life of Jesus   One of the major efforts of the higher criticism of the New Testament had been the effort to get a clear picture of "the historial Jesus" at the objective level of *Historie*. This was to be an accurate account of when he lived, of the chronology of the events recorded in the Gospels, of what he actually said and did.

We must recall the fact that Bultmann was a leading New Testament scholar. One of his major conclusions—a conclusion that is by no means original with him or limited to a small circle of his followers—is: "We can neither write a 'life of Jesus' nor present an accurate picture of his personality."[148] In other words, Bultmann does not think that there is sufficient historical evidence for any of the facts pertaining to the life of Jesus. He goes on to say that one cannot even be sure that Jesus actually claimed to be the Messiah, that is, the Christ. From the standpoint of *Historie* we must be sceptics about exactly what happened in God's decisive act in Christ because *all* the details of the *life* of Jesus of Nazareth are uncertain. They are not merely uncertain in the sense that historical knowledge *as such* is uncertain because no historical judgment can attain the degree of certainty of "Two plus three equals five." They are uncertain in a relative sense, that is, none of the facts of the life of Jesus are as well-established as many of the facts relating to the life of a Christian figure like Martin Luther.

One might think that his scepticism regarding the facts of Jesus' life might lead Bultmann to reject the claim that the Christian revelation is *historical*, but he does not do so. To understand his position we will have to consider the way he applies the *Historie-Geschichte* distinction to the holy history of the Christian community.

Heilsgeschichte: The Holy History of Christianity   Christian *Geschichte* is a special case of the higher level of history at which the facts are woven into a subjective framework of interpretation. It is *Heils-geschichte*, which means holy history. Bultmann, like most Christian theologians, claims that it is the history of revelation. He follows Kierkegaard's pattern by shifting our attention from the objective and factual level to the subjective level of *Geschichte*.

In commenting on God's revelatory act in Christ, Bultmann explicitly claims that the statement cannot be grasped at the objective level. "That God has acted in Jesus Christ is, however, not a fact of past history open to historical verification."[149] This statement has two elements: 1) Bultmann rejects the view that in order to apprehend the revelatory significance of God's act in Christ one would merely have had to observe Jesus in the flesh. One might see the man Jesus of Nazareth and fail to realize that he is the Christ. "To every other eye than the eye of faith the action of God is hidden."[150] 2) God's self-disclosure in Christ cannot be objectively confirmed or disconfirmed. "No science of history can verify this assertion—either to confirm it or to reject it; for it is beyond the sphere of historical observation to say that in this Word and its proclamation God has acted."[151] In another context he insists that history as science (*Historie*) ". . . cannot perceive such an act [God's actions in history] and reckon on the basis of it, but as historical science it may not assert that faith is an illusion and that God has not acted in history."[152]

Bultmann, like other religious existentialists, thinks that fundamentalists make the mistake of emphasizing the observable details of the biblical accounts of the holy events such as those relating to Jesus' resurrection. The tomb of Jesus, which was guarded by Roman soldiers and sealed by a great rock, was empty and a visible angel used audible language to tell the women who had come to anoint Jesus that he is risen (Mark 16:1–8). By contrast, the only observable aspect of this account that Bultmann will acknowledge is the text of the New Testament itself. Yet this text, as it stands, is not revelatory. I will again vary an image of Martin Buber's by way of communicating the difference between the mere observable words recorded in the Bible and their revelatory power.[153] The Bible, as we have it, is like a recording of Beethoven's C Sharp Minor Quartet. The sounds emitted by the record—any time I play it—are objective. They can be measured for both volume and speed. Yet I do not experience the meaning that Beethoven intended to communicate unless the music comes alive for me in an I-You relation. So too the text of the Bible is observable, but unless it becomes a springboard for an I-You relation with God, it is not revelatory.

The reason that Bultmann insists that God's decisive act in Christ, as recorded in the Bible, is beyond verification and confirmation should now be obvious, even though Bultmann does not spell it out. It has been worked out in connection with Buber's account of the I-You and the I-It (see pp. 118 f.). Whenever the music on a record or the meaning that is enshrined in the Bible becomes a You for us, we experience the distinctive revelatory disclosure that is packed into *Heilsgeschichte*. However, verification and confirmation of this revelation can only take place in the I-It attitude of detachment in which the eternal You that was present to us in the revelatory encounter is, in principle, inaccessible. The revelatory disclosures of *Heilsgeschichte* are, therefore, beyond verification, falsification, and confirmation. This sort of analysis is implicit in Bultmann's statement that "human trust and love . . . are not based on any trustworthiness or lovableness in another which could be objectively ascertained, but upon the nature of the other apprehended *in* the love and *in* the trust. There can be no trust and no love without this element of risk."[154] In other words, God's love and trustworthiness comes through in the revelatory moments when the words of the Bible provide the individual with an encounter with the eternal You. There can be no guarantee that the God thus revealed is trustworthy and loving, or even that he exists; but neither can these claims be falsified or disconfirmed.

It would, of course, be easy enough to charge that Bultmann and the other religious existentialists want objective verification of revelation. Failing to get it, they claim that what they really want is the subjective appropriation, in fear and trembling, of objective uncertainty. But Bultmann, true to the spirit of Kierkegaard, insists that faith as subjectivity is not a matter of "sour grapes." Authentic faith involves risk, a risk that is eliminated where objective evidence is available to back one's beliefs. Faith involves commitment beyond, or even against, the objective evidence. It is in this sort of commitment that the individual achieves authenticity. "Thus, the fact that God cannot be seen or apprehended apart from faith does not mean that he does not exist apart from faith. We must remember, however, that the affirmations of faith in its relation to its object, to God, cannot be proved objectively. This is not a weakness of faith; it is its true strength. . . ."[155]

A CRITICAL LOOK AT BULTMANN'S EXISTENTIALIZED CHRISTIANITY

Bultmann is impressive because he takes the rise of science seriously; he is self-conscious about his method of biblical interpretation, and his existentialized version of Christianity stresses the element of risk that is a part of authentic faith. It is a radical restatement of Christianity, and it has been criticized in a variety of ways.[156] I will focus on three major issues: (1) Is Bultmann's version of the faith genuinely Christian? (2) Is Bultmann's analogical approach to talk about God less problematic than the mythological language he rejects? (3) How effective is Bultmann's two-level theory of history?

Is Bultmann's Demythologized Faith Genuinely Christian?

Many of Bultmann's critics think that the major problem with his thought is that it is not genuinely Christian. In challenging it, they focus on his radical approach to such central Christian teachings as the resurrection.[157] Bultmann, we have seen, thinks that it is inconceivable that a corpse should be restored to life (see pp. 176f.). He therefore rejects literalistic approaches and deals with the resurrection by linking it to the cross. He claims that they form one event of holy history in which salvation is offered to mankind.

Bultmann rejects, as an unfortunate mythological hangover in St. Paul, the passage in the First Letter to the Corinthians where the apostle refers to the list of those who saw the risen Christ, including himself. Yet St. Paul follows his appeal to the post-resurrection appearances with a statement that links Christ's resurrection to the hope for the resurrection of the dead (1 Cor. 15:12–15).

> Now if this is what we proclaim, that Christ was raised from the dead, how can some of you say there is no resurrection of the dead? If there be no resurrection, then Christ was not raised; and if Christ was not raised, then our gospel is null and void, and so is your faith. . . .

Thus, it is not surprising that theologians should devote entire books to the subject of the resurrection in an effort to show that it is an event that could have happened; indeed, they claim that it actually occurred.[158]

Bultmann rejects accounts of the risen Christ who was observable to the disciples. He insists that it is both inconceivable to men of our day as well as religiously inappropriate. This is a radical position. It has led many theologians to charge that Bultmann is not a Christian because he has jettisoned the kerygma. They think of his scheme as a special version of existential philosophy or as a misguided effort at theology.

There is no simple way of answering this charge. The more complex the phenomenon, the more difficult it is to come up with a definition that includes what you want to include and excludes the rest. A religious tradition like Christianity resembles a political party, like the Democratic party in the United States, in being a broadly gauged affair covering many different elements. It can be argued that the leaders of the Democratic party in this century have taken stands that were diametrically opposed to the stands that were taken by Thomas Jefferson and its other founders. New Dealers and other twentieth-century Democrats can admit that their specific proposals would have been frowned upon by the founding fathers; nevertheless, they can claim that they have been true to the *intentions* of the founders and have adapted them to changing circumstances.

Bultmann regards Jesus Christ as the focus of God's decisive act in history. His understanding of biblical teachings that are related to it, especially the resurrection, is radical. Yet Bultmann claims to be a Christian, and outside the confines of the Roman Catholic Church (where ultimately the Pope has a right to decide these matters), it is hard to know how to settle the issue.[159] There is no way that conservative Christians can prove that Bultmann's demythologized version of Christianity is illegitimate.

Is Analogical Language about God Less Problematic than the Mythological?

Bultmann consigns science to the lower (objective) level of truth. He claims that mythological language about God deals with God in categories—for instance, the spatial one—that are only appropriately used of observable beings. Therefore, mythological language is vulnerable to the criticisms of science (see pp. 174f.). By contrast, Bultmann deals with God in analogical language. The model for this language is existential; it involves categories like love and friendship. These attitudes are internal and involve an element of spontaneity. They cannot be observed objectively and their occurrence (we speak of *falling* in love) cannot be predicted or verified with scientific rigor. That is why Bultmann thinks that his existential understanding of faith and his analogical language about God are not vulnerable to empiricist criticism.

Bultmann's position is, however, vulnerable to the same criticism that Ronald Hepburn directed against Buber (see p. 127f.). It is true that the living core of relations like love, friendship, and trust are not observable in the sense that a face flushed scarlet is observable. There is a quality of inwardness about them. Furthermore, we have considered the privileged access into a person's character that a relation of trust may provide (see p. 140). Yet Hepburn is surely right when he claims that *in our experience* love and friendship always occur between beings that have observable aspects. This does not prove that love could not occur between an observable man and the nonobservable God. Yet it does uncover an inconsistency in Bultmann's appeal to experience.

Bultmann appeals to our scientifically oriented notions of experience to show that the resuscitation of a corpse is inconceivable. He appeals to the same evidence in order to show that a God who is located in a spatial realm called heaven is inconceivable. Yet surely that same scientifically oriented notion of experience may be invoked to say that a center of loving consciousness that has no body is inconceivable.[160] Someone might try to back the claim about a disembodied center of consciousness by appealing to psychical research on extrasensory perception. This would, however, face in the opposite direction from Bultmann. Like Kierkegaard before him, Bultmann turns away from science as a source of insight, into existential issues in general and God in particular.

Bultmann, like most religious existentialists, can therefore, be accused of trying to have it both ways. When he wants to establish the experiential basis of Christian faith, he refers to the way we talk about love and trust in ordinary language. In this context, he justifiably notes that they cannot be understood merely in terms of observable behavior. Yet, when he deals with God as a person who gives no signs whatever of observable behavior, ordinary language is left far behind. If there are any answers to this sort of problem lurking in the subtleties of philosophical analyses of the mind-body problem, they are certainly not invoked by Bultmann. He is content to let the matter rest in terms of an appeal to the risk involved in a subjectively oriented faith.

Problems Related to Bultmann's Two-Level Theory of History

The two-level theory of history, like the two-level theory of truth, is an important approach to understanding Christian views of faith and revelation. By consciously incorporating objective doubts and subjective risk into faith, religious existentialists help us to discriminate its authentic modes from a fanaticism which cannot accept the possibility of error and cannot tolerate honest doubts. Yet, in their rush to the higher level of truth and history, existentialists often overlook important distinctions that need to be made at the lower level; Bultmann is no exception.

The New Testament: Existentially Valid or Tragically Wrong?

Ronald Hepburn, one of the most perceptive critics of religious existentialism, calls attention to a fascinating aspect of Bultmann's approach to history: Bultmann considers features of the New Testament that critics would use to argue against the truth of Christianity, and he uses them as evidence for the validity of his existentialized version of Christianity.[161] To cite the crucial example: The disciples expected Jesus to return in glory and power. He failed to do so. The sceptic regards this as a falsification of the Christian claim. Bultmann does not even consider this disheartening option. He insists that the expectation of the return of a visible Christ in power and glory was mythological. The fact that it was disappointed is then invoked to show that the expectation of Jesus' second coming must be interpreted existentially. God's decisive act in Christ provided all human beings with a new power to be genuinely open to the future. However, Hepburn thinks that Bultmann should present reasons for dismissing the sceptical option before insisting that the false expectation of the second coming is evidence for his existential reinterpretation of the texts.

Hepburn's criticism is acute, but Bultmann is not under the obligation to take account of all objections to Christianity that are spawned by philosophers. After all, he is not trying to state an objectively convincing case for the truth of Christianity. He claims that the significance of the kerygma can best be appropriated in existential terms, and it can only be affirmed with a considerable element of risk. He neglects to explore the possibility that Christianity may be tragically wrong because he assumes it. He insists that Christians believe it despite the great odds against its being true. Once again, we find that Bultmann is a genuine disciple of Kierkegaard. The Christian is convinced of the truth of his faith but only subjectively. Objectively considered, nothing could be less certain. Hepburn's criticism is, therefore, not as devastating as it appears.

Geschichte Cannot Generate Characters   *Geschichte* is the scene of historical turbulence. Historians argue fiercely even when they share the same frameworks of interpretation. When their frameworks differ, their controversies are intensified. For example, think of the differences between a historian who advocates the "great man" theory of history and a historian who is a Marxist when they deal with a figure like Winston Churchill. Yet neither historian would use his interpretative framework to create additional characters. The characters whose lives they interpret are researched at the lower level of history by the objective methods of *Historie.*

Bultmann interprets the history of Israel as holy history with God as its central character. Yet God cannot be observed along with the other historical agents such as Moses, the Prophets, and Jesus. Theologians who apply the two-level theory of history to the Bible claim that the history of Israel may best be *interpreted* as one in which the transcendent God guides his people. The interpretative framework is not only being invoked to justify the *understanding* of a given character, that is, of God, but it is used to generate the *existence* of this character. God is not accessible at all on the level of *Historie*; he can only be discerned at the level of *Geschichte.*

Historical Interpretations Must Be Grounded in Facts   *Historie* is the lower level of history in which researchers can attain objective agreement on the facts. Bultmann regards this level as less important than *Geschichte*, the level at which the facts are enmeshed in a subjective framework of interpretation. Yet conflicts of historical interpretation are vital only if there are objectively established facts to be interpreted. By stressing the inescapably subjective character of *all* approaches to the texts of the New Testament, Bultmann deflects our attention from this important point. In this connection, a comparison of Jesus of Nazareth with Martin Luther should be helpful.

The New Testament presents many details about the life, teachings, and death of Jesus of Nazareth, and historians present a wealth of material relating to the teachings of Martin Luther and his central role in the Reformation. According to Bultmann, no interpretation of the facts regarding either Jesus or Luther can claim final validity because there are no objective procedures for resolving these differences. Bultmann is therefore justified in his view that on the level of *Geschichte* there are no crucial methodological differences between dealing with the life of Jesus of Nazareth and the life of Martin Luther.

When we compare Jesus and Luther at the level of *Historie*, we confront a radical contrast, which Bultmann fails to explore. Historians have objectively established a great many facts about Luther such as his posting the Ninety-Five Theses on the door of the Castle Church at Wittenberg on October 31, 1517. Although the interpretation of the events of Luther's life will generate controversies as long as there are historians around to discuss them, this does not alter the basic facts, which are established independently of the conflicting interpretations. According to Bultmann, the same does not hold true of *any* of the facts concerning the life of Jesus of Nazareth, even though he claims that the New Testament presents a reliable acount of Jesus' teachings. Because of Bultmann's scepticism about the historical accuracy of the New Testament details concerning the life of Jesus, his two-level theory of history cannot be applied to it. The point may be elaborated as follows: Since many of the facts of the Reformation are objectively established, a Lutheran historian who wishes to approach it in terms of the two-level theory of history can do so legitimately. He could acknowledge the subjectivity of his perspective on the Reformation while insisting that this ought not to count against its truth because all other perspectives—Roman Catholic, Marxist, and the rest—are also subjective. None of them can be objectively validated and the Lutheran historian can claim that his perspective is as legitimate as any other.

Bultmann might claim that even though his interpretation of the origins of Christianity is subjective, it is by no means to be disqualified. All other interpretations are equally subjective. Bultmann's case for adopting his version of the Christian interpretation can even be strengthened if we recall William James' analysis of the right to believe (see pp. 138 ff.). James maintains that (1) where the intellectual issues cannot be objectively resolved and (2) where practical benefits flow from the belief, the individual has a right to commitment beyond what the objective facts will support. Bultmann, obviously, thinks that Christian faith yields the enormous practical benefit of authentic existence. Therefore, since there are no objective procedures for resolving differences of historical interpretation, the individual has the right to opt for the Christian interpretation of the events recorded in the New Testament.

The pattern is a neat one, but Bultmann's scepticism regarding the factual details of the life of Jesus of Nazareth breaks it. When he deals with the New Testament, Bultmann seems to want to have *Geschichte*, a subjective framework in which the facts are interpreted, without being prepared to defend the accuracy of *any* of the facts that are to be interpreted. The moral of the story is that there can be no *Geschichte* unless it is grounded in *Historie*.

Bultmann, like all religious existentialists, is, however, happy to forego claims to objectivity based on the kinds of procedures that scientists use and the kinds used by historians at the level of *Historie*. Nevertheless, he claims objectivity for the revelation of God in Christ, in the sense that it is the experience of reality rather than the merely fictitious. In other words, he claims that it is objective in the first sense of the term (see pp. 91f.). He writes: "I would not call dying and rising again with Christ a subjective experience for it can only occur through an objective encounter with the proclamation and the act of God which it mediates."[162] Yet this appeal to an "objective encounter" is extremely limited, especially when we consider Bultmann's claim that God's act in Christ was historical. Suppose I were to say: "I would not call becoming aware of the meaning of spiritual freedom through reading Dostoevski's "The Grand Inquisitor," a subjective experience, for it can only occur through an *objective* encounter with the text of the novel *The Brothers Karamazov*." The encounter with the text of Dostoevski's *The Brothers Karamazov* is certainly objective in the sense that the novel is not a figment of my imagination. Yet this statement would not entitle me to claim that the characters in *The Brothers Karamazov* are historical rather than fictitious. The only kind of evidence that could entitle me to discriminate historical from fictitious claims is the evidence that is turned up by historical research at the level of what Bultmann calls *Historie*. Since Bultmann doesn't think we have any reliably established facts about the life of Jesus, he does not provide adequate grounds for his claim that God's decisive act in Christ is historical. An analytically oriented philosopher, I. M. Crombie, provides an excellent statement of the point:

> Granted then, that we might discover that our understanding of life was deepened by conceiving of it in Christian terms; in that case the Bible could

be regarded as the work of "serious" fiction. The Christian interpretation would vie with the Dostoevskian of Kafkaesque interpretation. It might indeed surpass them all. But success, even supreme success, in interpreting life could only confirm it as an interpretation of life. It would still be open to me, the critic may say, to admit its validity as an interpretation, but none the less to regard all reference contained in it to things beyond experience as simply the device by which the illumination is thrown.[163]

In other words, the sceptic may regard God as a fiction, that is, useful for promoting morality, authentic existence, or some other special virtues. Crombie, however, insists: "The critic is not only asked to conceive of the world *as if* it were the work of a supreme intelligence, but also to believe that it *is* the work of a supreme intelligence."[164] Crombie applies this point to other Christian doctrines such as the view that God disclosed his nature in the person of Jesus Christ.

Bultmann not only asks his readers to live as if God acted decisively in Christ, but he asks them to believe that God did act decisively in Christ. In other words, as far as Bultmann's intentions are concerned he affirms the independent reality of God and witnesses to God's decisive acts in history. Yet Bultmann fails to provide a basis in *Historie* for his judgments about *Heilsgeschichte*. This strips his view of its ostensible historical basis.

The dubious quality of so many of the claims that religious existentialists make in the name of subjectivity has led some contemporary religious thinkers to draw the conclusion that faith needs more objective underpinning than the existentialists were willing to seek. It might be argued that even if objective arguments for the existence of God cannot yield everything that believers want to say about God, at least they can provide a rational foundation for the affirmations of faith. With this in mind, I now turn to the three major "proofs" of the existence of God.

Part Four

Traditional Arguments for the Existence of God

Believers in God have been on the defensive for such a long time that it is hard to realize that theologians were once prepared to take on all comers by proving the existence of God. This was not only true in the Middle Ages, the attitude was maintained for centuries after. The teleological, ontological, and cosmological arguments were thought to be convincing demonstrations of the existence of God. The teleological argument is designed to render God's existence probable, in the sense that a well-established scientific hypothesis is probable. The ontological and cosmological arguments are intended to show that God's existence is certain. These proofs are modeled on the kind of ironclad demonstrations of a mathematical discipline like Euclidian geometry.

The traditional arguments for the existence of God differ from the approaches that have been considered so far. The appeal to religious experience and religious existentialism both rely on special sensitivities, that is, on the kind of subjective awareness that comes from being a member of a community of faith. By contrast, the traditional arguments for the existence of God are addressed to people of average intelligence who are only asked to reflect on the logical implications of common experiences such as the relation of cause and effect.

Thinkers who defend the traditional arguments for the existence of God are optimistic about the power of objective reason. They appeal to rules of logic in the effort to demonstrate the existence of God. To follow their reasoning it is important to consider the character of formal arguments and such basic logical notions as inference and necessity.

I shall call religious thinkers who claim that the arguments work, *teleologists*, *ontologists*, and *cosmologists*. It is important to note that all three terms have other uses.[1] The risk of confusion is preferable to the use of long-winded phrases like "theologians and philosophers who think that the ontological argument is convincing."

Important theologians of our time, especially Thomists, think that some versions of these arguments are valid proofs of the existence of God.[2] They regard them as coercive in the same sense that the statement "All bachelors are unmarried" is coercive. Once you understand it, you cannot (without consciously contradicting yourself) deny its truth. Most contemporary theologians do not think that this ideal of the coercive demonstration of the existence of God is attainable and the religious existentialists do not think it is even desirable.[3] A number of sophisticated philosophical theologians insist that religious thought is not in a special case in this regard.[4] They do not think that the ideal of a demonstration that is coercive to all intelligent people is attainable. Therefore, theology is no worse off than the philosophy of science, epistemology, the philosophy of mind, or any other philosophical discipline.[5] In order to appreciate this point a discussion of formal arguments in general will have to precede the considerations of the arguments for, or proofs of, the existence of God.

The arguments for the existence of God are similar to other arguments as far as their logical structure is concerned. In order to appreciate what is meant by logical structure consider the following syllogism. One of its best known forms is:

Major premise: All A's are B
Minor premise: x is A
Conclusion: Therefore x is B

The substitution of crows for A and of black for B yields the following syllogism: All crows are black; x is a crow; therefore x is black. The pattern of the syllogism would not be changed if we substituted canary for A and purple for B. It would then read: All canaries are purple;

x is a canary; therefore x is purple. The first argument would strike most people as valid because they know that crows are black. They would be likely to regard the second syllogism as faulty because canaries are not purple. Yet the second is just as valid as the first. It is a matter of the logical structure of the argument, which is independent of its content.

The *logical* validity of an argument is exclusively a function of the relation of the conclusion to the premises. If the conclusion follows from the premises, then the argument is valid. If the major premise were "No A's are B," the conclusion would definitely be false, since in that case, the mere fact that x is an A would disqualify it from being a B. If the major premise were "Some A's are B," as in "Some swans are white," then the conclusion would not follow necessarily. Within the limits of the argument we know nothing about "x" beyond the fact that it is a swan; there would be no way of telling whether x was a member of the group of swans that are white. It might or might not be. Given the major premise that "*All A's are B*," the argument is logically valid—regardless of what we substitute for A, B, and x.

As we have seen in the case of "All canaries are purple," the logical validity of an argument offers no guarantee of the truth of its conclusion. Even if the argument is logically valid, it is possible that one or both of the premises are false. If so, then the conclusion can be false even though it follows logically from the premises. In the context of a discussion of the proofs for the existence of God, Walter Kaufmann makes the point neatly. "The classical syllogism is: All men are mortal; Socrates is a man; therefore Socrates is mortal. It provides the recipe for proving with equal elegance that Socrates is immortal: All men are immortal; Socrates is a man; therefore Socrates is immortal." Kaufmann then applies the point to the arguments for the existence of God:

> Can one prove God's existence? Yes, but this does not mean that God exists. . . . We can construct an indefinite number of proofs for God's existence. If Jesus was trustworthy, God exists; Jesus was trustworthy; therefore, God exists. The construction of premises from which the existence of God will follow as a valid conclusion is a mere matter of ingenuity; [formally] valid proofs of God's existence are not hard to find. The crux is whether any such proof can be based on plausible premises.[6]

Formal validity is not enough to make an argument convincing. A proof can be formally valid merely because the conclusion follows from the premises. It can, nevertheless, be ridiculous if the formally valid proof yields an obviously false conclusion. To vary Kaufmann's example, we can derive the obviously false conclusion that "Horseflies are immortal" by setting up the following formally valid argument: All insects are immortal; horseflies are insects; therefore, horseflies are immortal.

Although the formal validity of an argument provides no guarantee of the truth of its conclusion, it is still important to check on the formal validity of an argument because, if you can show that it is *not* formally valid, you can dismiss it. In other words, formal validity is a necessary, but not sufficient condition for a convincing argument for the existence of God.

An argument can be convincing only if, at a minimum, it is formally valid and if we have reasonable grounds for believing that its premises are true.[7] The discussions of the classical arguments for the existence of God will demonstrate how difficult it is to get agreement as to what, in this area, constitutes reasonable grounds for the truth of the premises of an argument.

If the standard for a convincing proof is one in which the premises are to be plausible, it is important to raise the question "plausible to whom?" If the answer is "to everyone," then proof will prove almost impossible to come by. In mathematics, as in sciences like biochemistry and physics, convincing demonstrations cannot be directed to everyone. Frontier work is directed to other mathematicians and scientists, and usually to experts in narrow fields of specialization within the given discipline. When we move to fields like history and politics, we find that work in these disciplines is also directed to the experts rather than to *all* intelligent people. Therefore, it seems unreasonable to demand that proofs for the existence of God should be understandable by and convincing to every intelligent person. Charles Hartshorne, a contemporary philosophical theologian, asserts that if this was not clear in the Middle Ages it should be clear now.

> Concerning "proofs for the existence of God" there are two extremes which seem equally mistaken: (1) the proofs, and even the search for proofs, are vain; (2) the proofs are completely satisfactory and coercive. The first extreme is now fashionable; the second was the fashion in the Middle Ages. I shall propose a view intermediate between the two. . . . Arguments are useful only if they convince some who would otherwise not be convinced. But obviously between "convincing to all" and "convincing only to those already committed to the conclusion" there is ample room for intermediate possibilities.[8]

The question of how an argument for the existence of God succeeds in convincing someone is just as complicated as philosophy itself. There is no neat way of deciding whether or not these arguments are convincing or even of deciding the philosophical standards by which they should be evaluated. The demise of logical positivism has shaken up the philosophical scene. Contemporary philosophers are much less confident of being able to achieve a consensus about standards of evaluating arguments equal to that which is found among physicists, much less one that is comparable to mathematics and logic.

The only way to evaluate the arguments responsibly is to study them deeply and to set them against the full range of knowledge that has been acquired from other sources.

Studying and evaluating the arguments for the existence of God is a demanding exercise. Before proceeding with it, one issue must be faced. If, as is often charged, the arguments have no religious value, then the exertions involved in understanding them would be pointless.[9]

One way of formulating the charge that they are religiously worthless is to focus on the conclusions of the arguments. The arguments do not prove that the living God of the Bible exists, but rather, they demonstrate the existence of philosophical abstractions such as "necessary being," or "first cause." Norman Malcolm has provided an important reply to this charge. He was dealing with the ontological argument, but it applies to the others as well.

> Surely there is a level at which one can view the argument as a piece of logic, following the deductive moves but not being touched religiously? I think so. But even at this level the argument may not be without religious value, for it may help to remove some philosophical scruples that stand in the way of faith.[10]

Another criticism makes the opposite point. Sceptics charge that arguments are so deeply immersed in the religious outlook that they can only prove convincing to people who believe in God independently of the arguments. Malcolm acknowledges this point as well.

> At a deeper level, I suspect that the argument can be thoroughly understood only by one who has a view of that human "form of life" that gives rise to the idea of an infinitely great being, who views it from the *inside* not just from the outside and who has, therefore, at least some inclination to *partake* in that religious form of life.[11]

In the exposition of the arguments which follows I will stress the connection between the arguments and religious attitudes, thoughts, and practices (which, I take it, is what Malcolm means in using Wittgenstein's expression "form of life" in this context). "Wonder," which is a fundamentally religious response to the world, will be the central theme considered in connection with the teleological argument. "Perfection," which is central to the religious view of God, will be crucial to the ontological argument. A metaphysical view of "contingency," which has been traditionally associated with mortality, will be the main feature of the version of the cosmological argument that I will present.

The modes of reasoning in each of the three arguments is distinctive. The teleological argument begins with the observation of the intricate adaptation of parts to the whole in individual organs like the eye and in animals like the frog, and argues to God, the intelligent designer and producer of the world. The teleologist does not regard this conclusion as necessary, but merely as the most reasonable explanation; one that is probably true.

Ontologists reason in a way that contrasts sharply with the reasoning used by teleologists. Ontologists focus on the meaning of the word "God." They try to prove that anyone who understands it will, on reflection, realize that God's existence cannot be denied without contradiction. Ontologists reason along the a priori lines of mathematics in contrast with teleologists who reason along the a posteriori lines of science. For ontologists, the conclusion "God exists" emerges with the necessity that is characteristic of analytic statements as the positivists understood them.

The cosmological argument has elements of the other two. Like the teleological argument, it begins with observations of general features of the world. The example considered here will be the fact that all observable beings come into existence, change, and, ultimately, cease to exist. On the other hand, cosmologists are similar to ontologists in thinking that their argument yields a conclusion, "God exists," which is coercive in the sense that, once you have understood the argument, you cannot deny the truth of the conclusion.

Chapter 10

The Teleological
Argument: Wonder

Immanuel Kant called the teleological argument "the oldest, clearest, and the most accordant with the common reason of mankind."[12] It comes up frequently in arguments about religion because it is rooted in a basic response to the world. I remember many dormitory bull sessions in which believers assailed sceptics with exasperation, saying: "How can you look at the wonders of nature—the stars, the oceans, the mountain ranges—and deny God?" There seems to be a common sense appeal to the notion that the vastness and complexity of the natural order is the product of an infinite intelligence and power. Believers insist that it couldn't "just happen" that way. They insist that there must be some plan or purpose behind it. The name, "teleological argument" is derived from the Greek word *telos* meaning "end" in the sense of goal or purpose.[13]

There are two distinctive stages to this argument. The first is the pre-Darwinian version which will be discussed under the special title of "the argument from design." The second stage is the contemporary version of the teleological argument which takes account of the theory of evolution. In both stages it is an empiricist's argument; that is, they begin with observations and try, in the words of the twentieth-century teleologist, F. R. Tennant, to "let the actual world tell its own story."[14] Teleologists begin with the facts and try to reason to the most likely explanation of what has been observed. They do not even try to achieve the coercive certainty that characterizes demonstrations in Euclidian geometry. They are prepared to settle for the kind of probability that attaches to a well-established theory in science.

THE PRE-DARWINIAN ARGUMENT FROM DESIGN

The most influential statements of the argument from design were presented by the Scottish empiricist David Hume (1711–1776) in his *Dialogues Concerning Natural Religion* by the Anglican clergyman William Paley (1743–1805) in his *Natural Theology*.[15] I will focus on the statement in Hume's *Dialogues* because it is the one most commonly discussed.

Hume's *Dialogues Concerning Natural Religion* is one of the most successful examples of this important mode of philosophical writing. It is elegantly written and it is genuinely dramatic. The method of dialogue is appropriate to philosophy because in philosophy to state a point is not to make one; arguments in support of one's statement must be presented in order for it to qualify as a genuine point. In this dialogue many impressive statements are made, but the ebb and flow of the argument soon shows how hard it is to make them stand up under criticism. One of the results of the dramatic success of the dialogue is that contemporary philosophers argue over Hume's own position, some claim that he thinks the argument works, others that he destroys it.[16] I will not consider this issue but will explore the thinking on both sides of the debate.

Statement of the Argument

The main characters in the argument are Demea, an orthodox Calvinist believer, who serves as something of a straight man for the other two, Cleanthes, a philosophical empiricist, who presents and defends the argument from design, and Philo, a philosophical empiricist, who attacks it. I shall divide Cleanthes' major statement of the argument into two elements: (1) a statement of the way that the structural intricacies of natural organisms elicits a sense of wonder in us, and (2) the crucial logical move.

> Look round the world: Contemplate the whole and every part of it: You will find it to be nothing but one great machine, subdivided into an infinite

number of lesser machines, which again admit of sub-divisions, to a degree beyond what human senses and faculties can trace and explain. All these various machines [Cleanthes means organs such as the eye, and organisms such as the frog] and even their most minute parts, are adjusted to each other with an accuracy, which ravishes into admiration all men who have ever contemplated them.[17]

Cleanthes does not call our attention to the wonders of organisms for the limited purpose of ravishing us into admiration. He is concerned to make a rational point. We know from experience that intelligence is required to produce a technological wonder like a telescope; it follows that a far greater intelligence is required to produce a natural organ like the eye because the eye is far more intricate than the telescope.

The curious adapting of means to ends, throughout all nature, resembles exactly, though it much exceeds, the productions of human contrivance; of human design, thought, wisdom, and intelligence. Since therefore all the effects resemble each other, we are led to infer, by all the rules of analogy, that the causes also resemble; and that the Author of nature is somewhat similar to the mind of man; though possessed of far greater faculties, proportioned to the grandeur of the work, which he has executed.[18]

The argument pivots around a comparison between artifacts (man-made objects) and the organs and organisms that are found throughout nature. I will restate the main points in my own terms.

1 From experience we know that even the most primitive artifact such as a knife requires an intelligent being to design and produce it for some purpose. This is even truer of complex artifacts such as telescopes and watches which have many parts that are designed to work together toward functions like increasing our power of vision and recording the time.

2 From experience we also know that organisms are far more complicated than even the most complex artifacts. This is true of relatively simple organisms like the earthworm, as it is of enormously complex ones like horses and human beings. Not only do their many parts work together toward such functions as movement, feeding, and reproducing, but they sustain themselves in the face of dramatically changing circumstances.

3 No one has ever observed the design and production of organisms (that is, their design and production from scratch as distinguished from their natural reproduction).

4 Yet given the fact that intelligence is required to design and produce artifacts, it is reasonable to conclude that a far greater intelligence is needed to design and produce organisms.

5 Indeed, the range and number of organisms that we can observe in our world make it reasonable to conclude that the being that designed and produced them is much greater than human beings, namely, the God worshiped by believers through the ages who created the natural order and who sustains it.

Induction and Analogy

The most distinctive thing about teleologists, ontologists, and cosmologists is that they think they can prove the existence of God by means of technical arguments rooted logic. In his presentation of the argument from design Cleanthes appeals to "the rules of analogy" to justify his inference to God and he concludes it by stating: "By this argument *a posteriori*, and by this argument alone, do we prove at once the existence of a Deity, and his similarity to human mind and intelligence."[19]

Inference is so basic to logic that I am tempted to say that it is simply what we do when we think logically. The kind of reasoning done in detective stories is replete with inferences. The victim's body was cold and stiff when it was found and the inference is that he must have been dead for some time. A comparison of the verb infer with another verb, to ingress, may prove helpful. The awkward and stilted expression to ingress means to enter a space; to go from where you are to where you are not. No by-your-leave is required, merely movement. Inference also involves going from where you are to where you are not, but when you infer, the movement is mental. Furthermore, a valid inference greatly depends on a by-your-leave. The person whc makes it must be prepared to provide justification that supports it. For instance, the inference from the observation of *rigor mortis* in a corpse to the conclusion that the person had been dead for hours is clearly justified by what we know about the rate at which a dead body stiffens and cools. In justifying his inference to an intelligent Author of Nature, Cleanthes appeals to a form of reasoning known as analogy, which is a part of inductive logic.[20]

Induction The simplest way to define induction is to say that it is contrasted with deduction. The most direct way of getting at both modes of logic is to draw on the distinction between the analytic and the synthetic as it was formulated by the positivists (see Chapt. 1). Deductive logic is used in the analytic. It is a priori, in the sense of being independent of observations. Its conclusions follow of necessity, in the sense that to deny them involves contradictions. Deductive reasoning draws out the logical implications of a set of statements, but the conclusion does not add anything to them. Therefore, it does not add to our knowledge of states of affairs. It only informs us of something that is necessarily packed into the statements and of something that we might not have realized without the application of deductive reasoning. For example, 9,331 is necessarily packed into 43 × 217, but we would not be consciously aware of this unless we actually performed the multiplication.

Inductive logic is relevant to the kind of thinking that is related to the synthetic. In contrast to deductive arguments, the conclusions of an inductive argument are not necessarily true. It is possible for them to be either true or false. All that is claimed on behalf of a valid inductive argument is that its conclusion is probably true. Inductive logic, again by contrast with deduction, does not function independently of observations of states of affairs in the world. Indeed, one of its main functions is to *regulate* the *generalizations* we formulate on the basis of observations of states of affairs.

Generalization is indispensable to thinking. Consider a teacher who in the course of a lifetime uses chalk a great many times. He certainly wants to be able to say something more than: "I have used 5,037 pieces of chalk to write on blackboards and all of them have written." The mere enumeration of the number of instances we have observed is inadequate to many important purposes both in everyday routines and in science. We need to use the past experience of chalk to predict that "The next piece of chalk that I use will write," or even more broadly to make lawlike generalizations like "Chalk writes on blackboards." Obviously, the prediction that the next piece of chalk will write is more probable than the unqualified generalization about chalk which deals with *all* pieces. To appreciate the importance of induction to the increase of knowledge one need only reflect on how important both predictions and laws are to scientific work.

Inductive reasoning reaches to the unknown from the known. It draws probable conclusions about the future from observations about the past. The more data we have to work with and the more limited the conclusion, the more probable it is that the conclusion of the inductive argument will prove to be true. A statement like "The next piece of chalk I remove from a package will write on a blackboard" is maximally probable. The statement is based on numerous experiences and the fresh piece is like the others in all relevant respects. Furthermore, my conclusion is limited to the function of chalk that I have always observed. I am not referring to some new and hitherto untested use like its ability to plug holes in a ping pong table.

The conclusions of inductive arguments are often highly probable, but they are never certain. Even conclusions based on many observations of exactly similar circumstances may, in the event, prove to be false.

Bertrand Russell (1872–1969), the logician and philosopher, illustrated the point by means of the story of the inductive chicken.[21] Every day it observed a hand raising the lid of the coop and scattering food. The details never varied. One day it observed the hand raising the lid. On the basis of its repeated observations of identical circumstances, it rushed eagerly to receive the food and the same hand that had so often fed it, proceeded to ring its neck.

Inductive arguments underlie many of the most foolish statements that people make. They use the inductive pattern of argument without becoming sufficiently sophisticated about the need for qualifying it. John Hospers, a contemporary philosophical analyst, drives this home:

> Thus suppose that someone aged 20 argues that for every twenty years now everytime he has awakened in the morning he has been alive at nightfall, and therefore it is very probable that he will be alive at nightfall today. Now suppose that the same person at the age of 90 argues that now he has far more inductive evidence for the same conclusion than he did at the age of 20, since he has now been alive for 90×365 days instead of a mere 20×365 days.[22]

In reasoning inductively it is, therefore, important to formulate expectations on the basis of all relevant knowledge and not merely on the basis of the specific evidence that is considered in isolation. In the case of the ninety-year-old man, it is obvious that there is a great deal of available information about organic deterioration in human beings. Hospers' ninety-year-old man who, unlike Russell's chicken, is intelligent, should have been aware of it.

The situations in which inductive reasoning is used are rarely as simple as an inference about the writing ability of the next piece of chalk that I remove from a package. It often involves matters like the effects of cigarette smoking on health. Even where fairly plentiful statistics are available, say regarding the higher incidence of lung cancer among cigarette smokers, the inductive reasoning involved may be dubious. Human organisms are so complex, and the behavior of human beings is so varied, that it is hard to be sure that smoking alone accounts for the difference. Furthermore, when medical researchers investigate these matters, they are forced to use laboratory animals rather than human beings. Partisans of tobacco can, therefore, protest against conclusions that disturb them on the grounds that the relevant experiments have not been carried out on human beings. These experimental factors weaken the force of the inductive arguments that are advanced by medical researchers, and it renders their conclusions less probable than they would be if the research were carried out on human beings. The application of inductive reasoning to such complex matters as the behavior of the voters is even more problematical. The politicians and pollsters try to predict the future on the basis of the way voters have behaved in the past. Such a vast number of variables are involved that it can be argued that attaining a high degree of probability for predictions drawn from the statistics of previous elections is more of an art than a science.

Analogy The line between induction and analogy is a difficult one to draw. Analogy is primarily a form of inductive argument based on a comparison of *similarities* in *different* types of objects. An elaboration of a previous example should make the difference clear. On the basis of many experiences of using commercial chalk to write on blackboards, I make the inductive inference that "The next piece of chalk I withdraw from a package will write on a blackboard." Suppose that I cannot find a piece of commercial chalk in a classroom and that a lump of whitish material catches my eye. I pick it up, it is soft. On the basis of its similarity of color and texture, that is, its analogy to commercial chalk, I infer that it will write on a blackboard. In making this inference I dismiss as irrelevant the disanalogies or dissimilarities, such as the slight difference in color and the great difference in shape.

A contemporary logician, Irving Copi, defines analogical inference as follows: "Every analogical inference proceeds from the similarity of two or more things in one or more respects to the similarity of those things in some further respect."[23] He then presents an extended discussion of the rules that determine the tightness of an analogical inference.[24] I shall confine my selection to those that I think are most relevant to the argument from design:

1 The objects compared must definitely be similar.
2 There should be numerous instances of them.
3 The comparison must be made in respect to specific features.
4 The similarities considered should be relevant to the inference that is being drawn.
5 In the case of an inference from similarity of effects to similarity of causes, a two-sided view of the relation should be a part of the basis of the inference.

Analogy and Design

Cleanthes, the character in Hume's *Dialogues* who advances and defends the argument from design appeals to an inference based on the rules of analogy. He argues that two classes of objects—artifacts and organisms —are strikingly similar in displaying an intricate adaptation of parts toward some function of the whole. Treating them as effects, he then infers that since their central feature (functional adaptation) is similar, their causes are probably similar. He concludes that organisms are produced by an intelligence similar to, but far greater than, the human. The main issue in the argument from design is the validity of this inference. In exploring it I will momentarily shift the focus from Hume's *Dialogues* to Paley's well-known appeal to the watch and the watchmaker.[25]

He begins by imagining himself crossing a deserted area and stubbing his toe on a stone. If anyone asked him what the stone was doing there, he'd answer that for all he knew it had always been there. By contrast, if he found a watch on the ground and someone asked him what the watch was doing there, it would hardly do to give the same answer. The watch displays such an amazing adaptation of parts that function together to tell the time, that it would be ridiculous to say that it had always been there. Paley claims that the functional adaptation shows that the watch must have been designed by an intelligence and brought there by the human being who used it:

> This mechanism being observed—it requires indeed an examination of the instrument, and perhaps some previous knowledge of the subject, to perceive and understand it; but being once, as we have said, observed and understood—the inference we think is inevitable, that the watch must have had a maker—that there must have existed, at some time and at some place or other, an artificer or artificers who formed it for the purpose which we find it actually to answer, and who completely comprehended its construction and designed its use.[26]

Paley continues his argument by detailing the many evidences of functional design in natural organisms and organs, especially the eye. He insists that these are far more wonderful than the most intricate artifacts which are produced by human intelligence, and he concludes: "Were there no example in the world of contrivance except the *eye*, it would be alone sufficient to support the conclusion which we draw from it, as to the necessity of an intelligent creator."[27]

Paley's example raises many issues. First of all there is the question of comparison among artifacts, that is, of watches with other watches or of watches with telescopes. Then there are the comparisons that are drawn between artifacts like telescopes and organs like the eye. These two different types of analogies must be considered before considering the question of the inference from similarity of effects to similarity of causes.

Comparisons of Artifacts Paley introduces his example of the watch by locating it in an out of the way and uninhabited place. To intensify the element of the strangeness of the locale, let me vary his illustration by supposing that when Neil Armstrong—the first human being to do so—set foot on the moon, to his amazement he found an ordinary watch lying on its surface. He would be pretty secure in inferring that it had been caused (designed and produced) by an intelligent being, either earthly (someone had beat him to it) or lunar (intelligent beings inhabit the satellite). Because he would be comparing the watch on the moon with the many watches he had seen on the earth, he would be comparing them with respect to their cause, and he would have (or at least could have) seen watches produced many times by human beings. In other words, his judgment that watches are designed and produced by intelligent beings would be based on a comparison of (1) *similar* objects, namely, one watch with other watches and (2) he would have the experience of *many* other watches on which to base the comparison. In addition, his comparison would be based on (3) one *specific feature*, namely, telling the time, (4) which is certainly *relevant* to the conclusion that the watch he found on the moon was designed and produced by an intelligent being. This feature is far more relevant than, for example, the shape of the case or the length of the hands. Finally (5) the astronaut would have had (or at least he could have had) a *two-sided view* of watches. The experience of both the effect, that is, the watches, and the cause, that is, the human beings who manufacture them. Armstrong's inference to an intelligent designer and producer of the watch on the moon would, therefore, be maximally tight. This analogy conforms to all five of the rules that I cited from Copi.

To vary the illustration, suppose that instead of a watch the astronaut came upon a complex-looking object made of metals, which required a great deal of examination before it could be understood. He might finally discover that it was an instrument which indicated the position of the sun, even when the moon was in darkness. In this case, the inference to an intelligent designer and producer would be less secure than in the case of the watch. For one thing, the objects being compared, namely, watches and sun-trackers, would not be the same. He would only have seen the one instance of a sun-tracker, and he would never have seen one made; in other words, he would not have had a two-sided view. Nevertheless, the features being compared seem relevant. Watches are artifacts used to tell time, and the object found on the moon would seem to have been designed by an intelligent being for the purpose of keeping track of the sun. The inference would, therefore, be valid, even if not as secure as the inference made in the case of the watch.

Analogy of Artifacts and Organisms   The argument from design extends the analogy to the comparisons of artifacts and organisms. Checking it out according to Copi's rules of analogy we find that in some respects it checks out favorably. (1) There are a limitless number of artifacts and organisms to be compared. (2) The comparison does not range widely, it is confined to a specific feature, namely, functional adaptation. (3) This feature is certainly relevant to the inference to an intelligent designer and producer of organisms.

So much for the analogies. Critics of the argument stress the disanalogies or dissimilarities. (1) We do not have a two-sided view of the production (from scratch) of organisms, and (2) organisms and artifacts are not similar enough to be used as the basis of an inference like that made in the argument from design.

The Two-Sided View   Critics of the argument from design, beginning with Philo, have noted the absence of a two-sided view as a fundamental criticism of the argument.[28] The inference from a watch to an intelligent designer is valid because we have a two-sided view of the design and production of watches. The critics, however, claim that in the absence of any experience of an intelligent being designing and producing organs like the eye, organisms like the horse, or universes like this one, we have no basis for the inference to an intelligence that is similar to human intelligence.

Teleologists argue that their critics are being excessively rigid in the standard of legitimate inference that they apply to the argument from design. Science could hardly advance if all inferences had to be based on two-sided views. After all, no one can observe electrons causing certain patterns on photographic plates, but physicists draw inferences from the photographic evidence to the invisible cause. Yet the sceptics who reject the argument from design do not challenge physicists on the grounds that they have not had, and cannot have, a two-sided view of patterns on photographic plates and the electrons that cause these patterns.

Cleanthes, Hume's teleologist, goes so far as to accuse the sceptics of prejudice against religion:

> . . . refined and philosophical sceptics push their researches into the most abstruse corners of science; and their assent attends them in every step, proportioned to the evidence that they meet with. . . . [They accept that] light is in reality atomised [and that] the true system of the heavenly bodies [has been] discovered and ascertained. . . . These sceptics therefore are obliged, in every question, to . . . proportion their assent to the precise degree of evidence which occurs. This is their practice in all natural,

mathematical, moral and political science. And why not the same, I ask in the theological and religious? . . . Is not such an unequal conduct a plain proof of prejudice and passion?[29]

Teleologists can, therefore, concede that their inference from organisms (as the visible effects) to a supernatural intelligence (as the invisible cause) does not meet the demand for a two-sided view, without conceding that it is thereby invalidated.

Similarity Now we must consider the most important rule of analogy, namely, that the objects compared should be similar. It is clear that artifacts resemble one another far more than any of them resemble organisms, for example, the watch and the computer resemble one another more than either of them resemble organisms like the frog or organs like the eye.

Critics of the argument from design insist that the comparison between artifacts and organisms is a case of stretching things too far. They acknowledge the similarity of functional adaptation but then emphasize the many dissimilarities that, in their view, outweigh it. Wallace Matson, a contemporary analytic philosopher, lists some of these dissimilarities.[30] Artifacts are made of inorganic material, whereas organisms are, obviously, composed of organic compounds. Furthermore, artifacts show marks of artificial production. There are patterns that tools like lathes make on metals, and the decorative designs that handcraftsmen make on axes and other tools. In addition, organisms reproduce themselves whereas artifacts are either directly made by human beings, or they are produced by machines that are designed by human beings for that purpose. Matson sums up his point by claiming that these sorts of distinctions enable us to distinguish organisms from artifacts; therefore, signs of purposiveness (functional adaptation) are not the crucial factor. To support his point he claims that space explorers, confronted with strange objects on another planet, would have little difficulty in using marks of fabrication and other such dissimilarities as the basis of distinguishing artifacts from organisms.

Teleologists can reply that these *dis*similarities are presupposed by the very appeal to analogical argument. In a case where there are no significant dissimilarities, as in two pieces of packaged chalk, there is no need to reason analogously in predicting that the next piece I use will write on the blackboard. In cases like this, one reasons inductively. Sceptics in turn can concede the point that all analogous reasoning presupposes dissimilarities, while insisting that in this case the dissimilarities outweigh the similarities to the point where they invalidate the inference to God made by the teleologists. Teleologists can answer in terms of an appeal to: (1) the vast number of observations of functional adaptations in both artifacts and organisms, (2) the relevance of this feature to the inference to an intelligent designer and producer of nature, and (3) the fact that this inference is based on experience rather than on mere speculation. The point has been stated persuasively by Alvin Plantinga, an analytic philosopher of religion (who, it should be noted, goes on to criticize it):

> Everything that exhibits curious adaptation of means to ends and is such that we know whether or not it was the product of intelligent design, in fact was the product of intelligent design.
> The universe exhibits curious adaptation of means to ends.
> Therefore the universe is probably the product of intelligent design.[31]

Plantinga's reference to the universe as a whole provides another target for the sceptics.[32] In Hume's *Dialogues* Philo focuses on our limited knowledge of the world in order to claim that in effect there are two unknowns in the teleologists' scheme—the world and God.[33] Since I do not think that the reference to the world is required for the statement of the argument to design, I will present Philo's points without comment and then rework the argument to eliminate the reference to the world as a whole.

1   Effective analogies depend on the observation of many instances of the things being compared. The universe is neither an artifact nor an organism; it is unique. Since we have no experience whatever of the origins of universes as a class, we have no basis for an inference to the origin of this one.

2   Teleologists claim that the entire universe is characterized by functional adaptation, but we have only observed a small fragment of it. We have no right to assume that the vast regions that are unknown to us are also characterized by functional adaptation.

3   In experiencing a limited part of the universe we observe many types of causes. The design and production of artifacts by human beings is only one type, and a very uncommon one at that. Vegetative and animal reproduction are far more common causes of the effects we continually observe. In the absence of direct observation of the origin of the universe, it is more reasonable to think of it as having been produced sexually or by pollination than to think of it as designed and produced by a divine intelligence.

Philo then tries to make a total shambles of the argument from design by claiming that even if the argument works it does not yield anything like the God of theism.[34] On the basis of experience alone we would not be justified in concluding that it was produced by one infinite creator. In human experience, the larger the venture, the greater the number of individuals involved. If the origin of the universe is conceded to be divine, it would be more reasonable, on the basis of experience, to think that it was produced by many gods rather than one. Furthermore, from the moral standpoint, the universe is so imperfect that it is hard to imagine that it was produced by gods who were operating at their best. On the basis of experience we would most reasonably infer that it was designed and produced by a committee of gods who were over the hill.

Of course, a teleologist could answer that the greatest acts of human creativity, like Michelangelo's *Moses*, are not produced by committees but by individual creators and that the creativity of human geniuses reflects the creativity of God. This answer, however, hardly helps with the main problem, which is that, in the absence of any direct observation of the design and production of universes, anything goes; one man's guess is as good as another's. There are simply no parallels to the universe as a whole in our experience. Therefore, we lack all controls and any inferences drawn by teleologists are not drawn from experience—despite their best intentions—but are based on speculations.

Yet even here, caution is in order. Admittedly, teleologists have no conceivable basis for the comparative study of the origins of universes. It does not, however, necessarily follow that their inferences are invalid. After all, as far as we know, the human race is unique, but a contemporary philosopher, R. G. Swinburne, notes that anthropologists draw reasonable inferences about its origins.[35] Having conceded this much to the teleologist, it should again be noted that scientists and religious thinkers differ in important ways. The inferences of anthropologists are based upon limited observations, and they constantly test them against the facts. Religious thinkers draw inferences about the universe as a whole which seem to be compatible with all observable states of affairs. Therefore, statements of the conclusion of the argument from design like "The world was designed and produced by an intelligent deity" provide examples of what the positivists called pseudo-synthetic statements.

The Appeal to the Universe as a Whole Is Not Necessary

Comparing the universe as a whole to an artifact complicates the argument from design and provides the sceptic with extra targets. Yet, in Paley's statement of it, the appeal to the world as a whole is not made.[36] With this in mind, the formulation from Plantinga that I quoted can be reworked in the following way.

In all cases where we have observed functional adaptation and we know whether or not it was the product of intelligent design, it in fact was the

product of intelligent design. The eye exhibits functional adaptation.
Therefore the eye is probably the product of intelligent design.

Given the vast numbers of organs and organisms that we experience
and given their marvelous intricacy, it is reasonable to infer that the
cause of these myriads of wonders must be an intelligence and power that
is infinitely greater than the human.

This inference is based on the rules of analogy, and it appeals to
such knowledge as we have. The arguments that Hume and other
philosophers direct against it only serve to show that it is not a strong
form of induction; they do not show that the inference is based on an
invalid analogy. Indeed, John Stuart Mill (1806–1873), the utilitarian
philosopher who was a leading authority on induction, regarded it as a
valid argument.[37] Yet the discussion provided here should show that even
if the analogy is valid, it is extremely weak. The dissimilarities between
artifacts and organisms are considerable, a point acknowledged by Swinburne, who has made one of the best efforts at defending the argument:

> And even if there are no formal fallacies in the argument, one unwilling to
> admit the conclusion might still claim that the analogy was too weak and too
> remote for him to have to admit it, that the argument gave only negligible
> support to the conclusion which remained improbable. In defending the
> argument I will leave to the objector this way of escape from its conclu-
> sion.[38]

Swinburne's statement seems both appropriate and modest; yet
some contemporary philosophers would regard it as not being modest
enough. They would claim that Darwinian thought dealt the argument
from design a mortal blow by providing a scientific explanation for the
origin of natural species, that is, both organisms like the horse and
individual organs like the eye.

EVOLUTION AND THE TELEOLOGICAL ARGUMENT

The crucial element in the argument from design is the observation of
functional adaptation in organisms and individual organs. Hume and
Paley, who presented the most influential statements of it, lived before
Darwin's evolutionary theory revolutionized our view of the origin of
species and of the development of specialized organs. This theory
severely jolted the teleological argument, yet defenses are still being
offered.[39] Contemporary ones show three basic tendencies: (1) ignore
evolution and claim that the logic of the argument from design is valid,[40]

(2) cope with the challenge of evolution by claiming that it does not undermine the effectiveness of the argument,[41] and (3) modify the teleological argument to deal with the direction of the total process of evolution rather than with instances of functional adaptation that are to be found in the natural world.[42] The first approach has, in effect, been presented in the first part of this chapter. I will now deal with the other two.

To understand why evolutionary theory is supposed by many thinkers, religious and secular, to have destroyed the argument from design, we should recall the crucial inference. We know from experience that intelligence is required to design intricate artifacts like watches. Natural organisms, even the simplest ones, like worms, are far more complex than even the most intricate artifact. Therefore, we can reasonably conclude that a purposeful intelligence must have been at work to produce natural species like worms and horses.

Evolutionary theory challenged this argument by providing an account of the origin of species that seemed to eliminate the need for positing a purposeful intelligence for creating species. We have all studied replicas of the little foxlike creatures from which, according to Darwinian theory, the horse evolved. If we accept this account, there was no divine intelligence at work producing horses by command (in the language of the first chapter of Genesis: "Let there be horses") or to breed them consciously in the way that race horses are bred for speed. According to the Darwinian theory of natural selection, all species have natural enemies, and so, of course, did the fox-sized predecessor of the horse. The strains which were larger, stronger, and faster could escape their enemies and reproduce in greater numbers. Therefore, these stronger and faster strains that were better adapted to their environment survived while the others died out. With a sufficiently long span of time, this process of selection by survival culminated in the emergence of the horse. The evidence for this theory are the fossil remains of the various strains that emerged in the course of evolution. Subsequent refinements of evolutionary theory have not altered the picture as far as the argument from design is concerned.

Given the obvious challenge to the argument from design that is mounted on the basis of evolutionary theory, it is important to note that there is a sense in which evolutionary thought does not effect the argument. Teleologists claim that an intelligent being designed and produced the world. In order to accommodate evolution to this belief one has only to claim that God works in and through the evolutionary process. Yet as Philo, the sceptic in Hume's *Dialogues* notes, it is one thing to claim that the facts of experience are *compatible with* the existence of God and another thing to claim that the existence of God can be *inferred from* them.[43] In other words, if by means of faith (see Chapt. 8) or an a priori argument (see Chapt. 11) we could establish the existence of God independently of an examination of nature, then we could square God's existence with the facts as understood in terms of evolution and other scientific theories. However, to claim that the existence of God can be inferred from an examination of those facts, and from this examination alone, is another matter entirely. In order to defend the teleological argument the stronger claim of inference rather than the weaker one of compatibility must be made. If the teleologist confines himself to compatibility, he is not arguing for the existence of God, but merely witnessing to God's existence and spelling out its implications for our view of nature.

Contemporary defenders of the teleological argument who cope with Darwinian thought do so by shifting the focus from static instances of functional adaptation to the process of evolution.[44] Kenneth Nelson shifts it from the fully developed eye (which was the central organ dealt with by Paley) to the evolutionary process out of which the eye emerges. F. R. Tennant, A. E. Taylor, and Peter Bertocci deal with the entire process insofar as it ultimately spawns human beings and the values that are important to them. They claim that the emergence of intelligence, morality, and sensitivity to beauty demand explanation in terms of a divine agent who guides the evolutionary process toward the production of human beings.

Evolution as Supporting the Argument from Design

In presenting the argument from design I reworked one of Alvin Plantinga's statements of it in the following way:

> In all cases where we have observed functional adaptation and we know whether or not it was the product of intelligent design, it was in fact the product of intelligent design.
> The eye exhibits functional adaptation.
> Therefore, the eye is probably the product of intelligent design.

We have seen why evolutionary theory is supposed to have destroyed the effectiveness of this argument. It presents an account of the development of the eye that eliminates the need for an appeal to an intelligence with a purpose or *telos*. Random genetic variations provide prefigurations of the eye; these prove effective in the struggle for survival. Over periods embracing millions of years, cells that are only slightly sensitive to light finally evolve into the fully developed eye without the intervention of any intelligence, human or divine.

In defending the argument from design, Nelson accepts evolutionary theory and its account of the development of the eye. Since evolutionary thinking shifts the focus with regard to nature from the fully developed organ, which Paley dealt with, to the process of its development, Nelson follows suit with regard to artifacts. Instead of dealing with the fully developed cameras of our day, he deals with the development of the camera and draws an analogy between the development of the camera and the development of the eye. The point of his analogy is to claim that, contrary to a common assumption, when evolutionary theory and the facts on which it rests are taken into account, an inference to a divine intelligence is justified.

Nelson notes that the earliest cameras only produced an image on a screen set at the back of the camera. They were improved to the point where they were able to record silhouettes on paper, but the image lasted only for a short time. During the Civil War they were able to produce permanent images on paper, but only when subject to a complex process of development in elaborate darkrooms. This was a far cry from the very elaborate cameras of our day which—combined with flash bulbs, color film, and developing techniques—automatically produce prints in ten seconds.

Nelson compares the development of the eye to the development of the camera by noting that, like cameras of our day, the eye represents the culmination of a vast number of improvements. The simplest photoreceptors, as in certain of the simplest organisms, the protozoa, only discriminate the presence or absence of light. Later the protecting eye socket and the adjustable lens developed and with it binocular vision, which provided a more accurate sense of the distance of the light source; then color vision, and so on. Nelson then compares the process whereby the camera is improved with the evolutionary development of the eye. He argues that since the effects (development of the camera and of the eye) greatly resemble one another, the causes ought also to be similar. To rework his point:

> In all cases where we have observed a process of development culminating in an instance of greatly improved functional adaptation, and we know whether or not it was the product of intelligent design, it was, in fact, the product of intelligent design.
> The eye represents a process of development culminating in an instance of greatly improved functional adaptation.
> Therefore, the eye is probably the product of intelligent design.

Nelson's case (and that of the argument from design as defended by other thinkers) can be strengthened by references to selective breeding, as in the examples of race horses and corn. In these instances, intelligence, working over long periods of time, produced functional adaptations in organisms and organs that are comparable to the improvements that intelligence contrives with respect to artifacts.

Nelson, accepting evolutionary theory, claims that it justifies an inference to an intelligent being who improves organs and organisms for purposes of his own in a way that is comparable to human beings working with artifacts for purposes like photographic reproduction.

Sceptics accept evolutionary theory, but they reject the inference and claim, instead, that only pure chance is involved. Nelson quotes the following example:

> It was not necessary for any intelligence to plan suitable changes in the organisms, since blind, unintelligent chance would suffice to produce the random variations that Darwin required. The adaptation was a hit and miss affair, and it worked because the hit would be preserved as a matter of course in the struggle for existence.[45]

In dealing with the explanatory options—either the evolutionary process is guided by an intelligent being or it operates through chance—Nelson opts for intelligence. He admits that our experience is limited. We do not, for example, have a two-sided view of the evolutionary process; we only experience the effects—like the eye—and not the causes that bring it about. Yet he claims that we have an analogous experience which *is* two-sided, namely, the improvement artifacts by intelligent human beings. Therefore, Nelson opts for the hypothesis of divine intelligence as guiding the evolutionary process. As he puts it:

> Whereas we have no analogue of improved adaptation occurring ultimately from unintelligent chance, on the other hand, the gradual evolution of better and better adapted organisms resembles exactly, though greatly exceeds, the gradual production by human intelligence of better and better adapted artifacts.[46]

Although he opts for intelligence, Nelson regards evolutionary theory and the facts it interprets as compatible with both chance and intelligence. Yet he tries to turn the table on the sceptics by saying that when we deal with the question of justifiable inference from the theory of evolution and the facts it interprets, we have some basis for an inference to divine intelligence and no basis for an inference to chance. Therefore, he thinks that evolution, far from demolishing the argument from design, actually strengthens it. In making this point, Nelson recalls Paley's illustration of finding a watch in an uninhabited area and adapts it by noting that in finding only one watch, one might "conceivably think it was the product of chance and not contrivance; but to find a *series* of watches, each having gradual improvements over the former, it would be much more difficult to ascribe this to chance rather than intelligence."[47]

Teleology and Evolution: The Appeal to Value

Another type of post-Darwinian version of the teleological argument considers the process as a whole and regards human beings as its culmination. The leading exponents of it—F. R. Tennant, A. E. Taylor, and Peter Bertocci—claim that the emergence of intelligent beings with a sense of moral and aesthetic value justifies the inference to a divine intelligence who controls the process for purposes of his own.[48] I will present their basic argument in my own terms.

Survival Cannot Account for All Human Characteristics

According to Darwinian thought, evolution proceeds not by selection for conscious purposes, as in breeding race horses, but by selection for survival. Human beings represent the result of many thousands of years of selection in which the unfit were winnowed out. It follows that the features which are most characteristic of human beings today ought to be features of obvious survival value. Some, such as intelligence and morality, have survival value, others, like aesthetic sensitivity, do not.

Intelligence is one astonishing characteristic; it is also a feature whose survival value is obvious. It has enabled human beings to modify their environment and to force all other living species into subordinate roles.

Morality is one characteristic of human beings that may seem, at first glance, to lack survival value. Indeed, in certain circumstances moral considerations may lead an individual to lose his chance of surviving, as when a soldier fulfils his moral obligation to remain at a post and loses his chance to escape from an overwhelmingly powerful enemy. Yet morality may be regarded as serving the larger cause of the survival of the race. It may hold men together even when they are terrified by natural threats and by enemies; it may also serve to inhibit aggressive instincts that would lead members of given societies to destroy one another.

There are other characteristics of human beings which are harder to understand from the standpoint of survival. The sense for beauty in art and nature is one of the most striking features of human beings, yet Tennant, in particular, stresses the point that beauty is superfluous to the physical survival of human beings.[49] It is a special and astonishing link between man and nature that cannot be explained by the appeal to mere survival. Tennant claims that it points beyond itself to a link between man, in his spiritual capacities, and the divine author of nature. That is why some people come to God through apprehensions of beauty. Putting the matter in terms of Martin Buber's scheme of things, this is one important access to the eternal You.

The teleologists have a point, but they do not argue with the tough-minded rigor of scientists. Having decided that intellectual curiosity (of a theoretical kind, as in pure mathematics) and beauty do not contribute to survival, they do not challenge their own hypothesis. They do not, for example, think of ways in which the sense for beauty might have, at least, initially, served as an aid to survival. Suppose that, for the sake of argument, teleologists were to grant the point that beauty *does* contribute to survival; they would still claim that they have a case. From their standpoint the main issue is not mere survival. Their concern is expressed by the question, survival for what? In this context we may consider part of John Hick's definition of God as ". . . the unique infinite personal Spirit who has created out of nothing everything other than himself . . . his attitude towards his human creatures, whom he has made for eventual fellowship with himself, is one of grace and love."[50] Of course, human beings could not enjoy fellowship with God unless they both evolved and survived, but survival is for the *purpose* of loving fellowship with God. Teleologists can, therefore, argue that the reason some of the most distinctively human features are not conducive to survival is that they have another purpose. They are conducive to fellowship with the personal God.

The Odds against the Evolution of Man   Results that happen by purposeful design might also happen by chance. If dice are loaded, someone may find it relatively easy to throw ten double sixes in a row. With unloaded dice the same result might, in an extremely long span of time, occur by chance (it is even *possible* that someone might throw them right off, but it is extremely unlikely). The point of this observation is to call attention to the fact that in human experience an unlikely occurrence of this kind is not apt to be the result of chance. It is more plausible to assume that the result is the product of intelligence; someone has loaded the dice.

The teleological argument is based on experience. In its post-Darwinian versions teleologists consider the process of evolution as a whole. They consider naturalistic views like Bertrand Russell's which claim that man is "but the outcome of accidental collocations of atoms" to be radically implausible.[51] From their point of view it is like claiming that *Hamlet* was not produced by a creative and purposeful intelligence, but by a large number of children who were provided with dictionaries, scissors, paste, and paper—and who managed to put the words together in that order over a long period of time without having an aesthetic purpose in mind. It may be possible for *Hamlet* to be produced in this way—by possible I mean that no logical contradiction is involved in the notion— but teleologists insist that it is utterly implausible. It is far more likely that a genius produced it for dramatic purposes. In addition, teleologists argue that the odds against the emergence of human beings by pure chance ("the accidental collocations of atoms") are incalculably greater than the odds against a literary masterpiece like *Hamlet* being produced in that way. Therefore, teleologists claim that it is far more reasonable to assume that man was produced by the infinite God who has mysterious purposes of his own.

A. E. Taylor notes that the environment which produced both life and human beings depends on a vast number of factors. If any of them had been different, neither life nor man would have emerged. Yet, if pure chance was at work, the odds against things working out in exactly this way would have been overwhelming.

> With a different chemical constitution of the solar system, for example, the appearance of living organisms on our planet might have been impossible; even given the actual chemical constitution, it is easy to think of possible conditions of things which would have prevented our planet from being the habitat of creatures capable of attaining to science, or even to any experience or habit of customary expectation.[52]

At this point Taylor makes a crucial point against thinkers who accept nature and its laws as ultimate:

> Either we must be content to take it as an unexplained and inexplicable miracle that our environment should be one which has made the appearance of increasingly intelligent and purposeful species of organisms and the development of scientific knowledge possible, or we must carry back the presence of controlling and directing intelligence beyond the appearance of living species and admit that it has been at work throughout the whole history of the formation of the environment which is their indispensable background.[53]

Taylor's reflections appeared in 1945. They were the reflections of a philosopher with theistic views, and as such, they were apt to be somewhat suspect in circles oriented to the scientific outlook. Approximately two years later, a French physiologist, Pierre Lecomte du Noüy, provided scientific support for Taylor's type of teleological thinking. He produced a set of staggering figures, numbers that literally defy the imagination, to prove that even the formation of the simplest molecule required for life could not have been the product of mere chance.[54] More than 2,000 atoms are required to form one of these molecules. Simplifying the picture and reducing these atoms to two rather than five types, the odds against them forming, by chance alone, the required structure is the utterly unimaginable figure of 2.02×10^{-321} 2×10^{-321} or about two chances out of a number formed by 1 followed by a string of 321 zeroes! Lecomte du Noüy then produced further sets of astronomical figures to show that there could not possibly have been enough space or time to allow for the required numbers of "shaking-outs" to take place by pure chance. It is important to remember that this argument concerns only the simplest protein molecule; it does not deal with the unimaginably more complex factors required to produce living organisms. The odds against the chance formation of full living organisms, and especially against man with his intelligence, are literally, by the standards Lecomte du Noüy uses here, incalculable.

Lecomte du Noüy's conclusion is that an "anti-chance" factor was at work. If an intelligent being desires to operate against mere chance in the fall of dice, he can "load" them so that a string of double sixes will be produced. In the same way, an intelligent being, God, could choose the elements and order them in the required ways in order to produce the protein nuclei required for life. With the purpose of making an intelligent being in mind, God could—by using his own intelligence—create human beings.

The theistic view does not explain why God exists or why he has the purposes that he does have. Nevertheless, it explains more than is explained by the appeal to mere chance. Tennant makes this point explicitly in terms of one crucial point—man's ability to understand the world. He refers to it as the "adaptiveness [of the world] to understanding."

> If the world "made itself" . . . its adaptiveness to understanding has simply happened, and is part and parcel of the . . . [naturalist's] last irrationality. It gives him more to explain or to refuse to explain. . . . If, on the other hand, this be due to an intelligent Creator designing the world to be a theatre for rational life, mystery is minimised, and a possible and sufficient reason is assigned.[55]

The Sceptical Reply to the Appeal to Value

The theologians who advance the teleological argument are modest. They don't claim that they have a clinching argument that will convince every individual that God must exist. They only seek to persuade us that the facts of nature, as scientists uncover them, are better explained by an overall outlook oriented to belief in God than by a naturalistic worldview that appeals to "the chance collocations of atoms" as the basis of evolution. Yet sceptics deny the force of even these modest claims.

The Protein Molecule Was Not Made from Scratch Lecomte du Noüy calculated the astronomical odds against the simplest protein molecule being made from the beginning out of constituent atoms. As we have seen, the odds against it are held to be vast, indeed, unimaginably great. Yet scientists do not claim that the simplest of the protein molecules was produced instantaneously out of 2,000 atoms of five basic types. They did not come together in this way but were formed out of pre-existing substances much as salt (sodium chloride) is formed out of sodium hydroxide combined with hydrochloric acid. It is not formed out of the basic molecules of sodium and chlorine coming together from scratch.[56] Frederick Ferré makes the point colorfully and clearly:

> If I have never dropped a rubber ball and know nothing about the properties of rubber, it is quite useless for me to calculate the "probabilities" of its bouncing. For all I know it might shatter or splatter or run along the floor or do any of an almost infinite number of things when dropped. I drop it; it bounces. How amazing! Out of an almost infinite number of alternatives, this is what it did. And the first time, too. I drop it again; *again* it bounces. Incredible! Two vastly improbable results from just two "throws." I do it ten more times; each time the same result. My conclusion: there must be some "anti-chance" factor here disturbing the outworkings of pure statistical probability. And of course I am right. The "anti-chance" factor is the nature of rubber itself! The physical laws that govern it, the chemical bonds between its molecules. . . .[57]

Ferré rejects Lecomte du Noüy's thesis because the French scientist omitted a crucial factor: the "anti-chance factors present in nature itself." There are laws governing chemical valence and the influences of electrical charges on hypersaturated pre-organic solutions. This type of solution probably existed in the oceans of the earth at the earliest period of its existence. The properties of these solutions were the anti-chance factor that corresponds to the properties of the rubber in Ferré's example. Ferré's analysis does not prove that God does not exist, or that God did not influence the development of the protein molecule. It simply undercuts the reasonableness of the inference to *God* as the "anti-chance" factor that accounts for the formation of the protein molecule against stupendous odds.

Some readers will now ask: "Why were the hypersaturated solutions there? and why were the laws of nature what they were?" This is an interesting issue but is more relevant to the cosmological argument; it is dealt with in connection with the principle of sufficient reason (see pp. 231f.).

Odds Can Only Be Calculated on the Basis of Considerable Experience   The issue of the odds on the emergence of the protein molecule, the wing, or human intelligence is, in any case, a misguided one. The question takes us back to Hume's principles regarding analogy. In this context we can put it in a somewhat different way. The greater the similarity between occurrences and the more frequently we have observed them, the more accurately we can predict results. Upsets are common in sports because odds on the favorites are computed on the basis of relatively infrequent contests between opponents and these contests themselves take place under different circumstances. If two horses were rigidly controlled as to their training and general fitness, and if they raced constantly on the same tracks under the same conditions, we could, after 300 races between them, get very accurate odds. As horse players know, these ideal circumstances are never found.

The protein molecule and man have, as far as we know, emerged only on this planet. We have no comparable events that have been observed even once, much less on a large number of occasions. There is no way at all of computing the probabilities of proteins or human beings emerging. All we can say is that it has happened. We can be astonished at it and respond with deeply felt wonder, but that is quite a different thing from saying that it was improbable and stupendously improbable at that.

In the case of occurrences which as far as we know are singular, there are no odds at all.

Evolution and Design: Some Problems

Nelson claims that it makes more sense to attribute evolution to the guidance of divine intelligence rather than to pure chance. We have an analogue for the improvement of organs (like the eye) in the operations of human intelligence to improve artifacts (like the camera). There is no analogue to the operation of pure chance to produce an extended series of improvements in one type of functional adaptation.

Nelson's analogy of the development of the eye and the development of the camera is ingenious. It is impressive because he attempts to defend the argument from design at the very point at which most thinkers have found it vulnerable to evolution. Nevertheless, it seems to take

account of evolutionary theory without actually doing so. Nelson operates on the assumption that evolution simply involves the observation and
cataloguing of a series of stages in the development of an organ like the
eye or of an organism like the horse. In that case we must invoke
categories from outside evolutionary thought to account for the changes.
He takes over two explanatory categories from the debates over the
argument: chance and divine intelligence. Yet the appeal to these large-
scale types of explanations, and the effort to find analogies that make one or
the other more reasonable, mirrors the situation that existed in Hume's
time before the development of evolution as a scientific theory. At that
time they were simply ignorant of the way in which the eye developed.

    1   Biologists are now able to tell us a great deal about the way that
the eye and the horse developed. They show us, for example, the patterns
by which environment operates to affect the numbers and strains of
organisms. If white and black moths inhabit a certain area of England and
white moths prove more vulnerable to nighttime predators, then the black
moths will soon predominate. Evolutionary theorists have also dealt with
the mechanisms whereby changes in the structures of organisms are
effected. Earlier, the existence of chromosomes and genes were inferred
from observations of the way organisms varied over generations. In
recent years, the discovery of the DNA molecule and other developments
in biochemistry confirmed these inferences.

    Evolutionary theory is, therefore, able to account for the develop-
ment of an organ like the eye without reference to a purposive intelligence
that guides the process. In that case, no analogy is necessary. The
scientific account handles the data, and evolution undercuts the argument
from design.

    It is, however, always open to the theist to argue that the scientific
account does not explain why the original genetic pool existed or why that
particular pool rather than some other one existed. This line of argument
systematically excludes any scientific explanation, evolutionary or otherwise, as being adequate to the issue at hand. This point, however, is
germane to the cosmological argument and will be dealt with in that
context (see pp. 288f.).

    2   For the sake of argument a sceptic might acknowledge the need
to choose between chance and an intelligent deity as large-scale forces
that are operative in the process of evolution. Even so, Nelson's case for
choosing an intelligent deity would not be persuasive. In human affairs
(on which his analogy is based) the greater the intelligence, the fewer the
mistakes. The divine intelligence is supposed to be far greater than the
human. One would suppose that it would operate effectively to realize its
purposes. Yet evolution is, to put it mildly, messy. Species and individual

organisms prey on each other and certain lines of development, like the dinosaurs, wind up as blind alleys. If one assumes that nature is regulated by impersonal forces and that blind chance and adaptation to environment combine to produce new species and improved organs, then the messy aspects of the evolutionary scene do not represent a pressing problem. We can take them as a given aspect of the environment and adjust to them as best we can. It is harder to think of the evolutionary process as subject to the direction of an intelligent God who is working to bring human beings into a loving relation with himself.

It is again worth noting that if we had knowledge of the existence of a divine intelligence that was independent of the argument, the situation would be changed drastically. The facts of evolution not only could be squared with his existence, they would have to be squared with it since we would be certain that God exists. However, to claim that evolutionary theory and the facts it interprets, taken in themselves, justify an inference to an intelligent deity is a different matter.

Teleology as an Expression of Wonder

One way of dealing with the arguments for the existence of God is to dismiss them as logical demonstrations which adequately support their conclusions and to regard them instead as elaborate restatements of a basic religious attitude. In the case of the teleological argument the attitude involved is wonder at intricacies of nature and at the intelligence and sensitivity of human beings.

Thomas McPherson, a contemporary commentator on the argument from design, puts it this way:

> . . . the value of the argument from design is, as we might have expected, a religious one. Granted that a man believes in God already, it will be of great benefit to him to reflect upon the evidence of "contrivance" in the world; for this will have the effect of confirming him in his belief and in a religious attitude to the world.[58]

McPherson's statement about the value of the argument in confirming a religious view of the world is relevant to Wisdom's parable of the Invisible Gardener (see pp. 43 f.). Belief in the presence or absence of the purposeful activity of a gardener was found to be a matter of one's total response—emotional as well as intellectual—to the garden as a whole, rather than a difference of some facts about the garden. They both see the same things but the character who claims that a gardener is at work focuses on things like the special arrangements of some of the flowers. Martin Buber provides another interesting characterization of two basic responses to the world as a whole.

> In the history of the human spirit I distinguish between epochs of habitation and epochs of homelessness. In the former, man lives in the world as in a house, as in a home. In the latter, man lives in the world as in an open field and at times does not even have four pegs with which to set up a tent.[59]

Teleologists, in responding to the world, experience a sense of wonder at the intricacies of nature and the intelligence and sensitivity of human beings. Naturalists experience the same things but they do not find themselves in the "house" designed by a heavenly father. The two passages which close this chapter are expressions of wonder on the part of a nonbeliever who lives in a cosmic "open field" and the Psalmist for whom the wonders of the universe witness to the glory of God.

In *The Heavenly City of the Eighteenth Century Philosophers* the historian Carl Becker wrote:

> Edit and interpret the conclusions of modern science as tenderly as we like, it is still quite impossible for us to regard man as the child of God for whom the earth was created as a temporary habitation. Rather we must regard him as little more than a chance deposit on the surface of the world, carelessly thrown up between two ice ages by the same forces that rust iron and ripen corn, a sentient organism endowed by some happy or unhappy accident with intelligence indeed, but with an intelligence that is conditioned by the very forces that it seeks to understand and control. We do not know the ultimate cause of this cosmic process of which man is a part. Whatever it may be . . . it appears in its effects as neither benevolent nor malevolent, as neither kind nor unkind, but merely as indifferent to us. What is man that the electron should be mindful of him! Man is but a founding in the cosmos, abandoned by the forces that created him. Unparented, unassisted and undirected by omniscient or benevolent authority, he must fend for himself, and with the aid of his own limited intelligence find his way about in an indifferent universe.[60]

Here we have the spirit of a heroic naturalism that is apparently tough-minded. No one who shares this point of view would be sympathetic to the teleological argument. On the other hand, the believer might note the rational flaws in the argument and still respond to it favorably because it would strike him as a rationalistic restatement of the point that man is not a cosmic foundling. The sense of cosmic at homeness has been proclaimed eloquently in the eighth Psalm.

O Lord our sovereign
how glorious is thy name in all the earth!
Thy majesty is praised high as the heavens.
When I look up at thy heavens, the work of thy fingers,
the moon and the stars set in their place by thee,
what is man that thou shouldest be mindful of him
mortal man that thou shouldest care for him?
Yet thou hast made him little less than a God,
crowning him with glory and honour
Thou hast put everything under his feet. . . .
O lord our sovereign
How glorious is thy name in all the earth.

Chapter 11

The Ontological Argument: Perfection

The ontological argument received its most influential formulation from a theologian named Anselm in 1077.[61] Remarkably enough, it is a major topic of philosophical concern today. I say remarkably enough because two of the most formidable minds in the history of Western philosophy were supposed to have presented convincing refutations of it. In the twelfth century it was refuted by St. Thomas Aquinas.[62] Nevertheless, it enjoyed a revival in the sixteenth century. Descartes presented his own version of it, and it was also prominent in the thought of the other leading rationalists, Spinoza and Leibniz.[63] In the *Critique of Pure Reason* (1781), Kant subjected it to criticisms that were generally regarded as devastating.[64] As a result, for over a century and a half, it was largely neglected by theologians as well as by philosophers.

There are trends and fads in philosophy as well as in clothes. The recent revival of the ontological argument is a good example of it. In 1960, Norman Malcolm, a leading disciple of Ludwig Wittgenstein, published an essay defending it.[65] This challenging essay by a philosopher who represented an influential movement, provoked a flood of commentary. Reams of essays and a number of books and anthologies on the subject appeared in the next decade.[66] The ontological argument is now front and center on the philosophical stage, and the interest in it shows no sign of abating.

One reason for the renewed interest in the ontological argument is that it is peculiarly philosophical in character. The teleological argument appeals to common sense and it exploits the wonder that most of us feel in the presence of the grandeur and intricacy of nature. By contrast, the ontological argument restricts our attention to the concept of God and to standards of logical consistency. The object is to prove that when we think of an important aspect of the concept of God, we must (if we are to avoid contradiction) accept the existence of God.

BACKGROUND: CONCEPTS, DEFINITIONS, AND UNDERSTANDING

The jumping off point of the ontological argument is an important concept, namely, that God is "something than which nothing greater can be conceived." The term "concept" is a familiar one to college students. They are always being asked to discuss the concept of something or other—like freedom and tragedy. Ordinarily this can be done without paying attention to the meaning of "concept." In the context of the ontological argument this word is important, and I will spend some time on it.

Concept Does Not Mean Mere Definition

The term concept is intimately related to definitions. Even though they cannot be simply interchanged, dealing with definitions is of some help to understanding the meaning of concept.

One way of approaching the concept of God is to look up the word "God" in a dictionary and to memorize the definition. The ability to provide a definition of a term is part of what is required for understanding the concept of it, but it is certainly not enough. Students can easily memorize definitions of difficult concepts like "transcendence" and "inertia," but they can do so without understanding them. On the other hand, someone may understand a concept like "red" rather well, in the sense of being able to use the word properly and to justify his use of it and yet not be able to give a verbal definition of it.

As noted earlier, the word "concept" frequently appears on examinations. This is because it is intimately related to understanding. In order to show genuine understanding of a complex concept like religion a student has to be able to show an appreciation of where it applies, where it does not apply, and a sense of proportion in applying it. Suppose that a true or false examination read:

The concept of *religion* involves the following:

1 Belief in God
2 Special houses of worship
3 Clearly defined prayers and other rituals
4 Sacred texts
5 A company of authorized interpreters of the texts
6 Democratically elected interpreters of the texts
7 A community of the faithful
8 Thirty elders to run each house of worship
9 Belief in the afterlife
10 The use of incense in the house of worship

What if someone were to get seven of them right? Would that show that he understood the concept of religion? If he answered everyone of them correctly except for number eight, would this statement that having thirty (no more and no less) elders to run the houses of worship be so gross a mistake as to lead us to believe he was lucky at guessing the rest of them?

Clearly, true-false questions are a poor way of checking on whether or not someone understands concepts like religion. They not only permit a lot of guessing, but they do not show whether a person really knows the lay of the land. There are many controversial issues associated with the concept of religion. Consider, for example, the issue of "belief in God." If God is used in the way that Christians and Jews use the term, then at least one great religion, Theravadin Buddhism, doesn't involve belief in God. On the other hand, if God is used as Paul Tillich uses it, namely, as a symbol for the ultimate or the unconditioned, then God is what every religion is all about, and a Theravadin Buddhist definitely believes in God. Issues like this simply cannot be discussed on a true or false, yes or no basis. They must be written out. In order to deal accurately with concepts like democracy, religion, or God, a person must know some of their central features, and display a sense of relevance. That is why the ability to organize an essay around a concept is an important indication of whether or not it has been mastered.

Experience and the Concept of God

"God" is a term that is frequently used to stand for an agent, a center of power which has infinite knowledge of human affairs and infinite power in acting upon them. Yet God is not a physical object that can be pointed to.

The concept of God cannot then be learned as we learn the concept of "red," "round," or "hard." In our culture we learn about God as a character in biblical stories, which are technically called myths. In these stories God often operates as an invisible superman. As we grow older the concept is refined.

Believers learn about God in stories like that of the Garden of Eden in which he walks through it looking for Adam and Eve; or as someone jealous of the power of human beings, who in building the Tower of Babel, threaten to storm the heavens. The God of these portraits is crudely anthropomorphic. Believers are forced to think about what makes this heavenly being different from human beings. They then find other passages of the Bible which are anthropomorphic, but less crudely so. They learn about a God who demands that human beings achieve peace and justice. They refine their view of God in terms of the rest of their experience and at the same time have their view of God shape that experience. It is a process of continuing interaction which goes on in every religious community and in the minds and hearts of individual believers. The framework of reflection is as broad and complicated as human life and history. Out of it the concept of God emerges, or rather, various concepts of God emerge.

Any concept of God is the deposit of reflection on a vast body of experience, especially on experience that is set in the context of the life and history of a community of faith.[67] One concept of God appears throughout this book. It is captured in John Hick's definition: "A unique infinite omnipotent omniscient person who made the world out of nothing and created human beings whose ultimate destiny is to enjoy fellowship with him."[68] Like any definition, this is a shorthand statement which is a beginning not the end of a reasonable discussion of the concept. For example, it implies, but does not use, such key terms as transcendence and perfection.

Now we are in a position to appreciate what is meant by saying that the ontological argument takes the concept of God as its starting point rather than beginning with experience. Both concepts, "God" and "perfection," are products of experience. Yet Anselm ignores the wider human context—the experiences—that give rise to them and focuses on their logical implications. He focuses on the concepts that have been distilled from experience rather than on the experiences from which they have been distilled. He does not deal with existing things in the world like human beings in their moral interaction, glorious sunsets, or watches. He begins with "perfection", which is a very important feature of the concept of God, and tries to show that if we reflect on it, we will realize that God must exist.

Conceivability: Logic Contrasted with Imagination

In the teleological argument the conclusion "God exists" is merely probable. God's purposes are regarded as the *most likely* explanation of the intricate functional relations of natural organisms or of the evolutionary process considered as a whole. Teleologists do not, however, deny that other explanations are possible. By contrast, the ontological argument is a "hard" argument in the sense that it is supposed to be impossible for a person who understands it to deny the conclusion, namely, "God exists." As Matson put it, it involves "the inconceivability of the opposite."[69]

It is important to distinguish "inconceivable" from "unimaginable." To imagine something is to form an image or picture of it. Obviously, things we actually see, like men and horses, are both conceivable and imaginable. Yet, there are many things that are both conceivable and imaginable that we know we will never see. An example is a centaur. The concept involves a creature with the torso of a man and the body of a horse. Centaurs are easy to imagine; in fact, Greek artists both imagined and drew countless numbers of them. Although from what we know about biology, zoology, and physiology, centaurs cannot exist, yet their existence is not at all inconceivable. From the purely logical standpoint there might perfectly well have been creatures with the torsos of men and the bodies of horses in the world as well as in our minds.

There are other things which are conceivable, but not imaginable. Two excellent examples are the color ultraviolet and the chiliagon, a 1,000-sided figure all of whose sides are equal.[70] We cannot form a mental image of ultraviolet—when we try it we wind up thinking of a special shade of violet. Yet we know how to handle it conceptually. We know its wave length and all sorts of other things about its effects. In the case of the chiliagon, it is difficult to keep that many sides distinct. They blur into a circle. Yet in this case, too, we have no trouble operating with the concept. We know that it will have one thousand radii, all the radii will be equal, and all sorts of other things about it. The only thing that gives us trouble is the problem of forming a mental image of it.

Conceivable then, does *not* mean imaginable. In the standard use of the term, inconceivable means logically contradictory. There is no way of conceiving a five-sided square. The notion involves simultaneously claiming "both *A* and not *A*." *A* is the claim that the figure has four sides (this is part of the meaning of "square") and not *A* is the claim that it does *not* have four sides ("is five-sided"). Anselm and other thinkers who claim that the ontological argument works insist that once we think about the logical implications of the concept of perfection—which is an important part of the concept of God—we will realize that to deny the existence of God involves us in contradiction.

ANSELM I: GOD AS "SOMETHING THAN WHICH NOTHING GREATER CAN BE CONCEIVED"

In his essay, *Anselm's Ontological Arguments*, Normal Malcolm not only stimulated renewed philosophical interest in the subject, he also claimed that Anselm presented two significantly different versions of the argument. Malcolm claims that the first version is vulnerable to major criticisms but that the second is not (see pp. 261f., 269). The claim that there are two different versions of the argument is questionable.[71] What is beyond dispute is that in the second and third chapters of his *Proslogion*, Anselm uses two different *definitions* of God; both definitions reflect his understanding of perfection. The first, which I will refer to as Anselm I, is that God is "something than which nothing greater can be conceived." The second, which will be referred to as Anselm II, is that God is "something that is not conceivable as not existing." In this section I will present the ontological argument as formulated in terms of Anselm I and the major criticisms of it. The following section deals with Malcolm's effort to use Anselm II to meet these criticisms and thereby demonstrate the existence of God (see p. 258).

Statement of the Argument

Anselm's argument is directed against "the fool" who, in the words of the Psalmist, "says in his heart: 'There is no God'" (Psalm 14:1).

    1 The *definition* of God is: "something than which nothing greater can be conceived."
    2 The concept of "something than which nothing greater can be conceived" exists in thought because we are entertaining the concept in our minds as we discuss it.
    3 *Key assumption*: A being existing in reality as well as in thought is greater than if it exists only in thought.
    4 What is involved in the fool's statement that "there is no God" is the claim that "something than which nothing greater can be conceived" exists *only* in thought and not in reality as well.
    5 To say that "something than which nothing greater can be conceived" exists only in thought involves the fool in contradiction. Applying the key assumption, we find that we can then think of something greater than "something than which nothing greater can be conceived," namely, that same concept as existing in reality as well as in thought.
    6 To avoid this contradiction the fool need only concede that God exists.

Anselm's Strategy

Anselm's argument depends on a distinction between what can be verbalized and what can be conceived. A child can *say*, "I know that a square can have five sides!" Nothing prevents him from doing so but we realize that the child is merely mouthing words. He cannot possibly conceive of a five-sided square because the concept is self-contradictory. Anselm charges the fool with the same error: verbalizing what he cannot conceive. It is not quite as gross as the case of the five-sided square because "something than which nothing greater can be conceived" is not linked to the concept of God in the glaring way that the characteristic of having four sides is linked to the concept of a square. That is why it takes a considerable amount of reflection to see that Anselm's "fool" is involved in a contradiction.

The bare statement of Anselm's argument is not enough reflection. The definition has to be examined to see whether it is religiously relevant as well as philosophically valid. The persuasiveness of Anselm's key assumption must also be argued for, and finally, the implicit contradiction in the fool's denial of the existence of God must be made explicit.

The Definition as Religiously Appropriate

Critics of the arguments for the existence of God often challenge their relevance to genuine religion. They claim that even if the arguments were effective, they would not yield the God of theism. I have, for example, already noted that Hume raised the question of whether the argument from design, if valid, would not yield the many gods of Mount Olympus rather than the one God of theism (see p. 225).

Anselm's definition of God is "something than which nothing greater can be conceived." On first exposure to this strange phrase it seems to fail religiously because it is utterly abstract, and also because it does not mention goodness, knowledge, or any of the other features that believers associate with the personal God of the Judeo-Christian tradition.

Reflection should change this initial impression. The key to an understanding of the religious relevance of Anselm's definition of God is provided by his interpretation of "greater." By greater he does not mean greater in size but better, that is, greater in value.[72] "Something than which nothing *better* can be conceived" is something that cannot be excelled in any respect by anything else. Anselm does not specify any of the respects in which the God of his definition is better. This seems to be a weakness in his definition, but it is actually a source of strength. By way of illustration, let me recall Buber's view of God as the eternal You (see pp. 110 ff.). To be a "You" in Buber's technical sense of the term is to be open and responsive to the other, any other, that one meets. From this

standpoint, any human being is very limited. Sometimes we are responsive and sometimes we are self-absorbed. By contrast, God, the eternal
You, is always present, always responsive. In other words, God is
"something than which nothing more responsive can be conceived."

This Buberian definition of God might be rejected on the grounds
that responsiveness is hardly the characteristic of God that believers
regard as most valuable. Some theologians might insist that God is more
appropriately characterized in terms of power, knowledge, goodness, or
still other qualities.

These objections only underscore the effectiveness of Anselm's
definition. He does not commit himself on the question of which specific
qualities can be legitimately attributed to God. His definition is designed
to show that, whatever they are or may be, God has them, all of them, to a
degree that cannot be surpassed by any other being whatever.[73] If
knowledge is appropriate then, according to Anselm's definition, God is
all-knowing. If responsiveness is legitimately attributable to God then,
according to this same definition, God is eternally responsive. In other
words, God possesses every perfection (valuable quality) that can be
conceived and he has them to the greatest possible degree. This is, at least
in part, what we mean by perfection, and Anselm seems to have isolated it
in a valid way. Furthermore, since perfection is something that religious
thinkers have traditionally attributed to God, "something than which
nothing greater can be conceived" is not an arbitrary definition that
Anselm concocted for the purpose of making his argument "go." It has
valid theological credentials.

Anselm's definition is also religiously potent; J. N. Findlay linked it
to worship, which is the most distinctively religious action performed by
believers. Findlay defines the attitude of worship as one in which we
revere and adore an object. We bend our knees and desire to fulfil its
demands. Almost all believers engage in worship, but very few of them
reflect on it. Findlay does. He sets up the following standard of what the
object must be like for the attitude and act of worship to be appropriate:
"We find it natural to say that such an attitude can only be fitting where the
object reverenced *exceeds* us very vastly whether in power or wisdom or
in other valued qualities. . . . To feel religiously is therefore to presume
surpassing greatness in some object."[74] By linking the God of the
ontological argument to the God of ordinary worshipers, Findlay demonstrates the religious power of Anselm's definition.

The Being as Existing in Thought   One of the stickiest points in
the argument is the second step in which Anselm claims that the concept
of God as "something than which nothing greater can be conceived"

exists in thought. It is odd that this point should be so problematic because, on the surface, it seems like an appeal to common sense. If someone, in the course of an argument, asks us to think of the concept of an isosceles triangle, we can readily do so. We think about a triangle with two equal sides, and it is then perfectly in order for the person who has asked us to think about it to claim that the concept of an isosceles triangle exists in thought. Anselm claims that the same holds true for the concept of "something than which nothing greater can be conceived." They can conceive of every existing thing, no matter how great—even the vastest galaxy—as something that could be greater. Just as of every number, no matter how great, they could conceive of a greater, just by adding any other number to it. Although they would concede that they can hear Anselm's words and try to figure out what they mean, they would deny that they genuinely understand his concept. Therefore they would deny that it exists in *their* thought.[75] This question can and does arise in the context of Anselm's first definition of God. Yet it arises even more urgently in the context of his second definition. For this reason, I propose to defer discussion of this issue until Anselm II is under consideration (see pp. 266 ff.). At this point, we may proceed as if the mere fact that we register Anselm's words and think about them is enough to establish his point that "something than which nothing greater can be conceived exists in thought."

Key Assumption: Its Plausibility Anselm's key assumption distinguishes the existence of a being in thought alone (that is, by my entertaining the concept of it in my mind) and the same being as existing in reality. To appreciate it, we ought to realize that while we can all entertain the concept of a unicorn (a one-horned white horse) in our minds, there has never been an instance of a "unicorn-find" in reality. The situation is different with the ninth planet of our solar system. An astronomer studied the data of our solar system and formed the concept of a ninth planet in his mind. It included the size, the orbit, and other details. Some years later, it was observed. It conformed to the astronomer's concept. This settled the question of its status. Until it was observed it might have been nothing more than a concept in the mind of the astronomer who first worked out the details. It might also have existed in the minds of other astronomers who read his work. After the observation it still existed in the minds of astronomers but, in addition, it was known to exist "out there" in the solar system.

It may help to look at it another way. We think of a being or a thing like a five-dollar bill. We can form the concept of this being in our minds, thinking of its size, the color of the bill, etc. We can also ask the question of whether the five-dollar bill is instantiated, that is, the question of whether there is an instance of it out there in the world.

We are now in position to appreciate the meaning and force of Anselm's key assumption. He claims that a thing is greater (more valuable) if it exists in reality than if it merely exists in thought. The assumption has a surface plausibility. Think of the haunting vision of St. Thomas More's *Utopia*. Initially it existed in his mind alone. Once he published the book it also existed in the minds of his readers. Yet we cannot live in Utopia in the way that we can live in Florence. If Utopia existed in reality as well as in the mind, it would be far more valuable. People could actually live in it in addition to being inspired by it. As we shall soon see, one of Kant's criticisms of the ontological argument was his challenge to the surface plausibility of this key assumption. But first, the fool's self-contradiction must be spelled out.

The Fool's Self-Contradiction   The statement "There is no God" or "God does not exist" has been made countless times throughout history and often by extraordinarily brilliant thinkers. Yet Anselm characterizes the person who makes it as a fool. It should now be apparent that it takes a great deal of reflection to understand how Anselm proposes to make good on his characterization. Yet, if we grant the cogency of his definition of God and of his key assumption, the person who denies the existence of God does contradict himself.

To deny the existence of God one must, on Anselm's analysis, think as follows: (1) entertain the concept of "something than which nothing greater can be conceived" in one's mind and (2) claim that it exists *only* in one's mind because one thinks about "something than which nothing greater can be conceived" and then insists that it is not instantiated.

At this point Anselm tightens the screws. He introduces his key assumption that a being existing in reality as well as in thought is greater than if it exists only in thought. The "fool" is then involved in self-contradiction even though he is not aware of it. The form of the self-contradiction is "I can conceive of that which cannot be conceived." Suppose that someone accepts both Anselm's definition and his key assumption. If he then says, "There is no God," he is, in effect, making the following statement, "I can conceive of something greater than 'something than which nothing greater can be conceived.'" That which is greater is precisely God as existing in reality as well as in thought. In order to avoid this contradiction "the fool" need only concede that God exists.

Criticisms of Anselm I

Initial exposure to the ontological argument results in a fairly typical set of reactions. The first reaction is one of bafflement ("I don't get it") but hard thinking generally yields a sudden flash of illumination ("Good grief! It works!") which is succeeded by suspicion ("There must be a catch somewhere").

The problem is that sitting in an arm chair and merely reflecting on a definition of God seems to yield a tremendously important conclusion. Very little study and knowledge is needed in order to support this reflection. Only two supporting points are required: the law of contradiction and the key premise. One philosopher, expressing the reaction of suspicion, asked: "Would it not be rather extraordinary if such a great conclusion could be got so easily?"[76] Yet another contemporary commentator on the argument—who was also suspicious—was forced to admit that "although the argument certainly looks at first sight as if it ought to be unsound, it is profoundly difficult to say what exactly is wrong with it."[77] This point is important because saying what is wrong with an argument—in the sense of giving convincing rational counter-arguments—is, for philosophers, the name of the game; hunches won't do. In the sections which follow we will see that it is, indeed, very difficult to show what is wrong with the ontological argument.

Gaunilo: If the Argument Works, It Works Too Well Shortly after Anselm's ontological argument appeared, a monk, Gaunilo, wrote his answer, *On Behalf of the Fool.*[78] In effect, Gaunilo tries to impale Anselm on the horns of the following dilemma. Either the argument doesn't work, or it works too well. One horn of the dilemma is obviously disastrous for Anselm because if the argument doesn't work, then he hasn't succeeded in proving the existence of God. The other horn is more intriguing. Gaunilo shows that if the argument is sound, it can be used to demonstrate the existence of "an island than which none greater can be thought."

The crucial point is that if "exists" is used in the ordinary sense of referring to an object that can be located in space and time, observed with senses, and (when one is in its presence) pointed to, then we can reason as follows:

1 Let us think of "an island than which none greater can be conceived."

2 A being as existing in reality as well as in thought is greater than if it exists only in thought.

3 If we claim that "an island than which none greater can be conceived" exists in thought alone and not in reality as well as in thought, we contradict ourselves.

4 Because we can then think of an island greater than "an island than which none greater can be conceived," we can think of this island as existing in space and time as well as in thought.

5 We will therefore have declared of "an island than which none greater can be conceived" that a greater *cannot* be thought and that a greater *can* be thought; this is a contradiction.

6 In order to avoid the contradiction we must declare that "an island than which none greater can be conceived" exists in reality as well as in thought.

This procedure can be generalized. It can be used to prove the existence of "a composer than which none greater can be conceived," or "a basketball player than which none greater can be conceived" and anything else that can be fitted into the formula of "an x such that none greater can be conceived." That is why I have characterized the second horn of the dilemma by saying that if the argument works, it works too well. It enables us to prove the existence "out there" of a perfect island, a perfect basketball player, and countless other things that we know perfectly well do not exist.

This is a clear example of the use of the *reductio ad absurdum* as the refutation of an argument. You provisionally accept it as valid and then bring out its absurdity by showing that utterly unacceptable consequences follow from it, thereby demonstrating that it is really invalid.

Gaunilo's criticism seems to be effective because, in this version of the argument, Anselm does not indicate the kind of existence that he attributes to God. In the discussion of Anselm II, it will be clear that Anselm makes an effort to show why Gaunilo's criticism does not draw blood. The answer to it is that islands are supposed to be observable; God is not. Therefore, in applying Anselm's line of argument to demonstrate the existence of a perfect island, Gaunilo misuses it. Anselm is not talking about something that is supposed to exist in space and time. He is using his argument to demonstrate the existence of the transcendent God who is, in principle, nonobservable. Gaunilo's criticism does not show that there is anything illegitimate about that (see p. 261).

Kant: Existence Is Not a Predicate   As noted earlier, as a result of Kant's criticisms, the ontological argument was philosophically eclipsed for over a century and a half. Kant's most telling point was that "existence is not a predicate."[79] This statement, which has been regarded as definitive and repeated by countless philosophers, is itself not clear. I hope to clarify it and to show the force that it has when directed at the first version of Anselm's argument. In the second part of this chapter, I shall show why Malcolm, Hartshorne, and others think that it does *not* score against the version of Anselm's ontological argument that uses the second definition.

The term *predicate* is primarily grammatical. In the sentence "Tom is tall," Tom is the subject and is tall the predicate. One of the confusions involved in the view that existence is not a predicate relates to the term "predicate" itself. The grammatical distinction between subjects and predicates is parallel to the philosophical distinction between particulars and universals, and, to compound the confusion, universals are sometimes called predicates.[80] In the sentence just quoted "Tom" is a particular entity that can be pointed to, and "is tall" is a general term whose function is descriptive. If someone who didn't know Tom asked us who he is, we might, if he were present in a room with other people, point to him and say: "Tom is the man standing next to the sofa." If Tom were not present we might describe him by means of a series of general terms or universals such as tall, blue-eyed, wide-shouldered, fat and grey-haired. These universals, which function grammatically as predicates (Tom is tall, blue-eyed, etc.) would enable someone who didn't know him to form the concept of "Tom." This individual could then pick Tom out of a group, point to him, and say: "There's Tom."

A further source of confusion is that *verbs* can also serve as predicates that help to describe a subject. If there were a group of men in a room, and all of them except Tom were sitting, then Tom could be described simply by saying: "Tom is standing." Grammatically, "Tom exists" seems similar to "Tom stands." Yet, we have already noted the fact that a statement may be grammatically proper, but philosophically invalid (see p. 14).[81] Kant analyzes "exists" philosophically and uses his analysis to challenge the key assumption of the ontological argument: something that exists in reality as well as in thought is greater than that same thing as existing in thought alone.

Kant's illustration of the point is financial. He claims that there is no difference between one hundred dollars as existing in thought alone and one hundred dollars as existing in reality as well as in thought. At first glance this illustration seems perverse. Far from undercutting Anselm's key assumption, it seems to support it. One hundred dollars as existing in reality as well as in thought certainly seem greater (better) than one hundred imaginary dollars, that is, one hundred dollars as existing in thought alone. We can buy things with one hundred real dollars; obviously, this cannot be done with one hundred imaginary dollars.

The point did not elude Kant. He said that the distinction between real and imaginary dollars would make a considerable difference to his financial status, but his point was that the *concept* of one hundred dollars is not affected by the claim that it exists. The position is very odd. Kant can take this provocative position because he is not concerned with home economics. He deals with the role of predicates in describing the particular subject that is under discussion; in other words, with their use as descriptive universals. To grasp Kant's point, imagine yourself in Germany, without any American currency available, trying to communicate the concept of a five-dollar bill. You tell your German friend about its color, shape, size, and describe the picture of Lincoln. You may add as many characteristics (or predicates) as you like; you can tell him about Lincoln's beard or the location of the serial number. Yet no matter how exhaustive you get in your list of descriptive characteristics, exists will not be one of them. It is not an additional characteristic that helps the German to know what to look for when he wants to find a five-dollar bill; therefore, exists is not, in that sense, a predicate. Once your German friend has a clear concept of a five-dollar bill, he can go out into the world to see whether something matches it. He will find one and see that it does. Then he can say of the concept of the five-dollar bill (that he has formed without the benefit of the term "exists") that it is instantiated. Something exactly corresponding to this concept has been observed to exist.

He can equally well form the concept of a unicorn in his mind and make the same test. He will find that nothing corresponds to this concept, or in other words, unicorns do not exist. In both cases, existence is something external to the concept; it is not a predicate or descriptive characteristic that is essential to forming the concept. "Five dollar bills exist" means there are things that match the set of descriptive characteristics that form the concept of the five-dollar bill. "Unicorns do not exist" means that there are no such things corresponding to the set of descriptive characteristics that form the concept unicorn.[82]

Now we can see why Kant insists that, conceptually speaking, one hundred real dollars is no greater, in the sense of being more valuable than, one hundred imaginary dollars. It cannot be more valuable, because the *concept* is, in both cases, precisely the same; there are ten thousand pennies in both of them. The difference is that in speaking of one hundred real dollars we declare that we have valid grounds for claiming that the concept of one hundred dollars is instantiated, that is, that something that corresponds to it can be found "out there" in the world. Obviously, when we speak of one hundred imaginary dollars, we make no such claim.

Kant uses this analysis to deny the validity of the key assumption of Anselm I, namely, that something existing in reality as well as in thought is greater than that same thing existing in thought alone. Kant insists that "something than which nothing greater can be conceived" as instantiated is *not* greater than as existing only in the mind. The concept is the same whether the thing exists only in thought or in reality as well. Kant also insists that the only way to determine whether anything exists in the world "out there" is to look and see. Therefore, the man who says "There is no God" is not a fool. "God" may mean "something than which nothing greater can be conceived," but this concept may or may not be instantiated. We cannot settle that by thought alone, anymore than we can settle the question of the existence of five-dollar bills or unicorns by thought alone.[83]

Contemporary philosophers have discussed Kant's view of existence and predication extensively. They have shown that there are a number uses of "exists" in which it serves as a predicate, in Kant's sense of a descriptive universal. I shall illustrate three of them.[84] The first is "Florence exists, but Utopia does not." A person who was unfamiliar with the concepts of both Florence and Utopia would be given information that would be useful in identifying them. If he came upon a city in a given geographical location, he would realize that it could not be Utopia, whereas, he would know that Florence is the sort of place that is to be found somewhere on this earth.

Another use of "exists" as a descriptive predicate may be illustrated by a statement that could have been made in 1962: "President Kennedy exists, but President Jefferson does not." In that case the listener would have realized that President Kennedy could be observed on the job in Washington, whereas, President Jefferson could only be found in history books.

A person who had a bad hangover might insist, "These bats exist!" In this case he would be warning us to keep our hair covered because they are not imaginary like those creatures that are seen by alcoholics suffering from *delerium tremens.*

These uses of "exists" are genuine descriptive predicates, but not indispensable ones. In each of them "exists" could be replaced by more precise predicates: "Florence is an actual city, but Utopia is 'fictitious'"; "President Kennedy is 'alive,' but President Jefferson is dead"; "These bats are 'not hallucinatory.'"

All these uses of "exists" as a descriptive predicate are legitimate, but they do not help Anselm I. We have seen that one of them means "living." Let us add this predicate to the concept of God. In that case, it would mean that God is living, not dead. It is easy to check on the truth of the statement, "President Kennedy is living." We check it by means of observations. It is now false; in 1962 it was true. God, however, is not supposed to be observable. Therefore, the tests that we use in checking on whether someone exists or not (is living or not) do not apply to God.

The same point applies to the ascription to God of the other predicates
that I have substituted for "exists," namely, "not fictitious" and "not
hallucinatory." Nevertheless, the fact that philosophers can come up with
valid cases where "exists" serves as a predicate weakens the force of
Kant's pronouncement that "existence is not a predicate." It can no
longer be trotted out as though it is self-evident and unexceptionable. An
examination of the role of mathematics will show that the situation is
even more complex.

Kant's analysis of existence and predication proceeds on the
assumption that instantiation is determined by observation. To appreciate
the point consider the logical formula for an existential claim, that is, the
claim that something exists: "There is an x such that. . . ." Kant claimed
that the only legitimate specifications that can be used to fill in the blank
are descriptive predicates like green, square, hard, and the rest. These are
the only kinds that enable us to go out into the world and to see whether
anything corresponding to the given concept of x is to be found. The
majority of contemporary empiricists share Kant's assumption.

In his extended comment on the question of existence and predication Alvin Plantinga, a contemporary analytic philosopher and logician,
proposes to fill in the blanks of the existential claim with numbers.[85] His
illustration deals with prime numbers, that is, with numbers, like seven,
that cannot be divided without remainder by any other whole number. He
uses the formula of the existential claim to make the statement, "There is
a prime number between fifty and fifty-five." The statement is true and
the number fifty-three instantiates the concept of "a prime number
between fifty and fifty-five." Furthermore, it does so in a way that
parallels Anselm's instantiation of the concept of God in his argument.
The procedure is a priori, and the statement "Fifty-three is a prime
number between fifty and fifty-five" is, according to the rules of mathematics, necessarily true.

Many philosophers, especially those with a positivistic bent, reject
the notion that numbers can be used to instantiate existential claims. They
object to a philosopher like Plantinga using numbers to fill in the blanks of
the existential formula because they resist all moves that bring the
treatment of numbers closer to the procedures we use for handling such
observable and independently existing things as tables, mountains, and
animals.[86]

Plantinga, obviously, disagrees. He claims that there is nothing
about the logical form of the existential claim, "There is an x such
that . . ." which restricts its use to observables. The formula is neutral. If
any philosopher insists that the blanks can only be filled in by descriptive
predicates, he has to make the case for it. This issue is very technical and

I will not pursue it further. Instead, for the sake of argument, let's accept Plantinga's position. In that case, fifty-three counts as an instantiation of the legitimate existential claim, "There is a prime number between fifty and fifty-five." Even so, it is hard to see how this helps the ontological argument. There are many philosophical arguments about the exact status of mathematicals like "forty" and "the square root of," but no philosopher suggests that numbers could possibly have the qualities that believers attribute to God. Numbers cannot be knowing, good, responsive, and the like. Therefore, even if it is legitimate, Plantinga's mode of instantiation merely yields another use of "exists" that seems irrelevant to the purpose of the argument.

To summarize: Kant's view that "existence is not a predicate" was regarded as sharply etched and authoritative. Its authority was invoked by generations of philosophers as sufficient reason for ignoring the ontological argument. Yet discussions of "exists" among contemporary philosophers diminish the effectiveness of Kant's case. They do not, however, demolish Kant's position by showing that it is mistaken or that it is irrelevant to the ontological argument. They merely erode the force of Kant's view of existence and predication by coming up with a variety of legitimate uses of existence as a predicate.

Where does that leave us? Admittedly, none of the legitimate uses of "exists" as a predicate is exactly like Anselm's. Clearly, if the word is to be applied to God, it is being used in a distinctive sense.[87] This observation should not startle religious thinkers. After all, they do not believe that God is an observable being like a horse, or that God is a nonobservable reality that can be dealt with in the same way as numbers. The transcendent God is unique and the peculiarities of "exists" that emerge in discussions of the reality of God are to be expected.

Ontologists are disposed to claim that the burden of proof is on the critics of the argument who have failed to come up with an unequivocal and authoritative use of "exists." They claim that critics must prove that "exists" cannot be used in the way that Anselm and other ontologists use it.

The critics, obviously, try to shift the burden of proof to the ontologists by stressing the radical dissimilarities between the way "exists" functions in the ontological argument and the way that it functions in ordinary contexts, like dealing with observable things, and even in some less ordinary contexts, like dealing with prime numbers. They challenge ontologists to clarify the use of "exists" in the ontological argument and to provide reasons for our accepting that use as legitimate.

In his essay "Anselm's Ontological Arguments" Norman Malcolm has, in effect, accepted this challenge. In what he calls the second version of the argument he finds a line of reasoning that develops the distinctive character of "exists" as applied to God, namely, that God necessarily exists. This mode of existence is not specified in the first version, for which reason Malcolm regards that argument as vulnerable to the criticisms of Gaunilo and Kant. He thinks that the second version works.

ANSELM II: GOD AS NECESSARY BEING

In Anselm I God is defined as "something than which nothing greater be conceived." Anselm tries to prove that to *deny* that God—as defined by this concept—exists in reality as well as in thought involves a contradiction. The problem with Anselm I is that his meaning existence is not clearly specified. This leaves the argument, at least on some readings of it, vulnerable to criticisms like those of Kant and Gaunilo. However, in the next chapter of his *Proslogium* Anselm provides another definition of God, namely, as "something that is not conceivable as not existing." This phrase is generally taken to mean that God's existence is necessary. The notion is difficult to understand and highly controversial. In order to grapple with the intricate tangle of philosophical issues involved, we need to come to grips with the terms "contingent beings" and "necessary being."

From Language to Being

The terminology of the logical positivists still dominates philosophical discussions in the English-speaking world even though this movement has passed from the scene. We have already considered the two categories of statements that were central to positivism, the analytic, and the synthetic. The most important philosophical consideration that is directed to statements is the question of truth and falsity. When we shift our focus from language to beings, we find that there are types of *beings* that correspond to the types of *statements* that the positivists considered. Existence is the most important philosophical consideration that pertains to beings.

Contingent Beings Correspond to Synthetic Statements
Synthetic statements are statements of fact. They may be either true or false. Consider the synthetic statement, "This book has white pages." It is true, but it *merely happens* to be true. The publishers might have used yellow pages; in that case the statement would have been false.

Now let us consider beings (that is, persons and things) instead of words. We would then focus on the pages themselves instead of on the statements about them. The pages, and all other beings that can be observed and located in space and time, are called "contingent beings."

Contingent beings are the sorts of things that *merely happen* to exist. There are further parallels between them and synthetic statements that are worth exploring.

The truth or falsity of synthetic statements is not a matter of necessity. It is possible for any synthetic statement to be either true or false and observation determines which is the case. It is possible for contingent beings to exist and not to exist, and in this case, too, observation settles the issue. Another parallel is that the synthetic or factual character of a statement is not a function of its truth or falsity. The false statement "This page is yellow" is just as synthetic as the true statement "This page is white." Similarly, it is not actual existence that determines the contingent status of a being, but rather the fact that it is the sort of thing that might or might not exist. Although unicorns do not exist, and horses exist, both species are contingent. There is nothing necessary about the nonexistence of unicorns. A herd of white one-horned horses might be found in some hitherto unexplored part of the world, and then we would realize that unicorns exist after all. Although horses actually exist, there is nothing necessary about their existence. Had every member of the foxlike species from which horses evolved been wiped out, horses would not have existed. What is true of the species is true of individuals. It is not necessary that any individual horse should exist.

Being and the Question of Correspondence with Analytic Statements

Turning to the question of the truth and falsity of analytic statements, we find ourselves dealing with necessity. Analytic statements are necessarily true. To deny them involves contradiction. Therefore, it is impossible for the denial of an analytic statement to be true. It is necessarily false.

The analytic statement "A quadrilateral is four-sided" is necessarily true, because "quadrilateral" means "a four-sided figure." Its logical form is the principle of identity; "A is A," that is "A four-sided figure is four-sided." The statement "A quadrilateral is five-sided," cannot possibly be true. It claims that "A four-sided figure is five-sided (not four-sided)" which is a contradiction that can be symbolized by "A is not A."

The correspondence of contingent beings to synthetic statements, which we just considered, is relatively unproblematic. The question of whether there is a mode or type of being which similarly corresponds to analytic statements (and their denials) is highly controversial. Indeed, the ontological argument itself is one important way of getting into the problem.

It seems as though there is a clear-cut parallel in *being* to the *denial* of analytic statements, that is, to the contradictions that are necessarily false.[88] We might say that the figure of a five-sided quadrilateral corresponds in *being* to the necessarily false *statement*, "A quadrilateral is five-sided." In other words, by the same a priori method which we used to show that the statement is necessarily false, we can show that the figure of a five-sided quadrilateral is necessarily nonexistent. A more common illustration of this sort of necessary nonexistence is the square circle.

Corresponding to analytic statements, which are necessarily true, we would have to posit a necessarily existent being. This being, is, as we shall see, the "God" of Anselm II, that is, God as "not conceivable as not existing." A sketch may help to emphasize the correspondences.

Statements	Beings
Mode of Possibility	

Synthetic	**Contingent**
Definition: It is possible for them to be either true or false	*Definition:* It is possible for them to exist or not to exist
Illustrations: "Unicorns exist" (false in fact, but might be true)	*Illustrations:* Unicorns (do not actually exist, but conceivable as existing)
"Horses exist" (true in fact, but might be false)	Horses (actually exist, but conceivable as not existing)

Mode of Necessity	

Analytic and Contradictory	**Necessary**
Definition: An *analytic* statement is necessarily true and its denial is *contradictory* (necessarily false)	*Definition:* Beings whose existence or nonexistence is necessary
Illustrations: "A square has four sides" (necessarily true)	*Illustrations:* God, i.e., necessary being (not conceivable as *not* existing)
"It is *not* the case that a square has four sides" (necessarily false)	A five-sided square (not conceivable as existing), i.e., its nonexistence is necessary

The Answer to Gaunilo: Islands Are Contingent Beings

What Malcolm calls the second version of Anselm's argument may not be another version at all but merely a clarification of the meaning of "greater" in the phrase, "something than which nothing greater can be conceived." In any case, the important question is not whether it is a different version of the argument but whether the points that Malcolm makes are valid and convincing.

Malcolm never states the argument in concise form with specific steps. Instead, he considers traditional objections to the argument such as those of Gaunilo and Kant and tries to answer them. His procedure is to state Anselm's second definition of God as "something which is not conceivable as not existing" and to explore its implications. I shall follow Malcolm's procedure, although I will use my own order and will state the points in my own terms, beginning with the reply to Gaunilo.[89]

Gaunilo's refutation of Anselm's argument depends on his ability to show that if the argument demonstrated the existence of God, it could also be used to demonstrate the existence of "an island than which none greater can be conceived." Islands, however, are observable and locatable in time and space; in other words, islands are contingent. Any island, or even islands as a class, might exist, and they might equally well not exist. Therefore, Anselm's second definition, which specifies God as "not conceivable as not existing," shows that his argument cannot be used to demonstrate the existence of any contingent being. It can only be used to demonstrate the existence of a necessary being, and such a being is not, by its nature, observable. Necessary being is part of what is meant by the God of theism, even though it is by no means exhaustive of this concept.

The Answer to Kant: Necessary Existence IS a Predicate

According to Malcolm's analysis, the sense of existence involved in Anslem II, "not conceivable as not existing," is necessary existence. Therefore, even if Kant is right in claiming that "existence is not a predicate" (and Malcolm thinks he is), this applies only to contingent existence. By contrast, "necessary existence" is a defining characteristic which distinguishes God from all other beings.

Malcolm also shows that necessary existence is a valuable characteristic or a perfection by linking the concept of necessary existence to independence.[90] Malcolm claims that in ordinary speech we regard dependence as a defect and independence as a characteristic that adds to the value of a thing. He uses the example of two sets of dishes that are the same in all respects except that one is more fragile than the other. The set that is more fragile depends on more careful handling for its continued existence. Therefore, it is inferior to the other set. Malcolm applies this point to the contrast between contingent and necessary beings. Contingent beings depend on something else both for coming into existence and for continuing to exist. Human beings are contingent, and we depend on our parents for coming into being and on parental care and food for continuing to exist. By contrast, "something which is not conceivable as not existing" cannot depend on anything to bring it into existence or for its continued existence because its nonexistence is inconceivable. It must exist independently of any state of affairs whatever.

Malcolm's exposition of the strength of Anselm's second definition of God clarifies the meaning of "greater" in "something than which nothing greater can be conceived" by showing that "greater" means "necessary existence." Necessary existence is not only a predicate, it is a perfection of incomparable value. Therefore, Malcolm claims that when the ontological argument is understood in terms of Anselm's second definition, it is not vulnerable to Kant's criticism that existence is not a predicate.

The Answer to Findlay: Necessary Being Is a Legitimate Concept

In different ways Gaunilo and Kant both attacked the key assumption of Anselm's argument, namely, that a being as existing in reality as well as in thought is greater than as merely existing in thought. J. N. Findlay adopts another tack. He ignores the premises of the argument and concentrates his fire on Anselm's second definition of God, namely, that God is necessary being.

As noted earlier, Findlay begins by claiming that Anselm's definition is religiously appropriate because it is implied in the distinctively religious act of worship. Findlay insists that this involves the tendency to "abase ourselves before some object, to defer to it wholly, to devote ourselves to it with unquestioning enthusiasm, to bend the knee before it, whether literally or metaphorically."[91] When Findlay looks for an appropriate object of worship, he decides that no contingent being will do: "We can't help feeling that the worthy object of our worship can never be a thing that merely *happens* to exist. . . . His own non-existence must be wholly unthinkable in any circumstances. There must, in short, be no conceivable alternative to an existence properly termed 'divine': God must be wholly inescapable . . . whether for thought or reality."[92] One could hardly hope for a clearer restatement of what is involved in Anselm's second definition of God as "something not conceivable as not existing."

Findlay's clear appreciation of Anselm's second definition, and his linking it to worship by way of showing that it is religiously appropriate, gives the impression that he is maximally sympathetic to Anselm. Ironically, Findlay sets matters up in this way so that he can launch what has been called "an ontological *dis*proof of God's existence."[93]

Findlay's Criticism Findlay's attack on the concept of necessary being is based on the kind of hard core positivism found in Ayer's *Language, Truth, and Logic.* This position has already been considered at length, but it may be worthwhile to rehearse the main points as Findlay deploys them.

All cognitively meaningful statements are either analytic or synthetic. The term "necessary" can only be legitimately applied to analytic statements; it has no application to beings. Analytic statements are necessarily true because of the rules of language. As Findlay puts it, "necessity in propositions [statements] merely reflects our use of words, the arbitrary conventions of our language."[94] As noted in connection with Humpty Dumpty's insistence on his right to use "glory" to mean "a nice knock down argument," the price of ignoring analytic necessity is the failure to communicate (see pp. 17f.).

Synthetic statements are used to refer to factual states of affairs, such as the existence or nonexistence of specific beings. It is possible for all such statements to be either true or false, necessity simply does not pertain to them. Since necessity cannot apply to a statement about any being whatever, it follows that nothing that exists, exists necessarily. A relatively trivial and ephermeral object like a horsefly and a great and enduring object like the sun are both the sorts of things that might or might not exist. If they exist, they merely happen to exist and their existence is only more or less probable, not necessary. Observation alone settles questions of existence. There is no object whose existence can be determined in the a priori way that Anselm tries to demonstrate the existence of God.

It follows that talk of necessary being or necessary existence is utterly illegitimate. If it does not involve self-contradiction, it is at least a "category mistake" like applying a word meant for colors to an utterly different domain such as a unit of time, as in the phrase "pink minutes." Findlay states his case this way:

> If God is to satisfy religious claims and needs, He must be a being in every way inescapable, One whose existence and whose possession of certain excellencies we cannot possibly conceive away. And the views in question [those of positivism] make it self-evidently absurd (if they don't make it ungrammatical) to speak of such a Being and attribute existence to Him. It was indeed an ill day for Anselm when he hit upon his famous proof. For on

that day he not only laid bare something that is of the essence of an adequate religious object, but also something that entails its necessary non-existence.[95]

Findlay, in effect, reverses Anselm's strategy. Anselm says that the atheist can say "There is no God," but that when he reflects on the meaning of his statement he must realize that he cannot conceive of it. By contrast, Findlay charges that the believer can talk about necessary being and can spout the words "God exists necessarily" but that, on reflection, he realizes that he cannot conceive of it.

Malcolm's Answer The charge that the concept of God as necessary being is self-contradictory was made most often when positivism was going strong. The best reply that can be given to this charge is to recall the considerations that led to the demise of positivism (see Chapt. 2). The positivists were unable to make a convincing case for their program and positivist positions that seemed so certain as to be unchallengeable were called into question.

The fact that the positivists were unable to make good on their central claims does not prove that these positions were wrong. It may well be that the concept of necessary being is self-contradictory, but the standard of what counts as an acceptable *argument* for this conclusion has changed. When the positivists were riding high, philosophers who invoked their major doctrines didn't have to defend them, they had only to mention them. Malcolm quoted a number of criticisms of the ontological argument which simply appealed to the notion that "necessary being is a self-contradiction" as a self-evident truth. The clearest statement was made by Kurt Baier: "It is no longer seriously in dispute that the notion of a logically necessary being is self-contradictory. Whatever can be conceived of as existing can equally be conceived of as not existing."[96] Ironically, this statement was made in 1957. This was about the latest date on which a thinker of Baier's acuteness would write it with this kind of assurance. Today, the issue as to whether the notion of a logically necessary being is self-contradictory is seriously in dispute. One of the arguments challenging the positivists' dogma that the notion is self-contradictory is the ontological argument. It follows that the ontological argument itself cannot be invalidated by a mere appeal to the positivists' dogma that no statements about existing beings can ever be necessary. Critics of the argument must now try to show where and how the argument goes wrong. They cannot get away with the mere assertion that we all know that its definition of God is self-contradictory.

It might, however, be argued that because the ontological argument appears to be so suspicious, the burden of proof is on thinkers who accept it as valid and convincing. In other words, the sceptic can claim that before he will even bother to take Anselm II seriously, its defenders ought to prove that the definition of God as necessary being is *not* self-contradictory. In considering this objection, Malcolm provides a clear example of Wittgenstein's influence on the philosophical scene. We may recall Wittgenstein's statement, "The meaning of a word is its use in the language." Malcolm invokes the spirit of Wittgenstein to challenge the legitimacy of the sceptics' demand that the defenders of Anselm II demonstrate that the concept of "necessary being" is not self-contradictory.

Malcolm notes that in the history of philosophy it has been claimed that a necessary being is self-contradictory and that the concept of seeing a material thing is self-contradictory. He argues that philosophers who deny that these concepts are self-contradictory need only refute specific arguments that try to demonstrate the contradiction. As long as "seeing a material thing" and "necessary being" are concepts with a history of meaningful use, thinkers who deny that they are self-contradictory are not under any burden to prove this, in *general* terms.

> With respect to any particular reasoning that is offered for holding that the concept of seeing a material thing, for example, is self-contradictory, one may try to show the invalidity of the reasoning and thus free the concept from the charge of being self-contradictory *on that ground*. But I do not understand what it would mean to demonstrate *in general*, and not in respect to any particular reasoning, that the concept is not self-contradictory. So it is with the concept of God. I should think there is no more of a presumption that it is self-contradictory than is the concept of seeing a material thing. Both concepts have a place [in Wittgenstein's terms, "a use"] in the thinking and the lives of human beings.[97]

It is worth repeating the point that the particular reasoning behind contemporary charges that a necessary being is self-contradictory is based on the positivists' standards of meaning. Since their position has been discredited, *this* particular charge of self-contradiction cannot be sustained. Therefore, Malcolm thinks that the burden of proof is on the critics. They are obliged to produce some other grounds for thinking the definition is self-contradictory, or else they ought to concede the point that it does not involve self-contradiction.

Kant's Criticism of Anselm II

Kant's criticisms of the arguments for the existence of God have been enormously influential. It is not an exaggeration to say that contemporary discussions of these arguments are commentaries on relevant sections of his book, *The Critique of Pure Reason*.[98] Kant's view that existence is not a predicate was directed against the key assumption of the first version of the argument (see pp. 252 ff.). He has also presented a searching criticism of the use of the concept of necessary being in what Malcolm calls the second version.

Statement of Kant's Criticism   Findlay and other positivists charge that the concept of necessary being is meaningless or self-contradictory. We have seen that Malcolm meets this difficulty by rejecting as dogmatic the positivists' claim that necessity applies only to statements and never to beings. Kant's criticism carries the discussion further because he claims that even if the concept of necessary being is accepted as legitimate, it cannot be used to guarantee its own instantiation. Therefore, the second version of the ontological argument does not prove that God exists.

To understand Kant's criticism we must focus on what I might call the hard view of concepts. By this I mean the view that is most at home in the domain of mathematics, namely, that there are certain essential or indispensable features that characterize a concept. As we have seen, it is the one that Anselm uses in his argument, and Kant appropriately replies by means of an illustration from the realm of mathematics. Kant claims that having three angles is an essential or necessary feature of triangles. This element of necessity in the concept of triangles does not, according to Kant, guarantee the necessary existence of triangles in the world. Of course, anyone who denied that there are such things as triangles would be making a statement that is, in fact, false. Kant is perfectly aware of that. What he insists upon is that, unlike the case of claiming that he has found a four-angled triangle, the person who denied that there are any such things as triangles would not be contradicting himself.

> To posit a triangle, and yet to reject its three angles, is self-contradictory; but there is no contradiction in rejecting [the existence of] the triangle together with its three angles. The same holds true of the concept of an absolutely necessary being. If its existence is rejected, we reject the thing itself [that is, we deny the existence of this being along] with all its predicates; and no question of contradiction can then arise.[99]

In contemporary philosophy Kant's point is restated as follows: "If anything is a triangle, then it has three angles." This principle is applied across the board. An existential claim, that is, a claim that some particular thing (with its specific defining characteristics) exists, can always be rephrased into the hypothetical form, "If . . . then . . ." as in the following examples. "If anything is a bachelor, then he is unmarried," or "If anything is a zebra, then it is striped," or "If anything is a unicorn, then it is one-horned." It is therefore necessary that bachelors should be unmarried, that zebras should be striped, and that unicorns should be one-horned; nevertheless, it is not necessary that such things as bachelors, zebras, and unicorns should exist.

Critics apply this analysis to the ontological argument in the following way. Anselm and contemporary defenders of his argument claim that the argument demonstrates that it is necessary that God exists. The critics claim that what the argument actually shows is that "If anything is God, then it exists necessarily." It does not demonstrate that any existing thing is God. Another way of putting the criticism is to say that the argument only shows that "If God exists, then he exists 'necessarily.'" It does not prove that God necessarily exists.

Malcolm's Reply to Kant This criticism, like the one that claims that the concept of necessary being is self-contradictory, is based on the appeal to a dogma of positivism. The critic charges that the ontological argument demonstrates only that "If anything is God, then it exists necessarily." He insists that to check this statement we must go out into the world and see if any existing thing corresponds to this concept of necessary being. This criticism depends for its validity on the positivist dogma that all existential claims are synthetic and that all synthetic statements are verified a posteriori by observations. The positivists insisted that no existential claims could be settled by a priori considerations. They reject the ontological argument because ontologists try to establish an existential claim (the necessary existence of God) on just this basis, that is, by a priori considerations alone.

For reasons we have just considered in connection with the charge that the concept of "necessary being" is self-contradictory, we cannot accept this appeal to positivist dogma. The procedure of the ontological argument, in establishing the existence of God on a priori grounds, cannot be declared invalid simply because it conflicts with positivistic standards of how we must proceed in verifying existential claims.

Malcolm therefore challenges the critics.[100] He claims that this is one case where an existential claim must be settled on a priori grounds. If the critics cannot demonstrate (independently of a mere appeal to the dogmas of positivism) that "necessary being" is self-contradictory (or that the argument has some other flaw), then the argument proves that God actually exists. Malcolm follows Anselm's pattern in trying to show the sceptic that his denial of the existence of God involves him in a contradiction. The critic claims that Anselm II merely demonstrates that "If God exists, then he exists necessarily." Let us now substitute the definition of Anselm II for the word "God." The result reads, "If 'something not conceivable as not existing' exists, then it exists necessarily." The contradiction glares at us in the first clause, namely, "If 'something not conceivable as not existing' exists." This clause involves the sceptic in simultaneously maintaining that he can and cannot conceive of the nonexistence of God. By accepting (as noncontradictory) the definition of God as "something not conceivable as not existing" he, in effect, admits that he *cannot* conceive of the nonexistence of God. Yet he simultaneously affirms that he *can* conceive of the nonexistence of God by saying, "*If* God, that is, 'something not conceivable as not existing' exists."

Malcolm's Two Uses of "Necessary Being"

It is important to note that Malcolm's defense of Anselm II involves two different uses of "necessary being."[101] Each of them appears in the context of his answer to a Kantian criticism of the ontological argument.

Logically Necessary Being   We have just considered Malcolm's reply to Kant's criticism of the use of necessary being in the ontological argument. Malcolm tries to show that the denial of existence to "something not conceivable as not existing" involves one in self-contradiction. In this context, "necessary" means logically necessary. In other words, it is necessarily true that God exists because his existence cannot be denied without self-contradiction, and this, as we have seen, is the mark of logical necessity.

Metaphysically Necessary Being   In replying to Kant's criticism that existence is not a predicate, Malcolm claims that "necessary existence" is a predicate, indeed a perfection. In laying this out he stresses the link between necessity and independence. He claims that because God is "something not conceivable as not existing," he cannot begin to exist or cease to be because no other beings can affect the existence of God. This sense of necessary being, which uses it as a contrast term with contingent beings, is the main issue that will be discussed in connection with the cosmological argument, so I will not elaborate on it here (see pp. 294f.). The important point is this context is that Malcolm uses two different senses of "necessary being" without acknowledging the shift.

Malcolm is therefore making a very strong claim: "The existence of God as metaphysically necessary being is logically necessary."

Malcolm-Hartshorne Strategy

Malcolm, and to an even greater extent, Charles Hartshorne, accuse critics of the ontological argument of making a basic mistake. The critics take categories that are applicable to contingent beings and apply them to necessary being. The way to determine whether any actually existing thing corresponds to the concept of a contingent being like unicorns or horses is to go out and look. This procedure is not, however, applicable to necessary being, that is, to God. In the case of this unique reality, the rules that govern synthetic statements about contingent beings do not apply. Furthermore, they cannot be made to apply by an appeal to the positivists' dogma that all existential claims are synthetic.

In this way, Malcolm and Hartshorne try to convert a traditional weak point of theism into a strength. The weak point has been the problem of reference. God is called the "infinite person," the "eternal You," and by other phrases that indicate that God is an existing reality. Yet there are no observable characteristics that enable us to identify God in the way that we identify finite persons. Therefore, sceptics deny that God is an existing reality, and they challenge religious thinkers to make good their claim that "God exists." Malcolm and Hartshorne use the ontological argument in an effort to turn the tables on the sceptic. They claim that sceptics make the mistake of treating the concept of God as though it were the concept of a contingent being. God, however, is not contingent. He is not the sort of being that should be observable but that somehow is never observed. God is unique. One sign of his uniqueness is that God's necessary existence can be demonstrated a priori by means of the ontological argument. This argument cannot, of course, be applied to contingent beings. The failure of Gaunilo's refutation shows that. Unfortunately, almost all the critics of the twentieth century are still making Gaunilo's mistake of treating the ontological argument, which demonstrates the existence of God as necessary being, as though it were intended to demonstrate the existence of a contingent being. Hartshorne makes the point in an outburst of philosophical pique:

> Will the reader admit that "existing" is identical with "not (not existing),"
> rather than with "not conceivable as (not existing)?" By what rules do the
> critics convert "not conceivable as" into a mere "not," or show that if the
> argument is invalid with the latter as premise, it must be so with the former?
> This is a challenge. I shall be inclined to take no answer as an admission that
> my point is correct, that the Argument does not depend on whether or not
> (mere) existing is a predicate. How much longer will ink—and the students'
> time in a thousand colleges—be worse than wasted on the supposition that it
> does?[102]

It is worth noting that this is the only instance I have found of a leading philosopher worrying about wasting the time of college students.

Is Anselm II Religiously Convincing?

W. P. Alston directed a criticism against the first version of Anselm's argument that is also relevant to the second one.[103] He claims that the ontological argument is effective religiously only insofar as people experience a flash of illumination and then think that it proves that God exists. The sense of "exists" they have in mind is the ordinary sense applied to both things and persons. God is, of course, an invisible person and if the argument is to have religious force it must demonstrate the existence "out there" of this invisible person.

We have seen that once the argument is subjected to philosophical scrutiny, this ordinary sense of "existence" won't do. It makes the argument vulnerable to the criticisms of Kant and Gaunilo. We have also seen that "exists" is used with reference to mathematicals like prime numbers. This too won't do; numbers cannot have attributes, like consciousness, that believers attribute to God. To counter these criticisms Hartshorne and Malcolm appeal to the second version of Anselm's argument and stress the special sense of "existence" that is expressed in the phrases "necessary existence" or "necessary being." Yet we don't know what we mean by "necessary existence" in the way that we know what we mean by the word "existence" in the context of statements about physical objects and even of mathematics.

In that case, it seems that the version of argument that is called Anselm II meets philosophical objections like those of Kant and Gaunilo at the price of losing its religious force. It no longer provides a demonstration of the existence of God in a sense of the term "exists" that is common to believers, religious thinkers, and sceptics.

This objection may be countered by insisting that it is based on a simplistic notion of religious belief. Obviously a child learns to think of the existence of God in the ordinary sense of "exists." The child thinks of God as some sort of invisible superman. The process of reaching a mature faith—for ordinary believers and not just for theologians—involves refining this sense of existence. On reflection, anyone should be able to appreciate the point that God, as the unique transcendent reality, would not exist in the way that tables, triangles, or numbers exist. God's mode of existence must reflect the distinctiveness of his reality. He is not imperfect in any respect, and one sign of his utter perfection is that he is "not conceivable as not existing." This is not a thought that would occur offhand to a believer; it even seems to elude many philosophers. Yet the fact that this notion of the necessary existence of God is not obvious does not preclude it from having religious force. Once a person reflects upon God (as Findlay reflected on attitudes that are involved in the act of worship) the concept of necessary being is seen to be religiously appropriate.

This discussion has only scratched the surface of the network of problems involved in the concept of necessary being. Further problems connected with this concept will be dealt with in the next chapter which deals with the cosmological argument.

Chapter 12

The Cosmological Argument: Contingent

Theologians who appeal to the cosmological argument try to prove the existence of God from reflection on certain features of the cosmos, that is, the world as a whole, or more simply, the universe. The name, "the cosmological argument," refers to the first three of the five ways by which St. Thomas Aquinas tried to prove the existence of God in his *Summa Theologica* and to the many restatements of them since his time. In order to focus more fully on the highly problematic notion of necessary being that we have already encountered in connection with the ontological argument, I shall restrict this discussion to St. Thomas' third version, "from contingent to necessary being."

EXPOSITION OF THE ARGUMENT

It will be useful to begin the consideration of the cosmological argument by comparing it with the two arguments we have already considered.

Comparisons between the Arguments:
Cosmological-Ontological-Teleological

The cosmological argument is similar to the ontological argument insofar as (at least in the Thomistic tradition) it is intended to be coercive in the sense that geometrical demonstrations are coercive. Once you have understood the rules of Euclidian geometry and followed the demonstration, you are forced to admit that the sum of the squares of the two sides of a right-angled triangle is equal to the square of the hypotenuse. Once you have followed the cosmological and ontological arguments, you are forced to acknowledge that necessary being exists. Supplementary arguments may then be used to persuade you that necessary being is a crucial aspect of God. By contrast, the teleological argument deals in probability. It is used to show that God is the most likely explanation for the order we discover in the world. This conclusion can be denied without contradiction; it is not coercive.

The ontological argument is used in an effort to squeeze the existence of God from reflection on the concept of God. Ontologists try, by thinking alone, to demonstrate the existence of God in reality as well as in thought. By contrast, the cosmological argument, like the teleological argument, begins with existing things that can be observed. The ontological argument moves from a concept to existence; the cosmological argument moves from existence to existence.

Theologians who use the cosmological argument reason from existence to existence. They do not, however, reason in common sense terms from physical existence to physical existence, as when Robinson Crusoe reasons from the physical traces of a human foot in the sand to the physical presence of another man on the island. In the cosmological argument the existence *from* which the theologian reasons are ordinary observable objects like tables, trees, persons, and mountains. Yet what he reasons *to* is not an observable physical existence but is rather a nonsensible existence. He reasons to necessary being, a reality that is not in principle observable. As Ronald Hepburn puts it: "The [cosmological] argument is metaphysical in that strongest (and most abhorred) sense: it tries to infer an unobserved and unobservable entity from some highly general fact about the world."[104] When Hepburn writes "most abhorred," he means, of course, by contemporary empiricist philosophers. Thomistic theologians are not at all unhappy with its metaphysical character.

Statement of the Argument

There are many versions of the cosmological argument, even of St. Thomas' Third Way that argues from contingent to necessary being. The one presented here differs from Aquinas' original statement but is typical of formulations of contemporary Thomists.

1 We observe countless existing beings.

2 Every existing thing that we observe is contingent, that is, it might or might not exist and it might be different than it is.

3 The existence and particular characteristics of contingent beings are dependent on other beings.

4 The cosmos (or the universe) consists of an unimaginably great number of contingent beings.

5 It follows that the cosmos is as contingent as any of the particular beings of which it is composed, and the cosmos is therefore *incapable* of accounting for its own existence.

6 In order to account for the existence of the cosmos we must acknowledge the reality of necessary being, that is, of a nonobservable being that is utterly different from contingent beings.

The above statement of the argument is not very helpful. It does not communicate the reasoning that has made it appear convincing to generations of brilliant men. Hepburn notes: "It is . . . important to reckon with the battery of supporting reflections . . . deployed by apologists in order to give imaginative and intellectual stiffening to the bare skeleton of the cosmological argument itself. These auxiliaries are often decisively important in determining whether the main line of reasoning will be found acceptable or not."[105] We must now consider some of these supporting reflections.

Contingent Beings

Observations provide the point of departure for the cosmological argument from contingent beings to necessary being. All around us we see beings, every kind of being there is, including human beings. All of them begin to exist; they change over shorter or longer periods of time; ultimately, they cease to exist. In the context of the ontological argument the term "contingent" has already been applied to the limitless number of changeable beings that we observe (see pp. 258 ff.). The main point in calling them "contingent" is to stress the fact that there is nothing necessary about their existence. They might or might not exist and their features could be different than they actually are. Think of the Empire State Building. It actually exists, but its existence is contingent; it need not have been built. It was built with certain specific characteristics, but there was nothing necessary about them. It has 102 floors; there might have been 100 or 120. It was built with a tower that has a rounded top. There was nothing necessary about this feature—it might have been otherwise—and, with the coming of television, it was actually changed. The old top was removed and a long thin antenna was substituted. In other words, the contingent/necessary contrast can be reformulated as the contrast between might be and must be.

In the context of the cosmological argument there is an important distinction to be drawn between two aspects of the term "contingent." The first is existential: it is the feature that enables people to regard the argument as personally and religiously important. The second is logical: it enables cosmologists to claim that the argument is philosophically sound and convincing. I shall deal with the existential aspect first.

Existential Power of Contingency Involves Change and Fragility In introducing the third version of the cosmological argument Aquinas wrote that ". . . we find in nature things that are possible to be and not to be, since they are found to be generated, and to be corrupted."[106] In other words, they come into being and change.

Change is a source of wonder and delight. It is also a threat. What is generated, ultimately, degenerates. To illustrate: in a metallurgy laboratory we used to assay for silver and gold. The ore, an ordinary-looking powder, would be heated until it bubbled like water. We then poured it into molds. As it cooled the metal dropped to the bottom and formed a button, leaving the rest of the ore above it to form beautiful ceramic cones. We removed the cones and admired them, but they were unstable. They would continue to cool, and in about half an hour, they would disintegrate. This is contingency with a vengeance. A process spawns a beautiful object, but it doesn't stop there; it continues and the beautiful object soon ceases to exist.

We are even more affected by the way the continuing process of change alters people. When we are young, change is on our side. We want to grow up and most of us do. As we age, change—which we welcomed earlier in life—becomes a threat. We experience the inevitable degeneration of our physical and mental capacities. Beautiful people age and their faces are ravaged by it. We become increasingly aware of death as members of our own generation die in increasing numbers. We are then bound to be struck by the fact that we need not be as we are, indeed, we need not exist. We are inescapably contingent.

It is not only deterioration that brings death to men. We are also extremely fragile. John F. Kennedy combined great personal vigor with the tremendous power of his office. He seemed as impervious to the ravages of capricious change as any man could be. Yet a psychopath with a cheap rifle killed him. The event made us face our fragility to the extent that in the hour that it took him to die, we aged by years. The contingency of human existence hit us with sickening force.

The notion of contingency has existential clout. It reminds us that we need not be as we are and that some day everyone of us will cease to exist.

Dependence and the Logic of Contingent The logical role of contingent in the cosmological argument is linked to the notion of dependence, a link that has already been considered in connection with Norman Malcolm's defense of the ontological argument (see pp. 261 f.). Every being that we actually observe or that we can, in principle, observe is changing. All such beings are also dependent. To return to the example of the Empire State Building, both its erection and its maintenance depend upon hosts of people: businessmen, architects, contractors, construction workers, and so on. Even in areas of the world where there are no human beings, the existence and sustenance of contingent beings depends on other beings. Animals depend upon the sexual activity of other animals for coming into being, and their particular characteristics depend upon the genes of their parents. They depend on food and water for their continued existence.

All observable beings are contingent. This is as true of vast mountain ranges, which seem impervious to change and independent of all other beings, as it is of human beings who change so drastically and are so obviously dependent on others. Mountains are dependent upon geological upheavals to come into existence, and they change dramatically over long periods of time. Wind and rain erode them until their peaks flatten out. They are as contingent as any fragile human beings.

The notions of change and dependence are crucial to the cosmological argument. The notion of change enables us to identify all observable beings as contingent. As we shall see, the notion of dependence enables cosmologists to claim that all contingent beings depend for their existence upon a reality of an entirely different order. This reality is unchanging and nonobservable; it is necessary being.

What Is True of the Parts Is True of the Whole: The Cosmos Is Contingent

All the beings that we actually observe are contingent. So too is any being that we could, in principle, observe. The cosmos, that is, the world as a whole or the universe, is nothing more than the aggregate of the observable, and therefore, contingent beings that make it up. In that case the cosmos itself is contingent. This ought not to be obscured by the vastness of the number of contingent beings that make up the cosmos. A limitless number of contingent beings is still contingent, just as a limitless string of zeros adds up to nothing more than zero.

From Contingent Beings to Necessary Being

The climactic move in the argument is from the contingency of the cosmos to the existence of necessary being. If the cosmos is contingent, then it too, even though it is unimaginably vast, cannot account for its own existence. It is dependent upon another reality to bring it about. We might initially suppose that this reality could be contingent. Yet, reflection will persuade us that this is not the case. If it were contingent, it would need to be accounted for, just as the cosmos needs to be accounted for. We must, therefore, acknowledge the reality of necessary being. Indeed, if necessary being did not exist, then there would be no cosmos and no contingent beings; there would be nothing at all.

At this point the "bare skeleton" of the argument is urgently in need of fleshing out. It is hard to understand why cosmologists claim that if necessary being did not exist, then no beings whatever would.

The auxiliary considerations with which the argument will now be fleshed out are: (1) the principle of sufficient reason and (2) the impossibility of an infinite regress of contingent beings.

The principle of sufficient reason is used to show the legitimacy of asking questions like "Why does the universe exist?" or "Why is there something rather than nothing?" The impossibility of an infinite regress is used to show that these questions cannot be answered in terms of contingent beings.

The Principle of Sufficient Reason

The principle of sufficient reason is a technical way of stating that human beings always ask the question "Why?"[107] We want to know why particular things exist and why they are as they are. We may confine our "why" questions to things that intrigue us like the arrangements of the great monoliths at Stonehenge or an upset in the world of sports like the defeat of the great Boston Bruins team in the Stanley Cup playoffs of 1971. Yet, there is no limit (at least no obvious one) to the things about which we can raise the question: "Why?" A member of President Eisenhower's cabinet during the fifties contemptuously defined basic research as the effort to find out why grass is green. His sarcasm boomeranged. This is a legitimate and important scientific question.

Asking "why" is so natural that it is hard to understand the need for embellishing it with a technical label like "the principle of sufficient reason." It is even harder to understand how philosophers—having formulated it—can uncover difficulties with this principle.

In the context of scientific work the principle of sufficient reason serves as an operative assumption or presupposition. Scientists assume that there must be an adequate explanation for the existence of any particular thing or state of affairs, i.e., an explanation of why it is so and not otherwise. They do not try to prove the validity of this assumption. It is simply packed into their successful enterprise. Whenever they study some specific thing, or state of affairs, or sequence of happenings, they find adequate explanations for them, or they keep on trying until they do (see p. 624). Yet, in the context of the cosmological argument, this principle plays a controversial role. It is used to show (1) that it makes sense to ask why the cosmos should exist and why it should be as it is and not otherwise, and (2) that the sufficient reason for the existence of the cosmos, as it exists, is that it was created by God.

Reasons: Causal and Purposive　Reasons are the statements made in answer to "why questions." In the context of his discussion of the cosmological argument, Wallace Matson presents a helpful discussion of two major types of reasons or explanations causal and purposive, and I will follow it closely.[108]

Causal　Causal explanations are the ones that provide the model for scientific work. They deal with laws or regularities of nature. An illustration of Matson's refers to an everyday occurrence: "Why did the lights go out last night? Because there was a storm up country, as a consequence of which a tree was uprooted and fell across the power line."[109] In this case, the principles of electricity are implicit rather than spelled out.

Purposive　The other major class of explanations deal with intentions, decisions, choices, and other activities we associate with intelligence. This sort of explanation is so common that we are not as self-conscious about it as we are about the causal explanations of science. No special theories are generally involved. We merely invoke common sense. If someone asks "Why is that book wedged under the leg of that bureau?" a perfectly reasonable reply is "Because one leg was short and John put the book there to even things up."

One of Matson's major points is: "Causal and purposive explanations are not always incompatible and are sometimes complementary. Why is Jones in the prison hospital? (*a*) [causal] Because a train hit the car in which he was riding and dragged it 300 yards. (*b*) [purposive] Because he tried to avoid the police by crossing the intersection just in front of the train."[110]

The complementary relation of the two types of explanation is especially relevant to the cosmological argument because philosophers have reflected on their relation down through the ages.

Gilbert Ryle, a leading analytic philosopher, claims that the classic example of causal explanation is the way a billiard ball moves in predictable patterns on impact with other balls and with the sides of the table. He acknowledges its validity in the following terms:

> Certainly from accurate knowledge of the weight, shape, elasticity and movements of the balls, the constitution of the table and the conditions of the atmosphere it is in principle possible, in accordance with known laws, to deduce from a momentary state of the balls what will be their later state.[111]

He then notes that this causal explanation is insufficient as an account of why and where the balls move in an actual game.

> But it does not follow from this that the course of the game is predictable in accordance with those laws alone. A scientific forecaster, who was ignorant of the rules and tactics of the game and of the skill and plans of the players, could predict, perhaps, from the beginning of a single stroke, the positions in which the balls will come to rest before the next stroke is made; but he could predict no further.[112]

Ryle uses the point to illustrate a general principle: "... a game of billiards provides one of the simplest examples of a course of events for the description of which mechanical terms [causal explanations] are necessary without being sufficient."[113] To offer a sufficient account of the game such matters as the purposes and abilities of the players must be taken into account.

Cosmologists employ this insight in a way that would make Ryle, a noted atheist, shudder (see p. 53). They regard explanations in terms of the purposes of intelligent beings as superior to causal explanations. In the context of the cosmological argument this involves two assumptions: (1) causal explanations of the kind used by scientists provide *in*sufficient reasons for the existence of the cosmos, and (2) the only sufficient reason can be the purposes of a divine intelligence.

The cosmological argument, as we have noted, does not yield a divine intelligence as its conclusion; instead, it yields necessary being. However, when we move beyond the bare statement of the argument and explore its auxiliary assumptions, we find that, under the guise of establishing standards of *sufficient* reasons or *adequate* explanations, the intelligence of the necessary being, that is, God, enters the picture.[114]

Sufficient   The term "sufficient" in the phrase "sufficient reason" means adequate. I shall begin with examples of *in*sufficient reasons where the reasons involved are purposive. The first set deals with a father's purposes in looking after the well-being of his son. The child asks his father: "Can I go out?" The father says: "No!" The child asks: "Why?" The father says: "Because it's too cold." The child says: "I'll put on my jacket." The father says: "Well you still can't go out because it's late and it must be dark outside." The son objects: "It's still light." The father answers: "There's no one outside to watch you so you still can't go out." The child now plays his ace-in-the hole. "Jimmy's father is out there." "Well," comes the reply: "you still can't go out!" The obvious response to that one is still another "Why?" and now on a note of total exasperation the father explodes: "Because I say so, that's why!"

The father is no longer trying to be reasonable. All the reasons have been *in*sufficient and the child is finally confronted with the fact of parental authority. If he tries to go out anyway, he would doubtless be confronted with the *brute force* of physical punishment.

As we ordinarily use the term, a *sufficient* reason is one that cuts off a series of why questions. It satisfies us because we understand the explanation we have been given, and it is sufficient to the context.

Many years ago I ran a lecture program in which a number of prominent speakers dealt with the role of morality in their particular careers. There were no fees. One of the men who had agreed to speak was a well-known actor. A month before the date we'd agreed on, I received a phone call from his agent who told me that his client could not keep the engagement; he was busy rehearsing a show. "All right," I answered naïvely, "let's change it until after the opening." That wouldn't do either. His client's part was sure to be revised after the opening, and he would be terribly busy mastering the revisions. I suggested that the talk be postponed until two months after the opening. He said that his client couldn't commit himself that far in advance. The argument continued, and I was playing the role of the boy showing his father that his reasons were insufficient. Finally, he shouted: "He's not going to do it because he doesn't want to do it, and that's that!" To which I answered: "Why didn't you say so in the first place?" Although I felt foolish at having missed the real reason for the cancellation when the conversation began, in terms of "the principle of sufficient reason," I was now satisfied. I understood why he was not going to speak. Even though I was unhappy at the outcome no further why questions were called for.

The Cut-Off Point of Why Questions   At around five years of age, children become conscious of themselves as individuals. They want to know where they come from. They can be told that the come from their parents. Then they want to know where their parents come from; they are then referred to their grandparents, and so on—back, back, and on back. Finally they develop a sense for the cosmos, the world as a whole, and they want to know where it comes from. They also want to know why things are as they are. They not only want to know why there is a cosmos, but why it is as it is and not otherwise. This is, as I have already noted, a natural tendency of the mind which philosophers call the principle of sufficient reason.

When we reach the outer limits of the cosmos, scientists provide us with theoretical statements that have the widest possible application, like the statement, the speed of light is 186,000 miles per second. It is always possible to ask, "Why is the speed of light 186,000 miles per second and not some other figure?"

The principle of sufficient reason cuts into the cosmological argument here and becomes controversial. From a scientific point of view, if the speed of light is established and there is no contrary evidence, then we have a fact about the universe. It doesn't make sense to ask questions like "Why does light have that speed?" It just has it, that's all, and other phenomena must be understood and explained in terms of this one. We have reached a cut-off point of "why's" and are confronted with an ultimate fact.

Cosmologists regard this appeal to fact as insufficient. They protest against this arbitrary limit on why questions when the father tells his son: "You can't go out because I say so, that's why!" his appeal is to arbitrary and unreasoning authority backed by force. Cosmologists often treat the appeal to the ultimacy of certain facts about the universe as though it were the same sort of thing. They refer to it as the appeal to *brute* fact.[115] They think that cutting off the sequence of why questions at this point sells man short. It denies him the right to the fullest exercise of his reason. It makes men more like animals who have to accept their environment without understanding it.

Cosmologists drive this point still further. They not only appeal to the principle of sufficient reason to justify "why questions" about the ultimate facts of the universe, they appeal to it in raising these same questions about the very existence of the universe. Richard Taylor demands "a sufficient reason *why* anything should exist in the first place."[116] Father W. Norris Clarke, S.J., a contemporary Thomist, links this question to the nature of intelligence itself:

> Here, it seems to me, is the truly decisive and fundamental question where two views of [the] nature and range of human intelligence clash head on.

Can or cannot the human intelligence raise the radical question about the very existence of the universe as a whole. . . . And if so, is there any legitimate schema or type of explanation which would render meaningful and possible an answer in the theistic sense? Personally, I believe that . . . not only can one *not* prevent someone from reasonably raising the question of the universe as a whole and its sufficient reason or ground, but to raise this question is the necessary fruition . . . of one's intellectual dynamism in depth.[117]

For the sake of argument let us concede that purposive explanations are superior to causal ones and that it makes sense to ask a question like "Why does the cosmos exist?" We must then consider the cosmologists' claim that this question cannot be answered in terms of an infinite regress of contingent beings.

An Infinite Regress of Contingent Beings Is Impossible

Cosmologists deal with the notion of infinite series. It is familiar to most of us from mathematics. We know that there is no limit to the series of whole numbers beginning with $1, 2, 3$. No matter how great any number in the series may be, the next number will be greater by one; the series is infinite. We can play out this same pattern with the series of even numbers, of odd numbers, and so on. Indeed, there are an infinite number of infinite series.

We can also set objects in a series. If we move forward in time, as with the offspring of a pair of fruit flies, then we are dealing with a progressive series. If, in the effort to trace someone's ancestors, we move back in time, we are involved in a regressive series. The notion of an infinite regressive series is not a problem in and of itself. We can conceive of time as an infinitely regressive series. We need only to think that before any given instant of time, there was an earlier instant, and an earlier one before that, and so on.

The infinite regress becomes a controversial matter in the context of the cosmological argument because cosmologists insist that it is impossible that there should be an infinite regress of contingent beings. They argue that the attempt to account for the existence of contingent beings by appealing to an infinite regress of them is a "vicious" use of the regress. John Passmore notes that when philosophers introduce the notion of a vicious regress, it is to "demonstrate . . . that a supposed way of explaining something or 'making it intelligible' in fact fails to explain . . . because it is, in the crucial respect, of the same form as what it explains."[118] Father F. C. Copleston provides a clear statement of this point in the context of cosmological argument:

What we call the world is intrinsically unintelligible, apart from the existence of God. You see, I don't believe that the infinity of the series of events—I mean a horizontal series, so to speak—if such an infinity could be proved, would be in the slightest degree relevant to the situation. If you add up chocolates you get chocolates after all and not a sheep. If you add up chocolates to infinity, you presumably get an infinite number of chocolates. So if you add up contingent beings to infinity, you still get contingent beings, not a necessary being. An infinite series of contingent beings will be, to my way of thinking, as unable to cause itself as one contingent being.[119]

It is perfectly clear that Father Copleston insists that an infinite series of contingent beings is, in the crucial respect ("unable to cause itself"), of the same form as what it is supposed to explain.

Cosmologists, like Father Copleston, claim that in order to give a sufficient reason for the existence of contingent beings, we must acknowledge the existence of necessary being. This makes us aware of an utterly different reality—the reality of "must be" rather than that of "might be."

The Vertical Thrust of the Argument

Father Copleston claims that an infinite series of contingent beings would not have a sufficient reason for its existence. He refers to the series as "horizontal," meaning that every member of the series goes back in time and with each member it makes sense to ask: "Why does this being exist?" Since the series is infinite or limitless, it would seem that the principle of sufficient reason is limitlessly applicable.

The mind keeps going along this horizontal track applying the principle of sufficient reason to one being after the other without reaching a resting place. Only when the mind moves vertically does it ultimately see, in a flash of intellectual illumination, that it must acknowledge the reality of a different order of being. It realizes that unless necessary being exists, there would be no contingent beings.

An illustration that is misleading insofar as it deals with physical objects may nevertheless help to communicate the sense of quest that leads the mind to move "vertically" to necessary being and the sense of rest that the mind finds when it reaches it.

In ordinary experience it is often understood that talking about objects at one level of reality implies realities of a different order. Dreams are an obvious example. To talk about the content of dreams—which are fantasies—implies that there is an actual person who is the dreamer. In the same way, to talk about a mirror image is to imply that there is some independent reality that is being reflected.

Imagine a man looking into a room through a door that is slightly ajar. His range of vision is restricted to one wall. On it is a large mirror with a series of reflections of a beautiful woman which diminish in size until he can no longer pick them up. He tries to open the door all the way, but it is held in place by a door jam. He is frustrated, because looking at the mirror, he knows that there must be a beautiful woman in the room. Even though he cannot see her directly he infers her presence from his knowledge of reflections. They are not the sort of thing that can exist on their own. In order for him to see the reflections on the wall there must be a reality of a different order that causes them. A beautiful woman who is not a reflection must be standing between the mirror he sees and another mirror on the opposite wall.

Cosmologists characterize this sort of reasoning as vertical. They are not reasoning back in time in a horizontal series of contingent beings. Rather, they claim that they could not *now* be observing the contingent beings that they actually see, unless necessary being, a being of an entirely different order, exists.

CRITICISMS OF THE COSMOLOGICAL ARGUMENT

The cosmological argument is a metaphysical web. One can be ensnared by considering contingency, but this leads to probes of the meaning of cause, purpose, dependence, infinite regress and the cosmos. No strand can be properly understood independently of the others. We cannot focus on one point and say that the argument stands or falls right here. In order to come to grips with it one has to develop a sense for the way the entire web hangs together and to appreciate why cosmologists think there is illumination at the center of it. Critics of the argument think the web is a tangled one that should be avoided altogether.

Many of the problematic aspects of the cosmologist's point of view have already been dealt with because it is simply not possible to present the argument without dealing with the special use of the terms involved in it. Similarly, there are an almost limitless number of interlocking points that are made as critics try to dismember the argument. My presentation will be confined to three major ones: (1) the principle of sufficient reason, (2) the empirical content of "contingent," and (3) the meaning of necessary being.

Sufficient Reason and the Cosmological Argument

The principle of sufficient reason is a philosophical statement of our natural tendency to ask "Why?" The first point that will be raised is the question of the consistency of cosmologists. The second, the legitimacy of asking "Why?" about the existence and the specific features of the cosmos, that is, of the world as a whole. Then I shall consider the question of what constitutes a sufficient reason or explanation for the existence of a particular contingent being or a specific state of affairs.

The Consistency of the Cosmologists in Applying the Principle of Sufficient Reason

One of the most common criticisms of cosmologists is: they defend the argument by insisting that the principle of sufficient reason must be applied to everything but they themselves fail to do so.[120] The sceptic cuts off the sequence of why questions when he reaches what he regards as ultimate facts, like the existence of the cosmos. He insists that there is no point to a question like "Why does the universe exist?" In opposition, cosmologists insist that these questions are both meaningful and important. As we have seen, Father Clarke asserts that raising these questions is a sign of using one's intelligence to the fullest degree possible. In that case, sceptics want to apply the principle of sufficient reason to the being whose reality emerges in the *conclusion* of the cosmological argument. They want to ask: "Why does God exist?" or "Why does necessary being exist?" Yet it is precisely at this point that the cosmologist cuts off the sequence of "why questions," and in doing so, seems to limit the applicability of the principle of sufficient reason.

Sceptics, therefore, charge cosmologists with a glaring inconsistency. In arguing *to* their conclusion, cosmologists insist that the principle of sufficient reason applies to *everything*. Once they arrived *at* the conclusion, that is, at necessary being, they make an exception. They insist that there is no point in asking why God or necessary being exists.

Father Clarke tries to answer this criticism. He claims that the principle of sufficient reason *can* be applied to necessary being. It makes sense to ask "Why does necessary being exist?" but, having asked it, a thinker realizes that the answer cannot be given in terms of *some other being that causes it*. Necessary being is independent of all other beings whatever; it is, in Father Clarke's term, "self-sufficient."

> To have reached this point of the affirmation of a self-sufficient being and then to ask of the cause of this being would simply make no sense, since in a self-sufficient being there is lacking by definition any basis for even raising the question of a cause [as he uses the term "cause" it means, "caused by some other being"], though the question of sufficient reason still applies since it allows of the answer "self-sufficient."[121]

Sceptics will probably regard Father Clarke's appeal to self-sufficiency as a bit of metaphysical term-juggling that does not meet the challenge. Thomists would be likely to find it a helpful clarification of a difficult point.

The Fallacy of Composition and the Cosmological Argument

As we have seen, cosmologists argue that what is true of every contingent being is true of the cosmos, namely, that it cannot account for its own existence. Sceptics charge that in arguing this way cosmologists commit the "fallacy of composition." This is the fallacy of attributing a property that can only be true of individual members of a class to the class as a whole. Bertrand Russell made this point in his debate with Father Copleston: "I can illustrate what seems to me your fallacy. Every man who exists has a mother, and it seems to me your argument is that therefore the human race must have a mother, but obviously the human race hasn't a mother—that's a different logical sphere."[122]

In Russell's illustration, the fallacy of composition is clearly committed. What is true of every member of the class of human beings is, in this case, definitely not true of the class of human beings as a whole. Russell's point, however, does not clinch the case: A counter example is easy enough to come by. If every member of the sophomore class is intelligent, then the sophomore class is an intelligent class. In this case we do not commit the fallacy of composition when we transfer a characteristic of each member of the class to the class as a whole.[123] The crucial point is the legitimacy of the move from the contingency of the individual beings in the world to the contingency of the cosmos. Is this an instance of the fallacy of composition?

The problem we encounter here has already been considered in the context of the teleological argument. We have ample experience of human beings and the different classes of them. This enables us to know when we do and do not commit the fallacy of composition. Since we do not have experience of the world as a whole, it is difficult to know which characteristics of the parts of the world apply to it.

Ronald Hepburn provides a clear discussion of this issue. He considers questions like "Has the universe a cause?" and claims that he does not know whether the fallacy of composition applies. It might and it might not. He is certain that cosmologists are overconfident when they argue that because things in the world have causes, therefore, the cosmos, which is the sum of all the things in the world, must also have a cause.[124]

Hepburn's certainty that this issue cannot be definitely resolved in the cosmologist's favor is based on his ability to come up with illustrations where he is certain that the fallacy of composition *does* apply. "No more can we," he writes, "argue from the fact that things in the world have tops and bottoms, insides and outsides, and are related to other things, to the belief that the universe has *its* top and bottom, inside and outside, and is related to a supra-cosmical something."[125] Many sceptics of Hepburn's analytic persuasion would proceed to argue that the cosmologists must be wrong. Hepburn's conclusion is more modest. "I cannot be dogmatic here; for I am not able to discover any clear principles on which to construct the list of things that one can and cannot sensibly say about the universe as a whole."[126]

Hepburn's tentativeness contrasts sharply with the assertiveness of Peter Geach, one of the leading contemporary commentators on St. Thomas. He claims that Aquinas, like Kant, was keenly aware of the problems of using the world as a whole as the subject and then ascribing predicates to it. Nevertheless, he insists: "What would have appeared to him [St. Thomas] not worth discussion at all is the idea that, though we can speak without contradiction of the world as a whole, we cannot raise concerning it the sort of causal questions that we can raise concerning its parts. Why should we not raise them?"[127] This is a provocative point; yet when Geach considers possible objections to his appeal to the obvious, the only objection he specifies is a fatuous one. "It would be childish to say that the world is too big for such questions to be reasonable."[128]

Geach is right to dismiss as childish the objection that the world is too big for such questions to be reasonable. For this reason, he might have examined the objections more carefully and found some that are not childish. In challenging the legitimacy of asking whether the cosmos has a cause, sceptics, like Ronald Hepburn, do not regard its size as the problem; rather, in good empiricist fashion, they note that we form our notions of wholes and parts from observing things inside the cosmos. We experience both whole apples and parts of apples, we experience both whole teams and individual members of teams, and so on. These experiences, of both ends of the whole/parts contrast, help us to understand the different kinds of wholes we encounter and the different kinds of relations that they have to their parts. In the case of the cosmos, we have no such all-encompassing view of the whole, and therefore, it is hard to understand its relation to the parts that compose it.

Given our inability to experience the world as a whole, Hepburn's tentativeness about these matters seems more appropriate than Geach's dismissal of the opposing view as "not worth discussion at all."

The Notion of a SUFFICIENT Reason In arguing from contingent beings to necessary being one can stress the need to provide a reason for the existence of the cosmos. As we have just seen, this approach is vulnerable to the charge of committing the fallacy of composition, or rather, as Hepburn explains, it is not clear that it avoids it. Another aspect of the argument from contingent beings to necessary being seems less vulnerable to this fallacy. It proceeds by emphasizing the insufficiency of our normal patterns of explanation.

In the case of an individual human being we can always give reasons or explanations for his existence in terms of his parents. Yet as soon as we have done so, it is natural to ask, "Why do they exist?" We can then move in a regressive series back through generations of ancestors to the evolutionary forebearers of the human race. We can equally well ask of every item that is brought forward in explanation: "Why does it exist?" We have seen that cosmologists claim that this confronts us with a vicious regress. If we cut off the process at any point, we are being arbitrary, because we appeal to an explanation that is deficient *in the same respect* as our original explanation, namely, the appeal to the man's parents as the explanation for his existence.

Cosmologists insist that the only sufficient reason or adequate explanation for the existence of any particular contingent being is a total explanation that leaves no loose threads hanging. It is an explanation that provides a rational cut-off to the series of "why questions" by taking the total cosmic context into account—and then moving beyond it to necessary being.

Critics of the cosmological argument accuse the cosmologists of being slippery in their approach to reasons or explanations. They claim that the cosmologists seem to be asking for straightforward explanations that will provide a reason for the existence of some ordinary and observable state of affairs. Yet, when explanations are offered, all of them are, in principle, rejected by cosmologists who insist that all explanations (with the exception, of course, of their appeal to necessary being) are insufficient on the grounds that further "why questions" can be raised. Sceptics protest that the cosmologists are using an utterly unreasonable standard of adequacy or sufficiency.

Milton Munitz has provided one of the best statements of the sceptic's protest. He imagines someone asking: "Why did the projectile land on this spot?" He insists that when we know the laws that govern the trajectory of projectiles and the initial firing conditions, we can provide a sufficient reason for a given projectile having landed on this spot. We can also, knowing those same laws and other initial firing conditions, *predict* where other projectiles will fall even before they are fired. Munitz insists that the statement of the scientific laws governing projectiles and the statement of the initial conditions provide a complete and sufficient answer to the question, "Why did the projectile land on this spot?"

If one should ask—and this is what those who use the cosmological argument, typically do—"But why were the initial conditions what *they* were?" or, "Why is the law of projectiles what *it* is?", new and different questions are now being asked. There may, or may not, be satisfactory answers to these new questions. But whether one does, or does not, have such answers, in no way reduces the completeness of the answer to the *initial* question.[129]

Munitz therefore undercuts the cosmological argument in a fundamental way.

1 Explanations of the existence of contingent beings in terms of the appeal to other contingent beings and laws are complete.

2 In that case, in seeking a sufficient reason for the existence of any contingent being we are not forced to embark on a regressive series of explanations.

3 Finally, we *need not* acknowledge the reality of necessary being in order to avoid a *vicious* regress.

"Contingent" Is Not Straightforwardly Empirical

To appreciate the sceptic's criticisms of the use of "contingent" in the argument from contingent beings to necessary being, it is important to recall the comparison of the starting points of the ontological and cosmological arguments. The ontological argument begins with the concept or idea of God. Cosmologists, from Aquinas on, have charged that this point of departure is inadequate. God, as existing in reality, cannot be generated out of a mere idea. They insist that in order to reason *to* existence in reality as well as in thought, we must reason *from* existence in reality as well as in thought. Therefore, cosmologists begin with observations of existing things in the world. I have italicized the key phrases in the following statements from Aquinas' *Summa Theologica.* "It is certain, and *evident to our senses*, that in the world some things are in motion." "In the world of *sensible things* we find there is an order of efficient causes." "We find *in nature* things that are possible to be and not to be."[130]

In beginning with observable features of existing beings cosmologists try to give their argument an empirical starting point. The discussion will be confined to the third version of the argument where St. Thomas argues from "things that are possible to be and not to be," which contemporary thinkers call "contingent beings." As noted, St. Thomas claims to find contingent beings "in nature." Yet sceptics regard this allegedly empirical starting point of the argument as deceptive for the following reasons.

1   Contingent is not a straightforwardly descriptive predicate like green. It applies to everything and is, therefore, incapable of picking out anything.

2   If, in answer to this first point, cosmologists claim that contingency is a characteristic that discriminates *all* observable beings from necessary being (which is, in principle, nonobservable) then the argument is circular in the vicious sense.

Contingent Applies to Everything and Does Not Discriminate Anything   In the argument from contingent beings to necessary being we reason *from* contingent beings. The starting point is supposed to be empirical, that is, it is based on observations of things "evident to our senses" that we find "in nature." Cosmologists then argue that we cannot account for these features of ordinary sensory experiences unless we acknowledge the existence of God. God is a transcendent reality who operates on a different plane of being, that is, necessary being, and is therefore capable of accounting for the existence of our world of contingent beings.

When we analyze the statement, "We find in nature things that are possible to be and not to be," that is, contingent beings, we find that it is peculiar. Its peculiarities have the effect of eroding the cosmologists contrast between the purely *conceptual* starting point of the ontological argument and the allegedly *empirical* starting point of the cosmological argument. We find that the term "contingent" is a relative of "exists." Just as exists plays havoc with the ontological argument, so too, contingent raises problems in the context of the cosmological argument.

The statement, "We find in nature things that are possible to be and not to be," seems as straightforward as the statement, "We find in nature things that are possible to fly and not to fly." They both seem verifiable, and what is more, they seem to be verifiable in the same way. When it comes to checking out the second statement, we find that birds fit the description very nicely. It is clearly possible for sparrows, pigeons, eagles, and the rest "to fly and not to fly" because sometimes they do and sometimes they don't. When we check the statement about "things that are possible to be and not to be," it seems equally easy to verify it, indeed, we confront an embarrassment of riches. We are not only able to observe *some* beings that have the capacity for both existing and not existing, but rather, we find that *all* beings we observe have this feature. In other words, every observable being is contingent. This shows the peculiarity of the term "contingent" when used as an empirical term, that is, as one that is rooted in sense experience. It seems to be a descriptive predicate like "fly" as in "birds fly," yet it doesn't distinguish any one thing in nature from any other.

Legitimate descriptive predicates must help us to discriminate among the things we can observe. If I say, "Please pass the green glass," then "green" helps you to pick out the glass I'm talking about from glasses of different colors. Suppose that, at a table with seven glasses of different colors and shapes, I say, "Please pass the contingent glass." It is obvious that this doesn't help; they are all contingent. Furthermore, so is every other observable being. If I asked you, "Bring me some contingent beings," you'd know (if you'd studied the cosmological argument) what to give me. Yet, if I simply asked, "Bring me some beings," the *same* batch you selected for the statement, "Bring me some contingent beings" would fill the bill.

Analytically oriented sceptics are therefore apt to charge that contingent only seems to have descriptive power because it functions *grammatically* in the same way as genuinely descriptive predicates like "green" and "can fly." Furthermore, it also has descriptive uses that are not indispensable but that give it the appearance of being a genuine descriptive predicate.

In discussing the question of whether "exists" is a descriptive predicate I claimed that, in certain uses, it is. I presented the following examples: (1) "Florence exists, but Utopia does not." Here "exists" means "not fiction." (2) "President Kennedy exists, but President Jefferson does not." If this statement had been made in 1962, "exists" would mean "is living." (3) An alcoholic, suspected of having *delerium tremens* says, "These bats exist," meaning, they are "not hallucinations."[131]

These uses of "exists" as a descriptive predicate were found to be legitimate, but dispensable. In each case, the translation into a word other than "exists" produces a more precise statement. In the context of the cosmological argument, the same point may be made about "contingent." There are genuinely descriptive uses of contingent, for example: (1) "The statement, 'There are mountains on the far side of the moon' is contingent," (2) "The arrangements for next year's conference are contingent on the plans of a number of members," and (3) "Human existence is a contingent affair, we are here today, gone tomorrow." We can now substitute other descriptive terms for "contingent." In the first example, we refer to a *statement* as contingent. This is the most clear-cut use of the term; it means that "it is possible for it to be either true or false." In the second example, we can substitute "dependent." In the third example, we can substitute "mortal," as in "Human beings are mortal." The last example has the most existential force.

The fact that "contingent" can be dispensed with by means of a substitution of other terms shows that it is not an indispensable descriptive term like "green." If we substitute other words for it, such as "dependent," "changeable," "mortal" and "either true or false," the term "contingent" has no irreducible meaning left. Its meaningful uses have been exhausted by the process of substitution. There is no similar way of substituting for the word "green" because it is a term that stands for an irreducible feature of experience. It is "evident to the senses" and observed "in nature." By contrast, "contingent" is a metaphysical term that seems to do the same sort of thing as "green," but philosophical analysis discloses that it is incapable of playing a similarly indispensable role.

The Use of "Contingent" as a Contrast Term Involves Circularity   If sceptics, on the basis of the kinds of considerations I've just presented, brand statements that use the term "contingent" as "pseudo-synthetic," cosmologists can reply that contingent does make a crucial discrimination. It distinguishes necessary being from all the contingent beings in the universe. If this move is valid, then "contingent" would operate as a descriptive predicate. It would stand in a contrast relation to "necessary," just as light is contrasted with dark and short with tall. Furthermore, if this contrast is allowed, then no other term could be substituted for "contingent." It would be every bit as indispensable as "green," "can fly," or "dark."

Although this move is intriguing, it would not help the cosmologists. In order for them to get the cosmological argument off the ground as an argument with an empirical starting point, "contingent" must be like "green"; it must be a quality of things that is evident to the senses. In a standard contrast pair like "light/dark" both terms stand for features of the world that are observable by the senses. In the paired terms "contingent/necessary" this is clearly not the case. As we have seen, necessary being is unobservable in principle. Therefore, it cannot be invoked to lend *empirical* content to the term "contingent."

It might be objected that the rejection of the empirical content of "contingent," and the charge that statements using it are pseudo-synthetic, represents a regression to positivistic standards of meaning. The objectors would claim that we are long past the day when the fact that a statement or term does not operate according to a fixed pattern, like the one governing the use of green or dark, provides sufficient justification for branding it as factually meaningless.

My criticism, however, does not depend on positivistic standards of meaning, even though in elaborating it, I have used one of the favorite labels of the positivists. The criticism of the cosmologists' effort to use "contingent/necessary" as contrast terms, involves the charge of circularity. There is nothing especially positivistic about this criticism; philosophers have leveled it at one another throughout the history of the enterprise. In this case the charge of circularity is formulated as follows:

1 "Contingent" is appealed to as an *empirical* starting point, suggesting that it is used as a straightforward descriptive predicate like "green" or "dark."
2 It is found that contingent cannot be used descriptively because it is not something "in nature" that is "evident to the senses"; it does not enable us to pick anything out.
3 In an effort to rectify this defect cosmologists may claim that "contingent" is contrasted with "necessary" and that it therefore *does* enable us to pick something out. By means of it we can discriminate necessary being from the countless numbers of contingent beings.
4 Yet in the absence of any possibility of our *observing* necessary being, we cannot accept it as real unless we are persuaded to do so by an argument like the cosmological argument.
5 However, if the previous line of reasoning is valid, the term contingent is not *empirical* unless necessary being can be invoked as a legitimate contrast term to it. In that case, the reality of necessary being must be presupposed for the cosmological argument to work. Here is circular reasoning in the vicious sense. In order to reason to the required conclusion cosmologists must assume its truth as part of their argument.

The cosmologists' claim that their point of departure is empirical is very dubious. They lay claim to the word, but, upon examination, their use of contingent turns out to be metaphysical rather than empirical. Indeed, Charles Hartshorne, a leading metaphysician, has said as much:

> My own view is that no theistic proof shuld be taken as empirical in the sharp sense . . . that its premises could conceivably conflict with observation. Thus, for example, to say, something contingent exists, therefore God exists as its noncontingent cause is not an empirical argument. For what conceivable experience could contradict its premise?[132]

The Metaphysical Meaning of Necessary Being

The ontological argument operates at the purely conceptual level. Its starting point is not any existing thing, but rather, the *concept* of "God" as "not conceivable as not existing." Given this starting point, and the way that the argument proceeds, it is easy enough to assume that when theologians use this argument to establish the existence of God as necessary being, by "necessary," they mean *logically* necessary." In other words, denying existence to God is like denying the characteristic "four-sided" to a square. In both cases, a contradiction is involved. It follows that the existence of God, like the four-sidedness of a square, is regarded as analytically true and logically necessary.

As we have seen, the positivists criticized the concept of "necessary being" as involving a contradiction in terms. They insisted that the existence, of anything whatsoever, can never be necessary but only contingent. Necessity, they thought, applied only to statements. With the demise of positivism and the abandonment of its central dogmas, this objection lost its force. It is no longer *assumed* that it is a contradiction to claim that something exists necessarily. The position must be argued.

In any case, even during the heyday of positivism, there were theologians who tried to instruct them on the theological use of necessary being. (For a discussion of this point in connection with the ontological argument, see p. 268.) The key to the meaning of "necessary" in "necessary being" is not the notion of contradiction, which is logical, but is the notion of independence, which is causal. The point has been made many times by philosophers such as A. C. A. Rainer, P. T. Geach, John Hick, and C. B. Martin.[133] The most helpful statement has been provided by Anthony Kenny: ". . . something is necessary if and only if it is, always will be and always was; and cannot nor could not, not will not be able not to be."[134] In other words, God does *not depend* on anything else to bring him into existence and he is *not dependent* upon anything else for his continued existence because, by his very nature, God cannot come into or pass out of existence. Nothing could *cause* God to cease to exist. Therefore, these theologians insist that God's existence is necessary, but not logically necessary. God's existence is metaphysically necessary. It is the existence of a reality that is not derivative and that neither needs to be, nor can be, explained in terms of the reality of anything else.

There is clearly a distinction between the definitions of "logically necessary being" and "metaphysically necessary being." Cosmologists would also stress the different methods that are involved in talking about them. To speak of God's existence as logically necessary is to claim that the denial of his existence is contradictory. To speak of God's existence as metaphysically necessary is to claim both that it is independent and that we cannot account for the cosmos unless we acknowledge his existence.

The contrast is sharply drawn, yet I maintain that the cosmologists' use of "metaphysically necessary being" is closer to "logically necessary being" than they think it is. One way of getting at the issue is to note that

John Hick, in writing of what I call "metaphysically necessary being," frequently uses the expression *factually* necessary being.[135] His use suggests the factual orientation of cosmologists and of other theologians who do not want to be saddled with the view that the existence of God is logically necessary. He is right about this, but the reference to factuality in connection with necessary being is highly misleading.

My discussion of the role of "contingent" in the cosmological argument was intended to undercut the cosmologist's claim that the term is factual or empirical. It is not an indispensable descriptive predicate like "green" or "can fly." As a result, cosmologists cannot claim that "necessary" is a factual term whose meaning becomes clear when it is paired with contingent in the contrast "contingent/necessary." Considering the relation of verification to these concepts is another way of getting at the point that the concept of "metaphysically necessary being" is no more factual than the concept of "logically necessary being."

The reference to verification may suggest that I am about to use the empiricist criterion of meaning in order to discredit the idea of necessary being. This is what the positivists did in their effort to show that language about God is cognitively meaningless. I am invoking verifiability for a different reason. I am only concerned to show that the cosmologists' contrast between the "empirical" character of the cosmological argument and the merely "logical" character of the ontological argument does not stand up. The cosmological argument is supposed to involve empirical data as its point of departure, and it is supposed to argue to metaphysically necessary being, a concept which is not merely logical but which is rooted in observation. The appeal to verification will show how heavily the cosmological argument relies on logical rather than empirical data.

The Definition of Necessary Being We have already considered Anthony Kenny's definition of metaphysically necessary being. Another one has been provided by C. B. Martin. "Let us," he writes, "suppose a being of the following sort: (1) A being for whose existence nothing else need exist. (2) A being that has always existed. (3) A being upon whom everything else depends for its existence."[136] In Martin's presentation God is necessary being because his existence is *independent* of the existence of all other beings, whereas their existence is *dependent* upon his. His definition is in line with the main emphases of the cosmological approach to the existence of God. God's existence is metaphysically rather than logically necessary.

Observation and Metaphysically Necessary Being Martin himself proposes the following way of stressing the empirical or factual content of this idea of metaphysically necessary being. "One can even have a kind of verification procedure for such qualities. For (1) take away all other things and the being would remain in existence. For (3) take away the being and everything else would pass out of existence. For (2) at *any* time in the past this being could be observed to exist."[137]

We can, using physical imagery, imagine these verification conditions. We could, for example, use our solar system as a model for them. For (1), take away the planets, and the sun continues to exist. For (3), take away the sun, and the planets as well as the sun pass out of existence. For (2), at *any* time in the past (or the future for that matter) the sun could be observed to exist.

Given the way Martin sets up his definition of metaphysically necessary being as well as his verification procedure, the example of the sun and the planets seems to be a valid one. In fact, he says that it would apply to a star.[138] This is enough to show that Martin's procedure is utterly misguided. One of the main points of serious religious thought is that the transcendent God of the Judeo-Christian tradition is not observable. It is fatuous for Martin to propose that God, understood in the sense of metaphysically being, could "at *any* time in the past . . . be observed to exist." It is part of the definition of the transcendent God that there is *no* point in time at which he could be observed to exist. Therefore, the concept of metaphysically necessary being is not linked to the observations of contingent beings because, as we have seen, the term "contingent" as used in the cosmological argument is not an observable feature of the world. It cannot be linked to the observations of necessary being because necessary being is, by definition, not observable.

Metaphysically Necessary Being and Time   God is not observable. Yet suppose, for the sake of argument, that God could be observed. From the standpoint of the cosmologists' claim that metaphysically necessary being has factual or empirical content, there would still be problems. Part of Anthony Kenny's definition of metaphysically necessary being is that God is, was, and always will be. How could one ever validate the claim that necessary being had no beginning and will have no end? Even if a cosmologist could prove that necessary being existed before the oldest galaxies, how could he show, *by observations*, that it had no beginning? The same is true of the claim that necessary being will have no end. A cosmologist could claim that at any point in the future necessary being will be observable (as long as, for the sake of argument, we grant the point that necessary being could be observed) but how could one prove that this claim holds good?

Actually, from the standpoint of factual content, cosmologists are in the same boat as ontologists. The cosmological argument depends for its effectiveness on a great many assumptions about reality, and it finally appeals to the fact that the concept of necessary being cannot be denied without contradiction. It is true that there is still some difference between the arguments because in the case of the ontological argument this appeal is more explicit. God is defined as "not conceivable as not existing." To claim that you *can* conceive of him as not existing is simultaneously to affirm *A* (conceivable as not existing) and *not-A* (*not* conceivable as not existing).

In the case of the cosmological argument, a number of assumptions—Aristotelian, Platonic, and theological—are packed into the premises. We are supposed to acknowledge (1) that every observable being is contingent and therefore incapable of accounting for its own existence, (2) that what is true of individual contingent beings is also true of the cosmos; it is incapable of accounting for its own existence, and (3) the conclusion—that only God, understood as metaphysically necessary being—could account for the existence of the cosmos. It follows that to admit the existence of contingent beings, while denying the existence of God, involves us in the simultaneous claim that *not-A* (the cosmos can*not* account for its own existence) and *A* (the cosmos *can* account for its own existence).

The cosmological argument may or may not be valid. This is difficult to evaluate without making a thorough exploration of the Thomistic or some other theological context. One thing should, however, be clear. Its point of departure is not empirical.

The Existential Function of the Cosmological Argument

There are religious thinkers who claim that the cosmological argument fails as a demonstration of the existence of God but that it nevertheless plays an important role in theology. They claim that it helps to clarify the meaning of "God" and of his relation to the world. It also calls attention to the kinds of experiences that lead men to talk of God. The analysis is similar to one that has already been presented in the context of the teleological argument (see pp. 238ff.).

Ronald Hepburn claims that the effort to argue to the necessary existence of metaphysically necessary being fails. Cosmologists make the mistake of drawing examples from our observation of ordinary states of dependence like the relation of a child to a parent and making ironclad inferences from them to the relation between God and the world. Instead, Hepburn proposes that these ordinary experiences serve as springboards to an awareness of the relation between God and the world.

> Let us put our whole emphasis on the utter uniqueness of the relation between God and the world. No examples of this relation can be reasonably demanded, for they would have to be drawn from the relations of finite,

created thing with finite, created thing. At best we could see the whole cluster of dependence-relations, such as cause-effect, parent-child, etc., as preparing one to make a final, and still sharp, transition in thought to the unconditional dependence of the cosmological relation itself. Because of this uniqueness, the fate of the cosmological movement of thought cannot be tied to the unhappy fate of arguments based on dependence-chains, such as cause and effect, that *are* exemplifiable in the world of ordinary experience.[139]

Hepburn is, however, aware that this version of the cosmological argument, which depends on the existential sense of contingency rather than on a formal argument, needs more experiential data to back it up. He appeals to Rudolph Otto's account of the numinous.

Numinous experience is characterized by a sense of out-and-out dependence, derivativeness, and creatureliness, and by a peculiar haunting strangeness—an awesomeness or weirdness. . . . We are in the sphere of the non-rational, the inexpressible: but it is just such an inexpressible and fundamental type of dependence that our sophisticated versions of the cosmological argument are concerned with. Could numinous experience be taken as an actual, privileged awareness of the world as related to God, of God as related to the world?[140]

Hepburn's answer is affirmative, and he thinks that the cosmological argument, taken in this way is "invulnerable to the usual criticisms."[141] Yet he recognizes that this invulnerability has been purchased at a price. The argument has been drastically changed.

It started its career as a rational proof of God's existence. But it was unable to prove God demonstratively. In shifting ground to the exploration of a possible *factual* cosmological relation, experienced, however transitorily and imperfectly, in numinous experience, we should be retaining some of the essential ingredients in the old argument, but thoroughly changing its status. It would no longer move from premises intelligible to any reasonable person to a conclusion, by way of a chain of inference open to logical scrutiny. It would be taken now as a form of words that evokes, or evokes the memory of, a special and elusive group of experiences, not obtainable at will, nor perhaps, *ever* actually obtained, by every one.[142]

The ground of these experiences is, of course, God, the Holy One.

Having recast the argument in this form, Hepburn claims that "the religious person is justified in saying that this elusiveness [of the numinous experience] does not necessarily invalidate the cosmological movement of thought—considering as one must, the unique nature of its object."[143]

Thomists and other cosmologists would not be inclined to thank Hepburn for his recasting of their argument. They would claim that he deals with such key concepts as causality and necessity in positivistic terms. They would insist that their metaphysical uses of these terms are valid and that the argument is a successful demonstration of the existence of God (see pp. 53ff. for Father Copleston's responses to A. J. Ayer). Hepburn, like other analytic philosophers of this post-positivistic era, would concede the point that metaphysical demonstrations cannot be dismissed out of hand in the way that the positivists dismissed them. Nevertheless, on the basis of the kinds of considerations that have been offered in this chapter, he would claim that the Thomists have not made a convincing case for their metaphysical demonstrations. They, in turn, might retort that they cannot make a convincing case for people who rule out metaphysical categories on positivistic grounds.

Paul Tillich, whose religious thought will be the subject of the concluding part of this book, deals with all of the arguments for the existence of God in the way that Hepburn deals with the cosmological argument. Tillich claims that they fail as proofs for the existence of God but that they can serve as a springboard to a valid relation to the object of religious experience (see pp. 319f., 325ff.).

Part Five

Paul Tillich: Religion as Ultimacy

Paul Tillich (1886-1965) was a distinctive thinker who put his personal stamp on everything he touched, and he was a comprehensive thinker who touched just about everything. In his philosophy of religion he dealt with religion and science, verification, religious experience, existentialism, revelation in history, and metaphysics. His thought is therefore both an enormously impressive achievement taken in itself, and it provides an invaluable overview of the issues that have been considered throughout this book.

Tillich was a cultivated intellectual with a passion for the arts, and he drew on all aspects of Western culture in expressing his message. He was primarily a philosophical theologian whose classical education in his native Germany provided him with the kind of resources that are rarely to be found in the United States, where he lived and taught from 1933 until his death.[1] His great impact on the American scene in the thirty years after World War II was, in large measure, attributable to his existential perspective on the entire sweep of Western thought.

Tillich's immersion in the tradition of Western thought (especially the Platonic tradition in philosophy and its Augustinian offshoot in theology) is such that even his most startling claims involve restatements of points that have been made by one or another great figure, and his effort to weave them together in a coherent and consistent fabric.[2] This accounts for a peculiarity of his style. He often writes in a kind of shorthand; that is, he makes a point in a sketchy way and refers to his agreements and differences with great thinkers of the tradition, as in the following account of courage:

> Looking at the history of Western thought one finds the two meanings of courage indicated almost everywhere, explicitly or implicitly. Since we have to deal in separate chapters with the Stoic and Neo-Stoic ideas of courage I shall restrict myself at this point to the line of thought which leads from Plato to Thomas Aquinas.[3]

Yet Tillich does not restrict himself in this way because, in the same paragraph, he also deals with Descartes and Kant. The reader is expected to fill in Tillich's sketches on the basis of his knowledge (the reader's, that is) of Plato, the Stoics, and others. Reading him is made even more difficult because his interpretations of the titans of the Western tradition are often controversial. Furthermore, he does not always let the reader know that his shorthand sketches are backed up by arguments that have been carefully developed by someone else (see his discussion of the cosmological argument, pp. 323ff.).

Tillich is one of the most influential religious thinkers of our time. Although he himself is immersed in the history of Western thought, his influence is a function of the way he interacts with contemporary problems. I will, therefore, concentrate on his relation to analytic philosophers and to religious existentialists.

Tillich's desire to recast the Christian message into fresh terms and his concern to build bridges to the major figures of the Western tradition accounts for another peculiarity of his style. He uses clusters of terms where other thinkers might confine themselves to one or two words. At the center of his thought we find terms that he associates with what believers call God. The terms include being-itself, ground of being, power of being, the God above God, ultimate concern, the unconditioned, the infinite, and others. In using these clusters of terms he is addressing other thinkers, and in effect, saying, "Wherever you are and however you put it in your view of reality, you've got a place in my system. Here's how *I* use *your* language."

Tillich's use of clusters of terms makes it easy to score points against him by calling attention to inconsistencies in his terminology. He often uses the same term in different senses (for example, *God* as ultimate concern and *God* as being-itself; see Chapts. 14 and 15) and different terms in very much the same sense (for example the ultimate and the unconditioned; see Chapt. 14). Yet these inconsistencies are superficial.

In the larger sense, Tillich is a consistent thinker. His consistency is one of patterns rather than of individual terms. He begins at the level of routine experience where words like truth, concern, being, and courage are used in their ordinary senses. Then he tries to show that these ordinary uses presuppose uses that are not at all ordinary. When he discusses the extraordinary uses, he generally uses the word "itself" as a suffix as in being-itself or courage-itself. At other times he uses the adjective "ultimate" as in the phrase ultimate concern. The words "itself" and "ultimate" are landmarks that indicate that we are at what Tillich calls the dimension of depth or the religious dimension.[4] Once you develop a sense for this pattern, you can anticipate Tillich's analysis of any concept.

In the following chapters we will see how Tillich moves to the religious dimension by means of an analysis of a selection of terms. In Chapter 13 the focus is on the drive from ordinary knowing to the ultimate level of truth. His move from everyday cares to ultimate concern will be analyzed in Chapter 14. His most characteristic and important analysis, namely, his shift from observable beings to the reality of being-itself is presented in Chapter 15. His use of symbols to connect ordinary experiences with the dimension of depth is considered in Chapter 16. Tillich's distinctive view of verification is dealt with in Chapter 17, which culminates with my effort to summarize his thought by means of an extended allegory which I call "Tillich's Infinite Sea of Being." In Chapter 18 a number of criticisms that have been directed against Tillich's thought are discussed.

Chapter 13

Tillich's Three-Level
Theory of Truth

The two-level theory of truth is the major strategy of religious existential-ists in coping with the challenges of a scientifically oriented culture. They do not resist scientists in the name of religious authority. On the contrary, they hail scientific work as a great manifestation of the human spirit. Yet they insist that scientific work (at least in physics, chemistry, and other natural sciences) involves detachment of the human subject from the objects that are studied. It is a combination of the matters-of-logic that the positivists called *analytic* and of the matters-of-fact that they called *synthetic*. Within its limits it is the most successful knowledge game that human beings have played.

Religious existentialists, having paid their respects to science, then insist that the most important human activities like moral decisions, aesthetic appreciation, religious belief, and political commitment cannot be handled in an attitude of detachment. In these matters we are inescapably participants whose positions are saturated with personal and cultural considerations. If we try to avoid the implications of this, we delude ourselves. Therefore, in these domains we must abandon the pretense to scientific detachment and objectivity. We must instead think existentially, that is, by sweating out the most important decisions of life with a full awareness of their objective uncertainty and a willingness to take the risk of committing ourselves both to wrong beliefs and wrong actions.

Tillich explicitly articulates a two-level theory of truth and does so with a complicated array of terms. To begin with, I shall simply present his own version which claims only two levels of truth, but I will then show why I think that he actually operates with a three-level theory.

TILLICH'S STATEMENT OF HIS TWO-LEVEL THEORY OF TRUTH

Kierkegaard's contrast of the two levels is dealt with in terms of objective truth at the lower one, and subjective truth or faith at the higher. Buber's contrast is between the I-It (lower) and the I-You (higher). Bultmann contrasts scientific thinking (lower) with the existential (higher). Tillich's contrast is played out in terms of two fundamental modes of thinking.

Reasoning is a catchall term that Tillich sometimes uses to refer to all modes of knowledge that can be acquired through observation. It is used for the ordinary observations that go into common sense statements like "This page is white," and the extremely complicated combinations of observations and theorizing that go into scientific statements like "The helium atom has two electrons." Reasoning takes place at the lower level of truth and Tillich uses a cluster of terms in referring to it: formal, technical, and controlling. He explicitly refers to logical positivism as a movement that tried to claim that only reasoning could yield truth.[5] His term "controlling reason" is an excellent one for describing the positivists' enterprise. As we saw, they were dedicated to restricting the application of the words "true" and "know" to uses where the rules and checking procedures are clear (see pp. 14ff.). Reasoning, according to Tillich, yields knowledge that is adequate to science but not to life.

Reason is the broadest term that Tillich uses in referring to the method required for attaining to the higher level of truth (but at times he also uses it to embrace both levels). He refers to it by another cluster of terms: ontological, self-transcending, and ecstatic. In its application to religion this mode of thinking does not yield knowledge, in the positivists' sense of the term, but symbolic insight.

Like all thinkers who advocate the two-level theory of truth, Tillich draws on the distinction between the detached stance of objectivity and the involvement or participation that is characteristic of subjectivity.

The relation to the sciences . . . strengthens the detached objective attitude of the philosopher. . . . The theologian, quite differently, is not detached from his object but is involved in it. . . . The basic attitude of the theologian is commitment to the content he expounds. Detachment would be a denial of the very nature of this content. The attitude of the theologian is "existential."[6]

The Integrity of the Lower Level of Science and Logic

All thinkers who present the two-level theory of truth affirm the integrity of science and logic and Tillich is no exception. Science, of course, represents synthetic knowledge and Tillich states that "faith has no power to interfere with science."[7] Tillich regards the conflicts of science and religion as based on tragic misunderstandings. Religious authorities had no right to dictate what the findings of astronomy or biology should be. Tillich also insists that faith cannot override analytic knowledge which deals with mathematics and logic. "The doctrine of the Trinity does not affirm the logical nonsense that three is one and one is three. . . . Theology is not expected to accept a senseless combination of words, that is, genuine logical contradictions."[8]

In one especially clear statement Tillich warns religious thinkers against the danger of superstition that is involved when the lower level of technical reasoning is violated.

No truth is possible without the material given by sense perception [observations which are the basis of the synthetic] and without the form given by logical and mathematical rules [the analytic] which express the structure in which all reality stands. One of the worst errors of theology and popular religion is to make statements which intentionally or unintentionally contradict the structure of reality.[9]

The Higher Level Provides the Goals, the Lower Level, and the Means

Tillich also follows the two-level pattern in claiming that while science and logic are admirable, they are limited. He claims that formal, technical, or controlling reasoning is, for example, limited to determining the best means for achieving certain goals. It cannot, however, determine the goals themselves. They must be determined by the higher type of ontological, self-transcending, or ecstatic reason. "Technical reason, however refined in logical and methodological respects, dehumanizes man if it is separated from ontological reason . . . even in the means-ends structure of 'reasoning' assertions about the nature of things (that is, ontological statements) are presupposed which themselves are not based on technical reason."[10]

Far more than most religious thinkers Tillich is aware of and stresses the interaction between the two levels. He insists that we dare not allow technical reasoning about means to be cut off from ontological reason's determination of the authentic goals of human existence. As long as ontological reason operates critically—as in a theology like Calvin's or a moral philosophy like Kant's—on the realm of ends, then human beings are not given over to fanaticism. Once philosophers like the positivists succeed in limiting knowledge and truth to the products of technical reasoning they open the floodgates. "The consequence is that the ends are provided by nonrational forces, either by positive traditions or by arbitrary decisions serving the will to power."[11] Tillich, who lived through the period when the Nazis seized power in Germany, knew a great deal about the noncritical forces that could provide the goals of life for people who were rootless and limited their thinking about political affairs to technical reasoning about means.

Tillich is very explicit on the point that the higher level of reason involves participation, as in love, and that technical or controlling reasoning, which operates at the level of detachment, is inadequate to them. He has an interesting comment on Pascal's statement about "reasons of the heart which reason cannot comprehend."[12] Tillich writes: "Here 'reason' is used in a double sense. The 'reasons of the heart' [ontological reason] are the structures of aesthetic and communal experience (beauty and love); the reason 'which cannot comprehend them' is technical reason."[13]

The Higher Level Is Impervious to Criticisms from the Lower One

The key to the two-level theory of truth is that religious thinkers offer to abandon all imperialistic pretenses provided that scientists, and scientifically oriented philosophers (like the analysts), are prepared to do the same. Tillich recalls two of the most bitter disputes of science and religion in which religious authorities attempted to dictate the truth to scientists. One was the Church's efforts to force Galileo to change his views, the other was the violent rejection of Darwinian thought by religious thinkers who held the view that all the words of the Bible were divinely inspired and infallible. Tillich's view is that there can be no conflict provided that each side does not overstep its limits. Scientists should deal with limited matters like the origin of individual species, but Darwinian thought should not be blown up into a total world view that makes pronouncements about the nature and destiny of human beings. Tillich, in line with other religious thinkers who advocate the two-level approach, acknowledges the fact that biologists may find it fruitful to study human beings as animals, but this can only be a partial and limited view that is relevant to their research. They overstep these limits when they use their results to criticize theological views of freedom and of existential decision.

> Science has no right and no power to interfere with faith and faith has no power to interfere with science. . . . Science can conflict only with science, and faith only with faith; science which remains science [at the lower level] cannot conflict with faith which remains faith [at the higher level]. . . . The famous struggle between the theory of evolution and the theology of some Christian groups was not a struggle between science and faith, but between a science whose faith deprived man of his humanity [Darwinian thought reducing human beings to the status of mere animals] and a faith whose expression was distorted by biblical literalism [which treats the myths of the creation as though they were intended as journalistic or scientific accounts].[14]

The analysis that Tillich directs to the Darwinian controversy underlies his general view that God, the object of theology, is impervious to criticisms from the lower level of technical or controlling knowledge.

> First, the object of theology . . . is not an object within the whole of scientific experience. It cannot be discovered by detached observations or by conclusions derived from such observations. . . . Second, it cannot be tested by scientific methods of verification.[15]

ECSTATIC REASON TRANSCENDS THE SUBJECT-OBJECT DISTINCTION

Tillich's thought seems to provide a standard example of the two-level theory of truth. Yet, despite his claim that he deals with only two levels of truth (or reason or knowledge), I maintain that he actually presents a third level which sets him apart from religious existentialists. The central clue is provided by his statement about ecstasy:

> "Ecstasy" ("standing outside of one's self") points to a state of mind which is extraordinary in the sense that the mind transcends its ordinary situation. Ecstasy is not a negation of reason; it is a state of mind in which reason is beyond itself, that is, beyond its subject-object structure. In being beyond itself [that is, in being beyond technical reason] reason does not deny itself. "Ecstatic reason" remains reason; it does not receive anything irrational or antirational—which it could not do without self-destruction—but it transcends the basic condition of finite rationality, the subject-object structure.[16]

When Tillich writes of a mode of reason that transcends the subject-object structure, he introduces an element that is not to be found among other representatives of the two-level theory of truth. In order to appreciate this point we have to realize that his pairing or polarity of subject-object is linked to two others—self-world and knower-known. In all these polar terms a human being is consciously aware of both self and otherness, as when Martin Buber writes that the I-You "teaches you to encounter others and to stand your ground in such encounters. . . ."[17] Clearly there is no transcending the subject-object structure in this relation. What is true of Buber's I-You is true of all instances of existential approaches to truth. A knowing subject relates to moral, political, and other types of issues in which the degree of personal involvement is considerable. Yet at the higher or existential level the subject is just as much in the picture as he is at the level of objective knowledge where analytic and synthetic statements are made. It should, therefore, be obvious that despite the fact that Tillich explicitly restricts his analysis to two levels, a third level is involved: ecstatic reason goes beyond the polarity of subject and object.

It would seem natural to present an extended statement of Tillich's view of ecstatic reason at this point, but it would be a mistake. To understand it we must recognize the need for transcending the pattern in which an individual human being (a subject) thinks about another being that is independent of him (the object). Tillich is aware of the fact that all our ordinary reasoning conforms to this subject-object scheme, and that the reasons for departing from it are not at all obvious. They certainly cannot be made comprehensible, much less persuasive, when considered apart from his analysis of the way that human beings, in thinking about and relating to God, continually fall into idolatry.

In the following chapters Tillich's third level of truth is considered in terms of his two basic approaches to the religious dimension of depth. His analysis of human concerns and his insistence that a person's ultimate concern should be one that is beyond the subject-object distinction is presented in Chapter 14. His use of ecstatic reason to claim that the truly ultimate, which he calls being-itself, is beyond the subject-object distinction is dealt with in Chapter 15. It is important to realize that, from Tillich's standpoint, they are the same reality.

Subjectivity: God as Ultimate Concern

Tillich is more self-conscious about the problems of philosophical method than are the religious existentialists, as in the way he deals with verification (see Chapt. 17). Still, he does not deal with hard-core secularists, who are indifferent to religion and who dismiss its questions as meaningless, in terms of detailed epistemological issues. Instead he asks the broad-guaged question, "What is man?" His answer is that human beings have concerns. I would put it more simply and say that, for Tillich, man is an animal that cares. I choose the simpler phrase because what Tillich is getting at is not something technical and artificial, but one of the most common features of everyday life. We all have many things we care about: ourselves, family, friends, politics, etc. Each breaks down into an almost limitless number of factors, for example, caring about ourselves involves a concern for pleasures, for ambitions, and for many other things. All these cares or concerns are generally mixed in the haphazard way that differently shaped and colored bits fall together in the tube of kaleidoscope. They are transformed into fascinating and ordered patterns when we turn the tube and look into the lens.

When life is running in low gear we take our concerns for granted. We watch television, read books, put ourselves out for family and friends, and participate, to some degree, in that broad range of activities that come under the heading of citizenship. Each of these concerns demands something of us, but there doesn't seem to be any reason why we can't handle all of them, but when things heat up, we are forced to think about these different concerns and to decide how deep our commitments are.

CONCERNS ARE INESCAPABLY SUBJECTIVE

Existentialists stress the *how* of momentous decisions rather than the *what*, that is, they stress the subjective attitudes manifested in the process of decision making more than the content of the decision (see pp. 153f.). In his analysis of concern, Tillich is very much the existentialist: the focus is on subjectivity. In the sermon, "Our Ultimate Concern," he asks: "What does it mean to be concerned about something?" and answers: "It means that we are involved in it, that a part of ourselves is in it, that we participate with our hearts."[18] We are on the level of existential participation where objective approaches won't work.

Tillich is not out to provide us with a list of concerns that any self-respecting and rational human being ought to regard as: important, more important, and most important. Human concerns cannot be measured in an objective way, that is, in terms of accepted procedures that yield agreement on specific concerns. He does, however, distinguish authentic from inauthentic ways of dealing with concerns. The main clue to authenticity is that we have to rate our concerns. Otherwise, we will simply drift along, responding impulsively or instinctively to the things that we happen to care most about at any given moment.[19]

One of the best known illustrations in existentialist literature is Sartre's story of the student who came to him after the fall of France in 1940.[20] He sought advice regarding his live, momentous, and forced options of staying with his mother, who needed him desperately (she had already lost his father and brother) and joining the resistance. The student was driven to think about his concerns; both were great, but he was forced to decide between them. Hard thinking on the issues helped in some respects. He could, for example, check out the integrity of the resistance and also try to get some idea of how badly he was needed. The one thing his reflection could not do was to provide him with an objective scale on which he could quantify his concern for his mother and his concern for his country's resistance to tyranny. The judgments packed into the things we care about cannot be dealt with by techniques appropriate either to analytic or synthetic statements. We can only define ourselves as more or less authentic by the way that we handle them.

ULTIMATE CONCERNS

Most concerns are what Tillich calls "preliminary" by way of distinguishing them from what he regards as most important, namely, "ultimate concerns." As he uses it in this context, ultimacy is defined by three main features: it is integrating, unconditioned, and captures the religious spirit.

Integrating

The first feature I shall present is one that Tillich calls "the integrating center of personal life," I will make it explicit by using my own illustration.[21]

One way or another we rate our concerns. If we do not rate them self-consciously, we will rate them unconsciously; that is, instead of having a clear idea of which concerns are most important to us and why, we will not be self-consciously aware of them, but we will merely display our priorities by the way we act.

Pleasure is an important concern for everyone. Yet we cannot simply assume that pleasure is the ultimate concern. Everyone, in the name of other concerns, defers pleasures at one time or another. In order to study, a student might miss a great movie. His concern to study is attributable to the desire to graduate. The desire to graduate is related to the desire to get a good job, and this in turn, reflects a concern to earn money. Money is desired for the sake of luxuries, and the luxuries reflect a concern for pleasure.

In this series of concerns the set pattern is: "I do *x* (study, work, earn money) because I want *y* (diploma, good job, luxuries, pleasure)." The last concern on the list is pleasure. If the student is now asked, "Why do you want pleasure?" one possible answer is, "Doesn't everybody?" This is the answer of hedonism, the doctrine that pleasure is the highest good. In that case, the student would break the *because* pattern. For the hedonist, the point of ultimacy has been reached. Pleasure is not sought as a means toward some other good. Everything the hedonist does is, ultimately, for the sake of pleasure, and this reveals pleasure as his ultimate concern.

When we come to the point of ultimacy we recognize a kind of finality; a series has come to an end, there are no more "becauses." Ultimate concerns are not followed up in the name of anything else, rather they are the focus of all preliminary concerns; we build, or integrate, our lives around them.

Unconditioned

In talking of ultimate concerns Tillich often uses another term, "unconditioned," which is a good example of his using clusters of words in driving at a concept. "Unconditioned" means there are no strings attached. A hedonist would say, "I want pleasure come what may." The man for whom knowledge is the ultimate concern could never say that. He must hedge or qualify his concern for pleasure, for example, by saying, "I want pleasure, but only *on condition* that it doesn't mess up my research." It is this qualification that makes pleasure a preliminary concern for him, whereas knowledge is his unconditioned or ultimate concern.

The Religious Attitude

Tillich links the unconditioned character of ultimate concern to what he regards as the most characteristically religious attitude. The link is the biblical commandment: "You shall love the Lord your God with all your heart, and with all your soul, and with all your might" (Deut. 6:5; Mark 12, 29, 30). Tillich comments: "This is what ultimate concern means and from these words the term 'ultimate concern' is derived."[22] In other words, ultimate concern stands for the subjective pole of faith where the individual makes an unconditional commitment.

The link between ultimate concern and the religious attitude shows that causes—political and religious—are the concerns that absorb Tillich's attention. They structure life by giving individuals something that they are prepared to die for. As we shall see, one of Tillich's major points is that an authentic human being should have an ultimate concern which is the focus of his life, but he should not be fanatical in his relation to it (see pp. 382f.).

Tillich's Effort to Bypass Debates over the Existence of God

We can now appreciate one of Tillich's most controversial claims: everyone, including the atheist, believes in God and he, Tillich, can demonstrate this. "The fundamental symbol of our ultimate concern is God. It is always present in any act of faith, even if the act of faith includes the denial of God. Where there is ultimate concern, God can only be denied in the name of God."[23] If, for example, a philosophical atheist denies the existence of God, he denies it in the name of truth. In that case, by Tillich's standards the so-called atheist actually affirms God at the same time that he denies God. He denies the God of theism in the name of truth, his ultimate concern, and for Tillich a person's ultimate concern is his God.

The gambit irritated many people, among them Sydney Hook, the well-known pragmatist, who accused Tillich of "conversion by definition."[24] Tillich claims that God is an expression of ultimate concern and that everyone has a concern of this character. Hook fears that people who come across Tillich's claim that everyone believes in God will not realize that the God that Tillich refers to is one's ultimate concern. They will think that Tillich claims that everyone believes in the God of theism. Hook is surely justified in his nervousness, but Tillich agrees with Hook on an important point: the God of theism does not exist (see Chapt. 15).

Tillich regards the debate over the existence of God as sterile and misguided and he tries to bypass it by means of his definition of God as the expression of ultimate concern.

> It is obvious that such an understanding of the meaning of God makes the discussions about the existence or non-existence of God meaningless. It is meaningless to question the ultimacy of an ultimate concern. . . . The question is not this ["Does God exist?"] but: . . . which symbol of ultimacy expresses the ultimate without idolatrous elements?[25]

Tillich is updating Calvin. The Reformer regarded human beings as "idol-making" factories. They would worship come what may; the object was to get them to worship the true God.[26] Tillich deals with human beings as concern-spawning creatures who inevitably make one of them (or different ones at different times) ultimate. In doing so, they become idolatrous by making limited or preliminary concerns into unconditioned or ultimate ones (this analysis is also applied to symbols, see p. 350).

Tillich wants human beings to recognize idols for what they are: "In true faith the ultimate concern is a concern about the truly ultimate."[27] An authentic human being would therefore not be content with figuring out what his ultimate concern actually is; he would try to see to it that what he cares about most is really what is most important.

THE TEST FOR ULTIMACY

Tillich doesn't have a magic formula for pulling the true God out of the theological hat. In other words, he doesn't have a way of coercing anyone to adopt a specific ultimate concern and to regard it as truly ultimate. He does, however, have a negative test for ultimacy; he can tell when a candidate is not the real thing. His criterion or test for ferreting out illegitimate candidates is: "The finite which claims infinity without having it (as, for example, a nation or success). . . ."[28] The point of the criterion is suggested by his examples; people are often swept along by the power of ambition or by the appeal of their country. This is what Tillich means in using this odd phrase "the finite which claims infinity"; an individual is grasped by the power of these concerns and then treats them as ultimate or infinite. They are loved with all his heart, soul, and might. Yet they are not ultimate because they are finite and conditioned. A country is limited by other countries, and personal success is obviously limited and conditioned by countless factors, including the continued life of the individual.

Country, success, race, revolutionary movements, mankind, the Bible, the church, are all possible ultimate concerns. Yet they are limited things which are here today and gone tomorrow (even if, in some instances, tomorrow may be a long time coming). All of them are things which are good in some respects and which are limited by other things which may be good in the same or in different respects. None of them is worthy of unlimited and unconditional love, of unreserved care, and of unrestricted concern.

Tillich's analysis of the subjective pole of the faith relation yields a standard of idolatry. ". . . in an idolatrous faith preliminary finite realities are elevated to the rank of ultimacy."[29] In the literal sense of the term, nothing, that is, no individual specifiable being, can be a legitimate object of ultimate concern.

Tillich writes: "In terms like ultimate, unconditional, infinite, absolute, the difference between subjectivity and objectivity is overcome."[30] This is his shorthand way of indicating why he thinks that any specifiable object, whether of observation or thought, is not worthy of being regarded as truly ultimate. No particular object, whether of our senses or of our imagining and thinking, is worthy of being loved with all our hearts, with all our souls, and with all our mights, because any particular object is conditioned by other objects. A country is conditioned because it is limited by the physical boundaries and the interests of other countries. Even the ideals of a great movement like the French Revolution—freedom, equality, and brotherhood—are conditioned in the sense that they arise in history and are ideals that reflect the consciousness of particular groups of human beings in particular times even though, in Tillich's formulation, they claim universality. Tillich means that the human beings who proclaim these ideals regard them as universally valid. Yet, from his point of view, ideals of this kind can never be truly ultimate because our awareness of their historically conditioned character enables us to see that they are finite.[31] Any given ideal is limited by our understanding of it in relation to others. The ideals of the French Revolution are, for example, limited insofar as they may be thought about in comparison with other ideals. For instance, the ideals of the Russian Revolution expressed in the phrase, "From each according to his ability, to each according to his needs."

As Tillich formulates his criterion of true ultimacy it becomes clear that he associates particularity with finitude and that what is finite cannot be truly ultimate. It follows that anything that can be a particular *object* of awareness by an individual *subject* is disqualified. His somewhat confusing statement of his own standard of true ultimacy follows:

> The finite which claims infinity without having it (as, for example, a nation or success) is not able to transcend the subject-object scheme. It remains an object which is looked at by the individual believer, who is a subject. He can [therefore] approach it with ordinary knowledge and subject it to ordinary handling.[32]

Tillich insists that nothing, literally no specifiable particular, can be truly ultimate. As far as our ordinary knowledge and our ordinary language is concerned it might as well be the void, just plain nothing. As we shall see, Tillich maintains that this ultimate, which is beyond all characterization, is being-as-such or being-itself. Without the reality of being-itself, there would be merely nothing, and we would not be around to think about idolatry and ultimacy (see pp. 327ff.).

Tillich warns us not to make the mistake of treating any particular as though it were the truly ultimate because that makes it into a false ultimate, that is, an idol, and idols let us down. "The inescapable consequence of idolatrous faith is 'existential disappointment'. . . ."[33] In *The God That Failed* a number of ex-Communists wrote spiritual autobiographies. They told of being drawn into the Communist movement and of their disillusion with it.[34] The essays, especially those by Arthur Koestler and Ignazio Silone, are a moving statement of what Tillich calls "existential disappointment." They entered the movement thinking that it would bring salvation to all human beings. They experienced Stalinist terror and left it feeling that the movement was a demonic force that broke the back of its most idealistic adherents. Tillich insists that any movement, any ideal will eventually fail human beings in this way if we take it as the ultimate rather than as a symbol of the ultimate (for Tillich's view of symbols, see Chapt. 16).

The ultimate, which Tillich generally refers to as being-itself, cannot be anything particular, anything specific; that is why, unlike all particular and therefore finite things, it cannot let us down. Yet, because it is not specific, we cannot relate to it directly.

Tillich writes that "every faith has a concrete element in itself. It is concerned about something or somebody."[35] I'd like to elaborate on that by saying that for Tillich every faith must have a concrete focus or better, a specific focus, since he does not restrict himself to observables. It can be something as abstract as liberty or justice. The important point is that we ought not to relate to them as though they were the ultimate because if we make that mistake, they become idols.

Tillich's "ultimate" and "unconditioned" are limiting concepts. The terms do not designate particular objects. Their meaning is disclosed when Tillich shows how they function in relation to all objects.

In dealing with concerns we are at the subjective pole of the knower-known relation. The terms "ultimate" and "unconditioned" function by enabling us to develop a proper perspective on our personal concerns. At this pole the focus is inward. We are all aware of the stream of consciousness that moves through our minds like a film. To see what Tillich is driving at, imagine a person's stream of consciousness being projected onto a cinema screen. He plays the role of a director, critically examining the concerns that unfold. Every concern that can be projected onto the screen is conditioned in the sense of being limited. Each concern appears in the context of others. For example, concern for country limits the concern for family, and vice versa. No specifiable concern in the stream of consciousness is or can be unconditioned. None can, therefore, be the truly ultimate concern. We are, nevertheless, tempted to regard specific concerns as truly ultimate because we become passionately involved with them. Tillich expresses the point in the following dense passage:

> Man's experiences, feelings, thoughts [the stream of consciousness] are conditioned and finite. They not only come and go, but their content is of finite and conditional concern—unless they are elevated to unconditional validity. But this presupposes the general possibility of doing so; it presupposes the element of infinity in man.[36]

Tillich is not making the ridiculous claim that human beings are infinite; on the contrary, he continually emphasizes their finite character. He means that ultimacy or the unconditioned is inevitably used in our thinking. This accounts for our capacity for idolatry in which we misapply these notions by taking a limited and conditioned reality, like the nation, for the unconditioned, that is, for the absolute or God. Another way of putting it is to say that Tillich thinks that the ultimate and the unconditioned are part of the conceptual apparatus of all minds, even of the minds of people who would just as soon ignore them.

The analysis of the element of ultimacy in human concerns discloses part of the role of ecstatic reason in Tillich's scheme. In dealing with the truly ultimate the individual should recognize the need for transcending the subject-object relation which is indispensible to technical reason. Tillich, therefore, also refers to technical reason as self-transcending.

When the individual using technical reason confronts the issue of ultimacy, he realizes that he must transcend technical reason.

Almost all the baffling things that Tillich says about the religious dimension can be understood in terms of his view that the subject-object pattern involves specificity and that specificity involves radical limitation.

1 Anything specific is limited. A specific thing (physical object) is limited by other physical objects; a specific person is limited by other persons; and a specific idea or ideal is limited by other ideas or ideals.

2 Whatever is limited cannot be the truly ultimate because, when we accept something limited as our ultimate concern, it results in existential disappointment.

3 Anything which a given subject thinks about as an isolatable object is a specific being. Therefore, the truly ultimate, which is worthy of being loved with all our souls, with all our hearts, and with all our might, cannot be an object which a given subject considers. Our ultimate concern must transcend the subject-object relation.

4 We cannot in anyway describe or imagine the truly ultimate because it transcends the subject-object relation and all our language is ordered to the routine experiences of an individual subject who contemplates objects or beings that exist independently of himself.

The pattern will come fully into focus in the context of the discussion of Tillich's view of being-itself (see Chapt. 15).

ULTIMATE CONCERN AND THE ONTOLOGICAL ARGUMENT

One of the most fascinating aspects of Tillich's thought is his treatment of the traditional arguments for the existence of God. He thinks that they are right, up to a point, and then they misfire. In the context of his treatment of concerns, that is, of the subjective pole, he deals with the ontological argument in terms of both agreement and strong dissent.[37]

At no other point is Tillich's indebtedness to the Platonic-Augustinian tradition as great as it is here.[38] I might add that at no other point in his work is his tendency to merely sketch or indicate arguments rather than developing them fully so maddeningly in evidence. I hope that the following restatement does justice to his intentions.

1 The dimension of ultimacy is an inescapable part of our mental apparatus. We know this because we all find ourselves manifesting passionate concerns and we all (if we are to be authentically human) try to order them in terms of importance. We rate them in terms of whether they are more or less conditioned, more or less ultimate. In other words, the truly ultimate and the unconditioned are concepts that we use as *standards* in judging the actual concerns we have.

2 We cannot eliminate these concepts (of the ultimate and the unconditioned) simply by noting that particular candidates for ultimacy—like the nation, success, or a given religion—are not truly ultimate. In other words, we do not jettison a criterion or standard simply because the individual items we consider do not measure up to it.

3 If the concepts of the ultimate and the unconditioned are indispensable elements of our thinking, then they must be indispensable elements of reality. To deny this connection would make truth impossible, since the link between thinking and being would be severed. He writes: "... every argument is based on the assumption that through the argument a character of the real is grasped."[39]

Tillich fails to develop this difficult point with clarity. He moves from ordinary uses of concepts to the highly controversial domain which he calls the dimension of depth. To illustrate, if you added three, eleven, eight, and ten you would get the answer thirty-two. If someone challenged it, you would check your addition. If you told him that it was correct and he answered, "I knew that your addition was right, but I don't agree that addition yields the correct result," you would be stymied. He would be responding in a way that makes mathematics impossible. Tillich claims that to say that concepts like ultimacy or the unconditioned are indispensable for thinking and then to claim that they are not real is to similarly destroy the integrity of a mode of reasoning—ontological reasoning. Of course the ultimate or the unconditioned are not real in the sense that physical objects like tables are real. They are certainly not observable. We become aware of them when we think about the underlying structures of being that enable us to order reality in reliable ways, as when we use them to rank our concerns.

Tillich's agreement with the ontological argument follows from this analysis. It involves the notion of limiting concepts, like the unconditioned, that are indispensable for thinking and, therefore, must be acknowledged as real. Anselm's definition of God as "something than which nothing greater can be conceived," is, from Tillich's standpoint, a limiting concept.

4 Tillich's point of disagreement with Anselm and other thinkers who regard the ontological argument as valid concerns the status of these concepts.[40] Tillich insists that the argument does not yield the existence of a specific reality, "necessary being" that is then characterized by such attributes (or perfections) as omnipotent and eternal. Thinking of this kind is appropriate to items within the world that are uncovered by technical reason, that is, to items like electrons and genes. It is not appropriate to limiting concepts that are *presupposed* in all our reasoning. We will have to consider his cosmological approach to being-itself to understand the status Tillich assigns to limiting concepts.

Chapter 15

The Objective Pole: God as Being-Itself

The presentation of Tillich's subjective pole of the faith relation, in which God is understood as ultimate concern, was deliberately toned down. The reader could come away from it thinking that Tillich stands in the great tradition of Christian thinkers, like Calvin, whose main point is to keep men from substituting limited beings for God. The assault on idolatry is indeed a central feature of Tillich's thought, but when we study his treatment of the objective pole in which God is regarded as being-itself, it will be obvious that he is an extremely radical Christian thinker.

Some years ago, after reading Tillich, a student declared: "If Christianity is what Tillich says it is, then I sure got gypped in Sunday school!" He was right. Anyone who accepts Christianity on Tillich's terms will certainly say, "Goodbye to Sunday school and all that." Yet in order to fully appreciate the radical character of Tillich's presentation of Christianity, it is important to realize that many clergymen could respond in the same way as that student. "If Christianity is what Tillich says it is, then I sure got gypped at my Seminary!"

In most Sunday schools teachers may be bothered by the passage about God walking through the Garden of Eden looking for Adam and Eve, but they do not balk at the idea that God gave the Ten Commandments to Moses or at the passages that represent God as demanding, righteous, and merciful. In other words, the Bible is explicitly anthropomorphic; so too is the God of the Sunday schools. The God of the seminaries is primarily the more sophisticated God of the theologians, who is a refined version of the biblical God of the Sunday schools. Most theologians claim that God is personal, but they try to purify this person. They claim that God is conscious of human beings but that God's consciousness does not operate through a body. A major goal of theological reconstruction is to purge God of all taint of a body which is an obvious symbol of the limited and the impure. He is then regarded as the perfect or highest being. God is all-powerful (but his power is not expressed by means of a body), God is all-knowing (but his knowledge does not work by means of a brain), and so on.

Tillich takes account of a wide range of idolatries. In crude forms, a tangible thing like a stone is treated as divine; in theological versions a "spiritual" being is treated as divine. From Tillich's standpoint the spiritual being of the theologians is as limited as the more obviously anthropomorphic God of the Sunday schools, therefore, the God of the theologians, too, is an idol. In fact, a more dangerous idol just because it is less obvious. Tillich's view of idolatry underlies his statement that "God does not exist."[41] In making it he allied himself with critics who, throughout the ages, have rejected the God of theism as a fantasy that has been pervasive in our culture because it has been supported by organized religion.

In declaring that God does not exist, Tillich does not think that he is sacrificing anything important to Christianity. Indeed, he thinks this God is an idol that must be rejected; it is not the ultimate which accounts for the existence of the world we live in.

The point of departure for an analysis of the radical character of Tillich's view of God is his understanding of being-itself. It is also the point at which he most obviously tries to go beyond the religious existentialists. He is as sensitive to the importance of subjectivity as any of them, but, unlike them, he is deeply troubled by the dangers of subjectivism. I have dealt with this issue at the end of the chapters on Buber, Kierkegaard, and Bultmann. In different ways, they try to establish the reality of God by means of analyses that are confined to subjectivity or inwardness. Buber, as we have seen, insists that God can only be known in the I-You relation and that no checking procedures can undermine the assurance of his reality that comes through in the relation itself (see pp. 118f.). I stressed the questionable character of this sort of thinking. An experience may be intense and illuminating, but when it claims to be an experience *of* another reality, then checking procedures that drive beyond the experience itself are in order.

Tillich tries to break out of the limits of the merely subjective by means of reasoning like that of the cosmological argument. Yet, true to form, he radically rejects the standard versions of this argument. A consideration of the grounds on which he rejects them, will help us to understand his distinctive approach to cosmological thinking.

TILLICH'S CRITICISMS OF THE COSMOLOGICAL ARGUMENT

A recapitulation of the second of Aquinas' Five Ways, the argument from efficient causality, will be a useful introduction to Tillich's criticisms of the cosmological argument.

We begin with observed beings, for example, human beings. They are caused by the parents who, in turn, are caused by their parents, and so on. At no point in this series—even if we go back beyond the human species to its evolutionary forebearers—do we come upon a cause that is capable of accounting for the existence of the series itself. Cosmologists conclude that since the series exists, there must be a cause that accounts for it, a cause that is of a different order of reality than all the members of the series. It will have to be a First Cause, in the sense of being only a cause and not also an effect of some other cause. The First Cause is, according to Thomists, what men call God.

Tillich's criticism of the cosmological and the teleological arguments for the existence of God is summed up as follows: "The so-called cosmological and teleological arguments for the existence of God . . . move from some special characteristics of the world to the existence of a highest being. . . . They are not valid in so far as they claim that the existence of a highest being is the logical conclusion of their analysis. . . ."[42] In other words, he rejects the pattern by which they move from the world to God, and he rejects the notion of God that appears in the conclusion, namely, the view that God is the "highest [or necessary] being."

Tillich rejects these arguments outright, but he does not discuss them at length. Instead, in a few brief strokes he presents, or rather, refers to, some of Kant's criticisms, as in his remarks on the causal version:

> The "first cause" is . . . not a statement about a being which initiates the causal chain [or rather, it is mistaken to consider it in this way because] such a being would itself be part of the causal chain and would again raise the question of cause.[43]

In other words, Tillich claims that it is illegitimate to reason to God as a being who is first cause in the sense that he initiates the causal sequence without himself being the effect of any cause. It is illegitimate because it does not cut off the sequence of "why questions." It would always be legitimate to ask, "And what caused the First Cause?"

Tillich locates the trouble in the method of the Thomists. He claims that they use patterns of reasoning, which he calls "arguing to a conclusion" that is ordered to experience within the world. In other words, Robinson Crusoe could reason from the existence of a footprint in the sand to the presence of a man on the island. This is legitimate because the footprint and the man are both observable realities within the finite world. Tillich, however, insists that it is illegitimate to use this method of reasoning in relation to God.

> The method of arguing through [to] a conclusion . . . contradicts the idea of God. . . . In arguments for the existence of God the world is given and God is sought. . . . God is derived from the world. . . . But, if we derive God from the world he cannot be that which transcends the world infinitely.[44]

In effect, Tillich, with as much impatience as any philosophical analyst, rules out of court all efforts to reason from the observation of features of the world to the God who transcends or who is utterly beyond the world. Ironically, his own reasoning is Hegelian.

Tillich's characterization of the reasoning involved in the cosmological argument would not be accepted by Thomists.[45] In effect, they would make the kind of responses that Father Copleston made to Professor Ayer (see p. 55). They claim that they are not misusing empiricist modes of reasoning but that they are using a distinctive and legitimate mode of reasoning, namely, metaphysical. It is reasoning that begins with observations within the world but that infers the existence of realities which are beyond the world. They claim that if there were no first cause, then the sequence of causes and effects could not exist.

Tillich is convinced that despite the best intentions of the comsologists they do misuse the ordinary modes of technical reasoning in arguing to the existence of God. Furthermore, once they have derived the existence of God by misusing ordinary modes of reasoning they compound their mistake. Robinson Crusoe could examine the footprint in the sand and not only conclude that there was another man on the island, but he could learn something about him. If the footprint is deep, he is heavy; if it is long, he is tall, and so on. So too the Thomists, having concluded that God exists, proceed to use (or, as Tillich would have it, to misuse) the same type of reasoning to conclude that God must be without limit or infinite, and that he must be all-knowing, and so on. Robinson Crusoe is a *subject* who uses both observations and reasoning to infer the qualities of the *object* of his investigation (the other man). Tillich claims that in similar fashion the Thomist reasons as a *subject* who uses observations and reasoning to infer the qualities of God—the *object* of his investigations.

Tillich insists that this pattern yields the wrong God, one derived by the wrong method. Inevitably, it results in the concept of God as "necessary being," the "highest being" or "perfect being." Despite the lofty and unique status that theologians wish to confer upon God by means of these attributes, Tillich charges that the result is the most sophisticated of idols. It is of this God, the God of the theologians that Tillich writes: "It is as atheistic to affirm the existence of God as it is to deny it."[46]

TILLICH'S COSMOLOGICAL APPROACH TO BEING-ITSELF

Tillich's criticism of Thomists and other thinkers who regard the cosmological argument as valid is that they use the wrong tools in getting to ultimate reality and, therefore, present a distorted view of it. *His* method is to use ecstatic reason rather than technical reason. His conclusion is that we reason to being-itself and not to the highest being or to necessary being.

The Question of Being

Tillich insists that the question of God must involve the question of being. "The question of God *must* be asked because the threat of nonbeing, which man experiences as anxiety, drives him to the question of being conquering nonbeing and of courage conquering anxiety."[47] The points have a technical ring: the question of being is philosophical and the question of God is theological, yet the roots of these questions are present in ordinary experiences. They come through poignantly in "To A Mouse" by Robert Burns. He destroys the nest of a mouse with his plow and, seeing the terror of the animal, he becomes painfully aware of the catastrophe he unwittingly causes. He thinks of the mouse's exertions in building the nest and makes his much quoted statement that the best laid plans of mice and men often go astray. What follows is relevant to Tillich's analysis:

> Still, thou art blest compared wi'me
> The present only toucheth thee
> But Och, I backward cast my e'e
> On prospects drear!
> And forward, thou I canna see,
> I guess and fear!

The mouse is totally locked into its environment; it lives in the moment. Through consciousness, human beings transcend immediacy and contemplate the past and future. Tillich has this sort of transcendence in mind when writing that ". . . reason is not bound to its own finitude. It is aware of it and, in so doing, rises above it."[48]

The ability to think about death (the contingency of the individual) and to imagine that the universe as a whole might not exist (the contingency of existence) is distinctively human. Tillich refers to it as "something like a 'metaphysical shock'—the shock of possible nonbeing."[49] Yet the questions we ask as a result of experiencing this shock are very odd: "Why should anything exist at all?" or "Why is there something rather than nothing?" Tillich insists that questions of this kind *cannot* be shown to be logically legitimate.[50] He agrees with the kinds of challenges mounted by analytic philosophers. The questions deriving from metaphysical shock are grammatically similar to ordinary questions like: "Why did George VI reign rather than Edward VIII?" The sceptic then criticizes the 'logic' of the ultimate questions. He notes that they are not answerable, not even in principle. Oddly enough, a philosophical analyst provided a superb statement of both Tillich's misgivings about these ultimate questions and of Tillich's reasons for keeping them at the center of his thought.

> Now let us ask, "why should anything exist at all?" Logic seems to tell us that the only answer which is not absurd is to say, "Why shouldn't it?" Nevertheless, though I know that any [effort to take it seriously by providing an] answer on the lines of the cosmological argument can be pulled to pieces by a correct logic, I still feel I want to go on asking the question. Indeed, although logic has taught me to look at such a question with the gravest suspicion, my mind often seems to reel under the immense significance it seems to have for me. That anything should exist at all does seem to me a matter for the deepest awe.[51]

The question "Why should anything exist at all?" reaches to the outer limits of human possibility. To shrug it off with the question "Why shouldn't it?" is, as far as Tillich is concerned, to truncate human being by making it more like that of animals. The question is there; it is both inescapable and serious. The person who dismisses the question as meaningless is like the one who refuses to get serious about the question: "How can I tell whether my ultimate concern is concern for the truly ultimate?" In both cases life is trivialized. Tillich regards people who trivialize existence in this way as inauthentic. He writes: "He who is not able to perceive something ultimate, something infinitely significant, is not a man."[52]

No Specifiable Being Can Provide the Answer to the Question of Being

In dealing with the subjective pole and its key question, "How can I tell whether my ultimate concern is concern for the truly ultimate?" I suggested that we might think of projecting our concerns on a film screen to see if any of them are worthy of being regarded as truly ultimate (see p. 318). In dealing with the objective pole and its key question, "Why is there something rather than nothing?" the same imaginative device can be used, but this time the camera must be turned outward. Film every being there is, project them all on a screen, and try to see if any one of them qualifies as the power that answers the question. Predictably enough, none of them do. Indeed, on reflection we come to realize that no observable being can possibly account for the fact that there is something rather than nothing. All observable beings that can be thought of as existing can also be thought of as not existing. In other words, to recall the central term of the cosmological argument, every observable being is contingent.[53] Furthermore, Tillich agrees with the Thomists and other defenders of the cosmological argument on the point that what holds for individual contingent beings also holds for the aggregate. The limitless number of contingent beings that make up the cosmos cannot account for there being something rather than nothing.

At this point, Thomists and other thinkers who regard the cosmological argument as valid draw the crucial inference. Since no observable being can account for the state of affairs in which countless contingent beings exist, they conclude that God, a nonobservable and necessary being, must account for it. Tillich rejects this inference. His reasons are similar to those we considered in connection with the cosmological argument. Tillich thinks that Thomists make the mistake of dealing with cosmic questions by means of technical reasoning. They misuse words like contingent by regarding the world as one great contingent thing and reasoning to God as the necessary cause of it.

The kind of thinking that underlies Tillich's treatment of the Thomists is captured in the following formulation by Ronald Hepburn: "The universe is not a limited thing like a box of biscuits or a galaxy. More helpfully, the word 'universe' is not a thing-word, and therefore it must not be expected to conform to the logical behavior of thing-words."[54] Tillich is convinced that if we are to reach the ultimate through an analysis of being, we must operate with a mode of reason oriented to ultimacy rather than with one oriented to contingent beings.

Begin with Technical Reason but Shift to Ecstatic Reason

Tillich maintains that if we wish to arrive at ultimacy by rational means, we must begin with technical reason operating in the ordinary way, but v e must not remain there. The person using technical reason in an effort to answer the question, "Why is there something rather than nothing?" comes to a sense of its limits. Reasoning of this kind can deal with contingent beings and the problems of explanation connected with them, but it cannot deal with the total state of affairs, the cosmos. The individual using technical reason finds that he simply cannot account for the existence of countless contingent beings.

The situation is not unlike the use of a magnetic meter. If it should be exposed to a magentic field that is utterly beyond its limits, the pointer would first move from zero to the maximum reading and then vibrate wildly. The vibrations would not give a true reading of the intensity of the magnetic field, but they would indicate two things: (1) the pointer in moving from zero to the maximum was going in the right direction; the wild vibrations do not cancel that and (2) the field in which it is set is too powerful for it.

The example of pointer readings is misleading in an important respect. It involves a continuity between most magnetic fields and the one that is too powerful for the meter to handle. In that case, a better meter might provide the desired reading. In Tillich's move from both technical and existential reason to ecstatic reason, there is no such continuity. The thinker using the other two levels of reason comes to a sense of their limits and recognizes the need for a different level of thinking to cope with ultimacy. He must probe the depths of reason represented by the limiting question, "Why is there something rather than nothing?" In doing so, he comes to see that being-itself is the *presupposition* of dealing with the existence and nonexistence of contingent beings.

Tillich claims that the reason we use in becoming aware of the presuppositions of rational arguments transcends the moves we make in using technical reason. As we have seen, he sometimes refers to it as self-transcending reason, and ecstatic reason—the term he commonly uses (literally means "standing outside the self")—is related to transcendence. When the individual transcends technical reason and uses ecstatic reason, he comes to an awareness of being-itself.

Again, we find Tillich using a cluster of terms to designate something that is important to his system. He also refers to being-itself as power of being and ground of being. Indeed, in contexts less specifically linked to his analysis of being, he will refer to being-itself as the ultimate, the unconditioned, the absolute, the infinite, and the God above God.

Being-Itself Is Not Reached by an Inference; It Is a Presupposition

Tillich's argument to being-itself as the presupposition of questions about the existence of contingent beings is similar to the cosmological argument from contingent beings to necessary being. Tillich agrees with the Thomists on the point that contingent beings cannot account for there being something rather than nothing. His disagreements with them largely pivot around the difference between inferences (used by the Thomists) and presuppositions (used by Tillich). Unfortunately, Tillich is not at all clear about the nature of presuppositions, and he uses the term in a number of different senses.[55] I shall try to achieve a clear understanding of his use of presupposition to show how it figures in his argument.

In making inferences we operate *inside* a given field of discourse. It may involve common sense, as when Robinson Crusoe sees a footprint and infers the presence of another man on the island. It may involve a specific science, as when a physicist observes certain marks on photographic plates and infers the existence of a subatomic particle. It may involve reasoning within a mathematical discipline like Euclidian geometry. In all these cases, the material from which the inference is drawn and the material involved in the conclusion are on the same plane.

In order to appreciate the considerations that Tillich has in mind in distinguishing presuppositions from inferences, imagine scientists running tests on the waters of a miracle shrine like Lourdes and discovering an unusual element that produces the cures (see p. 62). In doing so, they would make conscious suppositions or hypotheses, and they would draw *inferences* that were more or less probable. They would test (confirm or disconfirm them) by means of observations. The entire procedure is internal to science, and there is no radical shift of logical levels.

Tillich's major sense of *presupposition* involves focusing on general principles that are assumed in a specific activity like scientific research. Consider the following: any occurrence which can be observed by natural means can be scientifically explained. This presupposition is radically different from scientific inferences.

1 Scientific activity would make no sense (at least in Tillich's view) unless this principle were presupposed, but a given biochemist need not think about it when he analyzes the water. In other words, a presupposition is not consciously entertained during an activity; this is the point of the prefix *pre* in the word presupposition.

2 Conclusions are checked out by deductive or inductive reasoning, but the logic of presuppositions is unclear. They are not the conclusions of specific arguments. In using the term thinkers like Tillich seem to rest their case on an intuitive appeal to the idea that a specific practical activity like science does not make sense unless certain higher order principles are presupposed.

3   A statement about the content of the waters of Lourdes can be proved true or false by a specific chemical analysis, which is not the case with presuppositions like "Any occurrence which can be naturally observed can be scientifically explained." In proceeding with their investigations, scientists assume the truth of this presupposition. As we have seen, no matter how long they were frustrated in their search for a scientific explanation of an extraordinary cure at Lourdes, they would not conclude that the presupposition was falsified (see pp. 63f.). They would continue to assume that there must be a scientific explanation, but that it is very hard to come up with it. In other words, the truth of presuppositions is not checked out in the same way as we check on the truth of statements within the specific fields of activity.

The presuppositions that have been considered are relatively straightforward. We can easily understand a presupposition of science sucn as, "Any occurrence which can be naturally observed can be scientifically explained." By contrast, Tillich's use of presupposition with regard to being-itself is unusual. He writes that being-itself is ". . . that which is not a special being or a group of beings, not something concrete or something abstract, but rather something which is always thought implicitly, and sometimes explicitly, if something is said to *be*."[56] This statement indicates the radical character of Tillich's appeal to being-itself as a presupposition of any claim that something exists. In another context he indicates why he thinks this is the case.

> You can deny every statement, but you cannot deny that being *is*. And if you ask what this "is" means, you arrive at the statement that it is the negation of possible non-being. "Is" means "is not not". . . . You can deny anything particular whatsoever, but not being, because even your negative judgments themselves are acts of being and are only possible through being.[57]

Tillich, although he neglects to say so, is appealing to the kind of reasoning that is associated with the French philosopher René Descartes (1596–1650) whose exercise in systematic doubt was the beginning of the era of modern philosophy.[58] Descartes resolved to doubt the truth of all beliefs whatever, no matter how well established they seemed to be. The one thing that he found he could not doubt was his own existence. Any self, in the very act of doubting its own existence, affirms it, since the reality of the *I* is involved in "I doubt," (Descartes has "I think").

Tillich's move is similar. When we consider a specific being such as a tree or a person we may affirm its existence or we may deny it. Even if we deny it, we affirm the reality of being-itself. We do not affirm it by consciously thinking about it, rather, in the very act of dealing with questions of the existence or nonexistence of particular beings we presuppose its reality. We presuppose the reality of that which is not a particular being but is that which accounts for there being something rather than nothing. Being-itself alone accounts for the fact that human beings exist and for our ability to raise the question of the existence and nonexistence of particular beings.

Tillich does not say that being-itself exists. Instead he uses the strained phrase "is not not" in order to emphasize one of his major points, namely, that only contingent beings exist. Being-itself is not a limited and contingent being that exists alongside others; it is the presupposition of there being anything at all. Tillich thinks that Thomists, by applying the word "exists" to God, limit him, and make him into a being alongside others.

The Argument to Being-Itself is Not Intended to Be Coercive

Tillich differs from Thomists and other defenders of the cosmological argument on another important issue. The Thomists think that the argument is as coercive as a demonstration in Euclid. He does not think of his cosmological approach to being-itself as a coercive argument. Coerciveness can only be had in what the positivists called analytic statements. Tillich regards the analytic as a function of technical reason. At the other two levels, namely, existential and ecstatic reason, coerciveness is not attainable. Tillich agrees with the analysts: at the level of technical reason the question, "Why is there something rather than nothing?", is meaningless (see p. 326). Therefore, the sceptic can, by remaining at this level, reject Tillich's approach at the outset. Tillich does not even try to provide a coercive demonstration of the legitimacy of the question. He can only appeal to standards of human authenticity in urging us to take it seriously. When we do so, we drive beyond technical reason to ecstatic reason.

A brief summary of Tillich's argument should be helpful:

1 "Why is there something rather than nothing?" is a question that is both serious and meaningful; it is asked by authentic human beings.
2 Asking the question "Why is there something rather than nothing?" is one way of coming to realize that every observable being is contingent and that neither individual contingent beings nor the aggregate of them can serve as the answer to it. It is a limiting question about the world as whole and it points to a mystery.
3 We then realize that the question cannot be answered by means of technical reason, but rather, in trying to answer it this way, we come

upon the limits of technical and/or existential reason. We then transcend these limits by using ecstatic reason which is ordered to limiting questions that deal with the world as a whole.

4 The use of ecstatic reason uncovers being-itself as the presupposition of the existence or nonexistence of contingent beings. We realize that if being-itself were not real, there would be no contingent beings.

5 The argument is not a proof but a probe. There is no coercive way of demonstrating its validity.

Conclusion: God as Being-Itself Transcends the Subject-Object Scheme

Tillich uses an epistemologically distinctive move to drive to being-itself. It is not made within the normal pattern of thinking in terms of knowing subjects and known objects. It goes beyond technical reason in which a detached subject knows an isolated object, as when you know that this page is white. It also drives beyond existential judgments, as when two historians consider the Declaration of Independence and use radically different subjective frames of reference in interpreting it. The move to being-itself involves ecstatic reason at what I have called Tillich's third level of truth. It is made when the individual comes to realize the limitations of these other modes of reasoning. Tillich insists that being-itself, the reality we become aware of at the level of ecstatic reason, must be understood in terms that are appropriate to the distinctiveness of this mode of reasoning.

Being-Itself Is Not a Specifiable Individual

What is distinctive about being-itself is that it is not one specific entity. It is not *a* being, not even the highest being, necessary being, or perfect being. Tillich regards specificity as the mark of limitation. Any specific being is limited by the mere existence of other beings. They are what it is not. If God is *a* being, even necessary being, he is not the presupposition of being, but an individual. Therefore, he cannot be truly infinite because he is limited by myriads of finite beings. This is what Tillich means by his often quoted remark:

> The being of God is being-itself. The being of God cannot be understood as the existence of a being alongside others or above others. If God is *a* being, he is subject to the categories of finitude. . . .[59]

Tillich, of course, realizes that Thomists and other theologians who regard God as necessary being do not intend to subject God to the categories of finitude. They think that they can use metaphysical reasoning to show that God transcends these categories. What Tillich objects to is not their intention, but the effectiveness of the means by which they carry it out. By making God into one being alongside others, they present God in terms that are linked to categories of finitude like space and time, even though they then try to show that God transcends them. This is why he writes: ". . . the starting point is right, but the conclusion is wrong."[60]

The key to understanding why Tillich claims that being-itself cannot be *a* being alongside other beings is that he thinks the subject-object relation is an intrinsically limiting one. The subject is limited by the otherness of the object and the object is similarly limited by the otherness of the subject. When theologians, operating as subjects, deal with God as an object, they limit him. First they reason to his existence and then they think about his nature. To this extent they are not immersed in God but stand apart from him. And to the same extent, God is limited and cannot be infinite. Therefore, even though many theologians reason to God as an object and then try to talk about God as infinite and unconditioned, their effort is doomed from the start. They use the wrong mode of reasoning in getting to God, and the wrong mode of reasoning about God once they are there. They do not understand what ultimacy is about.

Tillich admits that when we talk about being-itself we, the subjects, are talking and thinking about it, which makes it into the object of our thought. Yet he (like the Thomists) distinguishes the study of the order of being (ontology) from that of the order of knowing (epistemology). In other words, Tillich acknowledges the point that we inevitably make being-itself into an *object* of knowledge. He insists, however, that one thing we know about it is that it cannot, from the standpoint of being, be an individual object. It cannot be a being that is separable from other beings. Tillich himself puts it this way:

> In the cognitive realm [the realm of knowing] everything toward which the cognitive act is directed is considered an object, be it God or a stone, be it one's self or a mathematical definition. In the logical sense everything about which a predication is made is, by this very fact, an object. The theologian cannot escape making God an object in the logical sense of the word, just as the lover cannot escape making the beloved an object of knowledge and action.[61]

So much for the order of knowing. Tillich then warns us of the danger of transferring the logical sense in which being-itself is an object of knowledge to the sphere of being or ontology.

> The danger of logical objectification is that it never is merely logical. It carries ontological presuppositions and implications. If God is brought into the subject-object structure of being, he ceases to be the ground of being

and becomes one being among others (first of all, a being beside the subject who looks at him as an object). He ceases to be the God who is really God.[62]

It is because technical reasoning is able to see that it cannot deal with being-itself in terms of the subject-object relation that Tillich claims that reason is able to transcend itself. In its ecstatic mode it recognizes a reality which cannot be handled by technical reasoning. Tillich's view of being-itself is one of radical transcendence. It transcends all distinctions based on the subject-object relation. Therefore, in Tillich's scheme, being-itself is no more a universal than it is a particular.[63]

Being-Itself Cannot Be Characterized

To arrive at the awareness of being-itself, the individual, as we have seen, must drive beyond both technical and existential reason in which subjects are aware of objects. When he arrives at being-itself, the conclusion of the argument, he must remember the route he took in getting there. Otherwise he will perform the ridiculous act of becoming aware of being-itself by driving beyond the subject-object relation and then trying to treat being-itself as though it were a specific object that is knowable by a subject.

Tillich is consistent. He does not reason to being-itself and then content himself with purging this concept of God of gross bodily associations like the one involved in the story of God walking through the Garden of Eden looking for Adam and Eve. He insists that the traditional understanding of the attributes of God, like holiness, omnipotence, and omniscience are badly misguided. The fundamental mistake is that the ordinary subject-object scheme of reasoning is used in deriving them. Tillich's rejection of the traditional view of these terms depends on his view that being-itself is not a specific object which can then be characterized by a set of defining features.

Tillich is, at this point, in the tradition of thinkers who have used "the negative way" in talking about God.[64] They claim that God is an utterly unique reality that cannot be characterized in the way that we characterize anything else. God is certainly not to be talked about in the way that we talk about observable beings as when we say, "This paper is white." Thinkers who argue for the negative way also insist that God cannot be talked about in terms of highly valued qualities as when we say, "Mary is good." All that we can say about God is that "God is *not* limited," or that "God is *not* locatable in space and time," and so on. The sustained use of the word "not" is the source of the title of the negative way for this kind of theology. Even though Tillich claims that his view of symbolism enables him to say more about God than can be said within the limits of the negative way, the following statements should indicate the extent of his agreement with it.[65]

1 *Holiness.* "The holiness of God makes it impossible to draw him into the context of the ego-world and the subject-object correlation. He himself is the ground and meaning of this correlation [remember that Tillich uses the ground of being as a synonym for being-itself], not an element within it."[66]

2 *Omnipotence.* "In popular parlance the concept 'omnipotence' implies a highest being who is able to do whatever he wants. This notion must be rejected religiously as well as theologically. It makes God into a being alongside others, a being who asks himself which of innumerable possibilities he shall actualize."[67]

3 *Omniscience.* "Omniscience is not the faculty of a highest being who is supposed to know all objects, past, present, and future, and, beyond this, everything that might have happened if what has happened had not happened. The absurdity of such an image is due to the impossibility of subsuming God under the subject-object scheme, although this structure is grounded in the divine life."[68]

All these criticisms of the traditional understanding of the attributes of God depend on Tillich's view that God, as being-itself, is not a distinct entity that can be characterized. He cannot even be characterized by means of special attributes, like holiness, omnipotence, and omniscience, which are supposed to be accessible only to reason and not to observation.

Now we are in a position to more fully understand Tillich's claim that "God does not exist" (see p. 322). Existence is a characteristic of specific entities that can be isolated either by observations or by thoughts. Existence is properly attributed only to individual entities that are limited by others. God, who is being-itself and not a being alongside other beings, cannot, therefore, exist.

Tillich, as we have seen, breaks with religious existentialists in his view of reason (Chapt. 13). He presents ecstatic reason as transcending the subject-object relation, which differs drastically from the view of the higher level of subjective reason found in religious existentialists from Kierkegaard to Bultmann. They present faith, or subjective truth, as a mode of reasoning that involves the relation of a subject to an object. Since Tillich's view of reason is different from that of the religious existentialists, it is not surprising that his view of the ultimate is also different from theirs.

Kierkegaard, Bultmann, Buber (and Otto, too, although he is not an existentialist) all, in their distinctive ways, talk of a personal God. Their God is a source of consciousness and power which is utterly beyond anything we can imagine. They differ from conservative supernaturalists and from fundamentalists insofar as they have a very sophisticated notion of *how* the intervention of this personal God into earthly affairs can be known. Conservatives and fundamentalists think that God intervenes in many ways but that his most dramatic interventions involve "one-shot" disruptions of the course of nature, as when the raging waters of the Red Sea divide and stand in walls. The existentialists reject this view of divine intervention and insist that God's interventions are confined to the inner life of human beings and to historical events. These interventions are subtle; they do not coerce the person who experiences them into accepting the religious point of view. They can also be interpreted in secular terms.

The religious existentialists present a pragmatic validation of faith (see pp. 163ff.). In doing so, they affirm traditional teachings like the view that God acts in history or that God entered history in the person of Jesus of Nazareth. They do not try to provide a theoretical account of how these beliefs can be true because they think that this is impossible. Instead, they appeal to the practical (pragmatic) benefits of these central teachings in order to justify belief in them. They draw on the resources of their various traditions for insights into the divine, and they use their existential perspectives to bring the texts to life. They do not claim that this yields secure knowledge of the nature of God and of his interaction with human beings. Quite the contrary, they insist that beliefs about God can only be appropriated in fear and trembling because, objectively speaking, these teachings run *against* the evidence.

Tillich is more radical than the religious existentialists. He insists that we must go beyond the subjectivities of existential reason (as well as beyond the objectivities of technical reason) and drive to ecstatic reason. We must, that is, transcend the subject-object relation. When we do, we will realize that the truly ultimate cannot be the personal God of theism, even when the approach to this God is as sophisticated as that of the religious existentialists. God cannot be an individuated and characterizable source of consciousness and power, that is, an individual person, because any such entity is, according to Tillich, necessarily limited. It cannot be the truly ultimate. Therefore, God cannot be a being alongside others to which the traditional theological attributes can be applied.

If No Being-Itself, Then Nothing at All

It would seem that Tillich's complex and many leveled analysis of the approach to ultimacy has left us without a reference for religious language. God as being-itself cannot properly be conceived as existing or as not existing, and there is nothing, literally no specific entity, that is ultimate. We may, therefore, ask, "What difference does the positing of being-itself make?" Tillich's answer, despite his difference with the Thomists, still has a cosmological ring (see pp. 325ff.). If being-itself were not, then we would not be here to ask the question of being. There would be nothing, nothing at all: ". . . everything finite participates in being-itself and its infinity [now understood as the unlimited which transcends the subject-object relation]. Otherwise it would not have the power of being. It would be swallowed by nonbeing, or it would never have emerged out of nonbeing."[69]

FINITE FREEDOM AS THE CLUE TO TRANSCENDENCE

Tillich's scheme is a difficult one. His view of transcendence is so radical that it is hard to see what can link being-itself, which is beyond the subject-object relation, to the limitless number of contingent beings. His answer is existentialistic in the sense that his link is not some feature that is common to all beings, but rather, the most distinctive aspect of human beings which he calls self-transcendence or finite freedom.[70]

Human beings are finite selves; we are limited and contingent. We can move, but only so fast; we rise above the limitations of our family and cultural background, but only so far. Ultimately, we confront the final limitation which is death. Yet, within the framework of the limitations that are packed into our very existence as identifiable selves, we exercise creative freedom. We achieve in ways that could not have been anticipated. The creative artist is the obvious model. In this sense, Tillich is close to Kierkegaard; he takes human beings as the clue to being as such, and he takes creative human beings as the key to the rest.

Picasso, Joyce, and Stravinsky are creative individuals who break with existing patterns of art in unforeseeable ways, thereby transcending the previous state of their art. Yet they remain identifiable selves. This is what enables us to refer to *The Rite of Spring* and subsequent neoclassical and twelve-tone works to Stravinsky—the one composer who is manifest in his many works. Clearly, as a creative individual he transcends his work. There is no way of knowing the limits of his capacity because this involves his freedom—within the limits of his being—continually to surpass what he has done before.

Tillich thinks that secularists and naturalists who identify reality with the sum total of contingent beings ("That's all there is, there ain't no more") miss the central clue to transcendence. They fail to note that contingent beings point beyond themselves to a limitless ground of being that infinitely transcends the sum of beings. Tillich does not claim that God is a creative being who transcends the world of contingent beings like

Stravinsky transcends his compositions. To think in these terms would involve the mistake of supernaturalism; it would reduce God to the status of *a* being beyond others. At the same time, Tillich claims that human beings could not exercise their finite freedom in a world of countless contingent beings unless being-itself infinitely transcended the sum total of contingent beings as well as any specific state of being. In other words, Tillich wants to reject the supernaturalistic picture that would model being-itself directly on creative artists who are specifiable individuals that can be dealt with in the subject-object relation. For example, Igor Stravinsky (subject) composed the *Rite of Spring* (object). Yet Tillich also wants to reject the naturalistic thinking which fails to see that all contingent beings point beyond themselves to a transcendent ground of being, to being-itself. In order to deal with this relation he focuses on symbols.

Being-itself is, for Tillich, the most adequate expression of the dimension of ultimacy. It is not, however, a religious term. It is a theoretical term that expresses the reality to which religious people orient themselves in their feelings, thoughts, and actions. It cannot be substituted for God. Think of saying, "You shall love being-itself with all your heart and with all your soul and with all your might." This formulation is not merely unfamiliar, like translations of the Bible that replace the language of the King James version with contemporary English. Rather, it is a mistake to use a technical term like being-itself in everyday religious language. We ask for a drink of water, not for H_2O. Furthermore, to love being-itself or to direct any other religious attitude to it would be to make being-itself an object of that attitude. This would destroy its status because it would then be sucked down into the level of the subject-object relation which is appropriate only to limited and conditioned realities. That is why Tillich states that "the unconditional element [being-itself] can become a matter of ultimate concern only if it appears in a concrete embodiment."[71] The concrete embodiment is what Tillich calls religious symbols.

Chapter 16

Religious Symbols as Expressions of Ultimacy

Symbols play a role in all religions. The major religions are often identified by them: the cross for Christianity, the tablets of the law for Judaism, the crescent for Islam, the lotus for Buddhism, and so on. Brand Blanshard provides a helpful introduction to the subject of religious symbols.[72]

Blanshard begins by presenting a conventional philosophical view of symbols in which he stresses the point that they have not, until recent times, been regarded as especially important. As he sees it, symbols serve two main functions:

1 They attract, and, hopefully, sustain attention as when a candidate's picture appears on a poster. The picture which symbolizes him is intended to keep his image before the voters.

2 Symbols are important as shorthand representations of complex ideas, which underlies the old saw about one picture being worth a thousand words. In doing geometry we constantly symbolize important intellectual relations by using representations like drawings of triangles and squares. In dealing with complicated ideologies and movements like communism, we can use nonverbal symbols like the hammer and sickle to stand for crucial features of complex historical developments.

Blanshard insists that the relation between symbols and what they symbolize is limitlessly varied, and that there is no point is systematizing them. Sometimes the symbols resemble the things they symbolize, as when a political poster resembles the candidate, and sometimes they don't, as when the crescent is used to symbolize the religion of Islam. Sometimes a symbol is associated with an important feature of what it symbolizes as when a flying horse is used to stand for the power of a gasoline; at other times, the association is historical as when Lincoln is used to stand for the Civil War.[73] In cases where the association of symbols with what they symbolize is not determined by resemblances, people vary greatly in the way they respond to them. The stars and stripes symbolizes national glory and idealism for Americans, but it symbolizes a hated imperialism for Cubans.

A further complication is that words are also symbols. They stand for realities which are obviously different from the shapes of the letters on the page. Justice stands for an extremely complicated set of ideas and relations which we couldn't even think about without the use of words. Even in cases where words stand for observables, the relation between the words and what they symbolize is complex; a person needs to know a lot of associated words before he can properly use even relatively simple words like those used for colors.

After detailing these points, Blanshard considers Tillich's effort to make symbolism central to his theology. He then etches his disagreement with Tillich.

> If symbols generally resembled their objects, one might throw some light on the object by scrutinizing the symbol, but since no such resemblance *in general* exists, one can secure such light only if one knows already that the object is like the symbol, and then the study of the symbol is needless.[74]

In other words, if we have studied communism thoroughly, we can use the hammer and sickle as a convenient shorthand, but we don't find out anything about communism by studying the symbol in isolation from the ideology. By the same token, if we have studied theology and have come to some important formulations of the character of God, we can then use the visual symbol of the cross or verbal symbols like the Eternal You as a shorthand for God. The symbols are, however, derivative. People use them because they are convenient, but they do not, in and of themselves, shed any light on God and his nature.

Tillich violently disagrees. His radical view of transcendence sets God beyond the subject-object relation. Tillich's God is just as inaccessible to ordinary modes of metaphysical thinking (as, for example, Thomistic thought) as to observation. The link between human beings and being-itself is the religious symbol. "It is almost a truism to assert that religious language is symbolic. But it is less of a truism to assert that for this reason religious language expresses the truth, the truth which cannot be expressed and communicated in any other language."[75] Tillich's effort to explain the relation between religious symbols and what they symbolize was a major preoccupation over a long period of years.[76] Yet he never succeeded in framing a comprehensive and adequate statement, and by adequate, I mean one that would be regarded as such by *sympathetic* interpreters.[77] His points are often sketchy and vague. His failure to probe his distinctions in order to see whether they stand up is due to his relative disinterest in symbols as such. He never attempted a thorough study of symbols that would enable him to handle them systematically in terms of the broad range of things and events that play symbolic roles and by considering the many functions that symbols serve.

Tillich was primarily concerned with the role that symbols play in religion. What he did was to create a mosaic. He noticed certain features of symbols: (1) their capacity to point to realities of a different order, (2) their participation in the reality of what they point to, (3) the fact that they cannot be changed at will, (4) their ability to open us up to distinctive insights into our surroundings and into ourselves, (5) their usefulness in helping individuals to achieve personal integration, (6) their role in making communities jell, and finally, the one that is most important to him, (7) their capacity to confront us with ultimacy. He pieced these bits together to form a pattern that enabled him to account for some of the crucial aspects of the religious life.[78] He used his theory of symbols to discuss such important matters as the ability of physical things like stones and the sun to point to God and idolatry, that is, the capacity of people to worship false gods.

When Tillich discusses the characteristics of symbols listed above, he presents a few examples of what he has in mind. He does not, however, press the issue to see whether counter-examples would nullify his distinction. As a result, his theory of symbols has been sharply criticized by a number of philosophers.[79] In what follows, I shall be as faithful as I can to Tillich's purpose in showing how his theory of symbols links the everyday world of contingent beings to being-itself.

SIGNS AND SYMBOLS

One of the main problems with understanding Tillich's approach to religious symbols is that he takes so many things for granted. Signs and symbols, as he puts it, "point beyond themselves."[80] However, he fails to contrast signs and symbols with things that point to realities like themselves. If we ask "Where's Tom?" and someone points to a man and says, "Over there," one person is pointing to another. This is literal communication. Tillich, in dealing with symbols, is concerned with the capacity of things and events to point beyond themselves by standing for realities of a different order.[81] A curved line on a road sign can point to or stand for a curve in the road; a rock can stand for the changelessness of God; and an event like the storming of the Bastille can stand for the ideals of liberty, equality, and fraternity. Within the limitless group of things that can point beyond themselves to realities of a different order, Tillich distinguishes two basic groups, signs and symbols.

Tillich's distinction between signs and symbols is one of the most vulnerable points in his thought. For one thing, Tillich's distinction is not consistent with ordinary English.[82] What we call mathematical *symbols* are, from Tillich's point of view, signs. This point is only of terminological importance, and it can be easily straightened out. More basic are two fundamental distinctions: (1) Signs do not participate in the reality of what they stand for, symbols do. (2) Signs can be changed at will with no loss of meaning, symbols cannot. These distinctions are highly problematical. In trying to make them good, Tillich, earlier in his career, took a more object-oriented approach. He stressed the character of the things or events themselves. Later, he shifted his emphasis, and, without losing sight of the nature of the things and events that play symbolic roles, he came to stress the way that people (subjects) respond to them.[83] His more subjective approach can be usefully compared with Buber's I-It and I-You distinction.

Signs are I-It: Conventional and Utilitarian

Tillich's favorite illustrations of signs tells us a great deal about them. They are the signs of mathematics and the signs of the road. Consider algebra: we perform a problem and begin by saying something like "Let x stand for apples and y for pears." Clearly, the signs chosen are arbitrary. We could reverse them or we could substitute other letters or other squiggles for them with no loss of effectiveness. There is nothing about the letter "x" that links it to apples. It does not participate in the reality of the apple to which it points. The same, obviously, holds true for the letter "y" and pears. The use of these particular signs (in Tillich's sense of signs) for apples and pears is purely conventional. As long as everyone accepts the convention, no misunderstanding will result. We simply use the signs to get the job done. They are "cold," that is, they do not engage us; we find it easy to take them or leave them. They are I-It; indispensable for certain functions but not important in themselves. Certainly, it would never occur to anyone to try to learn about apples and pears by studying these letters.

Symbols as I-You: Participation and Non-Exchangeability

Two of Tillich's major distinctions between symbols and signs are that, unlike signs, symbols participate in the reality of that to which they point and that, therefore, they cannot be exchanged without a loss of meaning and power. In his earliest essay on the subject, he tried to make this a function of the objective pole (the object of knowledge) of the knower-known relation. He claimed that the symbols, by virtue of their own objective characteristics, communicated insights about what they symbolize. He claimed that a symbol has "power inherent within it" or "innate power" and that it possesses "a necessary character. It cannot be exchanged."[84] This is true of some symbols. The caricature of a public figure that appears in political cartoons is obviously related to him in a special way. It participates in his reality by resembling him. It cannot be exchanged, not even for another caricature which also resembles him because the second caricature will stress different features. One cartoon, for example, might stress Richard M. Nixon's ski slope nose in an affectionate way, another might stress his heavy black beard in order to portray him as a villain. Yet both cartoons clearly participate in the reality of the man Richard M. Nixon.

This claim of the participation and nonexchangeability of symbols was clearly important to Tillich's analysis of religion. In the case of cartoons and political figures the symbol is relatively unimportant because the politician is observable. Although the symbol heightens our awareness of one feature of his character, it is not the only way we can get at it. In the case of God, the situation is radically different. God is not observable; therefore, there can be no direct access to his characteristics. In this case, the observable symbol must be linked to the nonobservable reality. If Tillich could make good his objective claim about the participation and nonexchangeability of symbols, then a symbol like a rock could tell us something about God. The changelessness of the rock (which is only apparent, it actually does change, but we do not see the changes) would participate in the changelessness of God. It could not be exchanged for a symbol like sand (which changes its appearance every time the wind blows) without loss of meaning.

Tillich was unable to make good on his claim that symbols possess characteristics which link them necessarily to that which they symbolize. An examination of two of his crucial illustrations will show the inadequacy of his objective approach to symbols. It will also enable me to explain why I think that Tillich's view of symbols boils down to something very much like Buber's understanding of the way different types of beings can become a You for us.

Tillich has illustrated his view that symbols participate in the power of that which they symbolize by talking of the institution of the strong monarchy.[85] The king stands for the state and he participates in its power by ruling. In this case the participation is functional and observable. It is also obvious that the symbol cannot be exchanged at will, that is, in the way that we might switch the letters that stand for apples and pears, or the colors that stand for stop and go. To change the symbol of the monarchy involves a revolution. So far, so good. Tillich is clear about what he means by participation, and it seems as though he has also provided a good illustration of why symbols cannot be exchanged. We can even say that the king, as the symbol of the state, bears some resemblance to it, in the sense that the state is composed of people and he is a person.

In the case of the strong monarchy, Tillich's objective approach to symbolization seems to work. Yet his more frequently used illustration of the symbol of a nation is the flag. An examination of its symbolic role will show how his objective approach breaks down.

Tillich insists that the flag participates in the reality of what it symbolizes, namely, the nation and that it cannot be changed at will. He is certainly right about the matter of exchanging the standard pattern for a totally different configuration. Although the design of a flag may be arbitrary when it is first adopted, once it is in use, it is hard to change it. It took an historical upheaval in the status of French citizens to change the Canadian flag. On the other hand, in the case of the flag, it is hard to see how the flag participates in the reality of what it symbolizes. It certainly does not exercise ruling functions like the king. Tillich's clearest statement on this issue is ". . . the flag participates in the power and dignity of the nation for which it stands. . . . An attack on the flag is felt as an attack on the majesty of the group in which it is acknowledged."[86] In this case, it is not the flag that visibly participates in the reality of the nation, it is the citizens who participate in that reality by honoring the flag.[87] This shifts the focus from the characteristics of the symbol itself (the objective pole) to the way it is taken by the group which regards it as a symbol (the subjective pole).

In any case, a flag, like the American, cannot now be changed for other configurations. The symbolic power is latent in that pattern. If an I-You relation to the flag takes place, then the individual who experiences it as a symbol *participates* in the power and ideals of the country.

Symbols Integrate Communities

Communities emerge in history; they do not endure forever. Fabrics of memory and concern bind the members. A symbol like the stars and stripes can elicit strong loyalties. I recall a European professor of politics expressing astonishment at the power of American symbols. Groups with interests as diverse as those of Maine and Texas accept the results of a presidential election and submit to executive leadership even when the leader seems to oppose the interests of their region.

The fabrics which bind communities can, however, all too easily be torn. There is nothing inherent in the symbol, that is, nothing about its actual characteristics, that enables it to integrate a community. It can have the power to do so at one period of time and lose it at another. It is a matter of whether it can become a You for the great majority of the people. This is why Tillich makes the seemingly absurd point that symbols are born, grow, and die.[88] Taking the American flag as an illustration, one can see the relevance of Tillich's organic image. The design of the flag is arbitrary, but the stars and stripes, having come into existence, grew in the power to integrate the new nation and maintained it for two centuries. Yet recent history shows the tenuous character of this power. During the American involvement in Vietnam the flag, which in previous wars was an integrating symbol, became partisan and divisive. It symbolized support for a war that was bitterly opposed by a considerable part of the population.

Symbols Open Us Up to Our Surroundings and Ourselves

It is always important to keep Tillich's analysis of religion front and center when dealing with his treatment of symbols; otherwise, some of the things he says do not make sense. He regards "opening-up" as one of the key functions of symbols because this is part of what some religious symbols do. By opening up he refers to both poles of the knower-known relation. The self is expanded in terms of awareness of the world and of self-awareness.

Religion, for Tillich, represents the dimension of ultimacy. It represents ultimate concern and being-itself. These are nonobservables. It is hard for the individual to relate to them. Indeed, he cannot do so directly because there is no identifiable entity to which he can relate. In Tillich's system the only possible link between the individual subject and being-itself (which is beyond the subject-object relation) is a symbol. One way of knowing whether the symbols are the real thing is to see if they open us up both to elements in the external world that we had previously missed and to elements of our own psyches.

The most common way of being opened up is through art: "in poetry, in visual art, and in music, levels of reality are opened up which can be opened up in no other way."[89] Once again, Tillich's sense of the symbol is strikingly reminiscent of Buber's I-You. Every You is unique and the relation with it is exclusive. What a specific poem communicates in the I-You relation cannot be communicated in a prose statement of the meaning of the poem. In talking of a Rubens landscape Tillich makes the same point.[90] You can talk about its balances of colors and the composition, but none of this communicates the unique meaning of the painting which gives the individual distinctive insights into nature.

Works of art enhance our experience of the world. Sometimes, as in the case of a Rubens landscape, we may be made consciously aware of things that we have often seen, but never really noticed. In other cases, like cubist paintings, the artist may discern and represent formal structures of things that underlie surface appearances. He provides an X-ray vision that then informs our subsequent perceptions. The result of this power of artistic work is that many people experience reality in terms of art as when they describe a woman as having a Botticelli face, a Rubens body, or a Modigliani neck.

Reading a story not only opens us to fresh insights into our environment, it may open us to fresh insights into ourselves. The technique is similar to the one the prophet, Nathan, used on King David. The king had just stolen the wife of one of his warriors, Uriah, and arranged for him to be killed in battle so that he would no longer stand in the way. Had Nathan simply excoriated the king for his immorality, David would, at best, have been defensive, and at worst, he would have had the prophet killed. So Nathan told the story of two men, one rich and one poor, who lived in the same town. The rich man had many sheep, the poor man only one lamb which he treated tenderly and treasured. When the rich man had a guest he decided to slaughter a lamb and, rather than diminishing his flock by taking one of his own, he slaughtered the lamb of the poor man. David had enough psychic distance from the story to miss the connection to his own behavior. With righteous indignation he said that the man who did that ought to be killed. Then, Nathan said: "You are that man" (2 Sam. 12: 1–7).

Tillich is right. Works of art open us to the world and to ourselves, but there are problems with his categorizing of works of art as symbols. One of them is that his theory seems to work for Rubens landscapes but not for other works. It is clear that he thinks the Rubens landscape is a symbol because it points beyond itself to the actual scene that Rubens painted, and it participates in that reality by way of resemblance. It would be hard to make these points with regard to a Jackson Pollack action painting or to Beethoven quartets. It is not at all clear that they point to something beyond themselves in whose reality they participate. Rather, as noted earlier, it would seem that when we have an I-You encounter with them, they open us to realities that are beyond our previous states of consciousness. *We* then participate in the revelatory experience.

Once again, I claim that the accuracy or consistency of the criteria that Tillich applies to symbols is relatively unimportant. What is important is an appreciation of the role that these various features play in Tillich's religious mosaic.

The Rubens landscape points to a scene that the artist *re*presents. He uses his creative powers to present a unique perspective on it, and then enables us to notice things that we had missed. Yet we can observe the scene itself independently of the painting. By contrast, in the case of religious symbols, the reality that is symbolized is not observable. In this case, Tillich claims that the symbols open us to elements of nonobservable reality. He claims that when we focus on the Torah or the Christ we experience insights that are not illusory. What Tillich is most concerned to stress is the capacity of religious symbols to open us to ultimacy.

RELIGIOUS SYMBOLS

In discussing some of the main features of symbols in general, I have already indicated Tillich's view of the overlap between religious and nonreligious symbols. He thinks that religious symbols also "point beyond themselves, participate in the reality of that to which they point, cannot be exchanged at will, grow by integrating individuals and communities, and die when they lose this power." Religious symbols also have distinctive features. Once again we find that Tillich's elaboration is both subjective (the experience of ultimacy) and objective (ontology or the analysis of being). On the objective side it is obvious that each and every being can point to being-itself because every contingent being must participate in being-itself or it would not exist. On the subjective side we find that each and every being or concept can serve as a symbol that engages individuals in what Buber calls the I-You relation.

Subjectivity and Religious Symbols: The Experience of Ultimacy

Throughout his career Tillich opposed narrow views of religion that confined piety to officially sanctioned objects or patterns of behavior. He insisted that the things and events that are labeled "religious"—churches, bibles, pictures of Jesus, hymns, and the rest—are often devoid of religious power. Christ may be absent from the manifestations of official religiosity, and he may be present in what is called secular art and in ordinary forms of experience in factories and farms. After all, Tillich claims that every being participates in being-itself, and it is not surprising that every being should, in his view, have latent symbolic power. "No thing, however is merely a thing. Since everything that is participates in the self-world structure of being, elements of self-relatedness are universal. This makes union with everything possible. Nothing is absolutely strange."[91]

On its subjective side Tillich's view of symbolic participation resembles Buber's view of the I-You relation. For Buber, anything whatever can be a partner of an I-You relation, just as for Tillich, everything that exists participates in the self-world structure of being. Furthermore, for Buber God, as the eternal You, is at the fringe of every I-You encounter even though the I is often unaware of the eternal You. For Tillich each being can serve as a medium whereby the self becomes aware of the dimension of depth, that is, of ultimacy. Yet many individuals relate to beings in routinized ways without ever becoming consciously aware of their symbolic power to disclose the sense of ultimacy.

Tillich differs from Buber insofar as Tillich tries to explore the objective side of the subject-object or self-world polarity in order to develop a scale of symbols. Tillich tries to see what there is about objects in themselves that would make them appropriate symbols of ultimate concern.

Symbols and Objectivity

Tillich deals with the objective qualities of beings in an effort to rate their potential for symbolizing the truly ultimate.[92] Basically, he applies the following standard: the more obviously limited the object, the less appropriate it is as a symbol of ultimacy. The point can be explained if we think of the ultimate concerns that individual symbols stand for. If an individual's ultimate concern is personal success, then his symbol may be the vice-presidency of a corporation. This symbol is extremely limited because it only relates to one individual. It is more limited than a political symbol like the elephant or the donkey because many people are involved in the political parties for which these symbols stand. The symbols of political parties are, in turn, more limited than the stars and stripes because they stand for a part of the nation whereas the flag stands for the nation as a whole, and so on. Tillich's effort to achieve an objective way of ranking symbols is balanced by his awareness of the element of validity in Buber's thought. Although some beings are more limited than others, it is, nevertheless, the case, that every individual being can serve as a symbol that brings us in direct confrontation with the truly ultimate, that is, with being-itself. In Tillich's scheme this follows from the fact that every being participates in being-itself. Therefore, Tillich's analysis allows for the possibility of direct confrontation with being-itself by means of one particular symbol, and it also allows for a chain of symbolism which culminates in that kind of confrontation.

Chains of Symbols Generally speaking, we consider signs and symbols on an individual basis. A skull and crossbones on a bottle of liquid stands for poison. Having registered the sign and responded with the appropriate sense of danger, we end the process of nonliteral awareness. This one shot type of response is also possible in dealing with religious symbols, as in Jacques Maritain's statement: "If we grant to a speck of moss or the tiniest ant the value of its ontological reality, we can no longer escape from the terrifying hand which made us."[93] Maritain is saying that any being, no matter how insignificant it seems, can trigger us to a direct sense of its origin in God. That is, as a conditioned creation, it can trigger us to a sense of its unconditioned Creator. As an effective religious symbol it becomes, in one of Tillich's favorite terms, *transparent* to being-itself.[94] We become aware of being-itself through it, that is, we retain a sense of what the ant itself actually is, even as we are aware of God by means of it.

Tillich claims that symbols also operate in chains. In that case, the initial symbol does not bring us to a direct experience of the truly ultimate but it points beyond itself to another symbol, which in turn, points to another symbol. The chain culminates in an experience of ultimacy but it is not the direct kind of encounter with the ultimate that takes place through a speck of moss (Maritain) or through an I-You encounter with a fragment of mica that provides a sense of the eternal You (Buber). Rather, in Tillich's scheme, intellectual analysis of the limitations of the individual symbols propel us further.

Tillich's sense of the way that symbols are linked is by no means confined to sets that are derived from the study of the symbols of organized religion.[95] The Marseillaise is a song which symbolizes the events of the French Revolution. The song is a very limited, and therefore, a conditioned affair; it may appeal to some people and not to others. Furthermore, the events of the French Revolution, for which the song may be taken as a symbol, can also be regarded as symbol. They symbolize the ideals of the Revolution: Liberty-Equality-Brotherhood. It might be argued that these ideals are not symbolic, which ends the chain. These ideals would then be an ultimate concern. In Tillich's scheme, however, these ideals cannot be truly ultimate because they are conditioned. For one thing, they are objects that are responded to as such, by individual subjects (see pp. 316f.).[96] Therefore, these ideals should be regarded as symbols of being-itself which alone is unconditioned and truly ultimate. It is beyond all conditioning and change; therefore, it does not result in existential disappointment. Tillich's scale of symbolism should then, be obvious. The Marseillaise is more limited or conditioned than the events of the French Revolution; the events are more limited than the ideals of liberty, equality, and brotherhood; and being-itself is alone unlimited and unconditioned because it is beyond the subject-object relation. Tillich explicitly applies this "chain" analysis to religious symbols.

> . . . the inner attitude which is oriented to the symbol does not have the symbol itself in view but rather that which is symbolized in it. Moreover, that which is symbolized can itself in turn be a symbol for something of a higher rank. . . . Devotion to the crucifix is really directed to the crucifixion on Golgotha and devotion to the latter is in reality intended for the redemptive action of God, which is itself a symbolic expression for an experience of what concerns us ultimately.[97]

Idolatry   When dealing with idolatry, we can see how Tillich combines his sense of the subjective power of religious experience with his analysis of the objective limitations of beings. Tillich's statements about the possibility of regarding the nation as a god shows that he realizes that any being, event, or social reality can confront an individual with the unconditioned. His statement about the idolatrous character of the nation (an idol that has been painfully potent in our day) shows his concern for objective analysis. Any object that is, by its nature, a limited affair that can be regarded as an object and discussed by subjects cannot be the appropriate object of ultimate concern. It is tragically misguided to love a conditioned reality with all one's heart and with all one's soul and with all one's might. Later, I will deal with his account of the destructive consequences of idolatry (see pp. 360f.). For the moment, it is important to note that any being whatever can provide an authentic confrontation with the unconditioned when it is treated symbolically. As long as it is taken as pointing beyond itself to less conditioned orders of reality, it can be religiously effective as a symbol. In that case, no idolatry is involved. As soon as the symbol itself is regarded as being unconditioned, it becomes an idol.

Myth as a Mode of Symbolism

Tillich regards all religious language as symbolic, and myths are, in his scheme, a special case. They are the narrative mode of religious symbols. "Myths are symbols of faith combined in stories about divine-human encounters."[98] A story like that of Adam and Eve in the garden of Eden or of the resurrection of Jesus of Nazareth cannot be understood today if it is regarded as a historical account of what actually occurred. Its deeper meanings can be approached only symbolically.

To some extent, Tillich is similar to Bultmann, who demythologizes the Bible into existential language. Bultmann, you may recall, denies that the resurrection can be understood in literal objective terms, that is, as a corpse restored to life. He translates the story into existential terms and talks about the way the disciples took heart after the crucifixion. It was their spirits that rose, not a corpse (see pp. 176f.).

Tillich goes a long way down the road with Bultmann and other religious existentialists. He is quite prepared to talk about the meaning of a myth like Adam and Eve in existential terms.[98] Eating the apple for him is not something that two people did way back then in a magnificent garden. It is the gradual recognition that comes to all of us that we are not what we ought to be and that we are somehow responsible for this state of affairs. "The good which I want to do, I fail to do; but what I do is the wrong which is against my will" (Rom. 7:19).

Yet there are important differences between Tillich and Bultmann. The very term "demythologizing" suggests that for Bultmann translating objectifying language into existential language involves a total abandonment of myth. Tillich, by contrast, would never talk of going beyond symbolic language or of demythologizing. Rather, Tillich speaks of broken myths, that is, myths that are no longer taken literally, but which preserve their symbolic character. In his scheme of things, the story of Adam and Eve in the garden of Eden deals with fundamental and inescapable problems. It deals with what is involved in being human, and the problem of what concerns us ultimately. It points beyond itself to the unconditional element in human experience, and ultimately, it points to being-itself.

We are now able to appreciate Tillich's answer to Blanshard who claims:

1   There is no intrinsic link between a symbol and what it symbolizes; the connection is only a product of human conventions.

2   There is nothing one can learn from a symbol that cannot be better learned from direct focus on the reality that is symbolized.

3 Symbolism is such a chaotic affair that there is no point to trying to unscramble it in terms of some overall principle of interpretation.

Tillich could reply:

1 All religious symbols are linked to what they ultimately symbolize because every being or state of affairs participates in the truly ultimate, that is, in being-itself.

2 Being-itself cannot be observed or conceptualized because it transcends the subject-object relation, therefore, the only access we have to it is through symbols.[99]

3 Subjectively speaking, it is true that symbols seem to be chaotic. Any and every being can serve as a symbol that provides a direct confrontation with being-itself, the truly ultimate. Yet, when we consider the objective pole of the relation of symbol and symbolized, we find that things are not utterly chaotic. We actually operate with a negative scale of appropriateness for religious symbols. The more obviously limited a being is, the less appropriate it is to serve as a symbol of being-itself.

God as the Indispensable Symbol

"God," Tillich writes, "is the fundamental symbol for what concerns us ultimately."[100] On the level of subjective concerns when we come to God, we stop, because God is the symbol for that which is, ultimately, most important to us. In this sense, the term God does not, for Tillich, point beyond itself but, in this same context, Tillich also claims that "God is the symbol for God". A specific symbol—whether from organized religion, like the cross, or from nonreligious life, like the nation—is regarded as ultimate. It is, therefore, in Tillich's analysis, functionally serving as God. On the subjective level it symbolizes that which concerns us ultimately, and according to Tillich that is what God means. Thus, God (the cross or the nation) is a symbol for God (ultimate concern). On the objective pole of the knower-known relationship, the situation is more complex.

On the first, and relatively noncontroversial level, Tillich deals with the God of mythological literalism who is treated as an invisible superman in the sky. Most sophisticated believers agree that this use of the word "God" is symbolic. They think that "God," as used in Bible stories, is a symbol for the true God, which they think of as the God of the theological seminaries—the necessary or highest being.

The radical character of Tillich's theology is evident at this point. He holds that talk of God as necessary being or as the highest being is also symbolic. The God of the theological seminaries is less obviously limited than the God of biblical stories who walks through the Garden of Eden looking for Adam and Eve. Nevertheless, Tillich regards the God of the theologians as symbolic because they think about him in terms of the subject-object relation.

> The first and basic level of objective religious symbolism is the world of divine beings [God walking through the Garden] which, after the "breaking" of the myth, is [reinterpreted as a symbol for] "the Supreme Being," God. The divine beings and the Supreme being, God, are representations [symbols] of that which is ultimately referred to in the religious act. They are representations, for the unconditioned transcendent [being-itself which] surpasses every possible conception of a being, including even the conception of a Supreme Being.[101]

As noted earlier, God is, for Tillich, a symbol for being-itself, but being-itself is a category of ontology, that is, of the analysis of being.[102] It is not a part of the religious scheme of things. Religiously speaking, "God" is the supreme symbol. It is not, for Tillich, an abstract term which stands for the kind of being that is common to all things, but rather, it is the highest of the symbols that express both our scale of concerns and what it is that we are concerned about. In other words, God is the most heavily freighted symbol of all. Any chain of symbols that proceeds from the trivial to the important (this is the subjective pole) and from the limited to the infinite (the objective pole) culminates in God.

The word God is not only the most important of symbols, it is also the most problematical. It is easy enough to see that the nation can be an idol when we love it too fervently, but God, too, can be an idol. We can use the word and mean something limited and conditioned. That is why Tillich is nervous about the God of the theological seminaries as well as the God of the Sunday schools. Both treat God as an object that is knowable by subjects, and therefore, as a being alongside other beings. Thus, Tillich often avoided using the word God and substituted terms like being-itself, power of being, ground of being, the ultimate, the unconditioned, the infinite, or the absolute. In effect, he used this cluster of terms as a set of danger signals that are designed to keep us from falling into the pit of idolatry (see p. 378).

Tillich came to realize that God is an indispensable symbol: ". . . a symbolic word (such as the word 'God') cannot be replaced."[103] What is at issue has been eloquently expressed by Martin Buber when he rebuked a philosopher who wanted to avoid using the word God on the grounds that it had been so much abused through the centuries that it was almost sinful to use it with reference to the highest (or to what Tillich calls our ultimate concern). Buber replied:

Yes, it is the most heavy-laden of all human words. None has become so soiled, so mutilated. Just for this reason I may not abandon it. Generations of men have laid the burden of their anxious lives upon this word and weighed it to the ground; it lies in the dust and bears their whole burden. The races of man with the religious factions have torn the word to pieces; they have killed for it and died for it, and it bears their finger-marks and their blood. Where might I find a word like it to describe the highest! If I took the purest, most sparkling concern from the inner treasure-chamber of the philosophers, I could only capture thereby an unbinding product of thought. I could not capture the presence of Him whom the generations of men have honored and degraded with their awesome living and dying. I do indeed mean Him whom the hell-tormented and heaven-storming generations of men mean. Certainly, they draw caricatures and write "God" underneath; they murder one another and say "in God's name." But when all madness and delusion fall to dust, when they stand over against Him in the loneliest darkness and no longer say, "He, He" but rather sigh, "Thou," shout, "Thou," all of them the one word, and when they then add "God," is it not the real God whom they all implore, the One living God, the God of the children of man? Is it not He who *hears* them? And just for this reason is not the word "God," the word of appeal, the word which has become a *name* consecrated in all human tongues for all times?[104]

Buber's passionate statement goes a long way toward showing us that God is a powerful symbol which is *not contrived*. It *cannot be replaced* by fashionable concepts like the numinous, the eternal You, or being-itself. It serves to *integrate religious communities* within Judaism, Christianity, and Islam by *pointing beyond* all observable and conceptualizeable realities to the dimension of ultimacy. It *opens believers* to unique insights into themselves and to the potential for holiness in the world of everyday experience. Buber communicates the fact that no symbol has been as potent as God. Nevertheless, in our secular culture this symbol could lose its effectiveness.

Tillich, as I noted earlier, is fully aware of the distinctive symbolic power of the word "God." He does not, however, communicate its power by talking directly about symbols. He communicates it by analyzing human existence in a way that provides verification—he calls it *experiential* verification—of the claims of specific religions, especially of the Christian faith.

Chapter 17

Faith and Experiential Verification

A symposium devoted to Tillich's thought met in New York City. A group of philosophers and theologians had already assembled, but Tillich was late. As we chatted aimlessly to fill the time naturally we talked about him. Suddenly a logician sneered: "Tillich, Tillich! Why should we bother with him? He says that 'faith is the state of being grasped by the power of being-itself!' "[105] It was the shrug of his shoulders with which he finished the statement that did it; the room was swept by derisive laughter. There were a considerable number of philosophical analysts participating. Many of them hadn't studied Tillich, and those who had were disposed to dismiss many of his statements out of hand, rather than exploring them in the total context of Tillich's thought to see if he succeeds in using them in an illuminating way. Any philosopher can be made to seem like an idiot if a lecturer pulls a few of his strange-sounding statements out of context and reads them in an attitude of disdain. I hope to show that Tillich's understanding of faith is meaningful and powerful. The question we will

355

then confront is whether the character of experience as a whole is such as to compel us or even to enable us to be grasped by the power of Tillich's way of talking about existence.

FAITH AND BELIEF

The most confusing aspect of Tillich's view of faith is its relation to belief. In general, we think of faith and belief as almost synonymous; for example, faith in Jesus Christ is generally thought to involve belief that Jesus of Nazareth was the Messiah awaited by the Jewish people. Yet a reader of *Dynamics of Faith,* Tillich's most extended treatment of the subject, might well think he was reading a psychiatric manual on personal integration rather than Tillich's statement of distinctively Christian beliefs. Tillich does not ignore the element of belief; rather, he views Christian beliefs as only one strand in the fabric of faith.[106] It is an important strand, but the element of belief cannot be isolated from thinking, feeling, willing, and participating in a community that is unified by symbols. "Faith is the most centered act of the human mind. It is not a movement of a special section or special function of man's total being. They [thinking, feeling, willing, etc.] are united in the act of faith."[107] For Tillich the act of faith is the act of living in terms of ultimate concerns, of showing what, if anything, it is that we love with all our hearts, with all our souls, and with all our might. Many people do not achieve a stable faith. In Tillich's view they are not integrated; they flit from one concern to another without a true sense of the most important concern.

Once Tillich's view of faith as the basic integrating force of the person is understood, it is easier to follow the details. Belief is, for him, the intellectual element of faith. Where we can have assured knowledge at the level of detachment appropriate to what the logical positivists called the analytic and the synthetic, faith does not come into play. Yet most of our important beliefs do not fall within these rubrics. They involve personal concern or engagement. The positivists therefore consigned them to the realm of merely "emotive" meaning. Tillich, on the other hand, regards them as part of the higher level of receiving or ecstatic knowledge that is valid at a level which transcends the positivists' logical and factual claims.

FAITH AND ULTIMACY: THE ELEMENT OF RISK

For Tillich, faith is a word that links the individual to ultimacy. It is a link at both the subjective pole of concern and the objective pole of being. As we have seen, the main job for an individual is to see to it that his ultimate concern is concern for the truly ultimate. The only way that he can check this out is to be sure that his ultimate concern *cannot* be expressed in terms of the subject-object distinction. Therefore, authentic faith involves an awareness of being-itself, a reality which transcends all conceptual schemes that are ordered to the subject-object distinction.

The most important element of faith is the realization that the truly ultimate is not some particular being that can be designated as a particular object by some particular subject. This awareness can be attained in two ways. Most people get it by means of the immediate experience of concrete symbols which directly confronts them with a sense of the unconditioned. This awareness is not attained by philosophical reflection; rather, it is a result of realizing the changeable and limited character of all beings, even of the greatest galaxies. Yet, as we have seen, Tillich thinks that we can also arrive at an awareness of the truly ultimate by means of philosophical analysis. We can use the subject-object conceptual schemes at the levels of technical and existential reasoning to come to an awareness of the limitations of these modes of reasoning. At this point, ecstatic reason—which is ordered to the whole of reality rather than to the parts—takes over. It enables us to come up with the criterion for true ultimacy, namely, that the truly ultimate must transcend the subject-object distinction of knower and known.

There are emphatically existential elements in Tillich's thought. Therefore, it is especially important to note that he differs from religious existentialists like Buber and Bultmann with regard to faith. They think that the element of risk permeates the entire faith situation. To affirm God is something that can only be done in fear and trembling, or, as Buber would put it, in holy insecurity. In Tillich's scheme the affirmation of the truly ultimate, of being-itself, does not involve risk. It is an awareness that can be achieved through rational analysis (ecstatic reason) or directly through symbols (experience). Therefore, since God is being-itself, the mere affirmation of God's reality does not involve risk.

The element of existential risk, the risk of faith, enters Tillich's scheme in commitment to specific symbols. We have seen that ultimacy cannot, so to speak, be taken straight (see p. 338). Being-itself is not a religious category, but a philosophical concept that enables us to discriminate authentic faith from idolatry. We can no more relate to being-itself in a religious way than we can love "love-itself." To love we must be involved with a concrete "You," a person. To focus our faith we must, therefore, relate not to being-itself, but to a specific symbol. "There is no faith without a content toward which it is directed."[108] It is in committing ourselves to symbols like the cross, the hammer and sickle, or old glory that we take the risk.

Ultimate concern is ultimate risk and ultimate courage. It is *not risk* and needs no courage *with respect to ultimacy* itself [being-itself]. But it is *risk* and demands courage if it *affirms a concrete concern.* And every faith has a concrete element in itself. It is concerned about something or somebody. But this something or this somebody may prove to be not ultimate at all. Then faith is a failure in its concrete expression, although it is not a failure in the experience of unconditional itself. A god disappears; divinity remains.[109]

In another context Tillich makes the point succinctly. "The risk of faith is based on the fact that the unconditional element can become a matter of ultimate concern only if it appears in a concrete embodiment."[110]

The risk of faith comes into the picture where the individual integrates his life around a symbol that may fail. Today's Communists take the risk that the hammer and sickle may, in the course of human history, wind up being regarded as a symbol of demonic totalitarianism like the swastika. Today's Christians take the risk that the cross may wind up being as dead a symbol as the owl of Pallas Athena. The individual, however, cannot wait for the judgment of history. He is confronted by specific symbols in the here and now and must make the leap of decision.

People cannot shop for symbols as if they were vegetables, but rather, it is like Buber's I-You relation. We are addressed by an "other" that turns us around. Yet we have an element of control over our response. Faith, for Tillich, involves being grasped by the power of a symbol and this, like Buber's I-You, is a combination of planning-spontaneity-response in varying degrees at various times. There is simply no way of programming and quantifying the process because spontaneity is involved. Therefore, when it comes to the question of the power that a symbol exerts upon us, Tillich stresses the element of existential engagement: ". . . there is no way of having the content of faith [the responsiveness to the power of a specific symbol] except in the act of faith. All speaking about divine matters which is not done in the state of ultimate concern is meaningless. Because that which is meant in the act of faith cannot be approached in any other way than through an act of faith."[111]

EXPERIENTIAL VERIFICATION

Tillich's view of faith reflects the two poles of the knower-known relation that is relevant to the study of any aspect of his thought. The individual loves with all his heart, with all his soul, and with all his might. Authenticity is achieved when the symbol to which he commits himself in this love is truly a symbol of the ultimate. The obvious question arises: How can he tell whether the symbol around which he integrates his ultimate concern is a symbol of the truly ultimate? One answer is that he cannot do so, not if the standard for judgment on this issue is going to be taken from common sense. "The cross is a valid symbol of ultimate concern" cannot be checked out by direct observation like "This page is white." Furthermore, there is no crucial experiment, like Elijah's test of fire which can be used to check it out (see pp. 142f.).

Tillich does not appeal to the distinctiveness of being-itself as an excuse for avoiding the challenge of verification. He maintains that the demand for some mode of verification is a legitimate one. " 'Verification' means a method of deciding the truth or falsehood of a judgment. Without such a method, judgments are expressions of the subjective state of a person but not acts of cognitive reason. The verifying test belongs to the nature of truth; in this positivism is right. Every cognitive assumption (hypothesis) must be tested."[112] Tillich, however, thinks that positivism is wrong to take the "safest test," which is the repeatable experiment, as the model for all verification. These scientific experiments are, as we have seen, ultimately made good by observations that are objective, in the sense of being the sorts of things about which scientists can achieve maximal agreement among themselves. Tillich thinks that limiting verification to phenomena that can be handled by controlling reason is dangerous because it sets the most important issues beyond the range of rationality. In that case reason cannot provide sanctions against demonic movements like that of the Nazis (see p. 308). Technical reason is inauthentic because it fails to take account of the full range of human experience which involves the need to integrate thoughts, feelings, and actions. Therefore, Tillich insists: ". . . it is not permissible to make the experimental method of verification the exclusive pattern of all verification. . . . The verifying experiences of a nonexperimental character are truer to life though less exact and definite. By far the largest part of all cognitive verification is *experiential*."[113]

Tillich provided one of his clearest statements of his view of experiential verification in an answer to Walter Kaufmann, who asked him how symbols participate in God. "Symbolic statements about God, his attributes and his actions, are not false or correct [because we cannot observe God directly by way of checking them out] but they are 'demonic' [Tillich often uses the term 'idolatrous'] or 'divine' and in most cases, they are mixed (ambiguous). The criterion is whether their implications are destructive or creative for personality and community."[114] It is at this point that Tillich is most existential because he claims that "this criterion cannot be applied from outside in terms of detached observations."[115]

In order to show how symbols of ultimacy actually function, I'd like to focus on "the clenched fist"—the symbol of so many contemporary revolutionary movements. The example is instructive because (1) it shows that religious symbols are not passive things, just lying there waiting to be picked up, but they are events in which individuals are grasped by an ultimate concern through the symbol, and (2) this symbol, unlike the cross or the crescent, is not obviously religious. Therefore, we can use it to gain an appreciation of the functional character of Tillich's analysis of ultimacy. It need not involve the symbols of organized religions.

During the last half of the sixties campuses all over the United States were politicized and challenged by radicals. In broad terms the ultimate concern of the radicals was the overthrow of the capitalist system of what they called "institutionalized greed" and the substitution of a more humane and just social order. One of the gurus of the movement was Herbert Marcuse, whose books and speeches inspired a generation of radical students. In the Spring of 1970 he appeared on the Princeton campus during a period when a number of radical students were on trial for having disrupted a conference sponsored by the university. The charge was that they had prevented a speaker from receiving a proper hearing. The campus was divided and many students had been drawn to the radical cause by the eloquent speeches made by the students who were on trial. In this charged atmosphere Marcuse articulated the hopes and the vision that animated the New Left. At the end of his talk he raised a clenched fist and cried: "Power to the People!" At a moment like that a student who had been drawn to radicalism, but was holding back, might have taken the plunge by making a "leap of decision" or what might more accurately be called a "leap of commitment." In that case he would have joined the SDS or some other radical group, and shared their analysis of social evils and their plans for eliminating them. He would adulate heroes like Mao Tse-tung, Fidel Castro, and The Chicago Seven, and such victims as the Black Panther leader, Fred Hampton.

The student whose radicalization was confirmed by this event would have been attuned to the dimension of ultimacy and his symbol would be the clenched fist. The key question, in Tillich's terms, would be: "Is the clenched fist demonic or divine?" and we know that, for Tillich, the key factors in answering the question involve the issue of whether it is creative or destructive for community and personality.

Community

It might appear that the clenched fist must be creative. It stands for ideals like justice, equality, and the participation of all human beings in the important decisions that affect their lives. Yet, on reflection we realize that every demonic symbol has been able to operate destructively only if it succeeded in raising a genuine but limited good to the level of ultimacy. Once you convince great numbers of people that they are working for a good cause, you can get them to act more cruelly and destructively than they would ever act as individuals.[116] This is obvious in the case of nationalism. It is also true of causes like the French Revolution which was scarred by the guillotine and of the terrors of the Communist revolt in Russia. The statement "The revolution devours its children" refers to them. They enlist the best young people in a fervent rebellion for idealistic goals. These goals are then absolutized and the most sensitive and critical revolutionaries are eradicated for their deviations. They become blood sacrifices to noble ideals like liberty, equality, and brotherhood or "From each according to his ability, to each according to his needs."

Once the revolutionary period is over a consensus generally prevails. The swastika is regarded as a symbol that was definitely destructive; the Marseillaise is, by contrast, almost universally regarded as creative. The hammer and sickle is controversial. What about the clenched fist? A student listening to Marcuse and stirred toward commitment would not have the judgment of posterity to help him. He would have to commit himself knowing that this symbol might never catch on at all, or that if it did, it might one day be regarded as demonic. He could only verify his decisions on the basis of existential judgments about its creative or destructive role in his own life and in society. And we did not need Tillich to tell us that these judgments are radically subjective. In making them we put ourselves on the line knowing that it is not possible to achieve maximal agreement on these matters. The most we achieve is considerable agreement within revolutionary movements, or within the movements that oppose them.

Personality

Anyone who has known members of radical groups (or of reactionary ones for that matter) knows how often the members seem to be egotistical fanatics. They are incapable of hearing voices other than their own, and they use the movement as a vehicle for working out their aggressions toward their family or society. It is all too easy to identify these types with radicals in general and to use this identification as an excuse for not confronting the issues they raise. After all, we also find many personalities that achieve integration through radical movements. They give generously of themselves and focus on the cause without calling attention to the "nobility" of their motives and actions. It is clear that any cause, even a destructive movement like fascism, can be a source of creative integration for individual personalities. A further complication is that judgments as to whether the individual is operating creatively or destructively are highly subjective. It is obvious that other members of the movement may see a given individual as "putting it all together," whereas observers who are hostile to the movement would see him as losing perspective, balance, and even sanity. It is worth recalling Tillich's statement that "this criterion cannot be applied from outside in terms of detached observations." Ultimately, the individual living it through has to make the judgment of whether or not it is integrating and creative or disintegrating and destructive.

Tillich's view of experiential verification is applicable to many areas of judgment, for example, to psychoanalysis, politics, and aesthetics. Obviously, its applicability to religious symbols is the point at issue, and this may be better appreciated if we deal first with a sign like the skull and crossbones. There is no direct correspondence between the contents of a bottle of iodine and the skull and crossbones on the label. It would be ridiculous to look inside the bottle for a tiny skull and two crossed bones; this particular sign is verified by its effects. If you drink it the results are destructive—violent illness and possibly death.

The same functional analysis applies to religious symbols, but there are important differences.

1   We can understand the meaning of the skull and crossbones regardless of the existential stand we take in relating to it. We can only be grasped by the power of a religious symbol in an I-You relation.

2   Poison is always destructive if taken in excessive quantities, and "excessive" is subject to reasonably precise quantification. Yet the effects of a symbol like the cross cannot be neatly assessed, quantified, and labeled. These effects are not independent of the subjective circumstances of communities and individuals.

3   A religious symbol like the cross may be creative at one period of history (the early church) and destructive at another (the Crusades). Yet this contrast is not only one which draws a distinction between the function of the cross at various periods of history, it also discloses the subjectivity of the commentator. Some Christians would regard the Crusades as a creative episode in the history of Christendom.

4   An individual may vary as to his judgment of the effects of the cross on his life. He may—in retrospect—feel that it was an integrating force during adolescence when it enabled him to cope with the problems of puberty, and a disintegrating force during his college years when he used it to resist all subjects that challenged his scheme of beliefs. Here again, considerable disagreement is possible between the individual and his friends, and the individual himself may vary in his judgments in different moods or different situations.

5 Poison is consistent. An overdose will have destructive effects on the individual and an overdose (too much iodine in the communal well) will also have destructive effects on the community. Symbols of ultimacy are not consistent in this way. The swastika was utterly destructive on the social level, yet it had an integrating effect on some individual Germans who were inspired to idealistic self-sacrifice by this symbol. The same, obviously, is true of the cross. Those who agree that the symbol of the cross was socially destructive at the time of the Crusades, should be capable of recognizing that it played an integrative and constructive role in the lives of the individual Crusaders.

COURAGE: AFFIRMING BEING IN THE FACE OF THE THREAT OF NONBEING

It is now time to link, explicitly, Tillich's analysis of being (ontology) with his analysis of human existence. We have seen that being-itself is, for Tillich, the ultimate ontological category. There is nothing whatever that can be said about it because all our words are oriented to the subject-object scheme, and being-itself is beyond it.

Given the role that being-itself plays in Tillich's thought, the language he uses in talking about it seems very strange indeed. He talks about it in dramatic terms: ". . . the concept of being as being, or being-itself, points to the power inherent in everything, the power of resisting nonbeing."[117] Again, he writes: "If we speak of the power of being-itself we indicate that being affirms itself against nonbeing."[118] At the literal level this language is strange and seems to contradict everything that Tillich says about being-itself because he writes as though being-itself were an agent capable of resisting something. Furthermore, that which is resisted is "nonbeing," and this appears to be unqualified nonsense because "nonbeing" cannot be there to be resisted. Analytic philosophers have been quick to note that Tillich's references to nonbeing in contexts like this one have a somewhat Lewis Carroll quality. Paul Edwards makes the point by quoting the following passage from *Alice Through the Looking Glass*:

> "Who did you pass on the road?" the King went on, holding out his hand to the Messenger for some more hay.
> "Nobody," said the Messenger.
> "Quite right," said the King, "this young lady saw him too. So of course Nobody walks slower than you."
> "I do my best," said the Messenger in a sullen tone. "I'm sure nobody walks much faster than I do."
> "He can't do that," said the King, "or else he'd have been here first."[119]

Tillich's language leaves him open to barbs of this kind in which he is accused of confusing nothing, that is, the absence of anything whatever, with a particular that he labels "nonbeing." Yet it should be obvious that Tillich's entire scheme of thinking is opposed to this type of confusion. It is precisely because of his awareness of the total distinctiveness and transcendence of being-itself that he refuses to refer to it by means of the term "Highest Being" or by any other theological term that implies that the ultimate is a *particular being*. It is, therefore, absurd to suppose that Tillich is not equally well aware of the blunder involved in talking of nonbeing in language that can be appropriately applied only to particular beings. Yet, the appeal to Tillich's awareness of the problem does not resolve the difficulty presented by his dramatic references to being-itself "resisting nonbeing." Indeed, critics like Edwards may be right in charging that Tillich's use of this language is, ultimately, unjustified. This will be dealt with later (see pp. 386f.). At this point, it is important to see that Tillich is using this kind of language with reference to the existence of particular human beings. Here is the key to Tillich's extraordinary impact on American culture, especially in his frequent appearances on college campuses in all parts of the country. He spoke in terms of being, but he got through to people in terms of the way he applied this talk to human beings. He writes: "If one is asked how nonbeing is related to being-itself, one can only answer metaphorically, being 'embraces' itself and nonbeing."[120] Tillich's metaphor is never translated into less figurative language when he deals with the cosmic level of reality as such, but he does attempt to make it less figurative when he writes about the level of human existence. His statement about being-itself embracing being and nonbeing can be understood in terms of the kind of analysis that both Heidegger and Sartre use and which Tillich adapts to his purposes in *The Courage To Be*. As a statement about human beings it may be understood as follows: any human being (the equivalent here of being-itself) embraces both the actual states of his own existence (being) and the awareness of what he is not (nonbeing), especially of his own potential for development.[121] He is finite, that is, limited in his capacities, but he is also free—within those limitations—to transcend any particular stage of his own development.

The key term in Tillich's analysis of human existence is "courage." Characteristically, he takes this term and gives it a special use in his system. He acknowledges the usual meaning of courage as the virtue, for example, of a soldier standing by his post in the face of danger. He then notes that military courage is only an instance of something that is more profound and pervasive, namely, ontological courage which he defines as ". . . the state in which a [human] being is aware of its possible nonbeing."[122] He elaborates it by stressing the point that ". . . courage as the universal and essential affirmation of one's being is an ontological concept."[123] He adds: ". . . courage is self-affirmation 'in-spite-of,' that is, in spite of that which tends to prevent the self from affirming itself."[124]

We now have before us the key terms that Tillich uses to spell out the experiential verification of religious symbols, namely, courage, self-affirmation, and anxiety. He uses them to make good his claim that he will "interpret faith on the basis of courage."[125]

Self-Affirmation and Anxiety

The term "self-affirmation" seems easy enough to understand. To affirm something is to say "yes" to it. Therefore, the term involves the idea of approval, the approval of a self by itself, and others. Yet we have seen that Tillich claims that "self-affirmation of one's being is an ontological concept." This means that he regards it as a defining characteristic of human beings.

Human beings are utterly distinctive. We not only desire to persist in life and to gratify our basic drives, but we need to approve of or affirm what we do and what we are. This is because our self-awareness is characterized by a sense of possibility. We do not merely experience what is, we are conscious of what might be. We know that we can and must choose from a variety of possibilities—of possible courses of study, of possible careers, of possible mates. We also know that we can and must choose with more or less effort and more or less passion.

Anxiety is the key for the threats to self-affirmation. The word gained wide cultural circulation through the work of Freud who distinguished it from fear. Fear is realistic; it is directed to a danger of which we are conscious, for example, a fire in a crowded movie house. Anxiety (at least large doses of it) was, for Freud, a sign of mental illness or neurosis. The individual gripped by anxiety was responding to an unreal threat of which he was not conscious, and was, therefore, responding in an inappropriate way. An example of the neurotic anxiety that Freud had in mind is the anxiety that afflicts some premedical students in relation to organic chemistry. Since this course is crucial to their program, it is realistic of students to fear a failure in their examinations.

Neurotic anxiety, however, enters the picture in students who are programmed by their parents to believe that their worth as human beings is bound up with their ability to become doctors. For these students an examination in organic chemistry is not merely a hurdle on their path to a career, it becomes a threat to their ability to approve of themselves. The anxiety often becomes incapacitating. The student loses his ability to study for organic chemistry and for anything else. Since the root of it is buried in his unconscious, he is utterly unaware of the true reasons for his inability to function. A case of this kind requires psychotherapy. It is not realistic of the student to feel that he can only become an acceptable person if he becomes a doctor.

Tillich acknowledges the point that a great deal of anxiety is sick or, in the seemingly more technical term, pathological.[126] Yet he also insists that anxiety is an inescapable part of human existence.[127] It is a function of awareness that we need not exist at all, and also that the way we live may not be worthy of approval. Basically, Tillich deals with anxiety, the threat of nonbeing, in three basic modes: the threat to life, to moral self-approval, and to meaning. Courage is the ability to affirm one's self in spite of these threats. Tillich claims that the three modes of anxiety do not appear in isolation within any human being but that they overlap. Nevertheless, at any one moment, one or the other form may be dominant in an individual, and sometimes a given form of anxiety dominates a personality on a more enduring basis.[128] In broad terms, self-affirmation is the "yes" that we seek regarding what we do and are, and anxiety is the threat of the "no." We look for a "yes" when we put ourselves on the line by expressing love toward another human being; a "no" in response to that love is one of the most dreadful things we can experience. Therefore, love is haunted by anxiety, so too are our career activities. We pour ourselves into the work of a lifetime and hope for a "yes," and we are anxious about the fact that the community to which we address the work may respond with a "no." These "noes" deprive us of gratification and threaten our self-esteem, in other words, they threaten our ability to affirm, that is, to say "yes" to ourselves.

Morality, Anxiety, and Self-Affirmation

Tillich's discussion of the three major modes of anxiety is abstract. Consider, for example, his key statement of the moral aspect of it. "Even in what he considers his best deed nonbeing is present and prevents it from being perfect. A profound ambiguity between good and evil permeates everything he does, because it permeates his personal being as such."[129] This statement might be rejected as an illegitimate introduction of moral perfectionism into Tillich's scheme. After all, Tillich insists that all human beings are limited; therefore, it seems fatuous of him to suggest that we ought to feel guilt because we fall short of perfection. To answer this charge, Tillich's statement must be understood in the context of the Christian view of sin. Even after this has been done, there are readers who may find Tillich unreasonably perfectionistic, but its human context and religious importance will be clear.

Christianity, at least Christian thinking that is oriented to the letters of St. Paul, has always insisted that there is a radical "performance gap" at the moral level. They have done this by focusing on motivation: It is not good enough to do the right thing, it must be done for the right reason. The concern for motivation is not exclusively Christian. Rabbis who were roughly contemporary with Jesus of Nazareth insisted that the only proper motive for performing the acts prescribed by the Torah was *Lishmah*, which means, roughly, for the sake of God, or for the love of God. Yet they were *relatively* relaxed about this. They urged Jews to perform the commandments *Lishmah*, but failing that, to perform them anyway, even without the proper motivation.

By contrast, Christian thinkers, beginning with St. Paul, have agonized over this issue. They focus on the individual who is rejecting himself and whose very efforts to improve himself, so that he can affirm himself, make the situation worse rather than better. Imagine a student wanting to gain admission to a special fraternity. He learns that he's unlikely to fulfill this ambition because he's too self-centered. He accepts the judgment of his character and resolves to do something about it. He starts by forcing himself to be concerned for the well-being of others. He loans his car to one friend, plies another with cigarettes, takes over a stint at the library for a third. Yet he is suddenly shaken by a sickening realization. He has never been more self-centered than at this very period of his life when he is thrashing around so desperately in an effort to break out of this pattern. All his efforts to overcome self-centeredness are a function of his drive to get into the fraternity. In other words, he can control his actions, but he can't control his motivation.

Self-centeredness is an example of the kind of inner anguish that is typical of Christianity. Even if the student could fool his classmates and make the fraternity, he wouldn't be able to fool himself; therefore, he wouldn't be able to affirm his self. This is what St. Paul has in mind in saying: "For the good that I would do, I do not do, and the evil that I would refrain from doing is precisely what I do" (Rom. 7:19). The Apostle is not talking about committing rape and murder as the evil acts that he cannot refrain from doing, and he is not talking about donating to charity and working for good causes as the good that he is incapable of accomplishing. Rather, he claims that he was able to obey the law and to fulfill the commandments (Acts 22:3–4). His problem is that he cannot fulfill them for the right reason, for what the Rabbis of his own age called *Lishmah*. It is out of the anguish of this agony that he cries: "Wretched man that I am, who shall deliver me from the body of this death!" (Rom. 7:24). This death is obviously the death of the spirit. It is the threat of nonbeing in the form of moral guilt raised to such a great intensity as to threaten the individual with despair, the absence of hope.

St. Paul was afflicted with what Tillich calls existential rather than neurotic anxiety about his moral failures because he really was doing the right thing for the wrong reason. He was fulfilling the commandments in the spirit of pride. Anyone who is familiar with the procedures of Freudian psychoanalysis knows that for it to be successful, the patient must surrender the pretense of being healthy and able to take care of himself. It is while still in the throes of neurosis that the patient receives the acceptance from the analyst that ultimately enables him to accept himself. Once that is done the unconscious thoughts that are repressed can surface. The individual can face them and thereby strip them of their force and shed the neurosis.

St. Paul's experience of existential anxiety follows the psycho-analytic pattern. He discovers that Christ died for his sake, for the sake of *Paul the sinner.* "God shows his love for us in that while we were yet sinners Christ died for us" (Rom. 5:8). Paul claims that God lovingly accepted him while he was, on moral grounds, unworthy of being accepted. And it is, according to Christianity, only when we have faced up to our moral inadequacies, that we can accept God's forgiving love in Christ. "For God was in Christ reconciling the world to himself and not counting their trespasses against them" (2 Cor. 5:19).

In Tillichian terms, it is only when we have fully faced our failure to become the selves that we ought to be, that we can develop the courage we need, the courage to admit our failings. We can then be reconciled to reality by accepting ourselves as we are, by affirming ourselves. It is this pattern of Christian faith that Tillich captures in his otherwise incom-prehensible statement that one must have ". . . the courage to accept onself as accepted, in spite of being unacceptable."[130]

Translating Christian categories into Tillichian terms may seem strained. We do not usually think of sin as the presence of nonbeing in the self. Tillich knows this but he maintains that some degree of philosophical filtering is inevitable in dealing with biblical texts. Even the fundamental-ist, who is committed to the literal reading of biblical texts, applies words like "historical" and "true" to them. These words have a philosophical history and Tillich claims that by failing to take account of their many possible meanings, fundamentalists, and other types of anti-philosophical theologians, simply apply these terms haphazardly and carelessly.[131] We can concede this much to Tillich and insist, nevertheless, that his translation of biblical categories into ontological language is too forced. This charge may be valid, but, in fairness to Tillich, I should like to close this discussion of his view of faith and its experiential verification with an illustration that seems to show his way of translating biblical texts to its best advantage.

A Tillichian Reading of St. Paul

There should be no need to recall the fact that Tillich rejects Sunday school literalism in dealing with God and the afterlife. Faith for Tillich is not a matter of believing that an all-powerful and all-knowing being resides in a special heavenly space. Nor does he present courage, the ability to affirm the self in spite of the threats of nonbeing, as an attitude that is based on the belief in heavenly rewards. In other words, he does *not* urge us to stand up to the trials of this life on the grounds that in spite of all the miseries, one day we will reside—with all other "saved" human beings—in the Celestial City with Jesus Christ ruling over it.[132] Tillich translates the language of the Bible into existential categories, but he sets this existential analysis, including talk about God as he is in himself, into the framework of his special approach to being.

Tillich's view of faith emphasizes this world. Courage is self-affirmation in spite of the anxieties of life in the here and now, and they cannot be alleviated by belief in another world beyond this one. It is the ability to integrate one's life around a specific symbol of ultimate concern. With this in mind let us focus briefly on the career and faith of St. Paul.

Paul traveled through the ancient Near East proclaiming the glad tidings that redemption had come through his Lord, Jesus Christ. Clearly there was a great element of risk involved. He addressed two communities, Jewish and Greek, and both responded with a "no" where he hoped for a "yes." The Jews had many versions of the Messianic expectation, but none of them included a Messiah who was executed as a criminal (the cross is now a religious symbol, but in those times, as I noted earlier, it had the ring that the electric chair has today). On the other hand, the Greeks laughed scornfully at the idea that in order to experience salvation all human beings must relate to an individual who entered history at a particular time and among a special people. They thought that the most important truths were those that were equally accessible to all. Knowledge of the incarnation of God in Jesus of Nazareth could not have been accessible to many people, for example, to all those who lived before his time. This lies behind Paul's statement: "Jews call for miracles, Greeks look for wisdom; but we proclaim Christ—yes Christ nailed to the cross; and . . . this is a stumbling-block to Jews and folly to Greeks" (1 Cor. 22, 23).

Paul suffered many rejections. He was denounced and imprisoned, he was whipped and he was near death many times, having survived shipwreck as well as conspiracy (2 Cor. 11:21–28). In other words, Paul received many "noes" where he sought to receive the affirmation of a "yes," and, as we have seen, he also was tormented by the "noes" he directed to himself. Here, if ever, was a man who knew how difficult it was to have the courage to affirm himself in spite of what Tillich calls anxiety—in spite of threats to his life, to his moral self-acceptance, and to his structures of meaning, that is, to the validity of his symbol of ultimacy, Jesus Christ. Yet his response was a lifetime of courage that found expression in a powerful statement of faith.

> Then what can separate us from the love of Christ? Can affliction or hardship? Can persecution, hunger, nakedness, peril, or the sword? . . . in spite of all, overwhelming victory is ours through him who loved us. For I am convinced that there is nothing in death or life, in the realm of spirits or superhuman powers, in the world as it is or the world as it shall be, in the forces of the universe, in heights or depths—nothing in all creation that can separate us from the love of God in Christ Jesus our Lord (Rom. 8:35–39).

St. Paul is grasped by the power of being as manifested in Jesus Christ. He is grasped in the immediacies of his experience of this life with all its anxieties, with its rejections of others and of himself. Right at that moment, when he is suspended over 70,000 fathoms of doubt and discouragement, with no objective grounds to support him, he affirms the power of this symbol of ultimacy. The threat of nonbeing in the form of death loses its power because the scheme of meaning communicated to him by the symbol of Jesus Christ overcomes the anxiety of guilt and self-rejection. It does not do so by eliminating objective uncertainty, but by providing life experiences that are so fulfilling that they overcome it. In his experience of God's reconciling love in Christ, Paul resonates with all being. He has the courage to affirm himself and the created order in spite of the appearances and in spite of his anxieties.

Paul verifies his faith experientially. The verification is, as Tillich understands it, subjective. It does not, for example, yield information about a Celestial City where Jesus Christ rules at the right hand of God the Father. For Tillich, this sort of correspondence theory of truth is out of the question. He rejects it along with the literal reading of the Bible. His understanding is ontological, his faith is existential, and his verification is experiential. As far as Tillich is concerned that is all the truth we can have on earth, but he thinks that—fortunately—it is all we need.

ALLEGORICAL SUMMARY: TILLICH'S INFINITE SEA OF BEING

Tillich regards the truly ultimate as infinite; a term he associates with ultimacy again and again. The infinite means the unlimited or, as Jewish mystics have put it, the *En Sof* which means "without end." Tillich regards reality as an infinite sea of being. He refers to it as being-itself.

Critics often ask questions like "How does Tillich know that there is such a reality as being-itself?" To Tillich this question would make no sense. It is like fishes asking, "Is there such a thing as the sea?" The reality of the sea is presupposed by the fact of fishes swimming in water just as the reality of being-itself is presupposed by the fact of human beings living in this world of ours and discussing what exists and what does not exist. If there were no sea there would be no fishes, and if being-itself were not real then there would be no individual beings, and we human beings would not be here discussing the meaning of being-itself.

We human beings are for Tillich the fish who need to swim vigorously and daringly in order to carry out our life functions. And we must do so without having destructive encounters with other fish and with the other beings that also exist in the Sea of Being.

There is one crucial difference between Tillich's Sea of Being and our earthly seas like the great oceans. The earthly seas have surfaces so that even if we were immersed in the Caribbean Sea, we could develop a sense of its limits. Flying fish, for example, can break the surface of the sea by leaping into the atmosphere above it, and amphibians can crawl out of the sea onto the shore. But there is no way that any beings in Tillich's Sea of Being can get out of it to develop a sense of its limits. Everything we know about the Sea of Being we know by means of a study of the specific beings that we fish encounter in it.

We fish achieve technical knowledge of particular beings within the sea. We meet other fish and we can objectively measure their size and their speed. We observe their behavior by swimming around them. We also encounter and study vegetative matter and minerals. We classify them and predict the way that they will behave when certain types of currents hit them, and so on.

We fish cannot have technical knowledge of the Sea of Being itself, that is, the Sea as a whole. We cannot directly experience the entire sea and we make drastic mistakes about it if we think of it by means of the concepts we use in dealing with individual beings in the sea. All the individual things in the sea are particular objects that we as subjects can think about and compare with other objects. But the Sea of Being itself is not a particular object, not even for thought, much less for the senses. Therefore, we cannot have technical knowledge of the sea itself by means of which we could control it. We cannot for example, characterize the Sea of Being as aqueous, turbulent, sublime, mysterious, and so on. Rather, we cannot characterize it by means of these terms in a literal way because the things we can say literally only apply to individual and specific beings in the sea or in areas of the sea. We can, however, say that the sea itself is aqueous, turbulent, sublime, mysterious, and so on, in a *symbolic* sense. We can apply these terms to the sea because the parts of the sea that we observe display these features and because every part of the sea participates in the Sea of Being. If we come upon a turbulent area of the sea, we can legitimately say that turbulence symbolizes it because as a part of the sea it participates in it. Yet we cannot claim that we know that the Sea of Being is itself turbulent because the Sea of Being transcends, or is beyond, the individual turbulent areas of the sea. All the words we fishes have are designed to deal with individual objects in the sea and not with the Sea of Being as a whole.

There is one problem that is raised by this scheme. Since everything in the sea is a part of the Sea of Being, it would seem that everything in the sea can equally well serve as a symbol of the Sea of Being. Turbulence is just as good as tranquility, and dead vegetative matter would be just as good as a magnificent sailfish.

Yet there is a way of ranking symbols. The ranking is done in terms of the functions of fish, and for the purposes of this allegory, let me say that the most important thing for fishes is to swim out and to swim courageously.

It follows that fishes are dependent on light which enables them to see where they are going and to keep themselves from swimming destructively into other fishes or into objects, such as sharp rocks, that are found all over the sea. Every individual fish must orient himself to the sea by means of illuminated objects.

To step outside the allegory for a moment, let me remind the reader that Tillich uses a cluster of terms to express the dimension of depth. Being-itself is the most typical, but, among others, he also refers to goodness-itself and truth-itself.[133] Thus far I have dealt with the infinite Sea Being as an allegorical equivalent of being-itself or *that within which* we orient ourselves. Now I will shift to the Infinite Source of Light as the allegorical equivalent of Tillich's truth-itself or *that by means of which* we orient ourselves.

Human beings can swim underwater in actual seas and know that the source of the light is above the surface and that we can break out of the water and look directly at the sun. In terms of the allegory of the Sea of Being there is no way that fish can break the surface to look directly at the source of all illumination. In fact, there is not even a way of being sure of the direction that the light is coming from. All it can do is to swim around and be grasped by the power of light through its contact with individual illuminated objects.

The problem is which illuminated objects are the most important? Which ones provide the best guide to the nature of the Sea of Being itself? Which illuminated objects participate most fully in the nature of that sea? The fish is bound to ask these questions. A failure to ask them will mean that the fish flits around aimlessly from one illuminated object to another, never really deciding for itself which illuminated objects are enduringly valuable.

One obvious standard to use is to say that the bigger the illuminated object the more obviously it participates in the source of light and the more authentically it can guide us as to the way we ought to swim purposefully in the sea. Therefore, fishes naturally tend to form scales of importance or chains of illuminated objects. They are grasped more powerfully by bigger phosphorescent pieces of vegetative materials than by smaller ones and, similarly, by bigger phosphorescent fishes. When they swim near a great phosphorescent reef, they think: "Wow! This is it!"

Yet when philosophically reflective fishes swim around the great coral reef, they come to realize that it is not the ultimate light in which all illuminated objects participate. It is only a great illuminated object that points beyond itself to the ultimate source of light from which it receives its illumination. How does the philosophical fish know this? Well, for one thing, it can look at great reefs that used to be phosphorescent but which are now no longer glowing (these correspond to what Tillich calls dead symbols of ultimacy like Zeus and Apollo).

The philosophical fish comes to realize that no specific illuminated object, no matter how great and valuable, can itself be the ultimate source of light. All of them merely point to that ultimate source.

If any illuminated object whatever can, like the coral reef, participate in the light, how does the fish know which of these illuminated objects are more or less important? Tillich's answer is that we can only check it out by noticing how the fish swims in relation to it. If the fish swims creatively, then it is an important and valid way of providing orientation within the Sea of Being. If the fish swims destructively, then it is a bad clue to the nature of the Sea of Being and to the way that light functions within that sea.

How can a fish know whether he is relating to the coral reef in a creative or a destructive way? Remember that the Sea of Being is infinite; there is no surface to its limitless extension, no way of breaking out of it to see the ultimate source of light by means of direct observation. Therefore, in Tillichian terms, the only way that one can tell whether a fish relates to the coral reef in an idolatrous way or a creative way is to watch it swim. You have to see whether it swims well, that is, authentically, or whether, in swimming, it makes existential mistakes. What kind of mistakes are these? I'll illustrate two opposite ones:

1 The fish thinks the coral reef is itself the ultimate, the one and only source of light. He clings to it and never swims very far away. Since the coral reef is very bright, a lot of other fish make the same mistake and there is an ecological crush of too many fish, not enough food. Our fish lacks the courage to swim to uncharted waters where there aren't many bright phosphorescent objects but where there's plenty of food.

2   Another existential mistake that a fish can make in treating the coral reef as the ultimate rather than as a symbol of the ultimate is to think that the phosphorescent light of the reef is so powerful that it reaches far beyond the reef itself. It swims out well beyond the reef, but it thinks that no matter how far from the reef it moves the light will still be as bright as it is in the vicinity of the reef. This turns out not to be the case, and our fish experiences existential disappointment. Instead of adjusting to the light that is to be found in these further reaches of the ocean, the light that comes from the truly ultimate source of light, it curses the feebleness of the light, fails to see the food that's all around it, and dies.

Chapter 18

Why Talk Tillichese?

Tillich's religious thought is the most comprehensive system that has been produced in the twentieth century. It has, understandably, been subjected to a wide range of criticisms.[134] I shall ignore the ones that have been directed at him from within the Christian fold; for example, the question of whether his view of Jesus as the Christ is a valid account of Christian faith. The focus will be on the following issues:

    1 The justification of his claim that the God of theism is not truly ultimate but that it is at best a symbol for the ultimate and, at worst, an idol that is mistaken for it.

    2 The criticisms of analytic philosophers. They have had a field day in going at Tillich because he seems to commit some of the worst blunders that they attribute to metaphysicians and theologians. Yet a careful reading suggests that Tillich's thought is impervious to the kinds of criticisms that analysts generally direct against Christian thinkers. In the overall scheme of his system he knows what he affirms, what he denies, and why.

3 The question of whether Tillich's imperviousness to the more obvious kind of analytic criticisms has been achieved at too great a price. He may have absolutely eliminated the possibility, within his system, of talking about God or being-itself as realities that are independent of human beings. In other words, we will have to consider the problem of whether Tillich's system of Christian theology—which draws insights from all the philosophers and theologians in the Western tradition—does not, in the final analysis, boil down to an elaborate scheme of existential humanism, a school of thought which eliminates transcendence.

ECSTATIC REASON

Tillich's talk of ecstatic reason is, as far as contemporary empiricists are concerned, a matter of waving a red flag at a bull. Tillich uses the word "reason," but claims that this mode of reasoning transcends the subject-object relation. The obvious question that arises in connection with ecstatic reason is: "What knowledge can it yield?" After all, knowledge is constituted by the subject (knower) and object (known) polarity. It would seem that Tillich is guilty of using the word "reason" while stripping it of the very element that enables us to apply the word.

Tillich is perfectly aware of this objection. He does not think that ecstatic reason yields specific contents of knowledge in the way that technical reason can yield knowledge in fields like physics and biology. He insists that ecstatic reason does not tell us anything about specific beings in the world. It points to the mystery we confront when we drive beyond our knowledge of specific entities and ideas and deal with reality as such, that is, with being-itself.[135] As we have seen, Tillich does not think that logical argument can convert the metaphysical shock of asking "Why is there something rather than nothing?" into specific knowledge of a being called God (see pp. 334f.). Tillich's effort to make good on his talk of ecstatic reason cannot be isolated from the total context of his thought. Ecstatic reason functions as a danger signal that is directed to individuals who try to live exclusively on the level of technical reason. It warns them that, by restricting themselves in this way, they will fail to reach the ultimate dimension of human experience and, therefore, of reality.

Philosophers who are interested in the problems of knowledge will be impatient with this way of making good on the use of ecstatic reason. They want to check things out more directly and with less sprawl. Yet it is to Tillich's credit that he is not confused about the nature of his enterprise. He recognizes the strangeness of ecstatic reason and of his appeal to total life experience as the way of checking it out.

ULTIMATE CONCERN

Tillich claims that "God" is a word that symbolizes or stands for that which concerns us ultimately. The religious attitude which is captured in the commandment, "You shall love the Lord your God with all your heart, with all your soul, and with all your might," is an expression of this concern. The obvious criticism of this aspect of Tillich's thought is that (1) not everyone has something that he is ultimately concerned about and (2) even if everyone did, that would not prove that there is something in the universe which ought to be loved with all our hearts, with all our souls, and with all our might.

Tillich does not think that everyone has an ultimate concern in the sense of being consciously aware of it or in the sense of being consistent about it. He knows that countless people are unaware of their ultimate concerns while others have a number of serious concerns without having one that stands at the apex of the pyramid.[136] Tillich is not, therefore, making a *factual* mistake by stating (1) that everyone ought to have an ultimate concern and (2) that everyone actually has one. His assertions are based on his *theological view* of human nature.

Tillich insists that everyone ought to have an ultimate concern because having one, in a conscious sense, is vital to personal integration. If an individual has an ultimate concern at one period of his life—but has it in an unfocused and unconscious way—then the same individual will, without realizing it, shift his ultimate concern at other times. In Tillich's view, this is symptomatic of a disoriented and underdeveloped personality. It follows that everyone ought to try to have an ultimate concern that is the conscious focus of their lives.

Tillich's claim that everyone actually has an ultimate concern, whether they are consciously aware of it or not, relates to his analysis of idolatry. He thinks that, at any given moment, every individual actually loves something with all his heart, with all his soul, and with all his might. If he does not bring this concern up to the level of consciousness, and if he fails to reflect on it critically, then he will be susceptible to demonic forces like totalitarian movements.[137] He will accept these false ultimates as result of his failure to work authentically at developing an ultimate concern for the truly ultimate. Tillich's analysis of ultimate concern is highly subjective, and he knows it. He does not think that he can prove that everyone ought to have an ultimate concern, much less, does he think that he can prove that the one ultimate concern that everyone ought to have is symbolized by Jesus as the Christ. Yet, as an important piece in the mosaic of his thought, Tillich's view of ultimate concern makes sense. It should not be pulled out of the overall scheme in a way that makes Tillich look foolish.

BEING-ITSELF

When ecstatic reason drives beyond our ordinary modes of technical and existential reason, it triggers an awareness of being-itself. This is certainly the most problematic concept in Tillich's thought.[138] It is also the one that seems most vulnerable to analytic criticisms. All the problems that are associated with the God of the theologians, the God who is omnipotent, omniscient, etc., seem to be associated with Tillich's being-itself. There seems to be no way of checking out whether statements about being-itself are true anymore than we can check on the truth of statements about the God of theism. In addition, Tillich insists that being-itself is so utterly beyond all characterization, that we cannot even apply the traditional attributes of God, like the ones just mentioned, to it. Indeed, there seems no way of distinguishing being-itself from nothingness.

Being-itself is that to which all religious language, or symbolism, is referred. Yet, because it is not a being alongside other beings, far from helping with the problem of reference, it compounds it; that to which religious language refers is beyond all characterization. Tillich wants to preserve the meanings associated with the language of theism, but he rejects all theistic efforts to provide a reference for this language.

Tillich is fully aware of these problems. As was the case with ecstatic reason and ultimate concern, we find that he does not wait for his critics to call the peculiar features of his concepts to his attention. He emphasizes them himself and for reasons of his own. Being-itself has two functions: (1) It does provide a trans-physical reference for religious language. Being-itself is not a being, yet its reality is presupposed whenever human beings think about the existence of persons or things. Without the reality of being-itself, there would be nothing at all, and this is all that can legitimately be said about it. (2) Since being-itself is not a being alongside others, it is not a particular entity or a specific concept. It cannot be an object of knowledge that is registered by a knowing subject. Therefore, it provides an important check against idolatry. Consider any person who loves something with all his heart, with all his soul, and with all his might. If he finds himself thinking about that object as though it were itself the ultimate, rather than a symbol of ultimacy, then he is treating it idolatrously, even if the symbol is as lofty as the God of the theologians.

Tillich's functional approach to being-itself renders his system less vulnerable to analytic attack than are most systems of philosophical theology, especially if the analysts are prepared to accept his version of experiential verification as a way of checking it out. Yet Tillich's views are certainly open to attack on the part of theists who may rightly think that their position has received a quick brush off in Tillich's scheme.

In directing criticisms at Tillich in the name of theism, I am not arguing that theists can make their claims good. I have indicated some of my own problems with theism in the critical sections of previous parts of this book. The point of these criticisms is to charge Tillich with an almost casual dismissal of theism. A reader who was unfamiliar with religious thought would, in reading Tillich, get the impression that theists cannot make any sort of philosophical case for the arguments for the existence of God and that their characterizations of God, such as omnipotence and omniscience, are extremely crude. Since Tillich never argues points of this kind, but merely states them, his procedure is unfair to theists in general, but especially to Thomists.

1 As noted earlier, Tillich does not present a sustained and carefully reasoned case for the failure of the arguments for the existence of God. He refers to some of Kant's points in a few brief strokes and lets it go at that (see pp. 323f.). This approach is not so much a philosophical refutation of the arguments as it is an assumption that they have been conclusively refuted. His treatment of other issues related to theism is equally sketchy.

2 Tillich scornfully rejected theistic attempts to characterize God by means of traditional attributes like omnipotence and omniscience. I have already quoted his views on omnipotence. "In popular parlance the concept 'omnipotence' implies a highest being who is able to do whatever he wants. This notion must be rejected, religiously as well as theological-ly" (see p. 335). It is typical of Tillich's cavalier dismissal of theism in general and of Thomism in particular, that he does not note that theologians *have rejected* the popular misconception of God as a being who can do whatever he wants. They insist that if the idea of a square circle is contradictory then it cannot be made into a conceivable geometri-cal figure simply by saying that "God can make a square circle."[139]

Concepts like omnipotence may, as Tillich charges, rest on confu-sions about a super-being called God. Yet given the care with which theists and atheists have debated the point over the centuries it seems irresponsible of Tillich to dismiss the notion with a quick reference to popular misunderstandings.[140] The picture is not improved when we note that this treatment of omnipotence occurs in his most technical work, the *Systematic Theology.*

3 Tillich insists that God cannot be a being alongside other beings. This has been challenged by Charles Hartshorne, one of the few philosophical theologians of this century who has attained a stature comparable to Tillich's. Hartshorne may or may not be justified in asserting that God must be *both* being-itself and a being. This is not the point of citing him. In this context, I only wish to call attention to Tillich's failure to take serious account of counterarguments to his assertion that the truly ultimate cannot be a specific center of consciousness and power, rather, that it can only be being-itself.

> Consider . . . Tillich's denial that God is *a* being. This is argued for by taking the disjunction, "being itself or *a* being," as exclusive. But on what ground? [This is the key question; Tillich is systematically elusive on matters of this kind.] Can being-itself in no fashion constitute *a* being? Suppose the Berkeleyan formula, "to be is to be perceived," is in some sense true with reference to God as the universal perceiver. Then the content of the divine perceiver is *a* being. (As self-conscious, it will perceive itself.) Possible being is what God might perceive, actual being (including his own) is what he does perceive. Thus his perceiving [that is the perceiving of *this* being] is reality as such [that is, being-itself].[141]

4   Tillich admits that we cannot help thinking of being-itself in the subject-object relation because anything we think about thereby becomes the object of our thought (see p. 333). Yet he insists that Thomists and other theists not only make God an object of thought but that they make God into a specific entity, a being alongside other beings, and he claims that this involves limiting God. Thomists and other theists admit that they think of God as a center of consciousness and power, but they insist that this does not limit him in the way that particular beings are limited. They have, for example, insisted that God is both everywhere and nowhere. As one of the great Rabbis put it: "Where can I find You? And where can I not find you?" Throughout the course of Western history, theists have advanced detailed arguments to show that God is not limited. One would think that Tillich, who was thoroughly familiar with this history, would use equally detailed arguments to refute them, but he fails to do so.

5   Tillich's presuppositional approach to being-itself depends on the metaphysical shock involved in the question "Why is there something rather than nothing?" He insists that this question cannot be answered in terms of any individual entity or object. It can only be answered in terms of being-itself. It is at this point that his presuppositional approach most strongly resembles the cosmological argument from contingent to necessary being (see p. 327). He claims that the reason that no individual object, not even the greatest galaxy, can account for there being something rather than nothing, is that every individual object is contingent. Tillich agrees with the Thomists and other cosmologists on the point that contingent beings individually and as a total class cannot

account for their own existence. He does not offer fresh arguments for this position. He merely regards specificity as the mark of limitation, that is, of finitude, and he regards it as self-evident that the truly ultimate cannot be finite. Therefore, anyone who finds the metaphysical use of contingency unpersuasive when it is set in the context of the cosmological argument, is not likely to be more impressed with it in the context of Tillich's presuppositional approach to being-itself.

6 Given Tillich's immersion in the history of philosophy and theology, his failure to argue issues relating to the God of theistic theologians needs some explaining. In what follows, I offer my explanation.

We have seen that one of Tillich's main ways of testing for false ultimates is that they lead to existential disappointment of the kind that leads a Communist to break with the party (see p. 317). Tillich insists that the God of theism is a legitimate symbol, but that it cannot be regarded as the ultimate. It follows that Tillich thinks that this God, taken as the ultimate, will lead to existential disappointment. He never said so in so many words, but I think that the clue to his attitude is his own disappointment with this God. In his case, the disappointment was intellectual. He could not defend the God of theism philosophically against the criticisms of Kant and others. He could not defend it culturally against Freudians, Marxists, and other critics. He therefore accepted their criticisms and rejected this God. He communicated his rejection in terms of a shorthand that everyone who is familiar with anti-theistic arguments would recognize and that everyone who agreed with the anti-theistic position would gladly accept. This relieved him of the burden of arguing these points, but it also makes his own anti-theistic case one which is long on assertiveness and short on argument. It is not likely to impress Thomists or other metaphysically sophisticated theologians.

RELIGIOUS SYMBOLS

Tillich's view of religious symbols has been criticized severely by analytic philosophers.[142] The gist of the criticism is easily conveyed. They insist that the symbolic use of language has many functions. A figurative expression like "The sea is angry" arouses certain emotions. If it is also intended to be informative, analysts insist that it be translatable into literal language such as "The swells in the sea are more than ten feet high."

Analysts apply this pattern to religious language. Naturally, they concede the fact that the symbolic language of religions has many fuctions.[143] One of them is to arouse our emotions. If this is all that theologians intend by their symbolic use of language, then analysts would have no quarrel with the proposal that all language about God is symbolic. Referring to God as "eternal" would be for the purpose of providing emotional assurance against the fear of change (or other fears). Yet analysts insist that if symbolic language about God is intended to tell us something about reality or being-itself, then this language should be translatable into literal terms. Since it is obvious that Tillich does not think that this kind of translating is possible, they would regard his talk of being-itself as cognitively meaningless. The problem with this sort of criticism is that the analysts give the impression that they are using sophisticated philosophical techniques to expose flaws that will devastate Tillich. He, presumably, is unaware of them. Yet Tillich is not only aware of the extent to which his use of religious symbols departs from the standard model of symbolic language, he insists on it. If a religious symbol points, ultimately, to a specifiable entity like the cross, or to a specifiable concept, even as lofty a one as the God of the theologians, the religious symbol is idolatrous. It is the mark of a genuine religious symbol to point to being-itself which is beyond all characterization and specification.

Tillich's scheme is, therefore, psychologically strenuous, almost as much so as Kierkegaard's. He runs *against* the common sense view that either there is a God who is a specific ultimate—in which case one should be willing to love him with all one's heart, with all one's soul, and with all one's might—or there is no such ultimate, and this attitude of unreserved love is always inappropriate. Every individual should then resolve that he will never love anything whatever in this way.

As we have seen, Tillich regards human beings as animals with concerns (see p. 311). We inevitably care about a great many things, and we ought to be willing to put ourselves on the line for the most important ones. A professor who is an ardent believer in civil liberties was under fire during the McCarthy era. He told me that many of his liberal friends, who had often assured him of their devotion to this cause, were craven when the going got rough. They would see him coming about a block away and hurriedly cross the street. They were afraid that if they met, he might ask them to sign a petition or to do something else that might get them in trouble. Tillich would not admire these cowards and neither would anyone else. To be authentically human we must be willing to do more than mouth expressions of concern, we must be prepared to sacrifice for them.

Tillich thinks that we must not only have concerns for which we are prepared to take risks, but that we must integrate our lives around one ultimate concern. In other words, he claims that it is authentically human to love something with all your heart, with all your soul, and with all your might. It is obvious that he thinks that this attitude ought to be directed toward that which is truly ultimate. Since being-itself is truly ultimate, it would seem that we should love being-itself in this unreserved way. Yet, as already noted, Tillich does not think that being-itself can be loved at all because it is not a specific reality upon which human beings can focus. Instead, it performs the important function of serving as a brake on our tendency to idolatry by telling us how we ought to relate to the ultimate concerns we actually have. We must recognize them as symbols of ultimacy rather than treating them idolatrously, which means taking them as the ultimate.

Tillich is advocating a policy of faith without fanaticism. If it were widely adopted, it would not eliminate conflict, but it would humanize it. Think of recent wars in which the Israeli takes the star of David as his symbol of ultimacy and the Egyptian does the same with his flag. Provided that they realize that their flags are limited symbols of ultimacy, they will be able to acknowledge one another's integrity even in the bitterness of conflict. They will recognize idealism and self-sacrifice in the other who is temporarily the enemy, an attitude which makes healing possible after the fighting is over. In this respect, Tillich's view of being-itself is not devoid of consequences, even though his insights might be expressed in other terms, such as the tragic view of life.

Being-itself has another function in Tillich's system; it is a source of hope. Any specific symbol may ultimately fail its adherents (see p. 317). However, Tillich claims that ". . . it is not a failure in . . . the unconditioned itself. A God [the symbol of ultimacy] disappears; divinity [being-itself] remains."[144] In other words, because reality is an inexhaustible source of fresh and creative symbols we should never despair even if our nation, our religion, or some other symbols fail us.

To summarize: Tillich's scheme is strenuous because it demands an unreserved response in terms of commitment and action but not in terms of belief. To be authentically human we must commit ourselves to a specific symbol of ultimacy, like the cross, to the point of being willing to die for it. Yet Tillich also thinks that to be authentically human we must qualify our belief in its ultimacy by acknowledging the relative character of all specific symbols of ultimacy. It is a demanding program.

EXPERIENTIAL VERIFICATION

We have seen that the test of whether religious symbols, which are the expressions of our ultimate concern, are genuine or idolatrous is a matter of experiential verification. We organize our lives around them. If the results for individuals and communities are creative, they are genuinely religious; if the results are destructive, the symbols are idolatrous. However, judgments as to the effect of a religious symbol on individuals and communities are, as we have seen, highly subjective (see pp. 360ff.).

Tillich seems to burn the candle at both ends. He pays homage to the legitimacy of the analysts' concern for verification. Yet his view of verification involves radical subjectivity, which is precisely what the positivists, in designing the test of verification, were trying to avoid.[145]

Tillich's answer to this charge has already been given (see p. 359). Experiential verification (which is based on existential experiences) is, admittedly, not as tight as experimental verification (which is based on observations). Yet it is all we can have for the most important issues in life.

A BOMBASTIC REDESCRIPTION OF HUMAN EXPERIENCE

Tillich is not to be caught in the usual nets laid out by contemporary empiricists because the meshes are too large. Yet one of the empiricists, Paul Edwards, having advanced some obvious criticisms of Tillich's view of symbols, offers an argument that is more telling.[146] Edwards introduces an analysis of what he calls "the bombastic redescription of empirical facts."[147] His first example concerns well known facts about Sigmund Freud. Edwards presents the straightforward empirical statement that "Freud was born in 1856 and died in 1939." He then presents an ontological restatement of these simple facts, which he characterizes as bombastic. "In 1856 Freud migrated from nonbeing to being and then in 1939 he returned from being to nonbeing." Edwards tries to skewer the ontologist on the horns of the following dilemma:

1 The second statement is *nothing more* than a restatement of the first. In that case it is factually meaningful and even true, but the language of the second statement is terribly inflated if that is all it means.
2 The second statement expresses insights into the relation between being and nonbeing which go far beyond the mere statement of fact about the dates of Freud's birth and death. In that case, the ontologist is obliged to state just what this "extra" of meaning might be, and according to Edwards, his efforts fail dismally.

Having sharpened his knife with this clever example, Edwards then applies his analysis to Tillich's thought. He provides several illustrations. I will reproduce one.[148] It begins with a straightforward statement of what Edwards takes Tillich to be saying: "Selfishness and other unadmirable motives are involved in even the best human actions." Edwards quotes

Tillich's ontological statement of the same point (see p. 366): "Even in what he considers his best deed nonbeing is present and prevents it from being perfect. . . . Nonbeing is mixed with being in his moral self-affirmation as it is in his spiritual and ontic self-affirmation."[149] Edwards then confronts Tillich with the dilemma that has already been worked out. He must either admit that his ontological language amounts to nothing more than the statement of fact about unadmirable motives being involved in even the best human actions, or he must show the extra meaning that is involved in the ontological statement. Needless to say, Edwards thinks that Tillich utterly fails to come up with an adequate reply to this second challenge.

The exposition of Tillich that preceded this critical discussion provides ample grounds for seeing how tough Edwards' challenge is, even if his own statement of it is somewhat heavy-handed. In the first instance, if Tillich is bombastically restating something, it is not a "bombastic redescription of empirical facts." Tillich insists over and over again that what he deals with are not empirical facts but the presuppositions of being and truth which make it possible to experience empirical facts. Yet, if the criticism is modified to the claim that Tillich presents a "bombastic redescription of human experience" it is a hard one to shake.[150] Tillich's being-itself is utterly devoid of content. Tillich claims that it is the presupposition of things as they are. That may well be, but it is a presupposition that seems to add nothing to our total experience beyond the awareness that in important aspects of experience we confront regulative ideals. When we, for example, argue about complicated scientific theories, we argue as though there were, somehow, a chance of achieving eternal truths, even though we know that all scientific work is only provisional, that is, it is subject to revision on the basis of further evidence. When we argue about moral concerns, we argue as though there were some position that is absolutely right, even though we realize that no such position can be formulated. When we argue about religious matters, we argue as though it were possible to express a revelation that is the final expression of being-itself, final in the sense of being valid for all times and places, even though we know that this ideal is never, in principle, to be attained.

Tillich's God cannot, therefore, be criticized along the lines that are generally directed at the God of philosophical theologians, but only because he has emptied his God of metaphysical as well as of theistic content. Being-itself, Tillich's metaphysical ultimate, does not, on his account, seem to have independent reality. When Tillich talks in terms of the threat of nonbeing in our personal lives, we can make sense of what he says even if we disagree with his way of saying it. We can understand what he means by characterizing nonbeing as the threat of a "no" in situations where we are desperately seeking a "yes." When, however, Tillich cosmicizes this pattern and speaks of being-itself or of the power of being as resisting nonbeing, his analysis loses all persuasiveness. Despite his best intentions he suggests that nonbeing is a reality that is somehow there to be resisted. Sidney Hook has summed up the case against Tillich's ontology in the following terms:

> Since we can know God [that is, being-itself] only through religious symbols, and since the validity and truth of these symbols can in no way be judged by any ontological fact [independent of human beings] but only by human experience and its needs, why do we require the ontological reference at all?[151]

Tillich's God is empty of all theistic content because he is not an independent source of consciousness, power, and love. Tillich's God also seems empty of metaphysical content. It appears then, that Tillich's radical approach to transcendence is confined to language. God's reality, that is, being-itself, is beyond characterization by words. Yet Tillich seems to have eliminated the possibility of regarding God as a transcendent reality on the level of being. In order to appreciate what I mean by transcendence with regard to being, consider the following theistic claim: God minus the world equals God; the world minus God equals nothing.[152] It restates the theistic view that God created the world out of nothing and that if the world ceased to exist his infinite reality would remain.

Tillich refers to being-itself as infinite, and it would seem to follow that if the world ceased to exist, being-itself (like the theistic God) would remain. However, Tillich never spells out any reason for thinking that being-itself has a reality that is independent of the reality of the infinite number of contingent beings in the universe. Aside from some references to the Platonic tradition in philosophy and to the Augustinian tradition in theology he does not argue for the kind of metaphysical realism that would be required to make this sort of claim good. Again and again when he deals with reality as such, he seems to refer only to the totality of beings, but he focuses on human beings.

Tillich claims that all beings—both persons and things—can serve as symbols that are transparent to being-itself (see p. 349). In this case *I* propose to emphasize the connection to human being by means of the following analysis. Transparent is another of Tillich's metaphorical terms. A window is transparent; we can see a tree through it without losing our sense of the reality of the glass. Obviously, one side of the metaphor of transparence fits neatly. When a specific being becomes transparent to being-itself, we do not cease to be aware of it as an individual thing. The other side does not fit, since being-itself is not an observable reality that can be seen. What Tillich suggests is that specific beings—without ceasing to be themselves—can communicate what Tillich calls metaphysical shock, the shock of nonbeing (see p. 326). He fails to argue that this human attitude could not be manifested unless being-itself were real and independent of the reality of contingent beings. Yet, the awareness that one might not have existed and of the inevitability of one's own death is enough to account for the experience of Tillich's metaphysical shock. It need not be transparent to the metaphysical reality of being-itself.

Tillich's pattern of translating his language regarding the transcendence of God or of being-itself into language about human beings is also evident in the following discussion where Tillich rejects a spatial view of the transcendence of God:

> And if we ask about the meaning of the ever repeated assertion that God is both *in* and *above* the world and question the use of the spatial metaphors "in" and "above," we have asked the ontological question. If we then answer that the relation of God and the world is not spatial but must be expressed in terms of creative freedom, an ontological answer is given, but an answer in terms of freedom. The freedom of the creature to act against its essential unity with God [which in Tillich's scheme means against its own essential nature as human being] makes God transcendent to the world.[153]

He claims that human being is the key to being as such, but the content he provides for being resisting non-being is confined to human being, to anxiety, and to the responses to it on the part of finitely free human beings. Therefore, Tillich's use of being-itself does not provide a transcendent sense of the being of God. Transcendence, in his system, boils down to the fact that we cannot speak of ultimacy in literal terms.

Given Tillich's view of ultimacy, which is, on his own account, atheistic, it seems strange that he should be willing to use the word God to symbolize his ultimate concern. After all, this word seems to be inextricably associated with the doctrines of theism. Of course, he claims that secular statements lack the power to change human beings. Therefore, the symbol of God is necessary to provide saving power, the power that creatively integrates individuals and communities (see pp. 360ff.). To this the sceptic can reply that even if, in general, it is true that the symbol of God has saving power this would not apply to Tillich's use. Anyone who appropriates religious language from a Tillichian perspective will never again experience the power of religious language in a pre-Tillichian way. He will have seen through its mythological and symbolic character just as someone who undergoes psychoanalysis will have seen through his rationalizations.[154] A person, for example, who has a writing block may rationalize it away by thinking of "important" errands—like picking up a suit at the cleaners—each time he sits down to write. As long as he really believes in the importance of the various dodges he thinks up, he will successfully mask the writing block. Once he has seen through the rationalizations, he will have to probe more deeply into his unconscious motivations in an effort to come up with the real reasons for his anxiety about writing because the rationalizations will have lost their effectiveness. Similarly, a Christian who grasps the principles underlying Tillich's translation of Christian language into ontological and existential terms may still go to church, read the Bible, and pray. Yet it is doubtful that he will ever again think that there is an ear that hears his prayers, and it is doubtful that the language of the Christian faith would have the power to stir his emotions and affect his decisions in the old familiar ways.

I can summarize my reactions to Tillich's complex, subtle and labyrinthine approach to God by recalling a dialogue from E. M. Forster's *A Passage to India.* Two missionaries, the older and more conservative Mr. Graysford and younger Mr. Sorley, are discussing the problem of heaven. They think it would be disgraceful if heaven mirrored the exclusivism of earth so that some human beings could never get in. Mr. Graysford is ready to let it go at that, but Mr. Sorley is more resolutely open-minded. The dialogue, as recounted from Forster's ironical perspective, runs as follows:

> In our Father's house are many mansions, they taught, and there alone will the incompatible multitudes of mankind be welcomed and soothed. Not one shall be turned away by the servants on that verandah, be he black or white, not one shall be kept standing who approaches with a loving heart. And why should the divine hospitality cease there? Consider, with all reverence, the monkeys. May there not be a mansion for the monkeys also? Old Mr. Graysford said No, but young Mr. Sorley, who was advanced, said Yes; he saw no reason why monkeys should not have their collateral share of bliss, and he had sympathetic discussions about them with his Hindu friends. And the jackals? Jackals were indeed less to Mr. Sorley's mind, but he admitted that the mercy of God, being infinite, may well embrace all mammals. And the wasps? He became uneasy during the descent to wasps, and was apt to change the conversation. And oranges, cactuses, crystals, and mud? And the bacteria inside Mr. Sorley? No, no this is going too far. We must exclude something from our gathering, or we shall be left with nothing.[155]

The application should be clear. Tillich manages to avoid most of the pitfalls of Christian thought, but he pays a high price for doing so. In the end, his world seems indistinguishable from the secular world just as Mr. Sorley's heaven would be indistinguishable from earth. If this is the case, there would seem to be little reason to talk Tillichese, for anything that he says in terms of Christian symbols could equally well be communicated in terms of the symbols of another faith, especially that of existentialistic humanism. It is not, therefore, altogether surprising that one of the movements most strongly influenced by Paul Tillich, a Christian thinker, called itself the "Death of God Theology."[156]

Epilogue

Conclusiveness Is Hard to Come By

My personal conviction regarding the problems of religious thought is that they are philosophically inconclusive. J. N. Findlay suggests that this may be true of all philosophical problems. ". . . there can be nothing really 'clinching' in philosophy: 'proofs' and 'disproofs' hold only for those who adopt certain premises, who are willing to follow certain rules of argument, and who use their terms in certain definite ways."[1]

Even among philosophers, like the analysts, who do, for the most part, adopt the same premises and rules of argument, agreement is hard to come by. When philosophers of different schools deal with a subject as complex as the philosophy of religion, it is especially difficult to resolve issues conclusively. I'd like to present a dialogue that explores this difficulty. It takes place between an existentialist believer (EB) and an empiricist sceptic (ES).

EB: The trouble with most excursions into religious thought is that both believers and sceptics are still haunted by the medieval emphasis on proofs. Therefore, they look for arguments that will conclusively prove or disprove the existence of God. Kierkegaard helped us to see that religious thought is limited in power: "In all eternity," he wrote, "it is impossible for me to compel a person to accept an opinion, a conviction, a belief. But one thing I can do, I can compel him to take notice."[2] He compelled us to take notice by showing that faith involves affirmation in spite of the fact that the beliefs involved are radically implausible, even absurd. To attempt to base faith on the kind of demonstrations that are possible in mathematics, or on the kind of hard empirical data that scientists seek, is to debase it. The more sure-fire your beliefs, the less they involve the risk that is associated with genuine faith. Furthermore, authentic human beings don't try to base their lives on sure things, they are prepared to make leaps of decision that go against the odds.

ES: The existentialist ploy is the greatest one yet. You stress the point that faith is directed to the implausible in such a way that the sceptic cannot win the argument. It's a "heads I win, tails, you lose" strategy. If the Christian scores points against the nonbeliever, you naturally want them to count. But if the sceptic scores points against the Christian, you claim that this supports the point that Christianity, being utterly implausible, shouldn't be expected to come off well in arguments that are conducted from the detached or objective perspective.

EB: This isn't a clever strategy devised by existentialists in an effort to make Christian faith impervious to criticisms. Existentialists have just reemphasized the nature of Christian faith which is not, and has never been, demonstrably true, probable, or even plausible. Arguments about the truth of the faith don't settle the burning issues of the nature and destiny of man, they just determine who the best debators happen to be. In one period the sceptics may come off better, and in another, believers have the edge. Ultimately, though, believers don't base their faith on arguments, but on the grace of God which comes through to them in religious experience.

ES: What bothers me is that religious thinkers pretend to be interested in serious philosophical discussion, but they don't take it seriously. They use the form and technical terms of philosophy but they ignore its spirit, because they are unwilling to change their minds as a result of it. They have their results in advance in the form of the Nicene Creed, the Westminister Confession, or what have you. They then use philosophical terms in the effort to either back up their creeds or, failing that, in an effort to show that reason cannot undermine them. Come what may, religious thinkers will emerge believing the same creed they believed in at the start of the argument—even if they have to completely change its meaning.

It was Ian Crombie, a believer, who really let the cat out of the bag when he wrote that we religious thinkers ". . . deceive ourselves by a sort of conjuring trick, oscillating backwards and forwards between a literal interpretation of what we say when we say it, and a scornful rejection of such anthropomorphism when anybody challenges us."[3] When they think they can get away with it theologians defend the anthropomorphism of a God who literally hears prayer. When they don't, they use dodges like Tillich's being-itself, which is supposed to be what God symbolizes, but which has nothing to do with personal God of either ordinary believers or sophisticated theologians. Again, we have Rudolf Bultmann claiming to believe in the resurrection as a crucial part of God's decisive act in Christ but who doesn't think it possible for a corpse to be restored to life, even to supernatural life. So we find that some of the most sophisticated religious thinkers recognize the force of sceptical arguments, but they cling to the traditional formulas by changing their meaning. In doing so, they do just what Jesus warned against; they put new wine into old skins that are stretched tight and that aren't going to hold the wine once it starts to age. That's why many students at Christian seminaries who studied Tillich wound up leaving the fold. His new interpretations of traditional Christian teachings couldn't be contained in the old dogmatic formulas.

EB: I don't know whose qualified to judge whether Tillich, Bultmann, and other sophisticated thinkers have gone too far in reinterpreting Christian teachings. I suppose that in Roman Catholicism the Pope can serve that function, but in recent years we've learned that even Roman Catholic interpretations are less cut and dried than they seemed. Anyway, people who are quite tolerant of many shifts in the meanings of words, are utterly intolerant when it comes to religion. Take the word "Democrat" as it is used in relation to the Democratic party. Its meaning has certainly changed since the days of Jefferson and Jackson, yet people who know this still call themselves Democrats. Furthermore, among the vast numbers of people who designate themselves as Democrats, the meaning of the term varies from that of a senator from Mississippi's definition to that of one from New York. Yet people who go along with developments of the meaning of the word "Democrat" and the diversity of interpretations involved in it, often insist that word Christian should be saddled with its most rigid, dogmatic and even superstitious formulations. And they damn any deviations from this easily rejected brand of Christianity.

ES: OK! I concede the point that authentic Christianity need not involve fundamentalism or other conservative versions of the faith. Yet I would still like to echo Antony Flew's falsification challenge and ask whether the word Christian is, in your mind, limitlessly expandable. In the face of strong criticisms can you simply keep modifying the meaning of such key terms as God, incarnation, resurrection, and the Christ? Is there no point at which you are prepared to say: "You've got me. Now I see that Christian claims cannot be made good, and I'm not going to play the modification game. I'm going to get off the line and admit that, in light of the decisive arguments that have been advanced against the faith, I can no longer call myself a Christian."

EB: It's sad to see you trotting out that old gambit so long after the demise of positivism. Neither the positivists nor their analytic successors ever came up with a viable version of verifiability, and you know it. The various versions of verification and falsification that actually eliminated theological statements, eliminated key scientific statements along with them. Confirmation kept the scientific statements in, but it allowed for the legitimacy of theological statements as well. So why should religious thinkers scramble desperately to meet this challenge?

ES: You can celebrate the demise of positivism if you want to, but it's a pretty cheap way out. Leaving aside positivism's fate, unless you can specify a cutoff point of some sort, that is, a point where you are prepared to admit that the show has folded, then you're not really claiming anything. Once Tillich has finished his job of translating Christian symbols into ontological language it seems that passionate atheists go along with what he says, so there's something the matter with Tillich's Christianity. It is so expansive that it embraces everything. All I'm asking you to do is to be un-Tillichian in the sense of specifying circumstances which would lead you and other believers to opt out of the Christian faith.

EB: Well if that's all you're after, it's easy. People opt out of faith all the time. Sometimes it's because of the suffering and death of someone they love, sometimes because they move into a new frame of reference and the prayers and other forms of religion dry up on them. They may experience the loss of faith when they become scientists, when they move to the city, or when they become intellectually sophisticated. My main point is that philosophical arguments—in isolation from total life experience—never change anyone's basic position on anything. Let me see if I can illustrate this point by turning the tables on sceptics.

The charge is that religious thinkers never give up. When the philosophical going gets rough they either modify the meanings of their key terms, or they leave them as they are and keep hoping that Godot will come along and provide them with refutations of the toughest arguments. The one thing they never do is to admit that the critics' arguments draw blood. My counter-scenario involves a sceptic reading Normal Malcolm's effort to revive the ontological argument. He'd read it with the conviction that Malcolm couldn't possibly be right because we all know that the argument is invalid; after all, Kant proved it more than one hundred and fifty years ago. Now suppose that as he reads along he's intrigued; Malcolm's line of reasoning seems to hold up. He tries like the devil to crack it, reads all the criticisms that have been written against it, but nothing works. In the end he's convinced that Malcolm's version of the ontological argument is valid. Would he then convert to Christianity? Not likely. Malcolm himself admits that the argument—even when it is accepted as valid—can be taken as an exercise in logic and that it can fail to touch a philosopher religiously. So the sceptic could lay it aside, frustrated at his failure to find a flaw in it, but convinced that there must be one. Then *he'd* wait for a philosophical Godot to come along and show the weaknesses in the argument. It should also be obvious that the more well-known the sceptic, the greater his stake. Sceptics like Walter Kaufmann and Kai Nielsen have a vested interest in their scepticism. It would be hard for them to climb down and admit that they'd been wrong all along, just as it would be hard for a theologian like Rudolpf Bultmann to abandon his Christian commitment.

ES: I'll admit that we all have a vested interest in positions that we've staked out and defended over a period of time. I'll also admit that philosophical arguments, in and of themselves, don't lead us to change our basic positions. These fundamental ways of looking at the world are products of our entire life experience and philosophical arguments are only a part of them. Even so, Christian faith runs so much against the grain of common sense and conflicts so badly with the best knowledge we harvest from science, that anyone who sticks with it is condemned to a lifetime of intellectual wriggling. I would think that someone who is as much concerned with personal authenticity as you claim to be would worry about this.

EB: What you derisively call "intellectual wriggling" I'll call "the Dance of Faith." I don't think either phrase takes us very far. I just want to make the point that one man's authentic risk of faith is another man's superstition. What a sceptic might regard as intellectual sobriety strikes a believer as being so up-tight that no genuine commitment is possible. Perhaps I can, all the same, suggest a point on which we can agree. In the Parable of the Talents in Matthew 25 Jesus tells of a man who goes abroad and puts three of his employees in charge of different amounts of money. He instructs them to use it wisely and then leaves for a year. When he comes home he calls them in for an accounting. The one who received the most, invested it and doubled it, so did the one who received the next largest amount. Their employer rewarded both of them. The one who had received the smallest amount had a different story to tell. He had "clutched" at the thought that in investing it, the money might be lost. So he'd buried it in the ground and returned it to his employer just as it was, no more and no less. The employer was furious, took it away, and distributed it among the other two. In this context, the application should be clear. The person who receives a religious upbringing, or who comes to faith through some other route, dare not bury it in the sand. He's got to meet the intellectual challenges that develop in this cultural situation. Doing so may erode his faith, and, taken along with other personal and cultural factors, it may even lead him to abandon it. Yet a failure to take this risk results in a fanaticism that can't face up to doubt. Authentic faith embraces doubt; it always involves affirmation in spite of the fact that objectively considered, the odds run against the truth of religious claims.

ES: I agree with the point that philosophical issues must be faced by the believer and that they must be taken seriously. I just hope *you* are serious about risking the loss of faith. Otherwise philosophical discussion becomes a kind of window dressing that guarantees the believer that at the end of the process he'll still be affirming the old-time religion, but in theological polysyllables.

EB: I'm very serious about risking the loss of faith, but you've already conceded the point that the basic orientations we have toward life are not changed because one or two facts jar us. Shifting from the Christian faith to a secular position, or the other way round, involves cumulative life experiences—feelings and decisions as well as thoughts. And thinking about the factors that enter into such a shift shows us that there is a tension between the ideals of faith and the ideals of science.

Scientists are supposed to be tough-minded about evidence. The scientist is supposed to be the severest critic of his own pet theories. Even if he's spent a lifetime on them, when contrary evidence turns up, he is, according to the ideal, supposed to drop them. For the scientist, holding to the truth of a hypothesis in the face of contrary evidence, is a temptation; it ought to be resisted. Now I admit that science isn't all that simple. Individual scientists fail to live up to the ideal; they cling to cherished hypotheses because they've got an emotional stake in them. I'll go even further and admit that in some cases this unscientific stubbornness may pay off; the evidence may, on further reflection, turn out to be compatible with the truth of the hypothesis. Yet the ideal of tough-mindedness is, nevertheless, crucial to scientific work. A scientist ought not to affirm the truth of a hypothesis "come what may"; he ought to sit loose to it.

When we turn to religious faith, we find that the ideal is in sharp contrast to that of science. The faithful individual ought to persist in believing in God even in the face of evidence that seems to deny God's existence or his goodness. In the Book of Job, when he has been stripped of his possessions and of his health, his wife urges him to curse God and die. He answers: "If we accept good from God shall we not accept evil?"

(Job 2:10). Job persists in his faith in God's justice in spite of the evidence. There are obviously, abuses of the ideal of "faith as persistence in trust and love." Some people lose faith as soon as someone they love dies, or in the face of other calamities such as having their life's savings wiped out by a flood. Yet the ideal of persisting in spite of the evidence remains integral to faith.

Ironically, it seems as though the ideal of science is a temptation for faith and the ideal of faith is a temptation for science. That is why discussions of the relation of religious belief and scientifically oriented scepticism so often degenerate into name calling. Believers brand sceptics as godless materialists whose attitudes erode the fabric of society and sceptics label the faithful as dogmatists whose adherence to outmoded beliefs impedes progress.

You and I, at least, ought to be able to agree on one point. Both attitudes—tough-mindedness and faith—are extremely important to authentic living. It is impossible to live at either pole; we can't change our basic life attitudes in the face of each item of experience that doesn't fit into the most recent version of our basic view of the world. On the other hand, clinging to beliefs without regard for evidence is not faith but fanaticism. Reading books and listening to experts can help us to sharpen our sense of what's involved in these basic postures toward life, but no book can answer the big questions about life's purposes and about the nature of the universe. There are no successful "how to" manuals on the matter of authentic living. Each individual has to put it all together with whatever integrity he can muster.

Notes

INTRODUCTION

1 This definition is a variation on the one presented by John Hick, "Editor's Introduction," *The Existence of God,* Macmillan, New York, 1964, pp. 2f.

2 The classical definition of the God of theism presented here has been held by most religious thinkers as well as (implicitly) by ordinary believers. It has, however, come in for sharp criticisms from Christian thinkers as well as from sceptics. The most trenchant contemporary critic is Charles Hartshorne; see especially *The Divine Relativity*, Yale, New Haven, 1951. In the introductory sections of *Philosophers Speak of God*, University of Chicago Press, Chicago, 1953, which he edited with W. L. Reese, Hartshorne provides details of his differences with Christian thinkers who are oriented to what he calls "classical theism," that is, to the theism oriented to the definition I have provided. Hartshorne is primarily concerned to challenge the classical notion of the utter changelessness of God. Other thinkers have been concerned to challenge the

element of omnipotence in the classical definition and an excellent discussion is provided by John Stuart Mill in his *Theism*, Liberal Arts Press, New York, 1957, part Two, pp. 33ff.

PART ONE

1   Barry Gross, *Analytic Philosophy*, Pegasus, New York, 1970, is the best introduction to this broad movement. He sets the logical positivists in the larger context of analytic philosophy and notes that there were other positivistic movements in the history of philosophy. John Passmore, *A Hundred Years of Philosophy*, Basic Books, New York, 1966, is an excellent introduction because it also deals with the other philosophies with which the analysts were interacting. J. O. Urmson, *Philosophical Analysis: Its Development between the Two World Wars*, Clarendon Press, Oxford, 1956, is a more technical study. Finally, A. J. Ayer, et al., *The Revolution in Philosophy*, Macmillan, London, 1956, is a collection of essays that are geared to communicating the revolutionary ferment of the movement; they were originally radio broadcasts and are, for the most part, quite clear.

2   Alfred J. Ayer, *Language, Truth and Logic*, 2d ed., Gollancz, London, 1946, p. 115.

3   Walter T. Stace, "Metaphysics and Meaning," in P. Edwards and A. Pap (eds.), *A Modern Introduction to Philosophy* (hereafter cited as *Modern Introduction*), 2d ed., Free Press, New York, 1965, p. 694.

4   Elmer Sprague, *What Is Philosophy?* Oxford, New York, 1961, p. 29.

5   Immanuel Kant, *Prolegomena to Any Future Metaphysics*, Paul Carus, ed., Open Court, Chicago, 1949, p. 2.

6   This presentation will ignore an important element of the positivists' program, namely, the effort to construct an ideal language that would exclude metaphysical, theological, and other types of statements that do not conform to the positivists' standards. This effort is primarily associated with the work of Rudolf Carnap, see especially *The Logical Syntax of Language*, Routledge, London, 1937. For a useful introduction to Carnap's work on this issue, see Barry Gross, *Analytic Philosophy*, pp. 132ff.

7   David Rynin correlates declarative and nondeclarative statements in "Cognitive Meaning and Cognitive Use," *Inquiry*, 9: 121f, 1966.

8   Hans Reichenbach, *The Rise of Scientific Philosophy,* University of California Press, Berkeley, 1951, p. 308; Fredrick C. Copleston, S.J., *Contemporary Philosophy*, Newman Press, Westminster, Md., 1956, pp. 26–33.

9   George Mavrodes, "God and Verification," in M. L. Diamond and T. V. Litzenburg (eds.), *The Logic of God: Theology and Verification*, Bobbs-Merrill, Indianapolis, 1974, section 6.

10 Charles L. Stevenson, *Ethics and Language*, Yale, New Haven, 1944, chap. 1.

11 Hans Reichenbach, *Rise of Scientific Philosophy*, p. 34.

12 For a psychological explanation, see Kai Nielsen, *Reason and Practice*, p. 417.

13 Donald Evans, "Scientific and Religious Assertions," in Ian G. Barbour (ed.), *Science and Religion*, Harper & Row, New York, 1968, pp. 118ff. This essay will appear in Diamond and Litzenburg (eds.), *The Logic of God*, section 9.

14 Barry Gross, *Analytic Philosophy*, p. 107.

15 For an extended treatment of this issue, see A. C. Ewing, "Meaninglessness," in Edwards and Pap (eds.), *Modern Introduction*, pp. 705ff.

16 Carl G. Hempel, "The Empiricist Criterion of Meaning," in A. J. Ayer (ed.), *Logical Positivism*, Free Press, Glencoe, Ill., 1959, p. 124.

17 A. J. Ayer, "Demonstration of the Impossibility of Metaphysics," in Edwards and Pap (eds.), *Modern Introduction*, p. 692; see also Michael Tooley, "Theological Statements and the Question of an Empiricist Criterion of Cognitive Significance," in Diamond and Litzenburg (eds.), *The Logic of God*, section 10.

18 My presentation is heavily indebted to Carl G. Hempel, "The Empiricist Criterion of Meaning," in A. J. Ayer (ed.), *Logical Positivism*, pp. 108–129. As a positivist, Hempel earnestly hoped that these difficulties could be overcome, but he exposed them with rigor and clarity.

19 Alfred J. Ayer, *Language, Truth and Logic*, p. 36.

20 Karl Popper, *The Logic of Scientific Discovery*, Hutchinson, London, 1959, see especially pp. 32–42, 64–72, 78–92. The English version of the book is a revision of the German, *Logic der Forschuung*, Vienna, 1935.

21 Carl G. Hempel, *Aspects of Scientific Explanation*, Free Press, New York, 1965, p. 105.

22 Ibid., section I, 1; also, Israel Scheffler, *The Anatomy of Inquiry*, Knopf, New York, 1963, part III.

23 Donald Evans, "Scientific and Religious Assertions," in Barbour, *Science and Religion*, pp. 118ff.

24 Willard V. Quine, *From a Logical Point of View*, Harper & Row, New York, 1963, pp. 20ff, 44ff.

25 Important essays that deal with this issue are: H. P. Grice and P. F. Strawson, "In Defense of a Dogma," in L. W. Sumner and J. Woods (eds.), *Necessary Truth*, Random House, New York, 1969, pp. 145–159; Hilary Putnam, "The Analytic and the Synthetic," in H. Feigl and G. Maxwell (eds.), *Minnesota Studies in the Philosophy of Science*, vol. 3, University of Minnesota Press, Minneapolis, 1962, pp. 358–397. Gilbert Harmon, "Quine on Meaning and Existence," part I, *The Review of Metaphysics*, 21: 124–151, 1967.

26 Barry Gross, *Analytic Philosophy*, p. 113.

27 Gilbert Ryle, "Heterologicality," in M. MacDonald (ed.), *Philosophy and Analysis*, Basil Blackwell, Oxford, 1954, p. 51.

28 Morton White, *Toward Reunion in Philosophy*, Atheneum, New York, 1963, p. 290.

29 Ludwig Wittgenstein, *Tractatus Logico-Philosophicus*, 2d ed., Routledge,

London, 1961; *Philosophical Investigations* (hereafter cited as *Investigations*), 3d ed., Macmillan, New York, 1969.

30 Wittgenstein, *Investigations*, p. 20. The general discussion of "meaning as use" runs from pp. 10–31.

31 For discussions of this point, see Dallas M. High, *Language, Persons and Belief*, Oxford, New York, 1967, pp. 134f; Ronald Hepburn, "From World to God," in B. Mitchell (ed.), *Philosophy of Religion*, Oxford, London, 1971, pp. 168f, and for an effort to answer this charge, see D. Z. Phillips, "Religious Beliefs and Language Games," in B. Mitchell (ed.), *Philosophy of Religion*, pp. 121–142.

32 Ludwig Wittgenstein, *Lectures and Conversations on Aesthetics, Psychology and Religious Belief*, Basil Blackwell, Oxford, 1966, were published posthumously; pages 53–72 deal with religious belief.

33 Among thinkers on religion who have been influenced by Ludwig Wittgenstein are: John Wisdom, "Gods," *Philosophy and Psychoanalysis* (hereafter cited as *Philosophy*), Basil Blackwell, Oxford, 1953, pp. 149–168; see also his *Paradox and Discovery*, Basil Blackwell, Oxford, 1965, especially "The Logic of 'God,'" pp. 1–22; Dallas M. High, *Language, Persons and Beliefs*; Paul L. Holmer, "Wittgenstein and Theology," in Dallas M. High (ed.), *New Essays on Religious Language*, Oxford, New York, 1969, pp. 25–35; and Paul L. Holmer, "The Nature of Religious Propositions," in Ronald E. Santoni (ed.), *Religious Language and the Problem of Religious Knowledge*, Indiana University Press, Bloomington, 1968, pp. 233–247; W. D. Hudson, *Ludwig Wittgenstein, The Bearing of His Philosophy on Religious Belief*, John Knox Press, Richmond, Va., 1968; Norman Malcolm, "Is It a Religious Belief That God Exists?" John Hick (ed.), *Faith and the Philosophers*, St. Martin's, New York, 1964, pp. 103–110; D. Z. Phillips, *Faith and Philosophical Inquiry*, Routledge, London, 1970; James Richmond, *Theology and Metaphysics*, SCM Press, London, 1970; Paul van Buren, *The Edges of Language*, Macmillan, New York, 1972; Peter Winch, *The Idea of a Social Science*, Routledge, London, 1958. In the note following there is a reference to a collection of essays by the "Metaphysicals," an Oxford-based group of religious thinkers who were influenced by Wittgenstein. Kai Nielsen in "Wittgensteinian Fideism," *Philosophy*, **63**: 191–209, 1967, subjects the religiously oriented Wittgensteinians to searching criticisms. W. D. Hudson replies in "On Two Points Against Wittgensteinian Fideism," *Philosophy*, **63**: 269–273, 1968, to which Nielsen replies in "Wittgensteinian Fideism: A Reply to Hudson," *Philosophy*, **64**: 63–65, 1969.

34 Basil Mitchell, "Editor's Introduction," in *Faith and Logic*, George Allen and Unwin, London, 1957, p. 5.

35 There are many strands of analytic philosophy and the religious thinkers who write in that vein reflect them. What follows is only a selection. (1) Thinkers oriented to *logic* who often write with formal notation: Joseph Bochenski, O.P., *The Logic of Religion*, New York University Press, New York, 1965; George I. Mavrodes, *Belief in God*, Random House, New York, 1970; Alvin Plantinga, *God and Other Minds*, Cornell, Ithaca, N.Y., 1967; James F. Ross,

Introduction to the Philosophy of Religion, Macmillan, London, 1969; *Philosophical Theology*, Bobbs-Merrill, Indianapolis, 1969. (2) Thinkers oriented to *ordinary Language* (see also note 33 above for thinkers influenced by Wittgenstein): Donald D. Evans, *The Logic of Self-Involvement*, SCM Press, London, 1963; Fredrick Ferré, *Language, Logic and God*, Harper & Row, New York, 1969, and his very comprehensive *Basic Modern Philosophy of Religion*, Scribner, New York, 1967; Ian Ramsey, *Religious Language*, SCM Press, London, 1957; Ninian Smart, *Reasons and Faiths*, Humanities, New York, 1958, and *The Philosophy of Religion*, Random House, 1970. (3) Analytically sophisticated thinkers who work in a *Thomistic* vein: Peter Geach, *God and the Soul*, Schocken, New York, 1969; Anthony Kenny, *The Five Ways*, Schocken, New York, 1969; Victor Preller, *Divine Science and the Science of God*, Princeton, Princeton, N.J., 1966. (4) *Positivistic* religious thinkers: John Hick, *Faith and Knowledge*, 2d ed., Cornell, Ithaca, N.Y., 1966; Paul van Buren, *The Secular Meaning of the Gospel*, SCM Press, London, 1963 (note van Buren's shift to a Wittgensteinian position in *The Edges of Language*, cited in note 33 above); William Zuurdeeg, *An Analytical Philosophy of Religion*, Abingdon, Nashville, Tenn., 1958.

36   John Wisdom, *Other Minds*, Basil Blackwell, Oxford, 1952, p. 11.
37   Wisdom, *Philosophy*, pp. 154f.
38   Antony Flew, "Theology and Falsification," in A. Flew and A. MacIntyre (eds.), *New Essays in Philosophical Theology* (hereafter cited as *New Essays*), Macmillan, New York, 1955, pp. 96f. See also James Richmond, *Theology and Metaphysics*, pp. 63ff.
39   For a study that uses legal arguments and other arguments drawn from life rather than mathematical demonstrations as the model for logic, see Stephen Toulmin, *The Uses of Argument*, Cambridge, London, 1958.
40   This connection underlies Kai Nielsen's attack on what he calls "Wittgensteinian Fideism" which is dealt with in note 33 above; see Stanley Cavell, "Existentialism and Analytical Philosophy," *Daedalus*, vol. 93 (1964), pp. 946–974, for a perceptive essay that is largely devoted to a comparison of Wittgenstein and Kierkegaard.
41   Wisdom, *Philosophy*, pp. 154, 157ff.
42   Ibid., p. 153.
43   Ibid., p. 154.
44   Ibid., p. 159.
45   Ibid., pp. 160f.
46   Antony Flew, R. M. Hare, and Basil Mitchell, "Theology and Falsification," in A. Flew and A. MacIntyre (eds.), *New Essays*, pp. 96–108. It is also reprinted along with a retrospective essay by Antony Flew on two decades of controversy that it provoked in Diamond and Litzenburg, *The Logic of God*, section 7. This section also includes responses to Flew's retrospective essay by T. V. Litzenburg and Schubert Ogden.
47   A useful introduction to contemporary treatments of the problem of evil is Nelson Pike (ed.), *God and Evil*, Prentice-Hall, Englewood Cliffs, N.J., 1964, and see Alvin Plantinga, *God and Other Minds*, chaps. 5, 6. An important

contribution to the problem that sets it in the framework of the history of Christian thought is John Hick, *Evil and the God of Love*, Harper & Row, New York, 1966.

48 Antony Flew, "Theology and Falsification," in Flew and MacIntyre, *New Essays*, pp. 98f.

49 Ibid., p. 97.

50 Fredrick Waismann, "Language Strata," in A. Flew (ed.), *Language and Logic*, 2d ser., Basil Blackwell, Oxford, 1953, pp. 11–31.

51 R. M. Hare, "Theology and Falsification," in Flew and MacIntyre, *New Essays*, pp. 100f.

52 John F. Miller III, deals with this point at length in "Science and Religion: Their Logical Similarity," in Diamond and Litzenburg, *The Logic of God*, section 9. See also Alastair McKinnon, *Falsification and Belief*, Mouton, The Hague, 1970. The whole of this short book (106 pp.) is relevant to this point. Donald Evans, "Scientific and Religious Assertions," in I. Barbour (ed.), *Science and Religion*, pp. 101–132, is an important effort to discriminate the logic of the two.

53 Basil Mitchell, "Theology and Falsification," in Flew and MacIntyre, *New Essays*, pp. 103ff.

54 Antony Flew claims that Mitchell never intended to say that theological statements cannot be conclusively falsified; see " 'Theology and Falsification' in Retrospect," in Diamond and Litzenburg, *The Logic of God*, 7:3. However, many readers of the initial symposium on "Theology and Falsification" took Mitchell to be denying that theological statements could be conclusively falsified; Flew cites a number of them; see Howard R. Burkle, "Counting Against and Counting Decisively Against," *The Journal of Religion*, 64: 223–229, 1964.

55 I am indebted to Kenneth Nelson for bringing this point to my attention in conversation.

56 Antony Flew, "Theology and Falsification," in Flew and MacIntyre, *New Essays*, p. 99.

57 Ibid., p. 106.

58 Ibid., p. 107.

59 Gilbert Ryle, "Final Discussion," in D. F. Pears (ed.), *The Nature of Metaphysics*, Macmillan, London, 1957, p. 160; see also pp. 144f.

60 A. J. Ayer and F. C. Copleston, "Logical Positivism—A Debate," in Edwards and Pap, *Modern Introduction*, pp. 726–756. Sections relevant to theology appear in Diamond and Litzenburg, *The Logic of God*, section 3.

61 F. C. Copleston, *A History of Philosophy*, Burns and Oates, London, 1946–1966; the series has now reached eight volumes.

62 Ayer and Copleston, "Logical Positivism," in Edwards and Pap, *Modern Introduction*, p. 726.

63 Ibid., p. 743.

64 Ibid.

65 Ibid., p. 755.

66 Ibid., p. 754.

67 Ibid., p. 755.
68 Alfred J. Ayer, "Editor's Introduction," *Logical Positivism*, pp. 15f.
69 Carl G. Hempel, "The Empiricist Criterion of Meaning," in Ayer, *Logical Positivism*, p. 126.
70 Carl G. Hempel, *Aspects of Scientific Explanation*, pp. 120f. It should be noted that Wesley C. Salmon, "Logic and Verification," initiated a fresh departure in the effort to formulate an adequate statement of the test of verifiability. Michael Tooley relies heavily on it in his essay, "Theological Statements and the Question of an Empiricist Criterion of Theological Significance." Both essays are reprinted in section X of Diamond and Litzenburg, *The Logic of God*.
71 A. J. Ayer, *Language, Truth and Logic*, p. 16.
72 Alan Richardson, *Christian Apologetics*, Harper, New York, 1947, p. 154.
73 Robert Burns, *David Hume on Miracles in Historical Perspective* (Ann Arbor, Mich.: University Microfilm, 1972).
74 Raeburne Heimbeck, *Theology and Meaning*, Stanford, Stanford, Calif., 1971.
75 Ibid., pp. 154f., 172f., 196ff., 221f.
76 Austin Farrer, "An English Appreciation" [of Rudolf Bultmann], in H. W. Bartsch (ed.), *Kerygma and Myth*, Macmillan, New York, 1953, p. 222.
77 For a similar definition, see F. L. Cross (ed.), *The Oxford Dictionary of the Christian Church*, Oxford, London, 1957, p. 905.
78 F. R. Tennant, *Miracle*, Cambridge, Cambridge, 1925, pp. 67ff.
79 St. Thomas Aquinas, *Summa Contra Gentiles*, bk. 3, chap. 102. A convenient edition is V. J. Bourke, ed., trans., *On the Truth of the Christian Faith*, Doubleday, New York, 1956, bk. 3, part 2.
80 Karl Jaspers, "Myth and Religion," in Karl Jaspers and Rudolf Bultmann, *Myth and Christianity*, The Noonday Press, New York, 1958, p. 5.
81 James F. Ross, *Introduction to the Philosophy of Religion*, Macmillan, London, 1969, pp. 82f.
82 Ninian Smart, *Philosophers and Religious Truth*, SCM Press, London, 1964, pp. 42f.
83 Guy Robinson, "Miracles," *Ratio*, 9: 159, 1967.
84 Ibid.
85 David Hume, *Enquiry Concerning Human Understanding*, Open Court, Chicago, 1927, section X. For important studies by a contemporary empiricist, see Antony Flew, *Hume's Philosophy of Belief*, Routledge, London, 1961, chap. 8 and Antony Flew, *God and Philosophy*, Hutchinson, London, 1966. chap. 17. For a study of the historical background to Hume's essay on miracles, see Robert M. Burns, *David Hume on Miracles in Historical Perspective*.
86 David Hume, *Enquiry Concerning Human Understanding*, 10: 121 (final paragraph of part 1).
87 Ibid., pp. 122ff. (opening pages of part 2).
88 Van A. Harvey, *The Historian and the Believer*, Macmillan, New York, 1966, p. 88; Rudolph Otto, *The Idea of the Holy*, 2d ed., Oxford, London, 1950, p.

64; A. E. Taylor, *The Faith of Moralist*, vol. 2, Macmillan, London, 1930, p. 152.

89 Martin Buber, *Moses*, Harper, New York, 1958, pp. 74ff.

90 Donald Evans, "Scientific and Religious Assertions," in Barbour, *Science and Religion*, pp. 102ff.

91 Rudolf Carnap, "The Elimination of Metaphysics," in A. J. Ayer (ed.), *Logical Positivism*, pp. 66ff. Kai Nielsen has made the point a number of times, for example, "The Intelligibility of God-Talk," in *Religious Studies*, 6: 1ff. 1970, and "On Waste and Wastelands," *Perspectives in Education, Religion, and the Arts*, State University of New York Press, Albany, N.Y., pp. 120ff.

PART TWO

1 Abraham J. Heschel, *Man Is Not Alone*, Farrar, Straus & Young, New York, 1951.

2 Rudolf Otto, *The Idea of the Holy* (hereafter cited as *Holy*), 2d ed., Oxford, London, 1950, first published in German in 1917.

3 Rudolf Otto, *Religious Essays*, Oxford, London, 1931, p. 137.

4 Otto, *Holy*, p. 3.

5 Immanuel Kant, *Critique of Practical Reason and Other Writings in Moral Philosophy*, L. W. Beck (ed.), University of Chicago Press, 1949; see "Foundations of the Metaphysics of Morals" and "Critique of Practical Reason." See also *Religion Within the Limits of Reason Alone*, Harper & Row, New York, 1960. A contemporary and succinct statement of a moral interpretation of the meaning of religious language may be found in R. B. Braithwaite, "An Empiricist's View of the Nature of Religious Belief," in John Hick (ed.), *The Existence of God*, Macmillan, New York, 1964, pp. 229–252.

6 Otto, *Holy*, p. 4.

7 Ibid., p. 141.

8 Ibid., p. 8.

9 Ibid.

10 Ibid., p. 7.

11 Phenomenology is one of the most difficult philosophical positions now in vogue. What has been presented in this volume is not so much an introduction to the movement as a statement of some themes that appear in Otto's work. For a lucid introduction which provides ample bibliographical suggestions, see Robert C. Solomon, *From Rationalism to Existentialism*, Harper & Row, New York, 1972, chap. 5.

12 Ludwig Wittgenstein, *Philosophical Investigations* (hereafter cited as *Investigations*), Macmillan, New York, 1953, pp. 13ff.; see also, Wilfred Sellars, *Science, Perception and Reality*, Routledge, London, 1963, pp. 161ff.

13 Wittgenstein, *Investigations*, p. 31.

14 H. M. Paton, *The Moral Predicament*, George Allen and Unwin, London, 1955, pp. 137ff. involves a brief statement of Otto's misuse of Kant by a famous Kantian scholar. John P. Reeder, Jr., presents a sustained and detailed study of it in "The Relation of the Moral and the Numinous in Otto's Notion of the Holy" in G. Outka and J. P. Reeder, Jr. (eds.), *Religion and Morality*, Doubleday, New York, 1973.

15 Ronald Hepburn, *Christianity and Paradox* (hereafter cited as *Paradox*), Pegasus, New York, 1966, p. 205.

16 Gabriel Marcel, *Being and Having*, Beacon Press, Boston, 1951, pp. 154ff, is a classical source of the distinction between a mystery and a problem.

17 Martin Buber, *Eclipse of God* (hereafter cited as *Eclipse*), Harper, New York, 1952, p. 50.

18 Otto, *Holy*, p. 28.

19 Ibid., p. 9.

20 *The Bhagavad-Gita*, trans. by S. Prabhavananda and C. Isherwood, New American Library, New York, 1944, part 10, pp. 91ff.

21 William James, *Varieties of Religious Experience* (hereafter cited as *Varieties*), Longmans, New York, 1928, Lectures 4 and 5, but see also Paul Tillich, *Systematic Theology*, vol. 1, University of Chicago Press, Chicago, 1951, pp. 108ff.

22 Heinrich Zimmer, *Myths and Symbol in Indian Art and Civilization*, Princeton, Princeton, N.J., 1972, pp. 181ff.; see also illustrations 53 and 54.

23 Otto, for example, sometimes writes as though only the rational side of religion develops; at other times he writes as though our awareness of the numinous (the nonrational element) is also characterized by evolutionary development, *Holy*, pp. 6, 20, 110, 112. For a full and detailed account of this and many other inconsistencies in Otto (which provides citations of the relevant literature) see the essay by John P. Reeder, Jr., cited in note 14 above.

24 Otto, *Holy*, p. 137.

25 Ibid., p. 177.

26 Ibid., pp. 177f; the discussion of divination is on pp. 143ff.

27 Martin Buber, *Eclipse*, p. 51. The reference to Alfred N. Whitehead is to *Religion in the Making*, Macmillan, New York, 1926, p. 75.

28 Otto, *Holy*, p. 144.

29 Ibid., p. 149.

30 Ibid.

31 Ibid.

32 Ibid., p. 143.

33 Ibid., p. 177.

34 Donald Evans, "Scientific and Religious Assertions," in I. Barbour (ed.), *Science and Religion*, Harper & Row, New York, 1968, pp. 111ff. provides and extended discussion of objective as involving maximal inter-subjective agreement.

35 James, *Varieties*, p. 58, quoted in Otto, *Holy*, p. 10.

36 Ibid., pp. 10f.

37 Ibid.
38 William L. Rowe, in *Religious Symbols and God*, University of Chicago Press, Chicago, 1968, pp. 152–163, presents a sustained and illuminating discussion on this point; see also Roderick Chisholm, *Perceiving*, Cornell, Ithaca, N.Y., 1957, especially chaps. 3 and 4. For a discussion that is directly related to accounts of religious experience like the one presented by Otto see C. B. Martin, "A Religious Way of Knowing," in A. Flew and A. MacIntyre (eds.), *New Essays in Philosophical Theology*, Macmillan, New York, 1955, pp. 76–95; see also his *Religious Beliefs*, Cornell, Ithaca, N.Y., 1959, chap. 5. For a provocative criticism of Martin's work, see George I. Mavrodes, *Belief in God*, Random House, New York, 1970, pp. 74ff.
39 James, *Varieties*, Lectures 4–8 spell out the contrast.
40 Hepburn, *Paradox*, p. 47. It should be noted that Hepburn qualified his scepticism in "From World to God," in B. Mitchell (ed.), *Philosophy of Religion*, Oxford, London, 1971, pp. 168–178.
41 C. D. Broad, *Religion, Philosophy and Psychical Research*, Routledge, London, 1953, p. 190.
42 Stuart Hampshire, "Identification and Existence," in H. D. Lewis (ed.), *Contemporary British Philosophy*, 3d ser., George Allen and Unwin, London, 1956, p. 202.
43 Otto, *Holy*, p. 28.
44 Arthur Cohen, *Martin Buber*, Hillary House, New York, 1957, concentrates on Buber's view of the holy; see especially, p. 10.
45 Martin Buber, *I and Thou*, Scribner, New York, 1970, new translation with prologue and notes by Walter Kaufmann; see Kaufmann's "Prologue," pp. 14ff.
46 Martin Buber, *Ten Rungs*, Schocken Books, New York, 1947, p. 15.
47 For a philosopher who sets Buber's account of the relation with eternal You into the context of discussions of religious experience, see Paul Edwards, *Buber and Buberism: A Critical Evaluation* (hereafter cited as *Buber and Buberism*). The Lindley Lecture, University of Kansas, 1969, pp. 38ff.
48 Buber, *I and Thou*, p. 53.
49 Immanuel Kant, "Foundations" in L. W. Beck (ed.), *Critique of Practical Reason*, p. 87.
50 Buber, *I and Thou*, pp. 82f.
51 Ibid., p. 85.
52 Ibid., pp. 56f, 149ff.
53 Ibid., pp. 172ff.
54 Ibid., pp. 57f., 175.
55 Martin Buber, *Between Man and Man* (hereafter cited as *Between*), Routledge, London, 1947, pp. 22f.
56 For a straightforward exposition of the I-You that explores important philosophical questions in the context of expounding it, see Paul Edwards, *Buber and Buberism*, pp. 4–22.
57 Buber, *I and Thou*, pp. 146f.

58 Ibid., p. 62; see also pp. 124f.
59 Ibid., p. 59.
60 Ibid., p. 54.
61 Ibid., p. 83.
62 Ibid., p. 84.
63 Ibid., p. 126.
64 Ibid., p. 127.
65 Ibid., pp. 123f.
66 Ibid., p. 57; see also p. 123.
67 Ibid., p. 123.
68 Buber, *Between*, p. 15.
69 Buber, *I and Thou*, pp. 150, 143.
70 Buber, *Between*, p. 7.
71 Buber, *I and Thou*, p. 147.
72 Ibid.
73 Ibid., p. 68.
74 Ibid., p. 147.
75 Ibid., p. 126.
76 Buber, *Eclipse*, p. 165.
77 Buber, *I and Thou*, p. 148.
78 This issue is covered extensively in Malcolm L. Diamond, *Martin Buber: Jewish Existentialist*, Oxford, New York, 1960, pp. 64–96.
79 Buber, *I and Thou*, p. 182.
80 Buber, *Eclipse*, pp. 166ff.
81 Buber, *I and Thou*, pp. 57ff.
82 Ibid., p. 59, my quotation marks.
83 Ibid., p. 81.
84 Buber, *Eclipse*, p. 49; on p. 60 Buber suggests that philosophizing in the right spirit can itself be an I-You experience.
85 Ibid., pp. 67ff.
86 Buber, *Between*, p. 57. Buber's view of philosophical and theological approaches to God is criticized as unfair by Paul Edwards, in *Buber and Buberism*, pp. 43ff.
87 Martin Buber, "Reply to Critics" in P. A. Schilpp and M. Friedman (eds.), *The Philosophy of Martin Buber*, Open Court, La Salle, Illinois, 1967, p. 690.
88 Paul Edwards, *Buber and Buberism*, p. 30.
89 Buber, *I and Thou*, p. 147; *Between*, p. 52.
90 The phrase the eternal You is, of course, used throughout Part Three of *I and Thou*; the phrase absolute person appears in *I and Thou*, p. 181, but see also *Eclipse*, pp. 23ff.
91 For Buber's view of God's eternal openness, indeed of his eternal initiative in addressing human beings, see *I and Thou*, p. 182; *Between*, pp. 11, 117. For his view of God's capacity to be present to all human beings, see *I and Thou*, p. 181.
92 Buber, *Between*, p. 184.
93 Buber, *Eclipse*, p. 165.

94 Buber, *Between*, p. 81.
95 Quoted by Soren Kierkegaard in his *Concluding Unscientific Postcript*, Princeton, Princeton, N.J., 1944, p. 97.
96 Martin Buber, *Hasidism*, Philosophical Library, New York, 1948, p. 142; see also Buber, *Between*, pp. 69, 145.
97 Buber, *Between*, pp. 45ff., 204f.
98 Ibid., p. 71.
99 Buber, *I and Thou*, pp. 54, 84.
100 Hepburn, *Paradox*, pp. 91ff.
101 Buber, *I and Thou*, p. 69.
102 Ibid., p. 58.
103 Ibid., p. 91.
104 Hepburn, *Paradox*, pp. 35f.
105 Ibid., p. 34; see also Edwards, *Buber and Buberism*, pp. 38ff.
106 An excellent introduction and contribution to the philosophy of mind is provided by Jerome Shaffer, *Philosophy of Mind*, Prentice-Hall, Englewood Cliffs, N.J., 1968.
107 Hepburn, *Paradox*, p. 30.
108 Donald Evans, "Differences Between Scientific and Religious Assertions," in Barbour, *Science and Religion*, p. 103.
109 Hepburn, *Paradox*, p. 38.

PART THREE

1 There are, of course, existentialists who are not religious. They are best represented by Martin Heidegger, *Being and Time*, SCM Press, London, 1962 and Jean-Paul Sartre, *Being and Nothingness*, Philosophical Library, New York, 1956. Fernando Molina tries to dissociate the movement from its religious origins, in his *Existentialism as Philosophy*, Prentice-Hall, Englewood Cliffs, N.J., 1962. An introduction that does justice to both religious and nonreligious existentialists is Robert C. Solomon, *From Rationalism to Existentialism*, Harper & Row, New York, 1972.
2 For an introduction to religious existentialism, see David E. Roberts, *Existentialism and Religious Belief*, Oxford, New York, 1957. Eugene Borowitz provides a more popular and wide-ranging introduction to religious existentialists (including Gabriel Marcel, a Roman Catholic, Nicholas Berdyaev, who was Russian Orthodox, and the Jewish thinkers, Martin Buber and Franz Rosenzweig) in *A Layman's Introduction to Religious Existentialism*, Westminster, Philadelphia, 1965.
3 An excellent survey of the problems involved is provided by Van A. Harvey, *The Historian and the Believer*, Macmillan, New York, 1966.
4 Blaise Pascal, *Pensées*, no. 265.
5 For an excellent study of Kant that deals with him in the context of the

two-level theory of truth see Edward A. Langerak, *Orienting Oneself Rationally: Kant's Constructive Philosophy of Religion*, unpublished dissertation, Ann Arbor, Mich., 1972. Robert C. Solomon, *From Rationalism to Existentialism*, pp. 9–37 contains a chapter on Kant that is also helpful in showing his relation to religious existentialism.

6   William James, *The Will to Believe* (hereafter cited as *Will*), Dover, New York, 1956. For criticisms, see Wallace Matson, *The Existence of God*, Cornell, Ithaca, New York, 1965, pp. 202–215; Walter Kaufmann, *Critique of Religion and Philosophy* (hereafter cited as *Critique*), Harper, New York, 1957, pp. 82ff., 92f.; Fredrick Ferré, *Basic Modern Philosophy of Religion*, Scribner, New York, 1967, pp. 275–298; George Mavrodes, "James and Clifford on 'The Will to Believe,'" in K. E. Yandell (ed.), *God, Man and Religion*, McGraw-Hill, New York, 1973, pp. 524–528. The thesis of this essay is that James misrepresented his differences with Clifford. Mavrodes' presentation of James' main purpose is, however, compatible with the line followed in this chapter.

7   W. C. Clifford, "The Ethics of Belief," in Walter Kaufmann (ed.), *Religion From Tolstoy to Camus*, Harper, New York, 1961, p. 206.

8   Kaufmann, *Critique*, p. 84.

9   James, *Will*, pp. 4f.

10   Ibid., p. 11, James italicizes this passage.

11   Ibid., p. 3.

12   John Wisdom, *Philosophy and Psychoanalysis*, Basil Blackwell, Oxford, 1953, p. 50, makes a similar point with reference to paradoxes. He acknowledges that they may be symptoms of linguistic confusion but claims that they may also be instances of linguistic penetration.

13   Kierkegaard's phrase is "leap of faith." See Soren Kierkegaard, *Concluding Unscientific Postscript* (hereafter cited as *Postscript*), Princeton, Princeton, N.J., 1944, pp. 15, 105, 231, 262.

14   George Mavrodes challenges James on this point in "James and Clifford on 'The Will to Believe,'" in Yandell, *God, Man and Religion*, p. 526.

15   Kaufmann, *Critique*, p. 83.

16   James, *Will*, p. 29.

17   Ibid., pp. 23ff.

18   Kaufmann, *Critique*, p. 86.

19   James, *Will*, pp. 25ff.

20   Ibid., pp. 25, 27.

21   For one effort to unravel this problem, see Josiah Thompson, *The Lonely Labyrinth: Kierkegaard's Pseudonymous Works*, Southern Illinois Press, Carbondale, Ill., 1967. Alastair McKinnon in Kierkegaard's "Existentialism Revisited," *International Philosophical Quarterly* **9**: 165–176, 1969, uses an analysis of the pseudonymous authorship in an effort to show that Kierkegaard did not himself espouse the irrationalism that should only be attributed to the pseudonymous works. Stephen Crites, "Pseudonymous Authorship as Art and as Act," in J. Thompson (ed.), *Kierkegaard*, Doubleday, New York, 1972, pp. 183–229, is both clear and suggestive. So too is

Louis Mackey, *Kierkegaard: A Kind of Poet*, University of Pennsylvania Press, Philadelphia, 1971. He presents an excellent survey of the Kierkegaardian literature, pseudonym by pseudonym.

22 Stephen Crites, "Pseudonymous Authorship as Art and as Act," in J. Thompson (ed.), *Kierkegaard*, pp. 222ff. provides support for this point in the material he quotes from Kierkegaard, although Crites himself does not make it and would doubtless oppose it. Even if I am mistaken in my interpretation of the pseudonymous authorship, Kierkegaard's influence on twentieth century religious thought is based largely (though, of course, not exclusively) on two works, the *Philosophical Fragments* (hereafter cited as *Fragments*), 2d ed., Princeton, Princeton, N.J., 1955 and the *Concluding Unscientific Postscript* which carries the argument further. Kierkegaard attributes both works to the fictional author, Johannes Climacus. If many of the experts on the pseudonymous authorship are right, a revolution in twentieth century theology should be attributed to Climacus (and to a misunderstood Climacus at that) rather than to the author who conjured him up.

23 Soren Kierkegaard, *The Sickness unto Death*, Princeton, Princeton, N.J., 1970, p. 146.

24 Soren Kierkegaard, *Fear and Trembling* (hereafter cited as *Fear*), Princeton, Princeton, N.J., 1970, p. 27.

25 Soren Kierkegaard, *Training in Christianity*, Princeton, Princeton, N.J., 1947, pp. 162ff.

26 For a lucid introduction to Kierkegaard that deals with his attack on the thinking of F. W. Hegel (1770–1831), the German philosopher who was one of the most influential thinkers of the nineteenth century, see Robert C. Solomon, *From Rationalism to Existentialism*, pp. 77ff.; see also chap. 2, on Hegel. Claude Welch, *Protestant Thought in the Nineteenth Century*, Yale, New Haven, 1972, also deals with Kierkegaard's attack on Hegelianism, pp. 303ff., as well as presenting a chapter on Hegel himself, chap. 4.

27 Soren Kierkegaard, *On Authority and Revelation*, Princeton, Princeton, N.J., 1955, p. 59.

28 Kierkegaard, *Fragments*, p. 118, n. 1.

29 A penetrating analysis of the effectiveness of this type of strategy is presented by B. A. O. Williams, "Tertullian's Paradox," in A. Flew and A. MacIntyre (eds.), *New Essays in Philosophical Theology* (hereafter cited as *New Essays*), Macmillan, New York, 1955, p. 190.

30 Kierkegaard, *Postscript*, p. 182; see also p. 540.

31 Ibid., p. 182.

32 Ibid., p. 135.

33 Ibid., p. 136.

34 Ibid., p. 135. Kierkegaard claims that the major tendencies of western philosophy, empiricism and idealism, exemplify the objective approach. On p. 173 of the *Postscript*, there is a useful characterization of the objective.

35 Ibid., p. 118.

36 Ibid., p. 182.

37 Soren Kierkegaard, *Journal*, A. Dru (ed.), Oxford, London, 1938, no. 22.

38 Kierkegaard, *Postscript*, p. 174.

39 Ibid.

40 Kierkegaard, *Fragments*, "Interlude," pp. 89–110.

41 Walter Lowrie, *A Short Life of Kierkegaard*, Princeton, Princeton, N.J., 1942, pp. 131ff., 144ff.

42 In his essay "The Question to the Single One," *Between Man and Man*, Routledge, London, 1947, Martin Buber criticizes Kierkegaard's attitude. See especially p. 52.

43 Kierkegaard, *Fear*, pp. 39ff.

44 For a penetrating discussion of the relation of religion and morality in Kierkegaard's *Fear and Trembling*, see Gene Outka, "Religious and Moral Duty: Notes on *Fear and Trembling*," in G. Outka and J. P. Reeder, Jr. (eds.), *Religion and Morality*, Doubleday, New York, 1973.

45 Kierkegaard, *Fear*, pp. 64–77. A sharp criticism is presented by Martin Buber, "On the Suspension of the Ethical," *Eclipse of God*, Harper, 1952, pp. 149–156.

46 Kierkegaard, *Fear*, pp. 86ff.

47 Ibid., pp. 41, 46, 64.

48 Soren Kierkegaard, *Consider the Lillies*, C. W. Daniel, London, 1940, p. 60.

49 Kierkegaard, *Fear*, p. 86.

50 Ibid., p. 65.

51 Ibid., p. 84.

52 Ibid.

53 Kierkegaard, *Postscript*, p. 181.

54 Ibid., p. 182.

55 Ibid., pp. 179f.

56 Kierkegaard, *Fragments*, p. 130.

57 Kierkegaard, *Postscript*, p. 188.

58 Ibid., p. 327. See also Claude Welch, *Protestant Thought in the Nineteenth Century*, vol. 1, pp. 295f.

59 Kierkegaard, *Postscript*, p. 187.

60 Willard V. Quine, *The Ways of Paradox*, Random House, New York, 1966, p. 3.

61 Kierkegaard, *Fragments*, pp. 71f. See also, pp. 125ff. Kierkegaard clearly agrees with the position that Charles Hartshorne characterizes as "classical theism," a position which maintains that God is time-invariant. Hartshorne rejects the position by claiming that God's knowledge changes as events in the world change. See C. Hartshorne and W. L. Reese (eds.), *Philosophers Speak of God*, University of Chicago Press, 1953, pp. 18ff., 131ff. In this same vein, see Nelson Pike, *God and Timelessness*, Routledge, London, 1970, and Norman Kretzmann, "Omniscience and Immutability," in S. M. Cahn (ed.), *Philosophy of Religion*, Harper & Row, New York, 1970, pp. 89–103. The considerations advanced in these works hardly qualify the force of Kierkegaard's absolute paradox in which God, who is bodiless, enters human flesh and changes in the sense that human beings change, while yet remaining God who is bodiless and changeless.

62 Soren Kierkegaard, *On Authority and Revelation*, p. 59.

63 Kierkegaard, *Fragments*, p. 80.

64 Ibid., pp. 49ff., for Kierkegaard's treatment of the proofs.

65 Ibid., chap. 4.

66 Kierkegaard, *Training in Christianity*, p. 31.

67 Kierkegaard, *Postscript*, p. 189.

68 For an excellent discussion of Tertullianism by a contemporary empiricist, see Bernard A. O. Williams, "Tertullian's Paradox," in Flew and MacIntyre, *New Essays*, pp. 187–211; the quotation from Tertullian is discussed on p. 190, which is relevant to Kierkegaard's thought.

69 Kierkegaard, *Fragments*, pp. 32–43, 69.

70 Ibid., chap. 2. Actually, the faith situation is far more complex than is indicated here, because the acquisition of faith involves the grace of God. This topic is treated in relation to Bultmann, in chap. 9.

71 Ibid., p. 103.

72 Kierkegaard, *Postscript*, p. 192.

73 Ibid., p. 188.

74 Walt Whitman, "Song of Myself," section 32.

75 Kierkegaard, *Sickness*, pp. 215f.

76 Ibid., p. 216.

77 Ibid.

78 Kierkegaard, *Postscript*, pp. 503f.

79 Gertrude Ezorsky, "Pragmatic Theory of Truth," in Paul Edwards (ed.), *The Encyclopedia of Philosophy*, Macmillan, New York, 1967, vol. 6, p. 427.

80 Ibid. The quotation from William James is from *Pragmatism*, Longmans, New York, 1907, p. 299. John H. Randall, Jr., in "The Ontology of Paul Tillich," in C. W. Kegley and R. W. Bretall (eds.), *The Theology of Paul Tillich*, Macmillan, New York, 1956, p. 150, also links pragmatism and existentialism, although he is dealing with Tillich rather than with Kierkegaard.

81 These criticisms are advanced against Kierkegaard by David E. Roberts, *Existentialism and Religious Belief*, pp. 87ff.

82 Soren Kierkegaard, *The Point of View for My Work as an Author*, Oxford, London, 1939, pp. 5f.

83 Soren Kierkegaard, *Journals*, A. Dru (ed.), no. 922, as cited in R. Bretall (ed.), *A Kierkegaard Anthology*, "Editor's Introduction," Random House, New York, 1946, pp. xxf.

84 Quine, *Ways of Paradox*, p. 11.

85 Soren Kierkegaard, *Works of Love*, Princeton, Princeton, N.J., 1949, chap. 2, especially pp. 46ff.

86 Kierkegaard, *Postscript*, pp. 187–210.

87 Ibid., p. 196.

88 Ibid., p. 189.

89 Ibid. (my emphasis). See also pp. 187, 194f., 512ff.; *Fragments*, pp. 71f., 125ff.; *Training in Christianity*, pp. 28f., 31.

90 Kierkegaard, *Postscript*, pp. 182, 204, 209.

91 The quotations are from Kierkegaard's *Journal*, no. 1074, and P. A. Heid-

berg, V. Kuhr, and E. Torsting (eds.), *Søren Kierkegaards Papirer*, 2d ed., Gyldenalske Boghandel, Nordisk Forlag, Copenhagen, 1909–1948, vol. 10, 6A p. 79. They are discussed by Cornelio Fabro, CP.S. "Faith and Reason in Kierkegaard's Dialectic," in H. A. Johnson and Niels Thulstrup (eds.), *A Kierkegaard Critique*, pp. 182f., by J. Heywood Thomas, *Subjectivity and Paradox*, Blackwell, Oxford, 1957, pp. 132f., and by Alastair McKinnon, "Kierkegaard: 'Paradox' and Irrationalism," in J. H. Gill (ed.), *Essays on Kierkegaard*, p. 110.

92   Kierkegaard, *Postscript*, pp. 182–210, attacks Hegelians who convert Christianity into a philosophy.

93   Rudolf Bultmann, "The New Testament and Mythology," H. W. Bartsch (ed.), *Kerygma and Myth* (hereafter cited as Bultmann, *Kerygma*, which citation will also apply to Bultmann's other contributions to the volume, "Reply to Theses of J. Schniewind," and "Replies to his Critics"), Macmillan, New York, 1953, p. 4.

94   Karl Jaspers, "Myth and Religion," in Karl Jaspers and Rudolf Bultmann, *Myth and Christianity*, The Noonday Press, New York, 1958, pp. 5f.

95   Rudolf Bultmann, *Jesus Christ and Mythology*, Scribner, New York, 1958, pp. 37f.

96   Bultmann, *Kerygma*, p. 5.

97   Ibid., pp. 10, 210; see also, Bultmann, *Jesus Christ and Mythology*, pp. 83ff., Rudolf Bultmann, *Existence and Faith*, Meridian Books, New York, 1960, pp. 18f., Schubert Ogden, *Christ Without Myth*, Harper, New York, 1961, pp. 43f., 115, 171f.

98   Van A. Harvey, *The Historian and the Believer*, pp. 102f.

99   Bultmann, *Jesus Christ and Mythology*, p. 18.

100   Rudolf Bultmann, "The Case for Demythologization," in Jaspers and Bultmann, *Myth and Christianity*, p. 59.

101   Bultmann, *Kerygma*, p. 13.

102   Ibid., p. 11.

103   Rudolf Bultmann, *Theology of the New Testament*, vol. 1, Scribner, New York, 1951, part 2, and vol. 2, 1955, part 3.

104   Bultmann, *Kerygma*, p. 3.

105   Ibid., p. 9.

106   Ibid., p. 39.

107   Bultmann, *Jesus Christ and Mythology*, p. 38.

108   Bultmann, *Kerygma*, pp. 33f.

109   Bultmann, *Jesus Christ and Mythology*, pp. 71f.

110   Bultmann, *Kerygma*, p. 30.

111   Rudolf Bultmann, *Existence and Faith*, p. 81.

112   Rudolf Bultmann, *Essays*, Macmillan, New York, 1955, p. 15.

113   Rudolf Bultmann, *Theology of the New Testament*, vol. 1, pp. 263ff., 315ff.

114   Bultmann, *Essays*, p. 81.

115   Bultmann, *Jesus Christ and Mythology*, p. 39.

116   Bultmann, *Kerygma*, pp. 30, 33; *Existence and Faith*, pp. 93ff.; *Jesus Christ and Mythology*, p. 77.

117   Bultmann, *Kerygma*, p. 31.

118 Ibid., p. 19.
119 Bultmann, *Existence and Faith*, p. 85.
120 Bultmann, *Kerygma*, p. 41.
121 Kierkegaard, *Fragments*, chaps. 1, 2.
122 Bultmann, *Essays*, p. 177f.
123 Bultmann, "The Case for Demythologization," in Jaspers and Bultmann, *Myth and Christianity*, p. 59.
124 Bultmann, *Essays*, p. 79.
125 Bultmann, *Kerygma*, pp. 114f., 118.
126 Bultmann, *Jesus Christ and Mythology*, p. 77; see also *Kerygma*, pp. 113ff., 118f.; *Existence and Faith*, pp. 106ff.
127 Bultmann, *Existence and Faith*, pp. 19f., 80ff.; *Kerygma*, pp. 19f., 113, 118f.; *Jesus Christ and Mythology*, pp. 31, 77.
128 Bultmann, *Kerygma*, p. 21.
129 Bultmann, *Jesus Christ and Mythology*, p. 69.
130 Bultmann, *Kerygma*, p. 197; see also *Jesus Christ and Mythology*, pp. 61f.
131 Bultmann, *Kerygma*, p. 199.
132 Bultmann, *Essays*, p. 9; see also pp. 75, 91ff., *Existence and Faith*, p. 18.
133 Ibid., p. 16; see also *Essays*, p. 18.
134 Bultmann, *Kerygma*, p. 211.
135 Bultmann, *Kerygma*, p. 44; see also pp. 118, 201.
136 Ernest Nagel, *The Structure of Science*, Harcourt, Brace & World, New York, 1961, chap. 15, takes a sharply critical line on these claims. He is especially concerned to deny the subjectivizing conclusions that existentialists and the other philosophers draw from the peculiarities of historical method.
137 H. Richard Niebuhr, *The Meaning of Revelation*, Macmillan, New York, 1941, pp. 47f.
138 Soren Kierkegaard, *Training in Christianity*, p. 67. It should be noted that Kierkegaard continues this passage by stressing the need for subjective interpretation in order to get at "the real," that is, the deeper significance of what occurred. Thus, with regard to the two-level theory of history, as in so many other respects, Kierkegaard blazed the trail for subsequent generations of religious existentialists.
139 Among the works by religious existentialists that illustrate the two-level theory of history, see Rudolf Bultmann, *The Presence of Eternity: History and Eschatology* (hereafter cited as *History and Eschatology*), Harper, New York, 1957 and many of the essays in his *Existence and Faith*; H. Richard Niebuhr, *The Meaning of Revelation*, Macmillan, New York, 1941; Reinhold Niebuhr, *The Nature and Destiny of Man*, Scribner, New York, 1948, vol. 2 and his *Faith and History*, Scribner, New York, 1949; Soren Kierkegaard, *Philosophical Fragments* and *Concluding Unscientific Postscript*; Paul Tillich, *Systematic Theology*, vol. 2, University of Chicago Press, Chicago, 1957; Nicholas Berdyaev, *The Meaning of History*, Bles, London, 1936. For a penetrating criticism of this line of argument, see Ronald Hepburn, *Christianity and Paradox*, Pegasus, New York, 1966, chaps. 6 and 7.
140 Rudolf Bultmann, *History and Eschatology*, p. 122.

141   Ibid., p. 116.
142   Ibid., p. 119.
143   William H. Dray, *Philosophy of History*, Prentice-Hall, Englewood Cliffs, N.J., 1964, presents a philosophical discussion of differing approaches to the Civil War along with references to the relevant historical literature, pp. 47ff.
144   Bultmann, *Existence and Faith*, p. 295.
145   Bultmann, *History and Eschatology*, p. 115.
146   Bultmann, *Existence and Faith*, p. 59.
147   Ibid.
148   Bultmann, *Existence and Faith*, p. 52; see also Rudolf Bultmann, *Jesus and the Word*, Scribner, New York, 1958, p. 8. However, in the pages which follow, Bultmann claims that we do know a great deal about the *message* of Jesus. This qualification is important, but given the fact that Bultmann focuses on the *life* of Jesus (especially on the crucifixion-resurrection) as the point where God acts decisively in Christ, Bultmann's scepticism about the facts of the life of Jesus is more important than his positive view of the accuracy of the message. Another important discussion of this issue is found in Rudolf Bultmann, "The Primitive Christian Kerygma and the Historical Jesus," in C. E. Braaten and R. A. Harrisville (eds.), *The Historical Jesus and the Kerygmatic Christ*, Abingdon, Nashville, Tenn., 1964, especially pp. 20–25.
149   Bultmann, *Kerygma*, p. 207.
150   Ibid., p. 197.
151   Bultmann, *Essays*, p. 18.
152   Bultmann, *Existence and Faith*, p. 292.
153   Martin Buber, *Between Man and Man*, p. 7.
154   Bultmann, *Kerygma*, p. 202.
155   Bultmann, *Jesus Christ and Mythology*, p. 72.
156   For Bultmann in debate, see C. W. Kegley (ed.), *The Theology of Rudolph Bultmann*, Harper & Row, New York, 1966 and also H. W. Bartsch, *Kerygma and Myth*, vol. 1, as cited above and vol. 2, SPCK Press, London, 1962. For the purposes of this book, the most important criticisms are Ronald Hepburn, "Demythologizing and the Problem of Validity," in Flew and MacIntyre (eds.), *New Essays*, pp. 227–242, and Richard Cambell, "History and Bultmann's Structural Inconsistency," *Religious Studies*, **9**: 63–79, 1973.
157   Among other criticisms of Bultmann's view of the resurrection, see Julius Schneewind, "A Reply to Bultmann," in *Kerygma and Myth*, p. 69ff.; Karl Barth, *Church Dogmatics*, T & T Clark, Edinburgh, 1960, vol. 3, part 2, pp. 443ff.; Schubert Ogden, *Christ Without Myth*, pp. 83ff.; Richard R. Niebuhr, *Resurrection and Historical Reason*, Scribner, New York, 1957, pp. 47ff, 62f, 96.
158   Richard R. Niebuhr, *Resurrection and Historical Reason*; for criticism, see Van A. Harvey, "On Believing What It Is Difficult to Understand: A Dialogue," *Journal of Religion*, **39**: 219–231, 1959.
159   For a stimulating discussion of what constitutes authentic Christianity, see Paul van Buren's "Theology and the Philosophy of Religion from the

Perspective of Religious Thought," *The Union Seminary Quarterly Review,*
25: 467–476, 1970, with responses from Peter Putnam, James F. Ross, Tom
F. Driver, Paul L. Lehman, and a reply by van Buren, pp. 477–503.

160 Kai Nielsen, "On Fixing the Reference Range of 'God,'" in *Religious
Studies,* **1**: 23, 1960. Nielsen cites Richard Taylor, *Metaphysics,* Prentice-
Hall, Englewood Cliffs, N.J., 1963, pp. 25ff. See also Paul Edwards, "Some
Notes on Anthropomorphic Theology," in S. Hook (ed.), *Religious Experi-
ence and Truth,* New York University Press, New York, 1961, pp. 242ff.

161 Ronald Hepburn, "Demythologizing and the Problem of Validity," in Flew
and MacIntyre, *New Essays,* pp. 230ff. Hepburn cites Bultmann, *Kerygma,*
p. 5, but see Bultmann, *History and Eschatology,* chap. 4, for an extensive
discussion of this theme.

162 Bultmann, *Kerygma,* p. 112.

163 I. M. Crombie, "The Possibility of Theological Statements," in Basil
Mitchell (ed.), *Faith and Logic,* George Allen and Unwin, 1957, p. 79.

164 Ibid.

PART FOUR

1 The ordinary uses of teleologist, ontologist, and cosmologist (in sketchy
form) are: (1) Teleologists are thinkers who find evidence of intelligent
purpose in nature. They need not attribute this purpose to a personal God.
Henri Bergson's *Creative Evolution,* Holt, New York, 1911, is still a classic
example of a teleological philosophy that is not theistic. (2) An ontologist is a
philosopher whose primary concern is the nature of being. He may or may
not be theistic. Paul Tillich insisted on calling himself an ontologist rather
than a metaphysician (a term commonly used for philosophers who study
the nature of being-as-such), because the term metaphysician has, in his
view, associations with another world "above" this one; see his *Systematic
Theology,* vol. 1, University of Chicago Press, Chicago, 1951, p. 20. (3)
Cosmologists are thinkers who study the origins of the world; they can do so
in religious terms, but the term is often associated with secular scientists like
Fred Hoyle, whose book *The Nature of the Universe,* Harper and Brothers,
New York, 1950, was one of the early efforts in the field.

2 Fredrick C. Copleston, S.J., *Aquinas,* Penguin, Harmondsworth, Middlesex,
1957, chap. 3; see also Copleston's *History of Philosophy,* vol. 1, Burns and
Oates, London, chap. 34; Etienne Gilson, *The Christian Philosophy of Saint
Thomas Aquinas,* Random House, New York, 1954, part 1, especially, chap.
3; Jacques Maritain, *Approaches to God,* Harper & Brothers, New York,
1954; Eric Mascall, *He Who Is,* Longmans, London, 1945. Victor Preller, in
Divine Science and the Science of God, Princeton University Press, Princeton, N.J., 1967, pp. 108ff., claims that St. Thomas is radically misunderstood
when he is thought of as presenting a "natural theology" which yields proofs
of the existence of God and knowledge of God's attributes.

3   Soren Kierkegaard, *Concluding Unscientific Postscript*, Princeton University Press, Princeton, N.J., 1944, pp. 31, 485; Rudolf Bultmann, "The New Testament and Mythology," in H. W. Bartsch (ed.), *Kerygma and Myth*, Macmillan, New York, 1953, p. 44. Terence Penelhum, *Problems of Religious Knowledge*, Macmillan, London, 1971, pp. 45ff.

4   George I. Mavrodes, in *Belief in God*, Random House, New York, 1970, presents the most penetrating and extensive treatment of this topic; see pp. 3–48.

5   Charles Hartshorne, "Six Theistic Proofs," *The Monist*, **54**: 159ff., 1970; Alvin Plantinga, *God and Other Minds*, Cornell University Press, Ithaca, N.Y., 1967, pp. 3ff.; James F. Ross *Philosophical Theology*, Bobbs-Merrill, Indianapolis, 1969, pp. 3ff. George Mavrodes criticizes the formulations of Plantinga and Ross that are listed above in "Some Recent Philosophical Theology," *Review of Metaphysics*, **24**: 82–93, 1970; see also Terence Penelhum, *Problems of Religious Knowledge*, chaps. 2 and 3.

6   Walter Kaufmann, *Critique of Religion and Philosophy*, Harper & Brothers, New York, 1958, p. 120.

7   George I. Mavrodes, *Belief in God*, pp. 26ff., discusses further complexities that are involved in determining whether an argument is convincing.

8   Charles Hartshorne, "Six Theistic Proofs," *The Monist*, **54**: 159, 1970; Hartshorne explicitly acknowledges his debt to Mavrodes.

9   Among the most forceful exponents of the view that the arguments for the existence of God are religiously worthless are the religious existentialists who were considered in part 3 of this book. However, for brief statements see Miguel de Unamuno, *The Tragic Sense of Life*, Dover, New York, 1954, pp. 159ff.; the views of Blaise Pascal as presented in James Collins, *God in Modern Philosophy*, Regnery, Chicago, 1959, pp. 328ff.; Martin Buber, *Israel and the World*, Schocken Books, New York, 1948, pp. 53ff.

10   Norman Malcolm, "Anselm's Ontological Arguments," in Alvin Plantinga (ed.), *The Ontological Argument*, Doubleday, New York, 1965, p. 159.

11   Ibid.

12   Immanuel Kant, *The Critique of Pure Reason*, trans. by Norman Kemp Smith, St. Martin's, New York, 1965, p. 520.

13   The name "teleological argument" applies most properly to the fifth of the five ways by which St. Thomas Aquinas proposes to prove the existence of God in part 1, question 2, article 3, of his *Summa Theologica*. St. Thomas argues from the fact that inanimate objects function in purposeful contexts. In the case of objects like arrows, we see human intelligence direct them to some purpose. He claims that in the case of inanimate bodies, like coal, which operate in regular and useful ways, we can assume that a nonobservable superhuman intelligence, namely, God, directs them toward their end or *telos*. The best discussion of this version of the argument is found in Anthony Kenny, *The Five Ways*, Schocken Books, New York, 1969, chap. 6. The seventeenth- and eighteenth-century version of the argument with which I am concerned in this part is more properly called the argument from design, although in contemporary discussions the term "teleological argument" is often applied to both versions. Here, as at so many other points, philosophers of our day follow Kant's lead. In *The Critique of Pure Reason*, pp. 518ff., he applied the name "physico-teleological" argument to this argument, and it has been shortened to the teleological argument.

14 F. R. Tennant, *Philosophical Theology*, vol. 2, Cambridge, London, 1930, p. 78. Fredrick Ferré, in *Basic Modern Philosophy of Religion*, Scribner, New York, 1967, pp. 149ff., first discusses empiricism as a philosophical position and then presents the argument from design in that context.

15 David Hume, *Dialogues Concerning Natural Religion*. They were published posthumously in 1779. Nelson Pike, an analytic philosopher of religion, presents them with his commentary, Bobbs-Merrill, Indianapolis, 1970 (hereafter cited as Hume, *Dialogues*). Another extremely useful edition, which sets the *Dialogues* within the framework of Hume's views on religion, is Norman Kemp Smith (ed.), *Social Science*, 2d ed., New York, 1948. An abridged edition of William Paley, *Natural Theology*, has been edited by Fredrick Ferré for Bobbs-Merrill, Indianapolis, 1963.

16 In his edition of the *Dialogues Concerning Natural Religion*, pp. 60ff., Norman Kemp Smith claims that Hume's position toward the argument is that of an empiricist critic, which is the line taken by the character in the *Dialogues* named Philo. Nelson Pike, in section four of his commentary on the *Dialogues*, argues that Hume thought that the argument is successful, a position represented in the *Dialogues* by Cleanthes. In his commentary Pike also cites the relevant literature.

17 Hume, *Dialogues*, p. 22.

18 Ibid.

19 Ibid.

20 A good introduction to induction is provided in Irving M. Copi, *Introduction to Logic*, 2d ed., Macmillan, New York, 1961, part 3. A brief introduction is provided by Wesley C. Salmon, *Logic*, Prentice-Hall, Englewood Cliffs, N.J., 1963, chap. 3.

21 Bertrand Rusell, *The Problems of Philosophy*, Oxford, New York, 1959, p. 63.

22 John Hospers, *An Introduction to Philosophical Analysis*, 2d ed., Prentice-Hall, Englewood Cliffs, N.J., 1967, p. 133.

23 Irving M. Copi, *Introduction to Logic*, p. 340.

24 Ibid., pp. 343–348.

25 William Paley, *Natural Theology* (selections), pp. 3ff.

26 Ibid., p. 4.

27 Ibid., p. 32.

28 Hume, *Dialogues*, p. 30. Among the important criticisms of the argument from design are: David Hume, *Dialogues*; Fredrick Ferré, *Basic Modern Philosophy of Religion*, chap. 5, part 3; Antony Flew, *God and Philosophy*, Hutchinson's, 1966, chap. 3; John Hick, *Arguments for the Existence of God*, Macmillan, London, 1970, chap. 1; Wallace Matson, *The Existence of God*, Cornell University Press, Ithaca, N.Y., 1965, part 2, chap. 3; Thomas McPherson, *The Argument from Design*, Macmillan, London, 1972; Terence

Penhelum, *Religion and Rationality*, Random House, New York, 1971, chap. 5.

29 Hume, *Dialogues*, p. 14.

30 Wallace Matson, *The Existence of God*, pp. 127ff.

31 Alvin Plantinga, *God and Other Minds*, pp. 100f. Readers should note that I have ignored Plantinga scintillating discussion of sample and reference classes; it is, however, well worth careful study.

32 Hume, *Dialogues*, part 7, pp. 62f. Plantinga is, of course, aware of this problem, but I want to use his particular formulation to cut into the issue in my own way.

33 Ibid., see especially part 6, pp. 54ff., 59f., part 7 pp. 62ff.

34 Ibid., part 5.

35 R. G. Swinburne, "The Argument from Design," in *Philosophy*, 43: 208, 1968. The point is introduced in the course of an important discussion by Thomas McPherson, *The Argument from Design*, pp. 59ff.

36 William Paley, *Natural Theology* (selections), F. Ferré (ed.), chap. 5. Leon Pearl, in "Hume's Criticism of the Argument from Design," in *The Monist*, 54: 272, 1970, forcefully states the case that the argument from design does not depend on an inference from the world as a whole. See also, Thomas McPherson, *The Argument from Design*, pp. 19, 60f.

37 John Stuart Mill, *Theism*, Liberal Arts, New York, 1957, pp. 27ff.

38 R. G. Swinburne, "The Argument from Design," *Philosophy*, 43: 200, 1968.

39 I am greatly indebted to an as yet unpublished paper by Kenneth Nelson, "Evolution and the Argument from Design," which not only provides an imaginative defense of the argument from design against the claim that evolutionary thought destroys it but which also organizes the literature on this issue in a useful way. Ian Barbour, in *Issues in Science and Religion*, Prentice-Hall, Englewood Cliffs, N.J., 1966, part 12, discusses the main issues posed by evolution and teleology and also organizes the materials in helpful ways. For a discussion of functional adaptation and of purpose in the context of Darwinian thought, see Andrew Woodfield, "Darwin, Teleology and Taxonomy," in *Philosophy*, 48: 37, 1973.

40 Richard Taylor's fresh approach to the teleological argument in his *Metaphysics*, Prentice-Hall, Englewood Cliffs, N.J., 1963, pp. 94ff., provides the best example of a forceful defense of the argument that ignores evolution. Alvin Plantinga whose treatment of the argument in his book *God and Other Minds* was touched on in the first part of this chapter, offered interesting defenses of the argument while ignoring the issue of evolution; but his conclusions seem ambiguous rather than positive. R. G. Swinburne, in "The Argument from Design," the essay from *Philosophy*, 1968, cited above, and in his subsequent essay, "The Argument from Design—A Defense," in *Religious Studies*, 8: 193–205, 1972, also ignores the issue of evolution.

41 Kenneth Nelson, whose paper on this issue is discussed in this chapter, presents the best statement of the view that the argument from design can be successfully reformulated in a way that takes account of evolutionary theory.

42 The major figures are F. R. Tennant, *Philosophical Theology*, vol. 2, chap. 4; A. E. Taylor, *Does God Exist?* Macmillan, New York, 1947; Peter Bertocci, *Introduction to the Philosophy of Religion*, Prentice-Hall, New York, 1951, chaps. 13–15.

43 Hume, *Dialogues*, pp. 92, 96; see also pp. 196ff. Philo deals with the problem of evil in the passages referred to and he challenges Cleanthes to show that the existence of a powerful knowing and good God can be inferred from our experience of the mixture of good and evil, but the principle involved can readily be transferred to the experience of functional adaptation.

44 In "The Argument from Design," *Philosophy*, 53: 200ff., 1968. R. G. Swinburne presents an important discussion of this point by dealing with two kinds of order, spatial and temporal. He claims that Hume's version of the argument from design deals with spatial order but that the argument is stronger if it is presented in terms of regular succession or temporal order.

45 Alvar Ellegard, "The Darwinian Theory and the Argument from Design," *Lychanos*, 41: 182, 1956.

46 Kenneth Nelson, "Evolution and the Argument from Design"; see note 41 above.

47 Ibid.

48 For references to the work of F. R. Tennant, A. E. Taylor, and Peter Bertocci, see note 42 above.

49 F. R. Tennant, *Philosophical Theology*, vol. 2, 92f.

50 John Hick, "Editor's Introduction," *The Existence of God*, Macmillan, New York, 1964, p. 2.

51 Bertrand Russell, *Mysticism and Logic*, Doubleday, New York, 1957, p. 45.

52 A. E. Taylor, *Does God Exist?* pp. 56f.

53 Ibid., p. 57.

54 My treatment of this issue is heavily indebted to Wallace Matson, *The Existence of God*, pp. 107ff.

55 F. R. Tennant, *Philosophical Theology*, vol. 2, p. 105.

56 Wallace Matson, *The Existence of God*, pp. 106ff.

57 Fredrick Ferré, *Basic Modern Philosophy of Religion*, p. 321.

58 Thomas McPherson, *The Philosophy of Religion*, Van Nostrand, Princeton, N.J., 1965, p. 80; see also, John Hick, *Arguments for the Existence of God*, pp. 33ff. and Paul Tillich, *Systematic Theology*, vol. 1, pp. 208ff.

59 Martin Buber, *Between Man and Man*, Routledge, London, 1947, p. 126.

60 Carl Becker, *The Heavenly City of the Eighteenth Century Philosophers*, Yale, New Haven, Conn., 1957, pp. 14f.

61 Anselm, "Proslogion," chaps. 3–4, reprinted in A. Plantinga (ed.), *The Ontological Argument*, and in J. Hick and A. McGill (eds.), *The Many-Faced Argument*, Macmillan, New York, 1967.

62 St. Thomas Aquinas, *Summa Theologica*, part 1, question 3, article 3; Plantinga, *The Ontological Argument*, pp. 28–30.

63 In Plantinga, *The Ontological Argument*, see René Descartes, "Fifth Meditation," *Meditations*, pp. 31–49. Benedict Spinoza, *Ethics*, book 1, pp. 49–53.

Gottfried Leibniz, *New Essays Concerning Human Understanding*, pp. 54–56.

64 Immanuel Kant, *The Critique of Pure Reason*, pp. 500–507. It is reprinted in Plantinga, *The Ontological Argument*, pp. 57–64.

65 Norman Malcolm, "Anselm's Ontological Arguments," *The Philosophical Review*, **69**: 41–62, 1960, reprinted in Plantinga, *The Ontological Argument* and in Hick and McGill, *The Many-Faced Argument*. Charles Hartshorne, "The Formal Validity and Real Significance of The Ontological Argument," *The Philosophical Review*, **53**: 225–245, 1944 anticipated Malcolm's argument but it was ignored.

66 Hick and McGill, *The Many-Faced Argument*, Bibliography, section 7, pp. 366ff.

67 John E. Smith, *Experience and God*, Oxford, New York, 1968, pp. 122f, 128f.

68 John Hick, "Editor's Introduction," *Existence of God*, p. 2. I have paraphrased it.

69 Wallace Matson, *The Existence of God*, p. 45.

70 John Hospers, *Introduction to Philosophical Analysis*, p. 172.

71 John Hick, *The Arguments for the Existence of God*, pp. 90f.; see also, J. Brenton Stearns, "Anselm and the Two-Argument Hypothesis," *The Monist*, **54**: 221–223, 1970 where he both denies that there are two versions of the argument and cites the relevant literature. Norman Malcolm alludes to two versions but neglects to formulate the second one. Victor Preller, in *Divine Science and the Science of God*, in the context of an important discussion of the ontological argument, pp. 92–107, formulates a clear statement of the second version; see p. 100.

72 Anselm, "Monologion," in S. N. Deane (ed.), *St. Anselm*, Open Court, La Salle, Ill., 1948, pp. 61f.

73 Throughout his voluminous work, Charles Hartshorne insists that theologians have generally misunderstood this issue. God cannot be surpassed by anything else whatever, but he must continually surpass himself. His classic statement of the point is found in *The Divine Relativity*, Yale, New Haven, 1948, pp. 18ff.

74 J. N. Findlay, "Can God's Existence Be Disproved?" in Plantinga, *The Ontological Argument*, pp. 115f.

75 Thomas McPherson, *Philosophy of Religion*, pp. 37f., John Hick, *Arguments for the Existence of God*, pp. 73ff.

76 J. J. C. Smart, "The Existence of God," in A. Flew and A. MacIntyre (eds.), *New Essays in Philosophical Theology* (hereafter cited as *New Essays*), Macmillan, New York, 1955, p. 29.

77 Alvin Plantinga, *God and Other Minds*, p. 27; see also, Thomas McPherson, *Philosophy of Religion*, pp. 31ff.

78 In presenting Gaunilo's point I have reworked it. It is newly translated along with Anselm's reply by Arthur McGill in Hick and McGill, *The Many-Faced Argument*, pp. 9–32. In addition, for criticisms of Gaunilo's actual argument

as well as of sympathetic reconstructions of it, see John Hick, *Arguments for the Existence of God*, pp. 76ff.

79 Immanuel Kant, *The Critique of Pure Reason*, pp. 504ff., reprinted in Plantinga, *The Ontological Argument*, pp. 61ff.

80 Peter Strawson, *Individuals*, Methuen, London, 1959, chaps. 5, 6.

81 G. E. Moore, "Is Existence a Predicate?" and W. P. Alston, "The Ontological Argument Revisited" in Plantinga, *The Ontological Argument*; J. Shaffer, "Existence, Predication and the Ontological Argument," in Hick and McGill, *The Many-Faced Argument*.

82 Bertrand Russell, *Introduction to Mathematical Philosophy*, George Allen, London, 1919, chap. 16.

83 Jerome Shaffer, "Existence, Predication and the Ontological Argument," in Hick and McGill, *The Many-Faced Argument* criticizes Kant sharply, but then formulates Kant's criticism of the argument in his own terms by distinguishing between the "intension" and the "extension" of a concept.

84 Peter Geach, *God and The Soul*, Schocken Books, New York, 1969, pp. 54ff.; John Hick, *Arguments for the Existence of God*, p. 83.

85 Alvin Plantinga, *God and Other Minds*, pp. 44ff.

86 Jerome Shaffer, "Existence, Predication and the Ontological Argument," in Hick and McGill, *The Many-Faced Argument*, pp. 244f. Plantinga's point (cited in the previous note) was made in response to this section of Shaffer's essay.

87 Victor Preller in *Divine Science and the Science of God*, p. 179, presents a sustained discussion of the distinctiveness of the concept of God; the following is a sample:

The conclusions of natural theology form an ordered series of sententially vacuous statements which follow logically from the "packed" presupposition that reality must in all its aspects be measured by intellect. They consist either of an admittedly hypothetical application of transcendental predicates to a nonconceivable meta-empirical entity [called "God"] or of a denial to that entity of intrasystematically meaningful predicates, or a combination of the two.

88 A. N. Prior, "Is Necessary Existence Possible?" *Philosophy and Phenomenological Research*, **15**: 545–547, 1955; Richard Taylor, "Introduction," in Plantinga, *The Ontological Argument*, pp. xviff.; Anthony Kenny, "God and Necessity," in B. Williams and A. Montefiore (eds.), *British Analytical Philosophy*, Routledge, London, 1966, pp. 138ff.

89 Victor Preller presents a clear statement of the so-called second version of Anselm's ontological argument in his *Divine Science and the Science of God*, p. 100. Charles Hartshorne, in *The Logic of Perfection*, Open Court, LaSalle, Ill., 1962, pp. 56f., presents a statement of it in formal notation. A bibliographical note on responses to the second version is found in Hick and McGill, *The Many-Faced Argument*, p. 367, and, in this same volume, see

John Hick's reply to Hartshorne, "A Critique of the 'Second Argument,'" pp. 341–356.

90 Norman Malcolm, "Anselm's Ontological Arguments," in Plantinga, *The Ontological Argument*, pp. 142ff.

91 J. N. Findlay, "Can God's Existence Be Disproved?" in Plantinga, *The Ontological Argument*, p. 113.

92 Ibid., p. 117.

93 G. E. Hughes, "Reply to J. N. Findlay," in Flew and MacIntyre, *New Essays*, p. 64. Findlay's own essay, cited above, also appears in *New Essays*, pp. 47–56.

94 J. N. Findlay, "Can God's Existence Be Disproved?" in Plantinga, *The Ontological Argument*, p. 119. See also, J. J. C. Smart, "The Existence of God," in Flew and MacIntyre, *New Essays*, pp. 38ff.

95 J. N. Findlay, "Can God's Existence Be Disproved?" in Plantinga, *The Ontological Argument*, p. 120.

96 Kurt Baier, *The Meaning of Life*, Inaugural Lecture, Canberra University College, Canberra, 1957, p. 8, as quoted by Norman Malcolm, "Anselm's Ontological Arguments," in Plantinga, *The Ontological Argument*, p. 150.

97 Norman Malcolm, "Anselm's Ontological Arguments," in Plantinga, *The Ontological Argument*, p. 157; see also pp. 152f.

98 Immanuel Kant, *The Critique of Pure Reason*, pp. 500–524.

99 Ibid., p. 502.

100 Norman Malcolm, "Anselm's Ontological Arguments," in Plantinga, *The Ontological Argument*, pp. 154ff.

101 This point has been made by a number of philosophers, among them: John Hick, "A Critique of the 'Second Argument,'" in Hick and McGill, *The Many-Faced Argument*, pp. 352ff.; John Hick, *Arguments for the Existence of God*, pp. 91ff.; Terence Penelhum, *Religion and Rationality*, Random House, New York, 1971, pp. 367ff.; Kai Nielsen, *Reason and Practice*, Harper & Row, New York, 1971, pp. 161ff.

102 Charles Hartshorne, *The Logic of Perfection*, p. 158.

103 W. P. Alston, "The Ontological Argument Revisited," in Plantinga, *The Ontological Argument*, pp. 104ff.

104 Ronald Hepburn, *Christianity and Paradox*, Pegasus, New York, 1966, p. 156.

105 Ibid., pp. 156f.

106 St. Thomas Aquinas, *Summa Theologica*, part 1, question 2, article 3; it is conveniently reprinted in D. R. Burrill (ed.), *The Cosmological Arguments*, Doubleday, New York, 1967, p. 54.

107 William Rowe, in "The Cosmological Argument and the Principle of Sufficient Reason," *Man and World*, 2: 278–292, 1968, presents a sustained treatment of this point to which I am indebted, but whose intricacies I have not tried to reproduce.

108 Wallace Matson, *The Existence of God*, pp. 62ff.

109 Ibid., p. 63.

110   Ibid.
111   Gilbert Ryle, *The Concept of Mind*, Hutchinson, London, 1949, p. 78.
112   Ibid.
113   Ibid., pp. 77f.
114   St. Thomas Aquinas, *Summa Theologica*. The Five Ways appear in part 1, question 2, article 3. The derivation of the attributes of God follows in questions 3–26.
115   A. E. Taylor, "The Vindication of Religious Belief," in W. P. Alston (ed.), *Religious Belief and Philosophical Thought*, Harcourt, Brace & World, New York, 1963, p. 44.
116   Richard Taylor, *Metaphysics*, p. 92.
117   W. Norris Clarke, S.J., "A Curious Blindspot in the Anglo-American Tradition of Anti-Theistic Argument" (hereafter cited as "A Curious Blindspot"), *The Monist*, **54**: 199, 1970, my emphasis.
118   John Passmore, *Philosophical Reasoning*, Scribner, New York, 1964, p. 33.
119   Fredrick C. Copleston, S.J., a debate with Bertrand Russell, on "The Existence of God," in Hick, *The Existence of God*, p. 174.
120   Father Clarke, in "A Curious Blindspot," in *The Monist*, 1970, pp. 181ff., presents a survey of thinkers who have raised this objection; it should be noted that his discussion deals with St. Thomas' second way, rather than with the third one which is being considered here.
121   Ibid., p. 192.
122   Bertrand Russell, a debate with Fredrick C. Copleston, S.J., on "The Existence of God," in Hick, *The Existence of God*, p. 175.
123   Wallace Matson, *The Existence of God*, p. 79; see also Irving Copi, *Introduction to Logic*, pp. 79f.
124   Ronald Hepburn, *Christianity and Paradox*, p. 168f.
125   Ibid.
126   Ibid., p. 169.
127   Gertrude E. M. Anscombe and Peter T. Geach, *Three Philosophers*, Basil Blackwell, Oxford, 1961, p. 113.
128   Ibid.
129   Milton Munitz, *The Mystery of Existence*, Appleton-Century-Crofts, New York, 1965, p. 111.
130   St. Thomas Aquinas, *Summa Theologica*, part 1, question 2, article 3; reprinted in Burrill, *The Cosmological Argument*, pp. 52ff.
131   As noted in connection with the ontological argument, this discussion is heavily indebted to Peter T. Geach, *God and The Soul*, pp. 75ff. See also, Barry Miller, "The Contingency Argument," *The Monist*, **54**: 360ff., 1970.
132   Charles Hartshorne, "Six Theistic Proofs," *The Monist*, **54**: 161f., 1970.
133   A. C. A. Rainer, reply to J. N. Findlay, "Can God's Existence Be Disproved?" in Flew and MacIntyre, *New Essays*, pp. 68f.; Peter T. Geach, *God and the Soul*, pp. 54ff.; John Hick, "A Critique of the 'Second Argument,'" in Hick and McGill, *The Many-Faced Argument*, pp. 343ff.; C. B. Martin, *Religious Belief*, Cornell, Ithaca, N.Y., 1959, pp. 156ff.

134 Anthony Kenny, "Necessary Being," *Sophia*, 1: 8, 1962.
135 John Hick, "A Critique of the 'Second Argument,' " in Hick and McGill, *The Many-Faced Argument*, pp. 347f.
136 C. B. Martin, *Religious Belief*, p. 156.
137 Ibid.
138 Ibid., p. 157.
139 Ronald Hepburn, "From World to God," in Basil Mitchell (ed.), *The Philosophy of Religion*, Oxford, London, 1971, pp. 172f. The cosmological relation, which Hepburn sketches here, is the main focus of Austin Farrer's *Finite and Infinite*, Dacre, Westminster, 1943; see especially pp. 14ff.
140 Hepburn, "From World to God," in Mitchell, *The Philosophy of Religion*, p. 173.
141 Ibid.
142 Ibid.
143 Ibid., pp. 173f.

PART FIVE

1 For Tillich's concern with art, see Paul Tillich, "Existentialist Aspects of Modern Art," in C. Michalson (ed.), *Christianity and the Existentialists*, Scribner, New York, 1956, pp. 128–147; see also James Luther Adams, *Tillich's Philosophy of Culture, Science and Religion*, Harper & Row, New York, 1965, chap. 3, and Walter Leibrecht, "The Life and Mind of Paul Tillich," Walter Leibrecht (ed.), *Religion and Culture*, Harper & Brothers, New York, 1959, pp. 7ff. A brief autobiography appears in the opening chapter of Paul Tillich, *My Search for Absolutes* (hereafter cited as *Absolutes*), Simon and Schuster, New York, 1967.
2 For a discussion of Tillich's relation to major figures in the history of Western thought, see John Herman Randall, Jr., in "The Ontology of Paul Tillich," C. W. Kegley and R. W. Bretall (eds.), *The Theology of Paul Tillich*, Macmillan, New York, 1952, pp. 132–161. The one major influence on Tillich that Randall neglects is G. W. Hegel, and his influence on Tillich is discussed (to the point of overemphasis) in Leonard Wheat, *Paul Tillich's Dialectical Humanism*, Johns Hopkins, Baltimore, Md., 1970.
3 Paul Tillich, *The Courage to Be* (hereafter cited as *Courage*), Yale, New Haven, 1952, p. 3. See also Paul Tillich, *Systematic Theology*, vol. 1 (hereafter cited as *Systematic*, I), University of Chicago Press, Chicago, 1951, pp. 85f., where Tillich, in a page and a half, presents a history of philosophy and theology with some twenty references to individual thinkers or to philosophical and theological schools.
4 Paul Tillich, *Theology of Culture* (hereafter cited as *Culture*), Oxford, New York, 1959, chap. 1. For a more technical statement, see *Systematic*, I, pp. 79ff., where Tillich deals with the depth of reason, and p. 207, where he links

truth-itself to being-itself and goodness-itself. In *Love, Power and Justice*, Oxford, London, 1954, he deals with the dimension of depth in relation to these three concepts; in *The Courage to Be* he deals with the depth dimension of courage.

5   Paul Tillich, *Systematic*, I, pp. 19f., 73.
6   Ibid., pp. 22f.
7   Paul Tillich, *Dynamics of Faith* (hereafter cited as *Dynamics*), Harper, New York, 1957, p. 81.
8   Tillich, *Systematic*, I, p. 56. In his *Systematic Theology*, vol. 2 (hereafter cited as *Systematic*, II), University of Chicago Press, Chicago, 1957, p. 92, Tillich applies this point to the incarnation.
9   Tillich, *Dynamics*, p. 34.
10 Tillich, *Systematic*, I, p. 73.
11 Ibid.
12 Blaise Pascal, *Pensées*, no. 277.
13 Tillich, *Systematic*, I, p. 77.
14 Tillich, *Dynamics*, pp. 81f.; see also *Systematic*, I, pp. 74, 117, 130.
15 Tillich, *Systematic*, I, p. 44; see also pp. 74, 130.
16 Ibid., pp. 111f.; for further expressions of Tillich's *three*-level theory of truth, see *Systematic*, I, p. 214; *Systematic*, II, p. 92; *Dynamics*, pp. 11f.; and *Courage*, pp. 178, 184f. In all these contexts Tillich claims that being-itself, the truly ultimate, transcends the subject-object polarity of knower and known.
17 Martin Buber, *I and Thou*, Scribner, New York, 1970, p. 84.
18 Paul Tillich, *The New Being*, Scribner, New York, 1955, p. 153.
19 Paul Tillich, *Courage*, pp. 86ff.
20 Jean-Paul Sartre, "Existentialism Is a Humanism," in Walter Kaufmann (ed.), *Existentialism*, Meridian, New York, 1956, pp. 295ff.
21 Tillich, *Dynamics*, p. 106. In dealing with Tillich's view of ultimate concern, as in coping with all other aspects of his thought, I have been greatly helped by William L. Rowe's brilliant and painstaking study, *Religious Symbols and God: A Philosophical Study of Tillich's Theology* (hereafter cited as *Religious Symbols*), University of Chicago Press, Chicago, 1968. For Rowe's treatment of ultimate concern, see pp. 20f., 148ff.
22 Tillich, *Dynamics*, pp. 2f.
23 Ibid., p. 45.
24 Sidney Hook, *The Quest for Being*, Delta, New York, 1963, pp. 133f.; see also, Kai Nielsen, "Is God So Powerful That He Doesn't Even Have to Exist?" in S. Hook (ed.), *Religious Experience and Truth* (hereafter cited as *Religious Experience*), New York University Press, New York, 1961, pp. 277f.
25 Tillich, *Dynamics*, pp. 46f.
26 John Calvin, *Institutes of the Christian Religion*, Westminster, Philadelphia, 1949, book 1, chaps. 3–5. For important discussions of Tillich's view of idolatry, see Rowe, *Religious Symbols*, pp. 224ff., and William P. Alston, "Tillich on Idolatry," *Journal of Religion*, 38: 263–268, 1958.

27 Tillich, *Dynamics*, p. 12.

28 Ibid., p. 11.

29 Ibid., p. 12.

30 Ibid., p. 11.

31 Tillich, *The New Being*, p. 102; it should be noted that in this context Tillich does not talk of ideals as limiting one another, but of theologies and philosophies; the principle, however, is the same.

32 Tillich, *Dynamics*, p. 11.

33 Ibid., p. 12.

34 Richard Crossman (ed.), *The God That Failed*, Harper & Brothers, New York, 1950.

35 Tillich, *Dynamics*, p. 18.

36 Ibid., p. 9; see also Paul Tillich, "The Problem of Theological Method," in W. Herberg (ed.), *Four Existentialist Theologians*, Doubleday, New York, 1958, p. 249.

37 Tillich's sketchy treatment of the ontological argument is found in *Systematic*, I, pp. 204ff. and *Culture*, pp. 15f. William Rowe makes a heroic effort to fill in the sketch along different lines than the one I take here, in *Religious Symbols*, pp. 89ff.

38 *Systematic*, I, p. 101. For a fuller discussion of Tillich's Augustinianism, see John H. Randall, Jr., "The Ontology of Paul Tillich," in C. W. Kegley and R. W. Bretall (eds.), *The Theology of Paul Tillich*, pp. 146ff.

39 Paul Tillich, "Reply to Interpretation and Criticism," in C. W. Kegley, and R. W. Bretall (eds.), *The Theology of Paul Tillich*, p. 333; see also *Culture*, pp. 13ff., 24f.; *Absolutes*, pp. 65ff.

40 Tillich, *Culture*, p. 15.

41 Tillich, *Systematic*, I, p. 205.

42 Ibid., p. 208.

43 Ibid., p. 209. Kant's criticisms are to be found in his *Critique of Pure Reason*, trans. Norman K. Smith, Macmillan, New York, 1927, pp. 513f. John H. Randall, Jr., in "The Ontology of Paul Tillich," in C. W. Kegley and R. W. Bretall (eds.), *The Theology of Paul Tillich*, pp. 146ff., shows how Tillich's treatment of the arguments for the existence of God reflect both the Platonic-Augustinian tradition and Kantian epistemology.

44 *Systematic*, I, p. 205.

45 Kenelem Foster, O.P., "Paul Tillich and St. Thomas," in T. A. O'Meara, O.P., and C. D. Weisser, O.P. (eds.), *Paul Tillich in Catholic Thought*, The Priory Press, Dubuque, Iowa, 1964, pp. 97–105; on p. 307f., Tillich replies to Foster; see also Albert Dondeyne, *Contemporary European Thought and Christian Faith*, Duquesne University, Pittsburgh, Pa., 1958, chap. 5, especially pp. 148ff.,; Donald J. Keefe, S.J., *Thomism and the Ontological Theology of Paul Tillich*, E. J. Brill, Leiden, 1971, especially, pp. 59ff., 71ff., 84ff. For excellent studies by non-Thomists, see Lewis S. Ford, "Tillich and Thomas: The Analogy of Being," *Journal of Religion*, **66**: 229–245, 1966, especially pp. 238f., for Ford's discussion of continuities and discontinuities in being, and Rowe, *Religious Symbols*, pp. 78ff., and see pp. 82ff., for

Rowe's claim that Tillich's system commits him, despite himself, to the view that God necessarily exists.

46 Tillich, *Systematic*, I, p. 237.

47 Ibid., p. 208.

48 Tillich, *Dynamics*, p. 76. This section shows Tillich's debt to Martin Heidegger's *Being and Time*, SCM Press, London, 1962, original German edition, 1927.

49 Tillich, *Systematic*, I, p. 163.

50 Ibid., p. 163f. See also William Rowe, *Religious Symbols*, pp. 83ff. Elmer Sprague's "On Professor Tillich's Ontological Question," *International Philosophical Quarterly*, vol. 2, 1962, deals with this question; satirically on pp. 81ff., and with an effort to probe its possible meanings, on pp. 88ff.

51 J. J. C. Smart, "The Existence of God," in A. Flew and A. MacIntyre (eds.), *New Essays in Philosophical Theology* (hereafter cited as *New Essays*), Macmillan, New York, 1955, p. 46. Smart subsequently retracted his openness to this question in "Philosophy and Religion," *Australasian Journal of Philosophy*, **36**: 56ff., 1958.

52 Tillich, *The New Being*, p. 121.

53 Tillich, *Systematic*, I, pp. 196f.; see also Paul Tillich, *Biblical Religion and The Search for Ultimate Reality* (hereafter cited as *Biblical Religion*), University of Chicago Press, Chicago, 1955, p. 16.

54 Ronald Hepburn, *Paradox and Christianity*, Pegasus, New York, 1966, p. 169.

55 Tillich's fullest statement of his view of presuppositions is to be found in *Absolutes*, chapter II. He seems to have at least three different uses. One is similar to the one that I expound in this chapter. Another is the appeal to the logical structures of thought as the presupposition of thinking; in other words, we could not think without the law of contradiction, so that it is presupposed in our thinking. At other times he seems to appeal to the notion of a regulative ideal, let us say of truth or justice, as presupposed in our specific efforts to formulate true statements or to arrive at just social arrangements. In other words, our efforts to achieve justice in any specific society presupposes an ideal that is like the mechanical rabbit that the greyhounds chase in dog racing. Chasing it is the point of the game, even though it can never be caught.

56 Tillich *Systematic*, I, p. 163.

57 Tillich, *Absolutes*, pp. 80f.

58 René Descartes, "Meditations on First Philosophy," Meditation I, in *The Philosophical Works of Descartes*, vol. 1, Dover, New York, 1955, pp. 145ff. In this passage Tillich is also true to his Augustinian roots because St. Augustine makes the same point, *Of True Religion*, Henry Regnery, Chicago, 1953, paragraph 73, pp. 69ff.

59 Tillich, *Systematic*, I, p. 235.

60 Ibid., p. 207.

61 Ibid., p. 172.

62 Ibid.

63 For a superb discussion of why being-itself is not a universal, see Rowe, *Religious Symbols*, pp. 48–61.

64 The literature on the negative way is voluminous. For a helpful presentation by an analytic philosopher, see Terence Penelhum, *Religion and Rationality*, Random House, New York, 1971, chap. 7, which sets it in the context of Thomism.

65 Tillich acknowledged the importance of the negative way to his system in his "Reply to Interpretation and Criticism," in C. W. Kegley and R. W. Bretall (eds.), *The Theology of Paul Tillich*, pp. 334f. He qualified it by claiming that his symbolic approach to God is a compromise between the radical agnosticism of the negative way and the so-called positive way in which all valuable characteristics found in the world are attributed to God in the superlative degree.

66 Tillich, *Systematic*, I, p. 272.

67 Ibid., p. 273.

68 Ibid., p. 278.

69 Ibid., p. 237.

70 Paul Tillich, *Systematic*, II, pp. 5ff.

71 Tillich, *Culture*, p. 28; see also pp. 24f., and *Dynamics*, p. 18.

72 Brand Blanshard, "Symbolism," in Hook, *Religious Experience*, pp. 48ff.

73 David H. Kelsey, *The Fabric of Paul Tillich's Theology* (hereafter cited as *Fabric*), Yale, New Haven, 1967, p. 49.

74 Blanshard, "Symbolism," in Hook, *Religious Experience*, p. 49.

75 Paul Tillich, "Existential Analyses and Religious Symbols," in W. Herberg (ed.), *Four Existentialist Theologians*, p. 286.

76 David Kelsey, in *Fabric*, pp. 41f., note 23, provides a helpful account of the development of Tillich's thought on symbols. Tillich published five major statements on the subject between 1928 and 1956. I shall list them in their most convenient English editions. "Appendix" found in Hook, *Religious Experience*, pp. 301–321; "The Nature of Religious Experience," *Culture*, pp. 53–68; "Existential Analyses and Religious Symbols," in W. Herberg (ed.), *Four Existentialist Theologians*, pp. 41–55; "The Meaning and Justification of Religious Symbols," in Hook, *Religious Experience*, pp. 3–12; see also *Dynamics*, chap. 2, pp. 41–54; and "God as Being and the Knowledge of God," *Systematic*, I, pp. 238–241. There is a critical and historical exposition of Tillich's view of symbols in Lewis S. Ford, "The Three Strands of Tillich's Theory of Religious Symbols" (hereafter cited as "Three Strands"), *Journal of Religion*, **66**: 104–130, 1966. Rowe's *Religious Symbols* is the fullest discussion.

77 Kelsey, *Fabric*, p. 41.

78 Kelsey sees this point clearly; he presents Tillich's view of symbols in the context of Tillich's treatment of revelation, *Fabric*, pp. 40–50.

79 William P. Alston, "Tillich's Conception of A Religious Symbol," in Hook, *Religious Experience*, pp. 12–26; see also the contribution by Blanshard already referred to (note 70, above) and Paul Edwards, "Professor Tillich's Confusions," in Steven M. Cahn (ed.), *Philosophy of Religion*,

Harper, New York, 1970, pp. 215ff. As noted previously, Rowe, in *Religious Sybmols*, is critical of Tillich, but in a way that is refreshing inasmuch as he is an analytically sophisticated philosopher who tries as hard as possible to be fair to Tillich and who does not score easy critical points.

80 Tillich, *Culture*, p. 54.
81 Tillich, "Meaning and Justification," in Hook, *Religious Experience*, p. 4.
82 Walter Kaufmann, *Critique of Religion and Philosophy*, Harper & Brothers, New York, 1958, pp. 137f.
83 Kelsey, *Fabric*, p. 48.
84 Tillich, "The Religious Symbol," in Hook, *Religious Experience*, p. 302.
85 Tillich, *Culture*, p. 55.
86 Tillich, *Dynamics*, p. 42.
87 Virgil C. Aldrich, "The Outsider," in Hook, *Religious Experience*, p. 36.
88 Tillich, *Dynamics*, p. 43; Tillich, "Meaning and Justification," in Hook, *Religious Experience*, p. 5; *Culture*, p. 58.
89 Tillich, *Culture*, p. 57; see also, Paul Tillich, "The Word of God," in R. N. Anshen (ed.), *Language: An Enquiry Into Its Meaning and Function*, Harper & Brothers, New York, 1957, pp. 132f.
90 Tillich, *Culture*, p. 57.
91 Tillich, *Systematic*, I, p. 97; see also, pp. 239f, and Tillich, "Meaning and Justification" in Hook, *Religious Experience*, p. 7; *Dynamics*, pp. 12ff.
92 Tillich, *Systematic*, I, p. 118.
93 Jacques Maritain, *Distinguer Pour Unir*, as quoted by E. L. Mascall, *Existence and Analogy*, Longmans, London, 1949, p. xiii.
94 Tillich, *Systematic*, I, pp. 80, 121, 124, 154; see also, Ford, "Three Strands," *Journal of Religion*, **66**: 113ff., 1966, and Tillich's "Rejoinder," pp. 187f., where Tillich substitutes "translucent" for "transparent."
95 Tillich, "The Religious Symbol," in Hook, *Religious Experience*, p. 303.
96 Tillich, *The New Being*, p. 102.
97 Tillich, "The Religious Symbol," in Hook, *Religious Experience*, p. 301; see also, Ford, "Three Strands," *Journal of Religion*, **66**: 114f., 1966.
98 Tillich, *Dynamics*, p. 49.
99 Tillich, *Systematic*, II, p. 29.
100 Tillich, *Systematic*, I. p. 211.
101 Tillich, *Dynamics*, p. 46.
102 Rowe, *Religious Symbols*, pp. 24ff., 184f.
103 Tillich, *Culture*, p. 58.
104 Martin Buber, *Eclipse of God*, Harper & Brothers, New York, 1952, pp. 17f. Tillich reports that Buber once rebuked him for trying to avoid using the word God, see Paul Tillich, "Martin Buber and Christian Thought," *Commentary*, **5**:515, 1948.
105 Tillich, *Courage*, p. 172.
106 Tillich, *Dynamics*, p. 31.
107 Ibid., p. 4.
108 Ibid., p. 10.

109 Ibid., p. 18, my emphasis.
110 Tillich, *Culture*, p. 28.
111 Tillich, *Dynamics*, pp. 10f.
112 Tillich, *Systematic*, I, p. 102.
113 Ibid., my emphasis.
114 Paul Tillich, "On Symbolism," in S. Rome and B. Rome (eds.), *Philosophical Interrogations*, Holt, Rinehart and Winston, New York, 1964, p. 387.
115 Ibid.
116 Reinhold Niebuhr, *Moral Man and Immoral Society*, Scribner, New York, 1932, especially chap. 10.
117 Tillich, *Systematic*, I, p. 236.
118 Tillich, *Courage*, p. 179.
119 Edwards, "Professor Tillich's Confusions," in Cahn, *Philosophy of Religion*, pp. 233f. For another version of the charge that Tillich hypostasises nonbeing, see J. Heywood Thomas, *Paul Tillich: An Appraisal*, Westminster, Philadelphia, 1963, pp. 70ff.
120 Tillich, *Courage*, p. 34. See Leonard F. Wheat, *Paul Tillich's Dialectical Humanism*, pp. 232ff., for interpretations of passages of this kind in a Hegelian context.
121 For a similar equation of the individual human being with Tillich's being-itself, see Elmer Sprague, "On Professor Tillich's Ontological Question," *International Philosophical Quarterly*, **2**: 84f., 1962.
122 Tillich, *Courage*, p. 35.
123 Ibid., p. 3.
124 Ibid., p. 32.
125 Ibid., p. 9.
126 Ibid., chap. 3, see especially, pp. 66ff.
127 Ibid., chap 2; see especially pp. 35ff.
128 Ibid., p. 42.
129 Ibid., p. 52.
130 Ibid., p. 164.
131 Tillich, *Biblical Religion*, pp. 9f.
132 Paul Tillich, *Systematic Theology*, vol. 3, University of Chicago Press, Chicago, 1963, pp. 409f.
133 See note 4 above.
134 Leonard F. Wheat, in *Paul Tillich's Dialectical Humanism*, pp. 1–18, 242–257 presents a survey of the various modes of criticizing Tillich. I find his classifications of the critics useful even though I disagree with many of his judgments.
135 Tillich, *Systematic*, I, pp. 112f.
136 Walter Kaufmann, *Faith of a Heretic*, pp. 81, 95ff.; Leonard Wheat elaborates on Kaufmann's point in *Paul Tillich's Dialectical Humanism*, pp. 252ff. Tillich's clearest exposition of the integrating power of an ultimate concern is in *Dynamics*, pp. 105ff.
137 Tillich, *Systematic*, I, p. 73.

138   Rowe, *Religious Symbols*, chap. 2.
139   St. Thomas Aquinas, *Summa Theologica*, part 1, question 25, article 3.
140   For examples of careful philosophical defenses of the conceptual coherence
      of omnipotence, see Peter Geach, "Omnipotence," *Philosophy*, **48**: 7–20,
      1973. Alvin Plantinga, *God and Other Minds*, Cornell University Press,
      Ithaca, N.Y., 1967, pp. 168ff. Admittedly, Tillich could not have known of
      these treatments, yet he ignored all the sustained treatments of the topic that
      had been made by generations of theologians, especially Thomists.
141   Charles Hartshorne, "Tillich and the Other Great Tradition," in *Anglican
      Theological Review*, no. 3., **63**: 247, 1961; see also, Charles Hartshorne,
      "Tillich's Doctrine of God," in C. W. Kegley and R. W. Bretall (eds.), *The
      Theology of Paul Tillich*, pp. 164–195, and, for a different version of the point
      considered here, pp. 192f.
142   See note 83 above.
143   Fredrick Ferré, *Language, Logic and God*, Harper & Brothers, New York,
      1961, presents a comprehensive survey of uses of religious language that is
      set in the context of the challenge of verification.
144   Tillich, *Dynamics*, p. 18. See also *Courage*, pp. 186ff., where the point is
      made in terms of "the God above God," the symbol of the courage that
      endures when all other symbols have failed.
145   Jerry H. Gill, "Paul Tillich's Religous Epistemology," *Religious Studies*, **3**:
      484f., 1968, makes this charge.
146   Edwards, "Professor Tillich's Confusions," in Cahn, *Philosophy of Religion*,
      pp. 215–225, presents obvious criticisms of Tillich's view of symbols;
      Edwards' views are criticized by Rowe, in *Religious Symbols*, pp. 183ff.,
      190ff.
147   Edwards' more telling criticisms appear in his "Professor Tillich's Confu-
      sions," Cahn, *Philosophy of Religion*, pp. 225–235.
148   Ibid., p. 228.
149   Tillich, *Courage*, p. 52.
150   Leonard F. Wheat in *Paul Tillich's Dialectical Humanism* devotes the entire
      book to the charge that Tillich presents a bombastic redescription of
      experience. More accurately, he accuses Tillich of redescribing it by means
      of categories drawn from Hegelian dialectics. Wheat's central theses are
      clearly stated on pp. 20ff., 232ff., 257ff. Wheat's position is expressed by his
      title; as Nietzsche thought that Kant was an "underground Christian," so
      Wheat regards Tillich as an "underground humanist." He credits Walter
      Kaufmann, *Faith of a Heretic*, Doubleday, New York, 1963, pp. 116ff., with
      the basic insight that stimulated his study. Tillich presents his criticisms of
      humanism in *Dynamics*, pp. 62ff. Nevertheless, my basic agreement with the
      Kaufmann-Wheat position should be clear. I disagree with them on one
      important point. They deal with Tillich in terms of an exposé. Wheat, for
      example, finds the central clue to Tillich's thought in Hegel's dialectical
      method and he then reveals all. He claims (1) that *humanity* is being-itself,
      that is, that humanity is Tillich's God, and (2) that Tillich knows this but does
      not want the general public to catch on. I disagree. In the first instance,

Wheat ignores the broad range of Tillich's thought, especially its Platonic-Augustinian roots. He therefore refuses to acknowledge the metaphysical claims that run through Tillich's thought and that are so carefully and clearly developed throughout Rowe's *Religious Symbols.* My own view is that Tillich's philosophical theology is an effort to deal with theistic categories in metaphysical terms but that ultimately it fails, and that he actually presents us with a form of existential humanism. Sidney Hook in "The Atheism of Paul Tillich," in Hook, *Religious Experience,* pp. 59–64 makes the point with the right balance. He understands Tillich's program of philosophical theology, he sees where it misfires, and calls attention to these problems without attributing conscious deception and all sorts of other unworthy motives to Tillich.

151 Sidney Hook, "The Atheism of Paul Tillich," in Hook, *Religious Experience,* p. 61.
152 William Temple, *Nature, Man and God,* Macmillan, London, 1934, p. 480.
153 Tillich, *Biblical Religion,* pp. 74f.
154 Alisdair MacIntyre, "Is Understanding Religion Compatible with Believing?" in J. Hick (ed.), *Faith and the Philosophers,* St. Martin's, New York, 1964, pp. 115–133.
155 E. M. Forster, *A Passage to India,* Random House, New York, 1924, pp. 38f.
156 For an introduction to this theological tendency, see T. Altizer and W. Hamilton (eds.), *Radical Theology and the Death of God,* Bobbs-Merrill, Indianapolis, 1966.

EPILOGUE

1 J. N. Findlay, "Can God's Existence Be Disproved?" in A. Flew and A. MacIntyre (eds.), *New Essays in Philosophical Theology* (hereafter cited as New Essays), Macmillan, New York, 1955, p. 71.
2 Soren Kierkegaard, *The Point of View for My Work as an Author,* Oxford, London, 1939, p. 35.
3 I. M. Crombie, "Theology and Falsification," in Flew and MacIntyre (eds.), *New Essays,* p. 110.

Index

Page numbers in *italic* indicate main discussion.